D1086919

REGNUM STUDIES IN MISSION

Transformation after Lausanne

Radical Evangelical Mission in Global-Local Perspective

Series Preface

Regnum Studies in Mission are born from the lived experience of Christians and Christian communities in mission, especially but not solely in the fast growing churches among the poor of the world. These churches have more to tell than stories of growth. They are making significant impacts on their cultures in the cause of Christ. They are producing 'cultural products' which express the reality of Christian faith, hope and love in their societies.

Regnum Studies in Mission are the fruit often of rigorous research to the highest international standards and always of authentic Christian engagement in the transformation of people and societies. And these are for the world. The formation of Christian theology, missiology and practice in the twenty-first century will depend to a great extent on the active participation of growing churches contributing biblical and culturally appropriate expressions of Christian practice to inform World Christianity.

Series Editors

Julie C. Ma	Oxford Centre for Mission Studies, Oxford, UK
Wonsuk Ma	Oxford Centre for Mission Studies, Oxford, UK
Doug Petersen	Vanguard University, Costa Mesa, CA, USA
Terence Ranger	University of Oxford, Oxford, UK
C.B. Samuel	Emmanuel Hospital Association, Delhi, India
Chris Sugden	Anglican Mainstream, Oxford, UK

A full listing of titles in this series
appears at the end of this book

REGNUM STUDIES IN MISSION

Transformation after Lausanne

Radical Evangelical Mission in Global-Local Perspective

Al Tizon

Foreword by Ronald J. Sider

WIPF & STOCK · Eugene, Oregon

Wipf and Stock Publishers
199 W 8th Ave, Suite 3
Eugene, OR 97401

Transformation after Lausanne
Radical Evangelical Mission in Global-Local Perspective
By Tizon, Al
Copyright©2008 Tizon, Al
ISBN 13: 978-1-60608-109-9
Publication date 7/23/2008

This Edition published by Wipf and Stock Publishers by
arrangement with Paternoster

I dedicate this book to my mother, Dr. Leticia A. Cvarak, MD, my father Francisco A. Tizon, Jr., and to my father-in-law, the Reverend David H. Weed, in memoriam.

Contents

Tables

FOREWORD

A dramatic change of enormous importance has occurred in evangelical circles in the last fifty years. And this book offers one of the best – perhaps the best – overviews and analyses of that historic transformation.

Fifty years ago, most evangelical leaders would have agreed with the statement: "The primary mission of the church is saving souls." Mission equalled evangelism and evangelism was the primary task for biblical Christians. If one had a little time or money left over, modest engagement with social issues was, perhaps, permissible. But social action was certainly not a primary concern for evangelicals. That was what liberal Christians did.

Today it is difficult to find an evangelical leader who still thinks that way. Almost all evangelical leaders now believe that evangelism and social ministry are both important parts of biblically shaped mission. Nor is the change merely conceptual and theological. All around the world, there are more and more local evangelical congregations and other ministries that are enthusiastically combining word and deed, effectively linking evangelism and social action in holistic ministries that both lead people to personal faith in Christ and transform broken people and impoverished communities.

Fifty years ago the generalization that "evangelical Christians do evangelism and liberal Christians do social action" was largely accurate. Today that is no longer even close to matching reality. At least in more and more evangelical congregations, denominations and para-church ministries, holistic ministry is the norm.

This book is an excellent guide to how and why this momentous transformation took place. It helps the reader understand the key conferences, prominent leaders and significant publications and organizations that led the way.

This book, however, is not merely descriptive. It also contains solid theological analysis plus a helpful discussion of how the "local" and "global" interact. Part of the story is precisely how local evangelical leaders like Bishop David Gitari in Kenya and Rev. Vinay Samuel in India developed successful holistic grassroots ministries and then built on that experience and insight to help the larger global evangelical community embrace holistic ministry. Building on that analysis of how in this story the local and global have interacted, the author develops a helpful vision for a "glocal" approach to mission in the twenty-first century.

Transformation after Lausanne combines solid historical analysis, vigorous theological discussion and helpful guidance for the future – in short, an excellent book about one of the most important changes in global Christianity in the last one hundred years.

Ronald J. Sider
Professor of Theology, Holistic Ministry, and Public Policy
Palmer Seminary at Eastern University
January 2008

PREFACE

In his seminal book *Pedagogy of the Oppressed*, Brazilian educator Paulo Freire defined the word "praxis" as "reflection and action upon the world in order to transform it" (1970:36, 66). Vision consultants tell us that the more customized one's mission or purpose statement, the better. But as I familiarized myself with Freire's treatment of "praxis," it instantly became my favourite word, and its definition, my personal mission statement. I simply could not improve upon it as an articulation of my own sense of Christ's call to be at once a practical thinker and a thinking practitioner, committed to knowing and serving a God who is heaven-bent on transforming the world according to God's rule and reign.

This book marks where I have been on the journey of praxis. It is extended reflection upon over twenty years of mission, pastoral and academic work both in the Philippines and in the United States with, for, and among the poor. It is theological construction with my personal experiences, lessons learned from the poor, and dialogue with mentors who have gone before me as the building materials. It is the way forward for my continued commitment to praxis for the sake of the Gospel in the twenty first century. It is very personal, but I would consider it a gratifying bonus if it encourages others in similar ways.

While in the thick of the action-reflection-action process as a cross-cultural community organizer and pastor in the Philippines and in the United States, I have realized that my missionary engagement resembles the work of many other evangelical theologians and practitioners around the world. Many of these practical scholars (or scholarly practitioners) have begun formulating a theology called Mission as Transformation, which resonates with my own sense of mission. So in the desire to understand more fully the theology that fuels my own journey of praxis, I decided to shine the light of academic scrutiny upon the historical, theological and cultural processes that have produced Mission as Transformation. What is it? How did it come about? How is it expressed around the globe? And how has it expressed itself in a particular context— namely, the Philippines? The following pages represent my findings.

I have so many people to thank. I know it is customary to end with acknowledgments to the family, but I feel compelled to begin with them; for it was actually my wife Janice who encouraged me to undertake this project in the first place. And then, during times of discouragement, it was Janice again who lifted me up and gave me strength, even when she knew that my continuing in the project came with a price. My children Candace, Christian, Corazon and Zoey certainly deserve my deep appreciation for allowing me the space and time that I needed to conduct this study with excellence. I vow to make it up to you all.

Certain friends have kept up with me too, taking genuine interest in my work and constantly asking me how I was doing personally. Special thanks to Craig Rusch, Jeffrey Buhl, Rob and Robi Fairbanks, Carrie and Chuck Strawn, Greg and Debbie Scroggins, Justin and Valerie Ensor, Rod Leupp, Andrew and Lynn Wollitzer, Steve and Rita Read, and Brian and Mary Ellen Gearin. Brian Gearin's determination regarding community development, during a time when that approach was suspect among many evangelicals, inspired me to seek long-term solutions to the problem of poverty. Thanks for letting me partner with you, Brian.

I could not have done this project without Dr. Philip Wickeri, my advisor and dissertation chair, at the Graduate Theological Union in Berkeley, California, USA. I am grateful that the one guiding the whole process was/is himself an experienced missionary, committed to both scholarship and practice. The other members of the committee - Fr. Eduardo Fernandez, SJ, Dr. Susan Phillips, and Dr. Ben Silva-Netto - contributed greatly to the shaping of this work. I cannot count the number of times I barged into their lives with my requests to get together, which they always graciously granted. Dr. David Lim provided extremely valuable insight into how Mission as Transformation developed globally as well as locally in the Philippines. As a pioneer in the movement, especially in the Philippines, I relied heavily upon David's input. I also want to thank Drs. Mariano Apilado, Melba Maggay, Vinay Samuel, Ronald Sider, and Tom Sine busy scholar - practitioners who agreed to be interviewed for this project.

The metamorphosis from dissertation to book could not have happened without the advice and encouragement of my former mission teacher and friend Dr. Doug Petersen at Vanguard University in Southern California. I also extend my sincere appreciation to Robin and Nancy Wainwright, who believed in this project enough to back it up with financial support. Thank you!

My thanks go out to Wonsuk Ma, Chris Sugden and the rest of the diligent folks associated with the Oxford Centre for Mission Studies in the U.K. But a special thanks to Dr. Sugden, who read the manuscript with an editor's eye, not once, but several times. I would especially like to thank Danuta Wisniewska from Regnum / OCMS for all her expert and patient work in typesetting the final manuscript. Without these folks, I do not think this work in its present form would have seen the light of day. Having said that, I take full responsibility for any oversights, mistakes, and ideas in the book that some may deem wrong-headed.

The bulk of my research happened while I served as pastor of the Berkeley Covenant Church in Berkeley, CA, and much appreciation goes out to the good people there, as they gave me as much time as I needed to make steady progress on the project, even when it knew the undertaking would take me away from my pastoral responsibilities. The gracious members there supported me, encouraged me, and celebrated with me upon the project's completion.

I cannot forget the good people of Action International Ministries, under whose auspices I engaged in mission in the Philippines for almost ten years. Thank you ACTION, for allowing me to work with and through you and for granting me an extended study leave that made this academic endeavor even possible. Of course, I am forever grateful to those who faithfully supported us the years while we were with ACTION. I hope you somehow see your influence in these pages.

I also sincerely thank the network of kingdom co-workers in the Philippines - Corrie De Boer and the Transformational leaders of the National Coalition for Urban Transformation (NCUT), Melba Maggay and the entire Institute for Studies in Asian Church and Culture (ISACC) staff, and especially Ronnie "Bong" Mapanoo and the staff of LIGHT Ministries in Zambales province. Under Bong's faithful leadership, LIGHT workers have been faithful to grow the community transformation ministry that I had the privilege of co-establishing with them in the aftermath of the 1991 eruption of Mt. Pinatubo. LIGHT embodies much of what I write about in these pages, and its leaders exemplify genuine, grassroots transformation in Christ's name.

Finally (although I am certain I have forgotten some), I extend my thanks to my friends and colleagues at Palmer Theological Seminary in Wynnewood, PA and to the staff of the Evangelicals for Social Action/Sider Center for Ministry and Public Policy. A special thank you goes to Dr. Ron Sider, a giant of sorts in the area of holistic ministry and an exemplar of what it means to be a scholar-activist. I cannot wish for a better mentor to take me to the next level. Working with you all has enabled me to continue on my journey of praxis here in the United States; which demonstrates even more that mission is not an enterprise done in some exotic far away land (though it certainly can be), but is rather a calling that we live out wherever the poor and the lost reside.

For the sake of the Gospel, to which the aforementioned people are wholly committed, I hope that this work amounts to more than an academic exercise. I hope that it contributes somehow to the advancement of the *missio Dei*. I hope that it demonstrates and encourages action, reflection, and then action again for the transformation of the world.

F. Albert "Al" Tizon
Wynnewood, PA
January 2008

Abbreviations

ACDA	Alliance of Christian Development Agencies
ATS	Asian Theological Seminary
CCT	Centre for Community Transformation
CMED	Christian Micro-Enterprise Development
COWE	Consultation on World Evangelization (1980 Lausanne in Thailand)
ESA	Evangelicals for Social Action
IMC	International Missionary Council
INFEMIT	International Fellowship of Evangelical Mission Theologians
IEMILIF	*Iglesia Evangelica Metodista en las Islas Filipinas* (The Evangelical Methodist Church of the Philippine Islands)
IFI	*Iglesia Filipina Independiente* (Philippine Independent Church)
INC	*Iglesia ni Cristo* (Church of Christ)
ISACC	Institute for Studies in Asian Church and Culture
IVCF-Phil	Inter-Varsity Christian Fellowship Philippines
KONFES	*Konsensiya ng Febrero Siete* (Conscience of February 7)
LATF	Latin American Theological Fraternity
LCWE	Lausanne Committee on World Evangelization
NCCP	National Council of Churches Philippines
NCUT	National Coalition for Urban Transformation
OCMS	Oxford Centre for Mission Studies
PCEC	Philippine Council of Evangelical Churches
PIM-Asia	Partnership in Mission Asia
PJM	Philippines for Jesus
RBI	Regnum Books International
SANGKOP	*Samahan ng mga Kristianong Organisasyong Pangkaunlaran* (Alliance of Christian Transformational Agencies
SLC	Simple Living Consultation (1980 in London)
CTD	Consultation on Theology of Development (1980 in London)
UCCP	United Church of Christ in the Philippines
WCC	World Council of Churches
WEF	World Evangelical Fellowship

INTRODUCTION

'On behalf of the National Coalition for Urban Transformation Secretariat, I welcome you to our first major urban consultation on how we can transform our cities for Jesus Christ'.[1] With these words, Corrie Acorda-De Boer ceremoniously opened a momentous event in 1998 - perhaps the first organized, strategic, cooperative effort in the Philippines between evangelicals, mainline Protestants and Roman Catholics for the purpose of reflecting upon the Church's role in transforming society.

Social activist and professor of urban ministry at Asian Theological Seminary in Manila, Acorda-De Boer identifies herself as an evangelical, a fact that may surprise many - at least those who take too seriously the stereotype that all evangelicals continue to ignore the social dimension of the Gospel. Indeed a socially informed missiology known as 'Mission as Transformation' has developed over the last thirty years at the hands of a group of radical evangelicals around the world that does well to foil any attempt at wholesale evangelical caricaturing.

What is an Evangelical?

The term 'evangelical' has evolved enough through the centuries that it behooves us to define it before proceeding any further. The Greek linguistic root of the word 'evangelical' simply refers to someone who believes in the Gospel, the *euangelion*, and who has a 'burning passion for the communication of the Gospel'.[2] The term came into historical prominence during the Protestant Reformation under Martin Luther, who first used it to describe 'all Christians

---

[1] Corrie Acorda-De Boer, 'Hope for the City', *Signs of Hope in Manila '98,* a booklet distributed at the first Metro Manila Urban Consultation of the National Coalition for Urban Transformation (NCUT) in Manila, Philippines in June 1998, 6.

[2] Orlando Costas, 'Evangelical Theology in the Two Thirds World', in Mark Lau Branson and C. Rene Padilla (eds.), *Conflict and Context: Hermeneutics in the Americas* (Grand Rapids, Mich.: Eerdmans, 1986), 312.

who believed that the Gospel was the basis of salvation by grace'.[3] To be evangelical meant affirming the classical Reformation leitmotifs of *sola Scriptura, sola gratia, and sola fide.* By implication, it also meant rejecting Roman Catholicism, as 'evangelical' became the label for those who protested against the abuses of the Church of Rome.

This simultaneously affirming and rejecting nature has come to characterize the development of evangelicalism in the centuries following the Reformation. The three movements with which historians associate the continuation of the evangelical spirit in the seventeenth and eighteenth centuries - German pietism, Methodism, and the Great Awakenings, which together make up the so-called Second Reformation - all underscore this tension. These movements stressed, on the authority of the Bible, personal conversion and experience, holy living, and spiritual and social vitality over and against what they perceived as the religiosity, impiety and sterility of the established churches of their day. This affirming-rejecting tension intensified in the late nineteenth and twentieth centuries, especially in America, as 'evangelical' came to mean at once the affirmation of the fundamentals of the faith and the rejection of all things 'liberal Protestant'.

In light of their rich Reformation (and Second Reformation) heritage, evangelicals at least bear the following identifying marks: 1) the desire to maintain fidelity to the Bible, 2) the belief that God in Christ is accessible by faith alone, which results in salvation, 3) the goal to lead a holy, moral, disciplined life as a result of that salvation, 4) the passion to share the good news with everyone everywhere, and 5) a critical posture towards any version of the Christian faith that is perceived to be unbiblical, impersonal, powerless over sin, and lacking in missionary zeal.

Evangelical missionaries have done well in spreading their understanding of the faith as the global movement represents 'the most energetic and fastest growing section of the church in the world today'.[4] Evangelicals, summarized recently by Timothy George,

> are a worldwide family of Bible-believing Christians committed to sharing with everyone everywhere the transforming good news of new life in Jesus Christ, an utterly free gift that comes through faith alone in the crucified and risen Savior. ... Evangelicals are gospel people and Bible people. We do not claim to be the only

---

[3] Philip L. Wickeri, Al Tizon and Hee Mo Yim, 'A Survey of Evangelical Missiological Concerns with Particular Reference to Asia', Philip L. Wickeri (ed.), *The People of God Among All God's People* (Hong Kong; London: Christian Conference of Asia; Council of World Mission, 2000), 291.

[4] Wickeri, Tizon, and Yim, 'A Survey of Evangelical Missiological Concerns', 289. The truth of this statement hinges upon the inclusion of the explosive worldwide growth of Pentecostalism, which most missiologists consider a part of the greater evangelical movement.

true Christians, but we recognize in one another a living, personal trust in Jesus the Lord, and this is the basis of our fellowship across so many ethnic, cultural, national, and denominational divides.[5]

What is a Radical Evangelical?

Because the movement has developed so diversely, the term 'evangelical' needs the help of adjectives to distinguish one type of evangelical from another, and typologies abound. Gabriel Fackre, for example, identifies five classifications for evangelical: 1) *Fundamentalist* (stress on biblical inerrancy, sectarian, in defense of doctrine); 2) *Old or Traditional* (stress on conversion and personal holiness reminiscent of old German Pietism); 3) *New or Neo -* (stress on social relevance but not at the expense of personal faith, compassion, intellectual development); 4) *Charismatic and Pentecostal* (signs and wonders, the power of the Holy Spirit, experience); and 5) *Justice and Peace*, which we identify here as 'radical evangelical'.[6]

Radical evangelicals come out of Anabaptist, Anglican, Wesleyan, and Reformed backgrounds, and based on their understanding of the demands of the Gospel, 'they call into question the accommodation of today's culture and churches to affluence, militarism, and unjust social and economic structures'.[7] This brand of evangelicalism refers to the unlikely combination of conservative evangelical theology and a radical orientation to faith and society.[8] Referring specifically to radical evangelicals in North America, the late Orlando Costas described them as representing

a new generation of scholars and critics with special interests in and ties to the Two Thirds World. Their criticism of North American religious culture and socio-economic policies, their commitment to a radical discipleship, and their solidarity with the Two Thirds World have made them natural allies of some of the most theologically articulate evangelical voices in that part of the globe.[9]

---

[5] Timothy George, 'If I'm an Evangelical, What Am I?' *Christianity Today*, 9 August 1999, 62.

[6] This typology is cited in Wickeri, Tizon and Yim, 'Survey of Evangelical Missiological Concerns', 292-293. Whereas Fackre lists Charismatic and Pentecostal evangelicals last, I have taken the liberty to list Justice and Peace evangelicals last simply for convenience, since it is this very classification of evangelical that we will focus upon in this book.

[7] Costas, 'Evangelical Theology', 313.

[8] Richard Tholin and Lane T. Dennis, 'Radical Evangelicals: Challenge to Liberals and Conservatives' *Explore* 2.2 (Fall 1976), 45-46.

[9] Costas, 'Evangelical Theology', 314. Costas defines 'Two Thirds World' as 'that planetary space which is the habitat of most of the poor, powerless, and oppressed people on earth, which is to be found in Africa, Asia, the Pacific, the Caribbean, and

It is in the hands of radical evangelicals worldwide that the development of a significant, post-Lausanne movement called Mission as Transformation has emerged and developed.

Lausanne I and Mission as Transformation

Like most stereotypes, the caricature of the evangelical has elements of truth to it. Evangelicals have indeed suffered from a kind of myopia for the last eighty years, viewing mission narrowly in terms of verbal proclamation (evangelism) and church planting at the expense of social justice. Scholars across disciplines have offered their respective views to explain this myopia, but they share at least one common explanation. They all agree that it largely developed as a reaction to ultra-liberal definitions of mission in the early part of the twentieth century that emphasized social justice at the expense of evangelization - a myopia of another sort.

The first Lausanne Congress on World Evangelization in 1974 marks the first serious corporate attempt to correct this shortsightedness among evangelicals. The Lausanne Covenant, the official resultant document of the Congress, includes 'Christian Social Responsibility' as one of fifteen key articles.[10] This inclusion started a lively debate among evangelicals between those who wanted to retain the primacy of evangelism and those who saw works of compassion and justice as equal to evangelism. For many, this debate has found resolution as social concern now occupies an integral place in the theology and practice of mission, albeit in varying degrees.

The Lausanne movement spawned many other gatherings among evangelicals. One of them occurred nine years later in 1983 in Wheaton, IL under the theme banner, 'I Will Build My Church'. Compared to Lausanne '74, the Wheaton '83 Consultation, sponsored by the World Evangelical Fellowship (WEF),[11] could not boast of huge numbers of participants nor of monumental worldwide notoriety. But in terms of the radical evangelical journey toward holistic mission, Wheaton '83 looms large. Organized into three tracks, Track III of Wheaton '83 with the sub-theme, 'The Church in Response to Human

---

continental Latin America' (311-312). I would add impoverished and oppressed communities of North America and Europe as well. Given the inclusivity of the term, I prefer it over the more common term 'Third World'. Moreover, it seems to be the term of choice among Transformational missiologists who claim that it is the oppressed peoples' self-definition.

[10] 'The Lausanne Covenant', in John R.W. Stott (ed.), *Making Christ Known: Historic Mission Documents from the Lausanne Movement, 1974-1989* (Grand Rapids, Mich.; Cambridge: Eerdmans, 1996), 24.

[11] As of January 1, 2002, WEF changed its name to the World Evangelical Alliance (WEA). But for the purpose of rendering an historical account, I will continue to refer to it as WEF throughout the book.

Need', took significant strides toward holistic mission by developing a biblical, theological, and practical understanding of the term 'Transformation'.[12] According to the Wheaton '83 Statement, the official document resulting from Track III, 'Transformation is the change from a condition of human existence contrary to God's purposes to one in which people are able to enjoy fullness of life in harmony with God'.[13]

Since 1983, this definition has served as the basis of a holistic missiology among radical evangelicals. Vinay Samuel and Chris Sugden, arguably the leading systematic theologians of Mission as Transformation, have identified eight key elements that define the contours of this missiological understanding: '1) an integral relationship between evangelism and social change; 2) mission as witness and journey in the world; 3) mission in context; 4) truth, commitment to change and imagination; 5) theology, Christian mission and understanding are always local; 6) freedom and power for the poor; 7) reconciliation and solidarity; and 8) building communities of change'.[14] In Part II of this study, we will look much closer at each of these elements and attempt to develop and enrich them. I mention them now merely to introduce this missiology's basic framework.

Transformation: The Development of a Term

The many uses of the term 'transformation' notwithstanding, we will limit our examination to how a loosely-knit, international network of radical evangelicals has used and developed it. Names and institutions associated with this network include Vinay Samuel and Chris Sugden at the Oxford Centre for Mission Studies in the UK, Rene Padilla, Samuel Escobar and the late Orlando Costas of the Latin American Theological Fraternity based in Argentina, Ronald Sider, Miriam Adeney and Tom Sine of the Evangelicals for Social Action in the USA, Melba Maggay of the Institute for Studies in Asian Church and Culture in the Philippines and David Lim of China Ministries International and Centre for Community Transformation also in the Philippines, David Gitari and Kwame Bediako of the African Theological Fraternity based in both Ghana and Kenya, and many others.

---

[12] Since I focus on a specific movement identified as 'Transformation' or 'Mission as Transformation', I have chosen to differentiate it via capitalization from incidental general uses of the terms 'transformation' and 'mission' throughout the book.

[13] 'Wheaton '83: Statement on Transformation', in Vinay Samuel and Chris Sugden (eds.), *The Church in Response to Human Need* (Oxford: Grand Rapids, Mich.: Regnum; Eerdmans, 1987), 257.

[14] Vinay Samuel and Chris Sugden, 'Introduction', in Vinay Samuel and Chris Sugden (eds.), *Mission as Transformation* (Oxford: Regnum, 1999), xvi.

This particular understanding of Transformation has undergone its own transformations since its inception.[15] It emerged through reflections on social ethics but later expanded into reflections on a holistic missiology; thus, the name expansion from Transformation to *Mission* as Transformation.[16] This broadening, however, did not reduce the importance of social concern; on the contrary, it made social concern part and parcel of the Gospel and therefore part and parcel of the Church's mission. Proponents of Mission as Transformation refuse to understand evangelization without liberation, a change of heart without a change of structures, vertical reconciliation (between God and people) without horizontal reconciliation (between people and people), and church planting without community building. They point to the biblical paradigm of the reign or kingdom of God as the source and driver for this holistic understanding of mission.[17]

Mission as Transformation and David Bosch

Since many scholars across mission traditions associate the term 'transformation' with the late missiologist David J. Bosch, it seems important to understand Mission as Transformation in relation to him. Bosch in fact participated in Track III of Wheaton '83 as a member of the committee responsible for drafting the Statement.[18] So Bosch certainly did his part in contributing to the development of Mission as Transformation; and conversely, this particular understanding most probably informed his own thinking on the matter. He later praised the Wheaton '83 Statement as a significant step in the maturation of evangelical social consciousness.[19]

Bosch, however, never defined the term in his magnum opus *Transforming Mission*, except to say in the Forward that 'transforming' has two meanings. As an adjective in the title, 'transforming' describes mission as that which changes the object of mission, i.e., society, culture, reality. By implication, mission represents something that transcends reality in order to transform it. As a

---

[15] For developments on the definition of Transformation since 1983, see Chris Sugden, 'Transformational Development: Current state of understanding and practice', *Transformation* 20.2 (April 2003), 70-72.
[16] Vinay Samuel, 'Mission as Transformation', in Vinay Samuel and Chris Sugden (eds.), *Mission as Transformation* (Oxford: Regnum, 1999), 228.
[17] Some theologians have made a viable case to use the term 'reign' over 'kingdom' on the grounds that 'kingdom' has male, patriarchal overtones that the broader biblical reality of 'kingdom of God' did not necessarily intend to convey. For more on this, see Mortimer Arias, *Announcing the Reign of God* (Minneapolis, Minn.: Fortress, 1984), xvi. For this study, because the more familiar 'kingdom of God' overwhelms Transformational literature, I have chosen to retain it.
[18] 'Wheaton '83 Statement', *Transformation* 1.1 (January/March 1984), 23.
[19] David J. Bosch, *Transforming Mission* (Maryknoll N.Y.: Orbis, 1991), 407.

present participle, however, 'transforming' refers to mission itself as that which is being transformed.[20] So transformation in Bosch's thinking denotes a comprehensive, divinely inspired process that affects both the object and the subject of mission; all parties involved undergo transformation. Beyond that, he did not say much else about the term. Nonetheless, his thirteen point emerging ecumenical missionary paradigm has had such an impact upon contemporary missiology that the title of his book has apparently caused many to associate the word 'transformation' with Bosch.[21]

In relation to Mission as Transformation as it has been developed by the international network of radical evangelicals, Samuel and Sugden have pointed out some serious shortcomings in Bosch's work. They describe *Transforming Mission* in their Annotated Bibliography as 'a major text which covers the biblical material admirably but unfortunately neglects some aspects of evangelical missiology from the Two Thirds World in the last 25 years'.[22] Sugden expands upon this critique (only after paying due respect to Bosch's brilliant contribution to missiology) and summarizes the advances of Two Thirds World evangelicalism that Bosch either failed to acknowledge or accord proper credit, such as 'the epistemological priority of the poor, the categories of covenant and family, the integration of evangelism and social action, the understanding of the relation between reconciliation and restitution, the understanding of power, [and] the role of Pentecostalism'.[23] Such a lacuna, as Sugden calls it, cannot ultimately be justified, for these issues that Two Thirds World evangelicals have effectively addressed over the past twenty five years constitute the heart of what is truly emerging as a contemporary paradigm of mission. In Samuel and Sugden's estimation, Bosch's development of transformation does not so much veer off as it falls short. Sugden concludes, 'I still regard Bosch as required reading, but I would also require other reading [as a necessary Two Thirds World complement]'.[24]

Mission in Context as Transformation

From the beginning, Mission as Transformation has focused upon the integral role that culture plays in theological reflection and practice. This commitment reflects the advances made by the growing field of contextual theology. All

---

[20] Bosch, *Transforming Mission*, xv.

[21] Bosch, *Transforming Mission*, 368-510.

[22] Vinay Samuel and Chris Sugden, 'Annotated Bibliography', in Vinay Samuel and Chris Sugden (eds.), *Mission as Transformation* (Oxford: Regnum, 1999), 513.

[23] Chris Sugden, 'Placing Critical Issues in Relief: A Response to David Bosch', in Willem Saayman and Klippies Kritzinger (eds.), *Mission in Bold Humility: David Bosch's Work Considered* (Maryknoll, N.Y.: Orbis, 1996), 150.

[24] Sugden, 'Placing Critical Issues in Relief', 150.

theology is contextual theology. For all of their pitfalls, postmodernism, postcolonialism, and all other things 'post-' have enabled profound theological truths such as this to find daylight.[25] Contextual theology has done well to expose the faulty base out of which Euro- and North Ameri-centric theologies dominated the missionary scene. As old traditional answers from these once dominant theologies began to lose their relevance for the new questions arising from Africa, Asia, Latin America, as well as black, feminist and indigenous groups in North America, 'a new kind of Christian identity was emerging apart from much of the traditional theological reflection'.[26] Mission historians note the early 1970s as the beginning point for the proliferation of local or contextual theologies. With their emergence came the realization that the classical theologies of the West are no less contextual than any other. This realization gave the discipline of contextual theology not only the right to exist; it pushed it to centre stage as an absolute imperative.[27]

Mission as Transformation has developed consistently along contextual lines as myriad voices from all over the globe have informed it. The Wheaton '83 Consultation that announced the birth of this missiological understanding can boast that sixty percent of its participants came from the non-Western world.[28] Furthermore, the articles published in the journal *Transformation*, one of the primary academic forums through which this understanding has been explored, also demonstrates its multicultural development. Between 1984 and 2000, the journal published eighty five articles from Asia, fifty three from Africa, forty six from Latin America, eighty seven from Europe, a hundred and twenty from North America, fourteen from Australia and New Zealand and five from the Middle East. Although North America still registered more articles, these overall numbers indicate how seriously the architects of Mission as Transformation have taken the role of local culture for theological reflection and practice.

Kwame Bediako's *Theology and Identity* represents one of the most poignant book length treatises that has informed Transformational thinking on

[25] Hans Kung describes present reality as 'post-Eurocentric, postcolonial, postimperial, postsocialist, postindustrial, postpatriarchal, postideological, and postconfessional', cited in David J. Bosch, *Believing in the Future* (Harrisburg, Pa.: Trinity Press International, 1995), 1.
[26] Robert J. Schreiter, *Constructing Local Theologies* (Maryknoll, N.Y.: Orbis, 1985), 2-3.
[27] Stephen B. Bevans, *Models of Contextual Theology* (Maryknoll, N.Y.: Orbis, 1992), 5-7. Bevan's book serves as an excellent introduction to the major ways in which theologians have appropriated local cultural context in doing theology. For a more concise introduction to contextual theology, see Eduardo Fernandez, *La Cosecha* (Collegeville, Minn.: Liturgical Press, 2000), 95-130.
[28] A. Scott Moreau, 'Wheaton '83', in A. Scott Moreau, (ed.), *Evangelical Dictionary of World Missions* (Grand Rapids, Mich.: Baker, 2000), 1014.

culture.[29] It surely deals with the issues of Christianity in the African context from a variety of African voices, particularly the struggle for African Christian identity in the aftermath of hundreds of years of European colonization. But it transcends Africa as well, by establishing identity - who we are in Christ and in our cultural context - as fundamental to any theology that is relevant for any particular context. Furthermore, it transcends the African context in that it connects the story of Christianity in Africa with the story of Christianity in the second century, thus demonstrating the continuity of the one story, the story of God in all human contexts throughout time. Bediako's work typifies the way in which Mission as Transformation has reflected upon the practice of contextualization, namely, by holding in creative tension both the particularity of a peoples' lived experience in a given time and place and the transcultural nature of the Gospel.

Mission as Transformation in Filipino Context

In this book, discussion of local context will necessarily lead us to the Philippines, because first, it marks the location in which I engaged in mission from 1989 to 1998, first in the mega-city of Manila and then in the rural province of Zambales. Moreover, the fact that I am ethnically Filipino deepens the appropriateness of focusing upon this context. So like all worthwhile theological reflection, this book gets its inspiration from the researcher's personal experience and area of interest.

Second, the events of the mid-1980s in the Philippines surrounding the People Power Revolution offer a unique environment to look at Mission as Transformation; for the timing of those historical events correspond to the timing of the birth and subsequent development of this missiology. Filipino evangelical intellectuals/practitioners like Melba Maggay, David Lim, Corrie Acorda-De Boer, and many others appearing in the following pages provide rich sources for conducting this study, not only because of their impact in their particular context, but also because of their influence upon the global understanding of Mission as Transformation.

And third, the Philippines, with its colonial history, its present post-colonial situation, and its predominantly Christian population (eighty percent Roman Catholic), provides fertile ground to explore the local dimensions of this holistic missiology.

---

[29] Kwame Bediako, *Theology and Identity: The Impact of Culture upon Christian Thought in the Second Century and Modern Africa* (Oxford: Regnum, 1992).

The Global and the Local

Mission as Transformation, however, *does* share characteristics across cultures - characteristics that I identify later as its global dimensions. It is at once global and local.

The term 'global' refers to a reality made up of input derived from multiple locales; that is, a reality that owes its existence to local contexts.[30] In the case of Mission as Transformation, the shared convictions among the theologies and practices of local contextual realities give shape to its global dimensions. This understanding of the global has no relation to that which contextual theology has rightly rendered obsolete, namely, the claim of the dominant West to possess *the* theology to be applied universally to all. If the truth that theologies coming from the West are as contextual as any other then their claims to universality ultimately came from colonial ethnocentrism and should be discarded today. However, I do make the case in Part IV that the global does attain a universal quality that enables it to inform local situations. In light of the global attaining universal status (albeit given to it by the locales themselves), I will often use the two words 'global' and 'universal' together - global/universal - when speaking about the global nature or dimensions of Mission as Transformation.

The term 'local' in relation to mission refers to those tangible, concrete places in the world where the Gospel is lived out. In the Introduction to Part III, I argue that local theology, i.e., local churches doing theology, worship and mission according to the values and traditions of their own local cultures - results from authentic contextualization. Samuel rightly claims that 'Christian mission and understanding [are] always local'.[31] Local dimensions of Mission as Transformation come out of the experiences of God's people in specific historical situations. In that sense, those local dimensions are particularly true and right for that context. The obvious affinity between the terms 'local' and 'particular' justifies the use of the combination 'local/particular' throughout this book when dealing with the local Filipino dimensions of Mission as Transformation.

The claim that this missiology is at once global/universal and local/particular corresponds with the new way in which a discernible set of globalized processes - globalization - has necessitated a reconceptualization of the world across disciplines. The age of globalization, where both a market based homogenizing effect around the globe (McWorld) and an ethnic based assertion of cultural identity and resistance to globalization (Jihad) co-exist nervously,

---

[30] I elaborate upon this idea, what I refer to as 'globalization from below' in Part IV.
[31] Samuel, 'Mission as Transformation', 230.

have forced scholars to deal seriously with the global-local relationship.[32] As the world simultaneously extends, intensifies and speeds up, negotiating this relationship becomes an essential task certainly not just for philosophically oriented arenas like theology and religion, but for those domains that have more direct concrete bearing including at least economics, politics, culture, military, law and ethics.[33]

I assume here a certain symbiosis between the global and the local for missiology. Rather than making a case for a local Filipino missiology over and against a global conception - which would cater to the trendy and parochial tendencies of postmodernism, or re-asserting a global conception over and against a local Filipino rendering which would ignore the important advances of contextual theology, I hope to demonstrate how the global and the local inform each other in order to achieve a relevant missiology.

Robert J. Schreiter, who has done much in advancing the discussion of the relationship between the global and the local in theology, asserts,

> One thing seems clearly to have emerged out of this history [that traces the move from modernity to postmodernity]: any theology needs to attend both to its contextual and to its universalizing dimensions. ... Theology must not be reduced to context in a crude contextualism, for then it is likely to lose its critical edge as it becomes simply a product of its surroundings. ... It must be rooted in the context, yet be able to take stock of the context at the same time. ... Theology must also have a universalizing function, by which is meant an ability to speak beyond its own context, and an openness to hear voices from beyond its own boundaries.[34]

Transformation between the Global and the Local

Building upon Schreiter's view, I seek here to understand the history, theology and practice of Mission as Transformation through a global-local lens.

This global-local rendering of Mission as Transformation, both as an historical movement and as a coherent missiology, is timely and necessary for at least four reasons. First, it formalizes and therefore clarifies the features of an understanding that has done much to elevate social concern in evangelical mission thought. Samuel and Sugden note that this understanding of mission

---

[32] For more in-depth views of this tension, see Benjamin Barber, *Jihad vs. McWorld* (New York: Times Books, 1995) and Tom Sine, *Mustard Seed vs. McWorld* (Grand Rapids, Mich.: Baker, 1999).

[33] For a clear, comprehensive, historically informed treatment of globalization, see David Held, Anthony McGraw, David Goldblatt, and Jonathan Perraton, *Global Transformations: Politics, Economics and Culture* (Stanford, Calif.: Stanford University, 1999). Many consider this volume as the most definitive work on globalization to date.

[34] Robert J. Schreiter, *The New Catholicity* (Maryknoll, N.Y.: Orbis, 1997), 3-4.

'has formed the basis of the theological understanding of many of the leading evangelical relief and development agencies'.[35] To formalize this understanding can greatly advance holism within the evangelical mission tradition. Second, the contextual location of this study offers the potential for a positive contribution to the particular development of Filipino evangelical mission theology and practice. Third, it can create bridges to mainline or ecumenical Protestant and Roman Catholic mission traditions, for issues of social justice and globalization have proven a promising meeting ground on which Christians of all stripes can think and work together. By laying out a socially informed, holistic, integrative - in a word, Transformational - missiology, we encourage genuine Christian ecumenism. And finally, a global-local rendering of Mission as Transformation hopes to add to the ongoing creative thinking among theologians, missiologists, and social scientists concerning the tension between the global/universal and the local/particular.

At the core of these points of significance lies the desire to recognize a missionary movement that has contributed significantly to helping the 'whole Church ... take the whole Gospel to the whole world'. This formula for holistic mission first appeared at the 1963 conference of the newly formed Committee on World Mission and Evangelism (CWME) in Mexico City. Evangelicals revived this formula at the second major Lausanne gathering in 1989 in Manila, thus demonstrating the progress made by evangelicals on their journey toward holistic mission between the first and second Lausanne Congresses. Much of this progress can be attributed to the extensive theological reflections and practical commitments of the proponents of Mission as Transformation. As such, this holistic missiology warrants a careful study for the benefit not only of the evangelical missionary community, but also of the wider Church.

This study is divided into four main parts. Part I focuses upon the historical development of Mission as Transformation as a mobilizer among evangelicals toward a radically holistic approach to mission. Where did it come from historically? Who played key roles in its development? And what tensions existed within the evangelical community that produced it? Part II explores the global dimensions of Mission as Transformation. What features of this missiology do radical evangelical theologians and practitioners share worldwide? And who and what claims to serve as its 'global keepers'? Part III follows up by focusing on the local context of the Philippines, exploring the particular local dimensions that Mission as Transformation took on as it sought to be continuous with the best of Filipino church mission tradition. And finally Part IV seeks clarity on the interplay between global and local understandings

---

[35] Samuel and Sugden, 'Introduction', x.

and appropriates the idea of 'glocalization' as a way to see the symbiosis between the global and the local, particularly how it serves the cause of the Church's mission in the world.

PART I

A HISTORY

Introduction to Part I

Our historical task entails some necessary excavating into both the literature of evangelical social ethics and Protestant mission theology. As mentioned earlier, Mission as Transformation began as reflections on social ethics; before it was 'Mission as Transformation' it was simply 'Transformation'. Making this observation, however, can suggest that at some point a major shift occurred within the movement. But because this social ethic emerged out of a missiological context, its proponents could have heralded it as 'Mission as Transformation' from the beginning. The expansion of the term does not so much reflect a paradigm shift as it does the eventual realization on the part of its shapers that their discourse on social ethics related inseparably to the larger discourse on mission theology and practice.

The subtitle change in the 1991 issue of *Transformation* (8/4), from 'An International Dialogue on Evangelical Social Ethics' to 'An International Dialogue on Mission and Ethics', clearly demonstrates this realization. Similarly, Samuel seems wishful when he suggests that the Wheaton '83 Statement on Transformation could have had the subtitle, 'The Church's Call to Mission' instead of 'The Church in Response to Human Need'.[1] In any case, the journey from Lausanne '74 to Wheaton '83 represented nearly a decade of post-Lausanne I international reflections upon the integral role that social concern has played in the missionary task.

To begin, however, with Lausanne '74 for a history of Mission as Transformation would overlook some key historical antecedents that led to the missionary social vision articulated at the Congress. Chapter 1 tracks the social ethical and missionary journey of evangelicals prior to Lausanne '74 by identifying two principle historical roots. The history of the relationship between social concern and evangelism since the latter half of the nineteenth century constitutes the first root, especially how it impacted evangelicalism worldwide through the Protestant missionary movement. To be sure, an understanding of Mission as Transformation has resulted in large part from efforts to work out this relationship in the intercultural missionary context.

---

[1] Samuel, 'Mission as Transformation', 228.

The history of relief and development work among evangelicals, especially after World War Two, constitutes the second root. Evangelicals continued to engage in mercy ministries despite the temporary loss of theological moorings to warrant it. As this theologically rootless activism began to tax the more evangelical thoughtful, a search ensued for a biblical and theological basis for compassion and justice ministries, a search that eventually led a group of radical evangelicals to an understanding of Mission as Transformation.

Chapters 2 and 3 continue the journey from Lausanne '74 to Wheaton '83. If Chapter 1 identifies the roots of Mission as Transformation, then the next two chapters document the struggles that forced this missiological understanding to sprout. Chapter 2 traces the internal tensions that grew within the evangelical missionary community after Lausanne concerning the role of social concern in the task of world evangelization; for though Lausanne I opened the door for holistic mission thinking, many found themselves feeling uneasy about it. Indeed the affirmation of socio-political involvement at Lausanne brought out both the most creative and the most reactive thinking among evangelical missiologists. These tensions from within the Lausanne movement forced the more radical spirits to articulate their position, a process that involved a series of key statement producing consultations, culminating in the Wheaton '83 Statement on Transformation.

These tensions from within the movement had a match from without, namely, the growing, worldwide influence of liberation theology, the subject of Chapter 3. Faced with the prophetic challenges of liberation theology, prominent Latin American evangelicals like Samuel Escobar, Rene Padilla and Orlando Costas, grappling with the very real revolutionary struggles of their respective contexts, led the way in eventually forging an evangelical version of liberation. These internal and external tensions forced radical evangelicals to rethink the missionary task. The missiology of Transformation forged at Wheaton '83 articulated their findings.

Chapter 4 focuses on developments after Wheaton '83. Both internal and external tensions continued to apply creative pressure upon this new missiological understanding, but the direction of Chapter 4 no longer tracks these tensions, mainly because the issues raised by them had remained relatively unchanged. Therefore, rather than focusing upon debates occurring at the large international evangelical gatherings like Lausanne II in 1989 in Manila, Chapter 4 concentrates upon how Mission as Transformation took on a life of its own at the hands of radical evangelicals worldwide. How did this missiological understanding develop around the world since Wheaton '83?

This seemingly simple question leads to a complex web of local, regional and international conferences, the formation of fellowships and organizations, and educational and publishing initiatives, wherein theologians and practitioners alike covered a wide range of missiological issues from a Transformational perspective. Consequently, a simple chronological approach to the question cannot even begin to make sense of it. In an effort to gain some clarity, Chapter 4 attempts first to understand the structures that Transformationists put into place in order to facilitate the vision articulated in the Wheaton '83 Statement. These structures include the local and regional networks that make up the International Fellowship of Evangelical Mission Theologians (INFEMIT), the Oxford Centre for Mission Studies (OCMS), publishing initiatives like Regnum Books and the journal *Transformation*, and continued participation at wider Christian gatherings of the Lausanne movement as well as of the World Council of Churches (WCC).

Through these structures, the Transformational vision developed and matured. Undoubtedly, the many local, national, and international conferences sponsored by the INFEMIT/OCMS network, as well as the many books released by Regnum Books and articles published in *Transformation*, serve as key sources to understand this vision. Chapter 4 reviews these conferences and publications as a whole and identifies major missiological advances in four areas, namely, the role of culture (both local and global), the impact of faith on economics, practical holism and the Holy Spirit in mission.

CHAPTER 1

Evangelical Social Concern and Mission Prior to Lausanne I: Roots of Transformation

Social Concern and Evangelism: A Look Back

The Lausanne Covenant defines evangelism as 'the proclamation of the historical, biblical Christ as Savior and Lord with a view to persuading people to come to him personally and so be reconciled to God'.[1] In all of their diversity, evangelicals worldwide essentially agree with this definition. In fact, the retention of the centrality of this kind of evangelism in the midst of religiously correct and universalist forces to the contrary defines in large part what it means to be an evangelical. The deliberations, therefore, concerning social responsibility among evangelicals occur with particular reference to its relationship to evangelism. Mission as Transformation has resulted from post-Lausanne efforts of radical evangelicals worldwide to work out the relationship between these two aspects of mission. Participants affirmed both of them at Lausanne I, but how evangelism related to social action and vice versa remained unclear, creating major tensions among evangelicals.[2]

Whereas affirming evangelism at an international evangelical missionary conference did not surprise anyone, including social responsibility among the fifteen key affirmations of the Covenant surprised many. But should it have? What developments in evangelical mission history signalled a more favourable spirit toward social concern? Such a question begs another one, namely, what occurred in the history of Protestant mission that led to the separation of evangelism and social concern in the first place? Alert to guiding questions such as these, a discussion concerning this relationship reveals the major root from which an understanding of Mission as Transformation emerged.

---

[1] 'Lausanne Covenant', *Making Christ Known*, 20.

[2] Tokunboh Adeyemo, 'A Critical Evaluation of Contemporary Perspectives', in Bruce Nicholls (ed.), *In Word and Deed: Evangelism and Social Responsibility* (Grand Rapids, Mich.: Eerdmans, 1986), 48-57. In this article, Adeyemo outlines nine different schools of thought among evangelicals since Lausanne I regarding the relationship between evangelism and social concern.

A Twentieth Century Phenomenon

Most mission historians agree that the debate concerning the relationship between evangelism and social concern is a twentieth century phenomenon. The debate assumes a dichotomy that finds its origins in something other than the Bible and most of the Church's experience throughout history. Bong Rin Ro surveys the relationship 'from New Testament times to 1960' and claims that prior to the mid nineteenth century, the Church engaged in these two missionary activities integrally and seamlessly.[3] Wilbert Shenk concurs and adds that the present dichotomy builds upon a modernist worldview. He writes,

> Our thinking about Christian witness in the twentieth century has been controlled by a paradigm stamped by the Enlightenment. This means we have identified that witness in terms of discrete components [evangelism and social concern] and then tried to determine the proper balance between them. ... This has precedent neither in the Bible nor in nearly nineteen hundred years of church history.[4]

Indeed, from the early Christians to the great revivalists of the nineteenth century, to follow Jesus Christ meant nothing less than to bear witness to him by the words they proclaimed and the deeds they conducted for the betterment of humanity.

Ro and Shenk as well as Bosch mention William Carey, 'the father of modern missions', as an example of the seamlessness between evangelistic aspirations and social reform.[5] In addition to preaching and planting churches in India, Carey spoke out against the caste system, protested slavery in Britain, organized a boycott against sugar imports from West Indian plantations cultivated by slaves, taught agriculture, and built systems of higher education. He conducted these activities in concert with his evangelistic efforts.

Factors in the Great Reversal

At least two undeniable factors led to what sociologist David Moberg has identified as the 'Great Reversal',[6] referring to the move of evangelicals from

---

[3] Bong Rin Ro, 'The Perspective of Church History from New Testament Times to 1960', in Bruce J. Nicholls (ed.), *In Word and Deed: Evangelism and Social Responsibility* (Grand Rapids, Mich.: Eerdmans, 1986), 13.

[4] Wilbert R. Shenk, 'The Whole is Greater Than the Sum of the Parts: Moving Beyond Word and Deed', *Missiology* 20.1 (January 1993), 73.

[5] Ro, 'The Perspective of Church History', 28 and Shenk, 'The Whole is Greater', 66. See also David J. Bosch, 'In Search of New Evangelical Understanding', in Bruce J. Nicholls (ed.), *In Word and Deed: Evangelism and Social Responsibility* (Grand Rapids, Mich.: Eerdmans, 1986), 68.

[6] David O. Moberg, *The Great Reversal: Evangelism Versus Social Concern* (Philadelphia, Pa. and New York N.Y.: J. B. Lippincott, 1972), 30-34. Credit for the

spearheading social reform in the eighteenth and nineteenth centuries to retreating almost totally from mainstream society by the late 1920s.[7] A strong reaction to the increasing sway of liberal theological developments, which included an emphasis on social concern, constitutes the first and primary factor. Evangelicals, primarily in North America, began to steer away from social concern when they perceived the popularity of the Social Gospel movement as eclipsing personal evangelism in the late nineteenth century.[8]

The preoccupation with defending orthodoxy against the liberal modernist tide produced what became known by the 1920s as fundamentalism, a movement that eventually came to represent 'the militantly conservative wing' of evangelicalism.[9] Martyn Percy has defined Christian fundamentalism as 'the unbudgeable belief in the word for word accuracy of the entire Bible and a spirit of hostility toward anything in the church or society that is thought to conflict with scriptural commands'.[10] This two - pronged description of the heart of the movement certainly describes the American fundamentalists of the 1920s, 30s and 40s, as they increasingly rejected anything the liberal modernists promoted, including unfortunately socio-political involvement.

---

term should ultimately go to historian Timothy L. Smith, as Moberg himself acknowledges (11, 30). Moberg, however, expands upon the phenomenon from a sociological perspective and deserves the credit for popularizing it.

[7] In Robert Krapohl and Charles Lippy, *The Evangelicals: A Historical, Thematic and Biographical Guide* (Westport, Conn. and London: Greenwood, 1999), the authors challenge the view that evangelicals retreated during the height of the fundamentalist-modernist controversy, if by 'retreat' we mean that evangelicals hid and remained silent. According to Krapohl and Lippy, they did no such thing. Although modernists occupied the major denominational posts, evangelicals remained active, outspoken, and influential (53).

[8] The Social Gospel movement, articulated by the likes of Washington Gladden and Walter Rauschenbusch, was generated by a combination of the desire to make the Gospel relevant to society in general and to address the complexities of the industrial revolution in particular. Advocates of the Social Gospel tended to accept the validity of the liberal science of biblical criticism and the emerging theory of evolution, against which evangelicals reacted most vehemently. For relatively recent treatments on the Social Gospel movement, see Christopher H. Evans, *The Social Gospel Today* (Louisville, Ky.: Westminster/John Knox, 2001).

[9] Fundamentalism derives its word usage from a series of tracts entitled *The Fundamentals* written between the years 1909 and 1915. The contemporary world now contains other forms of religious fundamentalism; in addition to Christian fundamentalism, Jewish and Islamic variations have reshaped their respective religious traditions. For a concise description of these variations in fundamentalism today, see Harriet Harris, *Fundamentalism and Evangelicals* (Oxford: Clarendon Press, 1998), 325-339.

[10] Martyn Percy, *Words, Wonders and Power: Understanding Contemporary Christian Fundamentalism and Revivalism* (London: SPCK, 1996), 7.

During these years, fundamentalism dominated the evangelical constituency. This explains in part why 'fundamentalist' and 'evangelical' are, for many, one and the same.

Of course, no one can tenably hold such a position today in light of the diversity that characterizes evangelicalism. But between the time when the reactionary seed of fundamentalism took root in the evangelical community in the late 1920s and the publication of Carl Henry's *Uneasy Conscience of Modern Fundamentalism*[11] in 1947 (more on the impact of this book later), the strength of the fundamentalist movement essentially defined what it meant to be an evangelical.

A shift in eschatology from a predominantly post-millennial to a pre-millennial orientation describes the second undeniable culprit that contributed to the Great Reversal. Inseparable to the reactionary impulse of fundamentalism, this shift had a devastating effect upon the involvement of evangelicals in social reform. Dispensational pre-millennialists preached at once the irredeemable depravity of the social situation and salvation from it through personal conversion. Men and women trapped on board the shipwreck of society described human existence, and offering the lifeboat of Christ to the doomed defined the mission of the Church. By the late 1920s, to be evangelical meant, for most, identification with pre-millennial fundamentalism that reactively erased social responsibility from the missionary agenda. And conversely, to be liberal or modernist meant placing little value on personal evangelism. By then, writes Bosch, 'All forms of progressive social involvement [among evangelicals] had disappeared. The "Great Reversal" had been completed. The polarization between the two main positions had become absolute. The position that one could have both evangelism and social action became virtually untenable'.[12]

The Fundamentalist-Modernist Debate and Protestant Missions

This polarization between fundamentalists and modernists occurred primarily in North America but diffused throughout the world by means of the West-to-East, North-to-South missionary movement during the first half of the twentieth century.[13] Lim notes that the dichotomy took several more decades before it took poisonous root in missionary circles, which then took the dichotomy to the

---

[11] Carl F. H. Henry, *The Uneasy Conscience of Modern Fundamentalism* (Grand Rapids, Mich.: Eerdmans, 1947).

[12] Bosch, 'In Search', 70-71.

[13] Historian William Hutchison, however, points out that the controversy was actually sparked on the mission field 'when a visiting theologian charged that most missionaries [in China] were Modernists'. Cited in Wickeri, Tizon and Yim, 'A Survey of Evangelical Missiological Concerns', 293.

ends of the earth.[14] Ro says it succinctly when he writes, 'The establishment of the Protestant church in the Third World was basically the fruit of Protestant mission from the West ... [And] both the western model of the liberal social gospel and the model of ... evangelical soul saving ... have been copied in the Third World.'[15]

This divide within Protestantism, however, did not intensify as heatedly in the Two Thirds World as it did in North America. In the Philippines for example, Protestant mission historians can easily find traces of the tension along the lines of the controversy, although early Filipino Protestants achieved an admirable ecumenism that included a basic unity between evangelism and social concern. For the most part, churches of the Two Thirds World spared themselves from the intensity of the controversy. Missiologists credit this to a number of factors. First, a less dualistic worldview, characteristic of most of the Two Thirds World, served well in avoiding the landmines of the debate. Referring to non-Western Christians, Bosch writes, 'Not sharing the Greek heritage of dualistic thinking to the same degree that Westerners do, [they] have a far more holistic understanding of the Gospel than do Western Christians'.[16]

Another factor had to do with the hard social realities of poverty, political instability, foreign oppression and exploitation, and human rights violations that needed desperate attention by both local churches and foreign missionaries even as they went about the countryside preaching the Gospel. Furthermore, as many nations declared independence from their colonizers after World War Two, as did the Philippines in 1946, so began declarations of independence on the part of many 'younger churches' from foreign missionary strings, thus eventually resulting in local missiological expressions that more reflected their culturally holistic orientations.

These factors notwithstanding, we cannot deny 'the strong presence and pressures exercised by Euro-American evangelicalism on the Two Thirds World through the missionary movement'.[17] Indeed, the effects of the North American fundamentalist-modernist controversy upon the Church worldwide, via the twentieth century Protestant missionary movement, went far and wide. The global reputation of the social negligence of evangelicals, in fact, attests to the eventual effective diffusion of the North American fundamentalist experience.

Such a claim does not contradict a recent equally valid claim by sociologist Paul Freston that Two Thirds World evangelicalism has developed quite apart

---

[14] David S. Lim, 'A Critique of Modernity in Protestant Mission in the Philippines', *Journal of Asian Mission* 2.2 (September 2000), 154-155.

[15] Ro, 'The Perspectives of Church History', 34.

[16] Bosch, 'In Search', 67.

[17] Costas, 'Evangelical Theology', 312.

from 'American right-wing forces'.[18] The fact that Freston's project deals with
the contemporary sociology of non-Western evangelical politics and not with
its history accounts for his conclusion.[19] Although historians cannot deny that
the American fundamentalists' lack of social concern adversely affected the
rest of the global evangelical community, they also cannot deny that today a
study of evangelical socio-political involvement requires contextual analysis in
order to draw out essential differences. Freston's project in fact opens the door
for more in-depth research in evangelical politics around the world today. The
undeniable historical impact of North American evangelicalism upon the Two
Thirds World, however, suggests that context - specific evangelical socio-
political involvement has resulted from each context uniquely working out the
imported fundamentalist-modernist controversy, which most certainly included
the relationship between evangelism and social concern.

Evangelicals versus Ecumenicals

The evangelism-social concern debate expressed itself in Protestant missions
amidst a larger debate over the ultimate meaning of mission between
evangelicals and mainline or ecumenical Protestants (or 'ecumenicals' for
short).[20] The publication of *Re-Thinking Missions* by William Hocking in 1932
ignited the debate in missionary circles. The 'shocking Hocking Report', as it
came to be called, summarized a two year project carried out by the Layman's
Foreign Missions Inquiry in the early 1930s. The report challenged what were
then basic Protestant missionary tenets, such as the uniqueness of Christianity
among the religions of the world and the necessity of preaching personal
conversion to Christ.[21] Consistent with this challenge, the report declared that
the purpose of mission was not to convert people, but to seek religious
cooperation toward a better world. Such a declaration sent shockwaves
throughout the Protestant missionary community. And needless to say,

---

[18] Paul Freston, *Evangelicals and Politics in Asia, Africa and Latin America*
(Cambridge: Cambridge University Press, 2001), 283-284.
[19] Unfortunately, Freston seems to make his case over and against the undeniable
historical fact concerning the global impact of North American fundamentalism. For
better or for worse, the most reliable historical sources continue to support American
evangelicalism's profound global impact.
[20]Alan J. Bailyes, 'Evangelical and Ecumenical Understandings of Mission',
International Review of Mission 85.339 (October 1996), 487-490. Bailyes identifies five
missiological points upon which the larger debate between evangelicals and ecumenicals
are based: 1) church and world, 2) the nature of conversion, 3) gospel and culture, 4)
Christology, and 5) hermeneutics.
[21] William E. Hocking, *Rethinking Missions* (New York ; London: Harper & Brothers,
1932), 3-78.

evangelicals strongly opposed the findings of the report, thus widening the polarization between evangelicals and ecumenicals around the world.

In the Philippines, the polarization manifested in the division of Protestantism into two main groups after World War Two, namely, the *mga Protestante* and the *mga Born Again*. The *mga Protestante* (the ecumenicals) represented 'the older denominational ecumenical bodies in the country like the United Church of Christ in the Philippines (UCCP) and the United Methodist Church', which carried on the liberal tradition of social concern in the country,[22] while the *mga Born Again* (evangelicals) represented the new post-World War Two wave of conservative, aggressively evangelistic groups. This division within Filipino Protestantism was representative of similar divisions in Protestant circles throughout the Two Thirds World, caused no doubt by North American missionaries who were embroiled in the Hocking Report controversy.

If the Hocking Report sparked the missionary evangelical-ecumenical polarity in the 1930s up through the 1950s, then the missiological developments within the WCC took the rift to unprecedented heights in the early 1960s through to the mid-1970s. Beginning with the official merger of the International Missionary Council (IMC) and the WCC in 1961 at New Delhi, evangelicals began to give the strongest expression to their growing sense of alienation from the WCC. By the mid-1960s, evangelicals poised themselves to launch their own international missionary conferences. In 1966, they met together not once, but twice, for the first time as a 'counter - World Council of Churches movement'.[23] Prior to the 1960s, David Tai-Woong Lee points out that 'both evangelicals and non-evangelicals had worked together to formulate missiology', the strength of fundamentalist missionary voices notwithstanding.[24] But with these two gatherings - first in Wheaton, IL for the Congress on the Church's Worldwide Mission and five months later in Berlin for the World Congress on Evangelism - evangelicals called the Church to

---

[22] The UCCP Statement of Faith includes the following: 'We BELIEVE God is working to make each person a new being in Christ and the whole world His Kingdom. The Kingdom of God is present where faith in Jesus Christ is shared, where healing is given to the sick, where food is given to the hungry, where light is given to the blind, where liberty is given to the captive and oppressed, where love, justice and peace prevail'. Cited in Melanio L. Aoanan, *Pagkakaisa at Pagbabago: Ang Patotoo ng United Church of Christ in the Philippines* (Quezon City: New Day, 1996), 138.

[23] Efiong S. Utuk, 'From Wheaton to Lausanne', in James A Scherer and Stephen B. Bevans (eds.), *New Directions in Mission & Evangelization 2: Theological Foundations,* (Maryknoll, N.Y.: Orbis, 1994), 101.

[24] David Tai-Woong Lee, 'A Two Thirds World Evaluation of Contemporary Evangelical Missiology', in William D. Taylor (ed.), *Global Missiology for the 21st Century: The Iguassu Dialogue* (Grand Rapids, Mich.: Baker, 2000), 134.

remain faithful in proclaiming the Gospel to all nations over and against the 'unfaithfulness' of the WCC.

Many identify the fourth WCC Assembly in Uppsala, Sweden in 1968 as the proverbial straw that broke the camel's back for many evangelicals. 'The great debate', as Roger Hedlund terms it, over the meaning of mission finally came to a head. With reference to the Uppsala meeting, Hedlund writes, 'Two basic theologies - two ideologies - were in conflict ... On the one side were the advocates of mission as humanization, on the other side ... [those concerned] with ... the evangelization of the lost.'[25]

But despite the distancing of evangelicals from WCC gatherings, issues that ecumenicals raised ultimately influenced the mission theology and practice of evangelicals in significant ways. And conversely, issues raised by evangelicals during that time period also influenced ecumenical mission thinking in equally significant ways. Indeed, although some may deny the mutual impact they have had on each other, the documents from their respective conferences of the '70s and '80s demonstrate 'a convergence of convictions'.[26]

Evangelical Diversity in Missionary Social Ethics

Although evangelicals demonstrated amazing unity in the 1966 World Congresses, largely held together by a common distrust of the WCC, the diversity regarding the way they viewed the relationship between evangelism and social concern eventually came to the surface. The united front of the fundamentalists and the 'new evangelicals' against the WCC in 1966, though genuine, could not permanently hold back the different convictions among them on this issue. Charles van Engen points out that even though the new evangelicals gained confidence after 1966 in helping to define mission theology and practice, a reactionary fundamentalism that never disappeared held them at bay.[27]

Who were these new evangelicals, and what did they represent? In 1947, Carl Henry jolted the evangelical world with the classic publication, *The Uneasy Conscience of Modern Fundamentalism* wherein he tactfully accused his fellow evangelicals of not proclaiming the whole Gospel. He wrote, 'Fundamentalism in revolting against the Social Gospel ... also ... revolt[ed]

---

[25] Roger Hedlund, *Roots of the Great Debate in Mission* (Bangalore, India: Theological Book Trust, 1997), 229. Hedlund's perspective is decidedly evangelical. For balance, see T. V. Philip, *Edinburgh to Salvador: Twentieth Century Ecumenical Missiology* (Delhi; Tiruvalla: ISPCK; CSS, 1999), 97-131.

[26] Bosch, *Transforming Mission*, 408.

[27] Charles van Engen, *Mission on the Way: Issues in Mission Theology* (Grand Rapids, Mich.: Baker, 1996), 135.

against the Christian social imperative'.[28] Such a statement may seem quite benign now, but in 1947 it had enough potency to have started a re-awakening of the evangelical social conscience in America and beyond. Henry continued to lead the charge to call evangelicals to re-engage society in the 'supernatural power of the Gospel'.[29] In a later publication, he labeled the evangelism - only posture as part of an unbiblical 'fundamentalist reduction'.[30]

Henry led the way in propagating this new kind of evangelicalism (which was not so much 'new' as it was a harking back to the pre-Great Reversal days) through a number of forums. The periodical *Christianity Today*, its premiere issue appearing in 1956, for which Henry served as the first editor, eventually established a wide readership that continues its influence today. Other forums, like Fuller Theological Seminary (1947), the National Religious Broadcasters (1944), the National Association of Evangelicals (1942) and Youth for Christ International (1944) also helped to promote a more moderate, less reactive, and to its proponents, a more biblically informed evangelical version of the faith, which most certainly included social concern. This new evangelicalism gained solid momentum in the 1950s and into the 60s, and it did its part in informing evangelical mission theology for years to come.

The reaffirmation of Christian social responsibility, which held a prominent place in the new evangelicalism, made its presence felt in the 1966 World Congresses at Wheaton and Berlin respectively, primarily by the likes of Carl Henry, Horace Fenton (then director of the Latin American Mission) and an itinerant evangelist named Billy Graham.[31] These and other speakers at the two Congresses made it clear, however, while reaffirming social responsibility, that evangelism must continue to hold a primary place in authentic biblical mission. In reaffirming social concern, they applied great caution not to replicate what they perceived as dangerous theological error being committed by the WCC. They assured the evangelical constituency that their understanding of social concern does not and must not eclipse the primary task of world evangelization.

Such prioritizing made many evangelicals from the Two Thirds World feel increasingly uneasy, and they gradually began to voice their discomfort at different gatherings. Padilla notes that the new concern for social problems shown at the 1966 Wheaton Congress 'was by no means unrelated to the

---

[28] Henry, *Uneasy Conscience,* 32.

[29] Henry, *Uneasy Conscience,* 44-45. Henry uses the term 'supernatural' in *Uneasy Conscience* as a polemic against the liberal, naturalistic view of humanity and society.

[30] Carl F. H. Henry, *Evangelical Responsibility in Contemporary Theology* (Grand Rapids, Mich.: Eerdmans, 1957), 33.

[31] For a selection of key documents from these Congresses with commentary on the major influences at the 1966 Congresses, see Hedlund, *Roots of the Great Debate,* 155-196.

presence of a good number of participants from the Two Thirds World'.[32] While gratified that their brothers and sisters from the West increasingly challenged the North American born, but globally diffused 'fundamentalist reduction', Two Thirds World evangelicals continued to press the international missionary enterprise to investigate further the integral place of social concern in the mission of the Church. As a result, the Church's social mission occupied major discussions at lesser known evangelical conferences held in Singapore in 1968, Minneapolis in 1969, Bogota also in 1969, and Amsterdam in 1971.[33]

A group of 'young evangelicals' from North America joined their brothers and sisters from the Two Thirds World and began expressing a similar kind of discomfort with what they interpreted as weak token affirmations of Christian social concern coming from the evangelical rank and file in the context of the volatile 1960s.[34] They called the nation to self-critique in general and the Church to a rediscovery of its prophetic ministry in particular. Their historic meeting in Chicago in 1973 produced the Chicago Declaration, which articulated a Gospel inspired commitment to compassion and justice, alongside evangelism, for a younger, radical generation of evangelicals.[35]

Meanwhile, the fundamentalist spirit remained strong as did the Henry-ian version of the new evangelicalism. These persuasions continued to exert themselves at all of the aforementioned conferences, promoting their respective views. So during the period between 1966 and 1973, we can identify three broad groupings that outlined the diversity of missionary social ethics among evangelicals: 1) the fundamentalists, who maintained the primacy of evangelism largely at the expense of social concern as a continued reaction against the 'apostate ecumenical movement', 2) the new or moderate evangelicals, who, while maintaining the primacy of evangelism, called for a return to historic evangelicalism that pro-actively engaged the social issues of

---

[32] C. Rene Padilla, 'Evangelism and Social Responsibility: From Wheaton '66 to Wheaton '83', *Transformation* 2.3 (April/June 1985), 28. Delegates from the Philippines at the Wheaton and Berlin Congresses of 1966 who contributed written reports included Gadiel Isidro, Max Atziena, Angel Taglucop, and Gregorio Tingson. Isidro's report is available in Harold Lindsell (ed.), *The Church's Worldwide Mission,* (Waco, Tex.: Word, 1966), 263-267. And the other reports are available in Carl F.H. Henry and W. Stanley Mooneyham (eds.), *One Race, One Gospel, One Task,* (Minneapolis, Minn.: World Wide Publications, 1967), 214-217, 526-527.

[33] Padilla, 'Evangelism and Social Responsibility', 28.

[34] Richard Quebedeaux, *The Young Evangelicals* (New York: Harper and Row, 1974), 99-134.

[35] Ronald J. Sider, 'An Historic Moment for Biblical Social Concern', in Ronald J. Sider (ed.), *The Chicago Declaration* (Carol Stream, IL: Creation House, 1974), 29-31. It is worth noting here that proponents of the new evangelicalism - the neo-evangelicals, or if one wishes, the not-so-young evangelicals! - like Carl Henry and Paul Rees were among the signers of the Chicago Declaration.

the day, and 3) the younger, radical evangelicals who called for an uncompromising socio-political commitment to biblical compassion and justice for the sake of the poor and oppressed in the world. Viewing it in one-two-three terms like this might give the impression of progressive development, as if the 'young radicals' phased out the 'moderates' who phased out the 'fundamentalists'. But missionary convictions die hard; these three strands not only continue to exist today, they also each have spawned variations of themselves, making evangelical missionary social ethics a very diverse and complex phenomenon.

Mission as Transformation emerged from the radical stream of evangelical social consciousness. Not satisfied with the language of the primacy of evangelism, radical evangelicals around the world continued to reflect upon the scriptures and their social situations, allowing their contexts of pastoral and missionary action among the poor to inform their reading. And vice versa: their reading of scripture informed how they went about their pastoral and missionary duties among the poor. In all of their social action and reflection (praxis), their vision for all to come to a saving faith in Jesus Christ never wavered.

Evangelical Relief and Development Ministries after World War Two

Alongside the historical root of the evangelism versus social concern debate grew a lesser root that also significantly determined the nature of Mission as Transformation. Calling it lesser simply means that it originated from, and therefore depended upon, the larger root of the evangelism versus social concern debate. This particular tension, however, created by the inconsistency between practice and theology among evangelicals warrants special attention because it was precisely the attempted efforts to relieve this tension that led to the affirmation of social concern at Lausanne I, a discussion that we will resume in Chapter 2.

Despite the North American 'fundamentalist reduction' that dominated the global evangelical missionary community, evangelicals continued to practice works of benevolence and social uplift in the service of the Gospel around the world. 'While it may be true that some evangelicals in the United States were uneasy about their response to their own social issues', write Samuel and Sugden, 'it would not be true to say that they have not responded to social needs on the mission field.'[36] David M. Howard, who chronicled the history of the World Evangelical Fellowship (WEF), states confidently that the leaders of WEF, as they represented the worldwide evangelical constituency, 'have

---

[36] Vinay Samuel and Chris Sugden, 'Introduction', in Vinay Samuel and Chris Sugden (eds.), *The Church in Response to Human Need* (Oxford; Grand Rapids, Mich.: Regnum; Eerdmans, 1987), viii.

always understood the obligation of Christians to reach out in love to those in need and give a cup of cold water'.[37] He then proceeds to list WEF's various humanitarian accomplishments among the world's needy, which included work among Vietnamese and Lebanese refugees, relief work among the poor in Latin America, cooperation with Development Assistance Services (DAS) and the International Institute for Development (IDAC), and the eventual formation within WEF of the International Development Assistance Commission.

Moreover, as mentioned earlier, Two Thirds World evangelicals eventually fought their way through false, Western imposed separations of the individual from the social and the spiritual from the physical, thus allowing themselves the freedom to get involved in their respective social and cultural struggles. For example, the story of Filipino Oseas Martin (as told by his daughter Viola) reveals a holistic ministry among the native Tingians of Apayao in the Philippines during an era when Western evangelicals were hesitant to get socially involved. He recounts that in addition to his evangelistic and educational efforts in the late 40s and early 50s, 'I became very interested in alleviating the lot of the Tingians, so I was enthusiastic when a group headed by the mayor ... planned to put up a Credit Union Cooperative and invited me to join.'[38] The point is, the disappearance of an evangelical social ethic during 'the dark ages of evangelicalism' failed to eliminate evangelical missionary social action.[39]

The inconsistency between missionary social practice and the lack of a social ethic increasingly distressed the more evangelical thoughtful. Did not continued social involvement betray the fundamentalist stand against the theology of the Social Gospel? If the liberal version of the Social Gospel stood to be rejected, how could evangelicals theologically justify the ongoing humanitarian work conducted by them? The attempt to bridge the gap between social practice and social ethic in the missionary context, to come up with a theological justification for compassion and justice ministries, constituted another root from which an understanding of Mission as Transformation eventually emerged.

---

[37] David M. Howard, *The Dream That Would Not Die: The Birth and Growth of the World Evangelical Fellowship, 1846-1986* (Exeter: Paternoster, 1986), 189.

[38] Oseas Martin, 'The Cause of Christ in Apayao', in Anne C. Kwantes (ed.), *A Century of Bible Christians in the Philippines* (Manila: OMF, 1998), 153.

[39] Athol Gill, 'Christian Social Responsibility', in C. Rene Padilla (ed.), *The New Face of Evangelicalism: An International Symposium on the Lausanne Covenant* (Downers Grove, Ill.: InterVarsity, 1976), 93.

Evangelical Missionary Humanitarianism

Evangelical social practice never completely left the missionary scene, but it did greatly diminish in the 1920s and 30s due to the pressures generated by the fundamentalist-modernist controversy.[40] The dip lasted for several decades until the period beginning at the end of World War Two to the aftermath of the Korean War.[41]

The post-war period, however, marked a significant increase in evangelical humanitarian ministries. For example, World Relief began in 1944 as the humanitarian arm of the National Association of Evangelicals in America. World Vision began in 1950 when Dr. Bob Pierce set out to help children orphaned in the Korean War. The Evangelical Relief Alliance or TEAR Fund (originally called 'EAR Fund') began in 1960 as evangelicals participated in World Refugee Year in the UK. In the Philippines, Christ for Greater Manila began in 1961 primarily as an evangelistic ministry but made the plight of street children a priority shortly thereafter. Indeed, evangelical relief and compassion ministries began to sprout globally during the post-war years. A short list would also include the Evangelical Fellowship of India Commission on Relief (EFICOR) and the Christian Relief and Development Association (CRDA) that brought together Christian organizations in Africa in 1973.

These and other humanitarian para-church organizations and coalitions attested to the growing freedom of evangelicals to respond to human need from the mid-1940s to the early 1970s. However, the consequences of the fundamentalist-modernist debacle lingered on, as a cloud of suspicion loomed over evangelicals who were involved in social ministries. The suspicion led to accusations that ranged from accommodating the liberal Social Gospel and thus compromising the evangelistic task to sympathizing with dangerous leftist groups. Even many of the evangelical social workers themselves deemed their ministries of compassion as secondary to the 'real' work of the Gospel of evangelism and church planting.

Evangelicals toward Development

Despite the sense of holding second class status within the evangelical community, socially involved evangelicals continued to mature in their practical response to the needs of the poor. Their humanitarian efforts began to broaden from primarily relief work to development work in the 1970s. Although it took several decades for evangelicals to implement what were

---

[40] Linda Smith, 'Recent Historical Perspectives of the Evangelical Tradition', in Edgar J. Elliston (ed.), *Christian Relief and Development: Developing Workers for Effective Ministry* (Dallas, Tex.: Word, 1989), 25-26.

[41] Smith, 'Recent Historical Perspectives', 26-27.

mainstream development activities in the 1950s and 60s, they did not summarily dismiss them.

The definition of development has evolved since World War Two, but in the immediate post-war period, the term referred generally to the assistance given by American and European countries (the 'developed' nations) to the less fortunate countries of the South and East (the 'underdeveloped' nations). The variations of development cooperation, development aid, community development or simply 'development' convey the same thing, namely, an empowering approach toward poverty alleviation, 'a second generational' approach from welfare relief in that it aims to 'help people help themselves' with the goal toward self-sustainability.[42] Post World War Two victors in the West adopted the term in an attempt to understand their new relationship with the 'less fortunate' nations. According to Jan Jongeneel, 'Developed and underdeveloped' replaced 'civilized and uncivilized', as the victorious nations campaigned to help war ravaged nations rebuild.[43]

Starting in the mid-1960s, many began to question the assumptions behind the development approach, eventually viewing it as just another form of Western imperialism that created a dependency relationship between rich and poor nations. To these critics, the assumptions behind development added up to an imposed modernization project that attempted to re-make countries in the Two Thirds World in the cultural image of the industrialized, technological West. Filipino nationalist historians Renato and Letizia Constantino exemplify this theory when they write,

> In the Philippines, the various aid programmes launched and implemented during the first twenty years of Philippine independence reinforced the neo-colonial structure of the economy. ... The propaganda and information campaigns for these programmes succeeded in making many Filipinos believe that their country could not exist, much less progress without foreign aid. Worse, many Filipinos still think of this aid in the semantic meaning of the word, oblivious of the onerous conditions attached to such programmes and the counterpart funds often required.[44]

---

[42] David C. Korten, *Getting to the 21st Century: Voluntary Action and the Global Agenda* (West Hartford, Conn.: Kumarian, 1990), 118.

[43] Jan A.B. Jongeneel, *Philosophy, Science, and Theology of Mission in the 19th and 20th Centuries: Part II* (Frankfurt-am-Main: Peter Lang, 1997), 148.

[44] Renato Constantino and Letizia R. Constantino, *The Philippines: The Continuing Past* (Quezon City: The Foundation for Nationalist Studies, 1978), 330-331.

Wolfgang Gern identifies two incompatible development theories that emerged since World War Two.[45] The modernization theory, which at the core believes that backwardness and lack of progressive vision causes poverty, views the process of development as poor nations simply catching up (with some assistance) to modern industrial global society. This theory informed the earliest of post World War Two development efforts, but needless to say, it continues its influence today.

The dependency theory, on the other hand, emerging out of the Two Thirds World, especially out of Latin America, directly challenges the modernization theory as it refutes the very categories of 'developed' and 'underdeveloped'. According to this theory, Two Thirds World nations do not represent an earlier or retarded stage of progress; rather, they represent simply differences in values and goals. And to better their lot requires not development aid as defined by their former colonizers, but rather the freedom to forge approaches that emerge out of their own respective cultures.

Not surprisingly, ecumenical Protestants and Roman Catholics participated in the development discussions. Jongeneel traces the priority of development in these mission traditions from as early as 1962 when the United Nations declared the 1960s as the 'decade of development'.[46] In fact, the theme of liberation within these traditions grew out of the practice of development in contexts of oppression, as they took up the pursuit of social justice with new vigor. Gern observes that after the first two WCC conferences on development, both held in Montreux, Switzerland, 'the struggle of the poor for liberation from oppression has been the new name for development and has become an integral part of ecumenical ecclesiology'.[47]

Evangelicals, on the other hand, remained primarily in relief work in their expression of social concern, although the winds of change in the direction of development blew all around them. Indeed evangelicals eventually caught the spirit of the patronizing but nonetheless well-meaning altruism that the victorious West extended to underdeveloped nations, and this undoubtedly played a key role in their seeing development activities as a good, right and perhaps even divinely directed endeavour. Caught up in the spirit of the times, they did not protest development activities. This non-polemical attitude toward

---

[45] Wolfgang Gern, 'Development', in Karl Muller, Theo Sundermeier, Stephen B. Bevans, Richard H. Bliese (eds.), *Dictionary of Mission: Theology, History, Perspectives* (Maryknoll, N.Y.: Orbis, 1998), 102-103.

[46] Jongeneel, *Philosophy, Science and Theology of Mission*, 148.

[47] Gern, 'Development', 105. See also Christian Smith, *The Emergence of Liberation Theology: Radical Religion and Social Movement Theory* (Chicago, Ill.; London: University of Chicago, 1991), 176-177, where the author claims the term 'liberation' replaced 'development' at the hands of Latin Americans Gustavo Gutierrez and Rubem Alves who were on their way to one of the conferences mentioned above.

such activities demonstrated a moving away from a social apathy of an earlier era.

It seemed like just a matter of time for the development approach (with traces of both modernization and dependency theories to be sure) to appear on the evangelical missionary agenda. And indeed by the mid-1970s, thanks to the social affirmations at Lausanne I, development became a major missiological activity. Many evangelical relief agencies became agencies of relief *and* development.

Increasing Need for a Theology of Development

As evangelicals moved from relief aid toward development aid in the years right before Lausanne I, the tension caused by the inconsistency between maturing social practice and a lack of a social ethic to warrant it came to bursting point; something had to give. Amid this tension, evangelical mission scholars and development practitioners finally woke up to their inevitable need for one another, and Lausanne I proved timely for such collaboration. Samuel and Sugden explain that 'the dialogue of mission theologians and workers in relief and development at the Lausanne Congress catalyzed a whole movement for the development of holistic ministry'.[48] Indeed Mission as Transformation grew from a root consisting of evangelical growth in relief and development ministries from the mid-1940s to the early 1970s and the consequent need for theological justification.

This root grew out of, and alongside, the larger root of the evangelism versus social concern debate. In fact, researchers can view this 'lesser root' as the practical expression of the first root. As the new evangelicals challenged the social blindness of fundamentalism in the 1940s and 50s, and as the radical evangelicals challenged the weakness of the social vision of all positions right of the political spectrum in the 1960s, the door increasingly widened for evangelicals to participate in works of relief and development. If the working out of the evangelism versus social concern debate constituted the theological root, then the theologically groundless growth of relief and development ministries among evangelicals constituted the practical root. Together these two roots eventually sprouted a socially informed missiology called Transformation.

---

[48] Samuel and Sugden, 'Introduction', *The Church in Response to Human Need,* p, ix.

CHAPTER 2

Lausanne '74 to Wheaton '83: Internal Tensions

Lausanne '74

By its sheer attendance and worldwide representation, by its ambitious scope yet clear evangelistic focus, and by its accomplishments in both theological reflection and strategic mobilization, the July 1974 International Congress on World Evangelization held in Lausanne, Switzerland stands alone in the annals of evangelical mission history. Representing a hundred and fifty countries and a hundred thirty five Protestant denominations, two thousand four hundred and seventy three participants gathered together for this watershed event. Furthermore, 'half of the participants were from the Third World'.[1] Of course, it has its antecedents including the gatherings at the two worldwide Congresses in 1966 in Wheaton and Berlin respectively and indirectly the formation of the World Evangelical Fellowship in 1951. But the theological and strategic impact of Lausanne I has set it apart from all other prior (and arguably subsequent) alliances and gatherings among evangelicals. The event of 1974 'became a movement, an inspiration, and a symbol for thousands of Christians all over the world'.[2]

The Lausanne Covenant, comprising fifteen key articles or clauses, encapsulates the many facets of the movement.[3] Rene Padilla, two years after the Covenant's adoption, described it as 'a little more than a detailed outline for an evangelical theology of mission',[4] and it has served since as the 'ongoing

---

[1] Philip, *Edinburgh to Salvador,* 107.

[2] Valdir R. Steuernagel, 'The Theology of Mission in Its Relation to Social Responsibility within the Lausanne Movement', (ThD thesis, Lutheran School of Theology at Chicago, 1988), 78.

[3] 'The Lausanne Covenant', *Making Christ Known,* 24-27. The drafting committee of the Covenant consisted of five members: John Stott, Samuel Escobar, James Douglas, Leighton Ford, and Hudson Armerding.

[4] Padilla, 'Introduction', 15.

basis for cooperation in mission among evangelicals the world over.'[5] Missiologists worldwide have analyzed and interpreted the Lausanne Covenant since 1974, as it continues to exert its enduring influence upon the direction of evangelical mission theology.

It behooves us here to review how the Covenant articulated the role of socio-political involvement in the missionary task, as well as how evangelicals interpreted it in different ways in the years that followed. Indeed consensus on the matter quickly eluded evangelicals after Lausanne, as tensions mounted regarding the still ambiguous relationship between evangelism and social concern.

Affirmation of Socio-Political Involvement at Lausanne

Billy Graham, the inspirational figurehead and catalyst of Lausanne I, listed four hopes in his opening address at the Congress, the third of which pertains directly to the social question.[6] He announced at the outset, 'I trust we can state ... the relationship between evangelism and social responsibility ..., [which] disturbs many believers. Perhaps Lausanne can help to clarify it.'[7] This opening statement demonstrates that by the time of the Congress, thanks to the factors discussed in Chapter 1, Graham and many others came prepared to settle this issue. Of course in retrospect, Lausanne did little to settle the matter, if by 'settle' we mean agreement, peace, and harmony occurred between parties. On the contrary, the issue of the relationship between evangelism and social concern intensified among them.

Lausanne I clearly recognized and affirmed social concern as essential to the task of world evangelization by making it an integral part of the Covenant. Article 5 entitled 'Christian Social Responsibility', which basically synthesized the papers presented at the Congress by Rene Padilla, Samuel Escobar and Carl Henry,[8] deals with the issue most directly.[9] In his analytical treatment of the

---

[5] James A. Scherer and Stephen B. Bevans, 'Wheaton Statement on Transformation', in James A. Scherer and Stephen B. Bevans (eds.), *New Directions in Mission and Evangelization 1: Basic Statements 1974-1991* (Maryknoll, N.Y.: Orbis, 1992), 253.

[6] Billy Graham, 'Why Lausanne?' in James D. Douglas (ed.), *Let the Earth Hear His Voice: International Congress on World Evangelization* (Minneapolis, Minn.: World Wide Publications, 1975), 34. The other three of Graham's stated hopes were: 1) 'I would like to see the Congress frame a biblical declaration on evangelism'; 2) 'I would like to see the Church challenged to complete the task of world evangelization'; the third is discussed above; and 4) 'I hope that a new "*koinonia*" or fellowship among evangelicals of all persuasions will be developed throughout the world'.

[7] Graham, 'Why Lausanne?' 34.

[8] Klaus Bockmuehl, *Evangelicals and Social Ethics* (trans. David T. Priestly; Downers Grove, IL: InterVarsity, 1979), 8-12. These papers to which Bockmuehl refers are available in James D. Douglas (ed.), *Let the Earth His Voice* (Minneapolis, Minn.:

contents of the Article, Klaus Bockmuehl extracts and then comments on the nine 'verbs of action' contained in it, offering a detailed interpretation of the social vision articulated at the Congress.[10]

At least two overall themes emerge from his analysis: 1) To act prophetically in society, denouncing injustices and calling governments to repentance, and 2) To demonstrate and promote the righteousness of the kingdom of God for and among the oppressed. This summary of the Lausanne social vision points out its two-pronged reactive and pro-active elements. But obviously, these themes only hint at a social ethic; it does not provide one. Article 5 of the Lausanne Covenant simply and officially affirmed socio-political involvement, thus validating it among evangelicals as part of the missionary task.

The strength of this validation gave evangelical theologians and practitioners alike a new sense of freedom to explore what social responsibility might mean for mission. Athol Gil comments that 'in expressing penitence "for having sometimes regarded evangelism and social concern as mutually exclusive" and in emphasizing that "evangelism and socio-political involvement are both part of our Christian duty", the Lausanne Covenant marked a turning point in evangelical thinking.'[11] Samuel and Sugden concur and add, 'Evangelical relief and development agencies around the world received fresh energy because they could now appeal to the evangelical constituency as "family" without the fear of either being rebuked for preaching the "social gospel" or being charged with compromising on evangelism.'[12] Indeed for both theological reflection and mission practice, the Lausanne Covenant, particularly Article 5, provided new impetus for evangelicals to engage in social ministries.

World Wide Publications, 1976), the official reference volume of Lausanne I. Padilla's address entitled 'Evangelism and the World' (116-146) and Escobar's 'Evangelism and Man's Search for Freedom, Justice, and Fulfilment' (303-326) were both plenary papers, while Henry's address 'Christian Personal and Social Ethics in Relation to Racism, Poverty, War, and Other Problems' (1163-1182) provided a foundation for the sessions of a special committee on ethics.

[9] C. Rene Padilla and Chris Sugden (eds.), *Texts on Evangelical Social Ethics* (Nottingham: Grove Books, 1985), 5-7. The editors discuss Articles 4 and 10 as also influencing the development of social ethics in evangelical mission.

[10] Bockmuehl, *Evangelicals and Social Ethics,* 17ff. The nine 'verbs of action' that Bockmuehl extracts from the Covenant are: 1) share God's concern for justice, 2) share God's concern for reconciliation, 3) share God's concern for the liberation of men from every kind of oppression, 4) respect the dignity of every person, 5) exploit no one, 6) serve every person, 7) denounce evil and injustice, 8) seek to exhibit the righteousness of the kingdom of Christ, 9) seek to spread the righteousness of the kingdom of Christ.

[11] Gill, 'Christian Social Responsibility', 89.

[12] Samuel and Sugden, 'Introduction', *The Church in Response to Human Need,* ix.

For the most part, evangelicals worldwide welcomed the Covenant, which by implication also welcomed the affirmation of the Church's social responsibility. In the Philippine National Strategy Group Report, for example, Fred Magbanua represented the fifty seven Filipino participants when he wrote, 'We wholeheartedly accept the Lausanne Covenant', and then later in the same report, 'We realize that we have emphasized the proclamation of the Gospel and neglected our social responsibilities. We affirm that evangelism and social concern are both parts of the mission of the church and must be carried out without sacrificing one for the other.'[13]

The Statement on Radical Discipleship

The Covenant's clear affirmation of social concern, however, did not go unchallenged at the Congress. Many conservatives saw it as a distraction from the original Lausanne vision of 'cross-cultural evangelism'. Others to the right of the conservatives went even further and accused Lausanne's stated social vision as being the old Social Gospel in evangelical clothing.[14] 'Most of [these critics] identified with the North American missionary establishment [while] the wholistic approach to mission continued to find support among evangelicals, especially in the Two Thirds World.'[15]

However for those left of centre, those identified here as radical evangelicals - the affirmation of socio-political involvement in the Lausanne Covenant did not go far enough. They claimed that even though Article 5 repented of past negligence and affirmed the inseparable relationship of social responsibility to evangelism, it did not define that relationship. Moreover, social concern still felt like an appendage to the 'real work' of the Gospel.[16] So a group of about two hundred people at the Congress formed an ad hoc committee to discuss the shortcomings of the Covenant's social affirmation in light of the implications of

---

[13] Fred Magbanua, 'Philippine National Strategy Group Report', in James D. Douglas (ed.), *Let the Earth Hear His Voice* (Minneapolis, Minn.: World Wide Publications 1975), 1424-1425. The Report mis-prints the author's name as 'Fred Magleanua'.

[14] See Steuernagel, 'The Theology of Mission', 151-156; Hedlund, *Roots of the Great Debate*, 294-299; and Padilla 'Evangelism and Social Responsibility', 29, to know who had problems with the Covenant's social affirmation. The list included Peter Wagner, Ralph Winter, Donald McGavran, Arthur Johnston, and Peter Beyerhaus. Hedlund mentions these individuals sympathetically from a 'church growth' perspective, which he shares, while Padilla discusses them from a radical evangelical perspective. Steuernagel attempts a more objective discussion, although he falls decidedly on the radical evangelical side.

[15] Padilla, 'Evangelism and Social Responsibility', 29.

[16] Chris Sugden, 'Evangelicals and Wholistic Evangelism', in Vinay Samuel and Albrecht Hauser (eds.), *Proclaiming Christ in Christ's Way: Studies in Integral Evangelism* (Oxford: Regnum, 1989), 33.

radical discipleship. They drafted an official response to Lausanne aptly titled 'Theology [and] Implications of Radical Discipleship'.[17]

Divided into four main parts, the official response challenged the Congress to declare more overtly the place of social concern in the mission of the Church by affirming the comprehensive scope of the Gospel of the kingdom of God.[18] '[The Gospel]', the paper read, 'is Good News of liberation, of restoration, of wholeness, and of salvation that is personal, social, global and cosmic.'[19] It ended with a resolution that affirmed both the spiritual and social dimensions of the task of world evangelization:

> We resolve to submit ourselves afresh to the Word of God and to the leading of his Spirit, to pray and work together for the renewal of his community as the expression of his reign, to participate in God's mission to his world in our generation, showing forth Jesus as Lord and Saviour, and calling on all men everywhere to repent, to submit to his Lordship, to know his salvation, to identify in him with the oppressed and work for the liberation of all men and women in his name.[20]

In sum, the Statement on Radical Discipleship repudiated the dichotomy between evangelism and social concern, challenged the language of the primacy of evangelism, and broadened the scope of God's salvific work in the world, all the while remaining wholly committed to biblical authority and world evangelization. Writing over ten years after the issuance of the statement, Padilla assessed that it 'provided the strongest statement on the basis for wholistic mission ever formulated by an evangelical conference up to that date.'[21]

Sugden reports that although the statement did not end up as part of the Covenant, convener John Stott presented it at the end of the Congress along with the final draft of the Covenant, thus giving prominent place to it.[22] Moreover, almost five hundred people, approximately a quarter of the number of official delegates, signed it before leaving the Congress. So between the Covenant's affirmation of socio-political involvement and the inclusion of the Statement on Radical Discipleship among the official papers of the Congress, the status of social concern within the evangelical constituency enjoyed a new

---

[17] 'Theology [and] Implications of Radical Discipleship', in James D. Douglas (ed.), *Let the Earth His Voice* (Minneapolis; Minn.: World Wide Publications, 1975), 1294-1296.

[18] 'Theology and Implications of Radical Discipleship', 1294-1296. The four parts begin with 'We affirm', 'We confess', 'We rejoice', and 'We resolve' respectively. See Appendix A of this study for the full statement.

[19] 'Theology and Implications of Radical Discipleship', 1294.

[20] 'Theology and Implications of Radical Discipleship', 1296.

[21] Padilla, 'Evangelism and Social Responsibility', 29.

[22] Sugden, 'Wholistic Evangelism', 34.

level of validation that it had not experienced since the days before the fundamentalist-modernist debacle.

Radical Discipleship as Precursor to Transformation

The broadness of the Lausanne social vision allowed for diversity in interpretation, and at the outset, this broadness served as a valuable point of evangelical unity. Valdir Steuernagel sees it 'as a sign of strength and of a rare and delicate moment of consensus. One step backwards,' he posits, 'and Lausanne would have lost the radical discipleship group; one step forward and it would have lost the conservative evangelicals'.[23]

But as much as its broadness proved valuable in the beginning, it eventually needed sharpening if socio-ethical thinking and practice had a future on the evangelical missionary agenda. Predictably, however, evangelicals went about interpreting and developing the Lausanne social vision according to their respective schools of thought. And as proponents of these various schools encountered one another at conferences, as well as on the mission field, an unprecedented level of tension intensified within the post-Lausanne evangelical missionary community. In the midst of this tension, proponents of the radical evangelical school took the Lausanne social vision down a specific path that eventually led to an understanding of Mission as Transformation.

These same radicals were responsible for drafting the Statement on Radical Discipleship at Lausanne. This strongly suggests that the Wheaton '83 Statement on Transformation finds its roots more in the Statement on Radical Discipleship than in the Lausanne Covenant itself.[24] To be sure, the drafters understood the Statement with reference to the Covenant, and indeed, the Covenant validated the Statement. So the link between the Statement and the Covenant remains organically intact. Therefore, saying that the Wheaton '83 Statement on Transformation has more affinity to the Statement on Radical Discipleship does not locate it outside of the Lausanne movement. Nevertheless, the convictions, the hopes, and the spirit of the Statement, viewed by its drafters as both an addendum and a corrective to the Covenant, set a course that was destined not only to go beyond the Covenant in affirming and defining socio-political involvement, but also to go a very different way than the conservative evangelical constituency.

---

[23] Steuernagel, 'The Theology of Mission', 156.

[24] In light of this, Samuel and Sugden's *Mission as Transformation* should have perhaps included the 'Statement on Radical Discipleship' as an Appendix rather than, or at least in addition to, the Lausanne Covenant. Chris Sugden's *Radical Discipleship* (London: Marshall, Morgan and Scott, 1981), in fact, does just that: Appendix 1 is the 'Statement on Radical Discipleship' and Appendix 2 is the Lausanne Covenant.

Tensions from Within: Evangelical Social Concern after Lausanne

Indeed an understanding of Mission as Transformation emerged from some very real tensions between 1974 and 1983. The prominence of the Statement on Radical Discipleship given at Lausanne probably led its supporters to believe that its convictions would eventually find their way into the evangelical mainstream. Confident declarations by Padilla, for example, that 'the Lausanne Covenant was a death blow to the superficial equation of the Christian mission with the multiplication of Christians and churches' and that 'evangelicalism is definitely getting over the "church growth" syndrome and over the unbiblical divorce between the *kerygma* and the *diakonia*' reflect more the high hopes of post-Lausanne radical evangelicals than the truth of the situation.[25] For in the decade that followed a theological battle ensued as to who will dictate the course of evangelical mission after Lausanne; it brought to the fore the different agendas of evangelicals corresponding to the various schools of thought.

At least three overlapping tensions related to socio-political involvement define the contours of the battle. These three tensions between 1974 and 1983 from within the Lausanne movement played a key role in leading a small worldwide group of radical evangelicals toward an understanding of Mission as Transformation.

Narrow View vs. Broad View

Narrow and broad views of the nature of mission characterized the first tension, which intensified as early as the first meeting of the Lausanne Continuation Committee in 1975 at Mexico City.[26] Meeting with the purpose of clarifying its role in continuing the efforts begun at Lausanne, conservative evangelicals fought for singling out and focusing on evangelism, while others pleaded that all facets of the agreed upon Covenant be taken seriously, especially the Church's social responsibility. After a week of intense deliberations, the committee tried to take into account both the narrow and the broad by concluding that its purpose was 'to further the total biblical mission of the church, recognizing that "in this mission of sacrificial service, evangelism is primary", and that our particular concern must be the evangelization of the 2.7 billion unreached people of our world'.[27]

A year later, the committee convened again in Atlanta, henceforth calling itself the Lausanne Committee for World Evangelization (LCWE). There it formed four working groups, one which the LCWE named the Lausanne

---

[25] Padilla, 'Introduction', 12.

[26] Steuernagel, 'The Theology of Mission', 173-179.

[27] Leighton Ford cited in Steuernagel, 'The Theology of Mission', 174.

Theology and Education Group (LTEG).[28] Mandated 'to promote theological reflection on issues related to world evangelization and, in particular, to explore the implications of the Lausanne Covenant', the LTEG sponsored or co-sponsored four consultations between 1977 and 1982.[29] These consultations provided the most open and free forum in which evangelicals could deliberate on given issues. As social responsibility continued to be a 'hot issue', two out of the four consultations dealt with various aspects of evangelical social concern: the 1980 International Consultation on Simple Lifestyle in London (SLC) and the 1982 Consultation on the Relationship between Evangelism and Social Responsibility in Grand Rapids, MI (CRESR).

The SLC in London sought to grasp both the theological and practical meanings of a conviction expressed in Article 9 of the Lausanne Covenant. After expressing shock by world poverty, Article 9 reads, 'Those of us who live in affluent circumstances accept our duty to develop a simple lifestyle in order to contribute to both relief and evangelism.'[30] In an attempt to take this conviction seriously, the participants of the SLC looked at the issue through the dual lens of 'the Word of God and world of need'.[31] They synthesized their findings in a statement they simply called 'The Commitment', which made the necessary and unavoidable connection between the personal and social dimensions of living out and proclaiming the Gospel in an unjust, needy world.[32] John Stott and Ron Sider, co-chairpersons of the consultation, report that 'although at the beginning we sensed some tension between representatives of the First and Third Worlds ... by the end, the Holy Spirit of unity had brought us into a new solidarity of mutual respect and love.'[33]

However, only the participants of the consultation experienced relief from the tension. For some of the leaders of the LCWE, the tension actually intensified as they expressed grave concern over the consultation's findings. As Steuernagel observed, 'Some of the Lausanne people were clearly not happy

---

[28] 'Historical Background of the Lausanne Committee', in *Billy Graham Center Archives*, www.wheaton.edu/bgc/archives/GUIDES/046.HTM#3 (accessed 2 April 2003). The other three working groups were the Communication Working Group (CWG), originally chaired by Thomas Zimmerman of the USA, the Strategy Working Group (SWG), originally chaired by Peter Wagner of the USA, and the Intercessory Working Group, originally chaired by John Reid of Australia. The LTEG was later shortened to the Theology Working Group (TWG), originally chaired by John Stott.

[29] Ford cited in Steuernagel, 'The Theology of Mission', 179-180.

[30] 'Lausanne Covenant', *Making Christ Known*, 34.

[31] John R.W. Stott and Ronald J. Sider, 'Preface', in Ronald J. Sider (ed.), *Lifestyle in the Eighties: An Evangelical Commitment to Simple Lifestyle* (Philadelphia, Pa.: Westminster, 1982), 10.

[32] 'The Commitment', in Ronald J. Sider (ed.), *Lifestyle in the Eighties: An Evangelical Commitment to Simple Lifestyle* (Philadelphia, Pa.: Westminster, 1982), 13-19.

[33] Stott and Sider, 'Preface', 10.

with the SLC.'[34] They accused it of being imbalanced in the selection of participants and therefore imbalanced in theological orientation, leaning on the side of the radical. Moreover, drafters of 'The Commitment' did not adequately connect the theme of simple lifestyle to the singular focus of the LCWE, namely, world evangelization. These concerns aggravated the conservative constituency, which interpreted the SLC's findings as the continued and deliberate 'torpedoing' of the specific task of world evangelization, a 'torpedoing' that began at Lausanne '74.[35]

Undoubtedly, this dissatisfaction strengthened the resolve of the LCWE to reassert its agenda at the 1980 Consultation on World Evangelization in Pattaya, Thailand (COWE), just three months after the SLC in London. If conservative voices decried the broader view of church mission in general and the findings of the SLC in particular, then they certainly celebrated the renewed emphasis on the more 'functional definition' of evangelism reached at the COWE. The facilitators of the COWE, the LCWE, towed the hard line of single focus evangelism and structured the consultation accordingly around the church growth concept of unreached people groups.[36] From the LCWE's first meeting in 1975 at Mexico City to the COWE in 1980 at Pattaya, the LCWE managed to set the official missionary agenda for evangelicals with the narrower view of world evangelization. Church growth strategist Peter Wagner applauded the fact that the COWE upheld 'the functional definition of evangelism agreed upon by the LCWE', which read:

> The *nature* of world evangelization is the communication of the Good News. The *purpose* is to give individuals and groups a valid opportunity to [hear]. The *goal* is the persuading of men and women to accept Jesus Christ as Lord and Savior.'[37]

---

[34] Steuernagel, 'The Theology of Mission', 185-186.

[35] C. Peter Wagner, 'Lausanne Twelve Months Later', *Christianity Today* 4 July 1975, 961-963. Wagner's use of the torpedo metaphor refers to the attempts on the part of what he considered misguided evangelicals whose agenda served to detract the Congress from its stated purpose of world evangelization. Undoubtedly, the findings of the SLC constituted the latest torpedo that 'attempt[ed] to confuse evangelism with social action' (961). The other two torpedoes were the 'attempt to confuse evangelism with Christian cooperation' and the 'attempt to confuse evangelism with Christian nurture' (961-963).

[36] Seventeen mini-consultations, entitled 'Christian Witness to _____', to be filled in with a people group like Chinese people, Marxists, Buddhists, etc. structured the COWE. These mini-consultations produced reports, which are available on-line at http://www.lausanne.org/documents.html.

[37] C. Peter Wagner, 'Lausanne's Consultation on World Evangelization: A Personal Assessment', *TSF Bulletin* 4.1 (October 1980), 3.

The official Thailand Statement reflected this narrow view of evangelism, while also claiming faithfulness to the whole of the Lausanne Covenant, specifically stating its affirmation of social responsibility. As a member of the LCWE, Wagner praised the COWE's steadfast maintenance of this kind of evangelization over and against the 'dangerous tendency' espoused by 'advocates of holistic evangelism', while at the same time believing that the Thailand Statement did not violate the broader social vision of Lausanne.[38]

These 'advocates of holistic evangelism' refer, of course, primarily to the radical evangelicals, who predictably considered this limited vision at the COWE as a deplorable step backward. They criticized the LCWE of not being true to the broad, holistic mission vision of the Covenant and of reducing evangelization once again to the verbal proclamation of the Gospel. Samuel and Sugden lament that the COWE 'seemed ... painfully unaware of all the developments in the Lausanne movement in seeking to communicate the whole Gospel to the whole world. The years of slow growth in sensitivity to the social dimensions of the Gospel and to the contexts in which it was proclaimed, seemed to be wiped out.'[39] Bediako describes the travesty in terms of theology and strategy and lamented, 'The victory of theology over strategy [won at Lausanne '74] was overturned at Pattaya.'[40]

Those who concurred with such sentiments joined forces and drafted a Statement of Concerns that nearly one third of the COWE delegates signed at the end of the consultation.[41] This statement basically challenged the LCWE to look at the world in terms of social, economic and political institutions in addition to the category of unreached people groups and to provide guidance for justice to Christians living in oppressed lands and for abetting oppressive regimes. The plea not to isolate verbal proclamation from the total demands of the Gospel drove the signers of the Statement of Concerns to challenge the LCWE to take more seriously the social dimensions of the missionary task. The statement demanded that the LCWE reaffirm its commitment to all aspects of the Covenant, encourage study and action in fulfilment of Lausanne's

---

[38] Wagner, 'Lausanne's Consultation', 3.

[39] Samuel and Sugden cited in Steuernagel, 'The Theology of Mission', 196-197.

[40] Kwame Bediako, 'World Evangelisation, Institutional Evangelicalism and the Future of the Christian World Mission', in Vinay Samuel and Albrecht Hauser (eds.), *Proclaiming Christ in Christ's Way* (Oxford: Regnum, 1989), 57.

[41] Orlando Costas, 'Report on Thailand '80', *TSF Bulletin* 4.1 (October 1980), 4-5. Costas gives details of the drafting of the Statement of Concerns. He reports that 'Africans and Black Americans who had participated in the drafting of the [Statement on Radical Discipleship at Lausanne]' also wrote the first rough draft of the Statement of Concerns, a delegation of Latin Americans then expanded it, and then, a committee of seven including Costas finalized it. The others who served on this committee were David Gitari of Kenya, Vinay Samuel of India, Andrew Kirk of England, Peter Kuzmic of (former) Yugoslavia, Clarence Hilliard and Ronald Sider both of the USA.

commitment to socio-political involvement, convene a world congress on social responsibility, and give guidelines for evangelicals living in oppressive situations.[42]

The chairman of the LCWE, Leighton Ford took their concerns seriously enough to call a meeting between the LCWE and representatives of the 'concerned group', namely, Orlando Costas, Vinay Samuel, and Ron Sider.[43] Tension no doubt filled the meeting. But as a result, claimed Costas, the official final version of the Thailand Statement, drafted by Stott, 'did address ... some of the issues that we were raising.'[44]

Costas, however, describes the subsequent formal response of the LCWE to the Statement of Concerns as 'cool and disappointing'.[45] Its overall response consisted first of all, of denying the charge that the LCWE undermined the comprehensive scope of the Covenant; second, that plans were already underway for a consultation on the relationship between evangelism and social responsibility (but a far cry from a world congress the radical evangelicals demanded in the Statement of Concerns);[46] and third, that it was not the place of the LCWE to give guidelines for evangelicals in oppressed and discriminatory lands. The disappointment of the signers of the Statement of Concerns was palpable. Costas wrote, '[The response] made us wonder how committed indeed was the LCWE to the whole of the Lausanne Covenant.'[47]

Proponents of the radical school took this hard, as their agenda seemed once again relegated to marginal status, to the fringes of the official institutionalized thrust of the LCWE. Whereas the Statement on Radical Discipleship at Lausanne I at least received publicity and relatively wide acceptance despite it not being an official part of the Covenant, the Statement of Concerns at Pattaya did not come close to the kind of consideration that its drafters thought it deserved. The tension between the narrow and broad views of evangelization came to a head at Pattaya, and the narrow view won the official battle. By the end of 1980, Steuernagel rightly observes that 'the evangelical family was more

---

[42] 'Statement of Concerns', in Rene Padilla and Chris Sugden (eds.), *Texts on Evangelical Social Ethics, 1974-1983* (Nottingham: Grove Books, 1985), 24-25.

[43] Costas, 'Report on Thailand '80', 5.

[44] Costas, 'Report on Thailand '80', 5.

[45] Orlando Costas, 'Proclaiming Christ in the Two Thirds World', in Vinay Samuel and Chris Sugden (eds.), *Sharing Jesus in the Two Thirds World* (Grand Rapids, Mich.: Eerdmans, 1984), 3.

[46] Furthermore, this small consultation in the works was assigned to a working group of the LCWE, the Lausanne Theology and Education Group (LTEG), that was formally disbanded at Pattaya. So the proposed consultation on the relationship between evangelism and social responsibility was given basically to a group that no longer formally existed! This added insult to injury to the agenda of the radical evangelical school.

[47] Costas, 'Proclaiming Christ', 3.

divided than [ever]. While the SLC was interpreted as speaking too much the language of the "radical evangelicals", COWE was being criticized not only because it had excluded "social responsibility" ... but also because it was embracing [too narrow] a definition and strategy of evangelization.'[48]

Prioritization vs. Holism

The narrowness or broadness of mission characterized the first tension; the relationship between social concern and evangelism in that mission described the second tension. These obviously interrelate, but whereas different answers to the question, 'Is social responsibility included in the task of world evangelization?' created the first tension, struggling with 'If social responsibility, then where does it fit into the overall scheme of that task?' created the second tension. Few missiologists at that point would have disputed that social responsibility has some role to play (in light of Article 5 of the Covenant), but how important a role with reference to the verbal proclamation of the Gospel? While conservatives maintained the primacy of evangelism, radicals questioned the very language of prioritization over and against the holistic demands of the Gospel.

If any hope existed for conservatives and radicals within the evangelical missionary community to find some level of consensus on the social question, it hinged upon the 1982 Consultation on the Relationship between Evangelism and Social Responsibility in Grand Rapids, MI (CRESR). Steuernagel's description of the CRESR as 'the most carefully planned, sensitive, feared and threatening consultation ever held by the LCWE' underscores what was at stake at this consultation, namely, unity or another tragic split of the worldwide evangelical family.[49] Co-sponsored by the LCWE and WEF, the CRESR gathered fifty evangelicals from around the world to understand better the relationship between evangelism and social responsibility in biblical, historical and missiological perspectives.[50]

For a full week, the delegates presented papers and responded to each other with openness and respect as well as with honesty and intensity, in what turned out to be, according to the CRESR chairpersons Bong Rin Ro and Gottfried Osei-Mensah, 'a model of how Christians should approach a ... divisive

---

[48] Steuernagel, 'The Theology of Mission', 18.

[49] Steuernagel, 'The Theology of Mission', 199.

[50] One delegate from the Philippines - Augustin 'Jun' Vencer, then President of the Philippine Council of Evangelical Churches (PCEC) - joined the consultation. Vencer later became the International Director of WEF.

issue'.[51] The CRESR produced a seven-chapter, sixty four-page document entitled 'The Grand Rapids Report on Evangelism and Social Responsibility: an Evangelical Commitment'.[52]

The strength of the report relied on the fact that it did not arrive at any one conclusion concerning the relationship; instead it offered a range of possibilities that it considered faithful to biblical and historic Christianity. According to the report, social action can be understood as 1) a *consequence of* evangelism - one of the principle aims of a changed life is to serve others; 2) a *bridge to* evangelism - with no need of manipulation, good deeds naturally create opportunities to share the Gospel; and 3) a *partner with* evangelism - the church must witness Christ in the world by both word and deed.[53]

Due to this range of valid views, delegates for the most part reached an important level of consensus on the subject. Both Wagner and Padilla, insofar as they represented the conservative and radical constituencies respectively, expressed satisfaction for what the CRESR accomplished, namely, recognizing the vital importance of socio-political involvement to the missionary task.[54] In light of the Grand Rapids Report, evangelicals of all persuasions could no longer ignore the Church's social responsibility. Those who retained the language of the primacy of evangelism could not allow that language to reduce, or worse, eliminate the mandate of social responsibility - that which makes credible the Church's witness to Christ in a needy world - from the missionary task.

As important a level of consensus as the CRESR reached, however, it still operated under a false North American nurtured dualism between body and soul, and social and spiritual, separating these two vital realities from each other and then falsely asking which one has priority over the other.[55] Radicals desired the evangelical community to see the falsity of this unbiblical dualism and then to begin to train its thinking, and therefore its doing, in more non-dualistic, i.e., holistic, terms. For the most part, those who adhered to these holistic notions remained somewhat marginalized from the mainstream of the Lausanne movement. The tension between the dualistic prioritization approach and the holistic approach to the relationship between evangelism and social responsibility enjoyed at best, only temporary relief.

---

[51] Bong Rin Ro and Gottfried Osei-Mensah, 'Preface', in Bruce J. Nicholls (ed.), *Word and Deed: Evangelism and Social Responsibility* (Grand Rapids, Mich.: Eerdmans, 1986), 7.

[52] 'The Grand Rapids Report', in John R.W. Stott (ed.), *Making Christ Known* (Grand Rapids, Mich.; Cambridge: Eerdmans, 1996), 167-210.

[53] 'The Grand Rapids Report', *Making Christ Know*, 181-182. Italics mine.

[54] Steuernagel, 'The Theology of Mission', 204-205.

[55] Mark Lau Branson, 'Striving for Obedience, Haunted by Dualism', *TSF Bulletin* 6.1 (September/October 1982), 11; Bosch, *Transforming Mission*, 406.

First World Theology vs. Two Thirds World Theology

The third notable tension between evangelicals in the decade after Lausanne had to do with power shifts in theology and mission. The proliferation of contextual theologies around the globe did not just occur within ecumenical Protestant and Roman Catholic circles. Indeed, Lausanne opened the door for Two Thirds World evangelicals to take seriously their respective contexts for informing their view of God, worship, church, and mission. As evangelicals in these parts of the world began to assert themselves, a tension emerged between Two Thirds World theology and the once dominant theology of the West, particularly of North America.

With regard to social responsibility, Two Thirds World evangelicals did not wait for the LCWE to 'see the light' of holism. In spite of the hesitancy of institutional evangelicalism, Two Thirds World radical evangelicals, those profoundly touched by Lausanne's broader vision, initiated local movements. Indeed some of the most significant fruit of the post-Lausanne period resulted not so much from activities emanating from LCWE headquarters but from 'local, national or regional initiatives'.[56] ISACC in the Philippines, for example, began 'in 1978 as a reflective arm of the church and a catalyst towards biblically based responses to political, social and cultural issues in the country'.[57] A gathering that occurred in Deveali, India in 1977 and then reconvened in Madras in 1979, specifically to address the social question, also exemplifies the initiative of local Two Thirds World evangelicals. Participants of these all-India meetings produced the Madras Declaration on Evangelical Social Action, which grounded social responsibility in scripture and integrated it with evangelization as an equal partner.[58] Another key evangelical gathering met in 1979 in Lima, Peru for the second Latin American Congress on Evangelism (CLADE II), where participants issued a 'Pastoral Letter' to the evangelical community in Latin America.[59] The letter urged evangelicals to address the issues of poverty, injustice, and human rights violations as part of their faithful witness to the Gospel. In Kenya, David Gitari's prophetic preaching, as both bishop of Mt. Kenya East District and archbishop of Kenya, against governmental injustice and corrupt voting practices inspired church action, which helped to change the way democratic elections were conducted in the country.[60] In South Africa, 'Concerned Evangelicals' drafted and distributed

---

[56] Steuernagel, 'The Theology of Mission', 170-171.

[57] See Appendix 3, which is ISACC's self-description.

[58] 'Madras Declaration', in Rene Padilla and Chris Sugden, *Texts on Evangelical Social Ethics, 1974-1983* (Nottingham: Grove Books, 1985), 11-15.

[59] 'Pastoral Letter', in Rene Padilla and Chris Sugden, *Texts on Evangelical Social Ethics, 1974-1983* (Nottingham: Grove Books, 1985), 15-17.

[60] See David Gitari, 'Church and Politics in Kenya', *Transformation* 8.3 (July/September 1991), 7-17, for a concise autobiographical summary of his encounters

the document, 'Evangelical Witness in South Africa', which reported on the inhumane situation of apartheid. It also more importantly urged both black and white evangelicals to re-think their theology, which at the time was enabling them to acquiesce to the evils of apartheid'.[61] These and other local and regional gatherings among radical evangelicals around the world demonstrate the advances of holistic mission, despite the tentativeness of institutional evangelicalism.

Consistent with these local initiatives, a second movement began with a discussion among many of the same people who signed the Statement of Concerns at Pattaya. In their disappointment for the way the COWE went, they 'resolved to meet again as a Two Thirds World consultation'.[62] Making good on their promise, the first consultation, framed and organized for the first time by theologians of evangelical conviction from the Two Thirds World, convened in 1982 at Bangkok to discuss Christology. This gathering led to the formation of the International Fellowship of Evangelical Mission Theologians in 1987 (INFEMIT). The significance of INFEMIT in the development of Mission as Transformation warrants more discussion, which the next chapter takes up.

A third movement among many of these same evangelicals began as they considered the implications of the Gospel to the growing practice of development. A significant meeting occurred in September 1978 between five concerned evangelicals who proposed a long-term biblical and theological reflection process on development.[63] From that brainstorming and planning session, another meeting convened with theologians and practitioners in April 1979 where the participants determined the need for a consultation on a theology of development. Hence in March 1980, a consultation of that title, sponsored by WEF's Theological Commission, convened just a week before, and in the same location as, the SLC.[64] The Consultation of a Theology of Development (CTD) not only forged ahead with exploring the meaning of evangelical socio-political involvement without the official backing of the LCWE, it also steered evangelical thinking in the decisive direction of

---

with government officials, especially 13-17. Gitari's sermons to which I refer can be found in David Gitari, *In Season and Out of Season: Sermons to a Nation* (Oxford: Regnum, 1996). See also Gideon G. Githiga, *The Church as a Bulwark Against Authoritarianism* (Oxford: Regnum, 2001) for a more detailed account of the responses of the churches in Kenya to governmental injustice, especially Gitari's role as catalyst.

[61] 'Evangelical Witness in South Africa', *Transformation* 4.1 (January/March 1987), 17.

[62] Sugden, 'Wholistic Evangelism', 38.

[63] Ronald J. Sider, 'Introduction', in Ronald J. Sider (ed.), *Evangelicals and Development: Toward a Theology of Social Change* (Exeter: Paternoster, 1981), 107. The 'five concerned evangelicals' were Wayne Bragg, Bruce Nicholls, John Robinson, Vinay Samuel and Ronald Sider.

[64] There were fifteen of the combined ninety participants who attended both consultations.

community development as the way to fulfil the Christian duty to be involved socio-politically as the Covenant stipulated.

The Statement of Intent produced at the CTD says, 'We recognize that the Bible teaches that the mission of the church includes the proclamation of the Gospel and the demonstration of its relevance by working for community development and social change.'[65] The CTD appointed a steering committee to continue reflecting upon the theme of development since the consultation only scratched the surface of this vital theme. This steering committee committed itself to a three year study process that culminated at Track III of Wheaton '83, which produced the Statement on Transformation. But more than culminating this particular study process on development, the Wheaton '83 Statement on Transformation also acted as a significant marker for the theological maturity of holistic mission thinking among many evangelicals after Lausanne. Indeed, even though its origin can be traced directly to the particular study process on development begun in 1978, the Wheaton '83 Statement on Transformation also settled for many the other internal tensions discussed in this chapter that threatened the unity of the evangelical missionary family.

---

[65] 'Statement of Intent', in Ronald J. Sider (ed.), *Evangelicals and Development* (Exeter: Paternoster, 1981), 15.

CHAPTER 3

Liberation Theology and Transformation: External Tension

Tension from Without: The Challenge of Liberation Theology

As these tensions within the Lausanne movement pushed from the inside toward an understanding of Mission as Transformation, an equally strong and influential tension pushed from the outside, namely, the challenge of liberation theology.

What Is It?[1]

Liberation theology took the Church by storm in the late 1960s and early 70s, and its enduring and far-reaching influence continues to inform the Church,

---

[1] To do justice to the multidimensional nature of liberation theology would go hopelessly beyond the main focus of this study. In light of the extensive scholarly works available on the subject, I am barely giving an introduction. For more serious researchers of liberation theology, a short list of standard primary texts should include Gustavo Gutierrez, *A Theology of Liberation* (Maryknoll, N.Y.: Orbis, 1973) and Jose Miquez Bonino, *Doing Theology in a Revolutionary Situation* (Philadelphia, Pa.: Fortress, 1976) for a systematic theological perspective; Enrique Dussel, *A History of the Church in Latin America* (Grand Rapids, Mich.: Eerdmans, 1981) for an historical perspective; Juan Luis Segundo, *The Liberation of Theology* (Maryknoll, N.Y.: Orbis, 1976) for a sociological perspective; and Paulo Freire, *Pedagogy of the Oppressed* (New York: Continuum,1970) for an educational perspective. For many, the definitive source on the movement in both English and Spanish is Ignacio Ellacuria and Jon Sobrino (eds.), *Mysterium Liberationis: Fundamental Concepts of Liberation Theology* (Maryknoll, N.Y.: Orbis, 1993).
Many scholars prefer the plural, speaking in terms of liberation *theologies* rather than *theology*. When stressing its contextual nature, theologians legitimately use the plural to highlight differences in how certain regions have expressed liberation themes. In Deane Ferm, *Third World Liberation Theologies* (Maryknoll, N.Y.: Orbis, 1986), the author generalizes that in Latin America, liberation theology focuses on oppression, in South Africa on racism, in Asia on the conflicts that arise from its religiously pluralistic setting, and so on (1). But in Christian Smith, *The Emergence of Liberation Theology: Radical Religion and Social Movement Theory* (Chicago, Ill.; London: University of Chicago, 1991), the author makes a legitimate case for the use of the singular in that regional differences do not erase the common starting point - a reality of social misery - and a common goal - the liberation of the miserable or the oppressed (26-27). Both singular and plural uses are legitimate.

despite the waning of liberation rhetoric among theologians today. This burgeoning movement, which flourished most aggressively in the fertile revolutionary soil of Latin America, rose to prominence at the Catholic Bishops' Conference in 1968 at Medellin, Colombia.[2] Although it originated among Latin American Catholics, the liberation vision did not respect cultural or ecclesial lines; it challenged all church traditions - Roman Catholic, Orthodox, ecumenical and evangelical Protestant - in all places.

Definitions for liberation theology abound, but they all essentially build upon the one offered by Peruvian priest - theologian Gustavo Gutierrez, whom many consider liberation theology's founding father. He writes,

> The theology of liberation attempts to reflect on the experience and meaning of ... [Christian] faith based on the commitment to abolish injustice and to build a new society; this theology must be verified by the practice of that commitment, by active ... participation in the struggle which the exploited social classes have undertaken against their oppressors.[3]

At least four basic, discernible tenets of this new way of doing theology come to the fore from this definition. First, the historical, concrete experience of the oppressed poor must begin the process, not a body of doctrinal truth. 'Theology ... is the second step. ... It does not produce pastoral activity [among the poor]; rather it reflects upon it.'[4] Second, active participation in solidarity with the poor and oppressed must accompany reflection. Gutierrez asserts that 'all the political theologies, the theologies of hope, of revolution, and of liberation, are not worth one act of genuine solidarity with the exploited social classes.'[5] Third, the Church must choose to serve the oppressed poor, and the oppressed poor must speak and be heard to inform the theology and mission of the Church. These two sides of the same coin basically define the well known but often misunderstood phrase, 'the preferential option for the poor'.[6] And fourth, using Marxism as a tool for social analysis, liberation theology

---

[2] C. Smith, *The Emergence of Liberation Theology,* 150-164.

[3] Gutierrez, *A Theology of Liberation,* 307.

[4] Gutierrez, *A Theology of Liberation,* 10.

[5] Gutierrez, *A Theology of Liberation,* 308. Gutierrez assumes these theologies' debt to European theologians from Karl Barth to Jurgen Moltmann as well as to North American theologians from Walter Rausenbusch to Thomas Altizer. To see how these various theologies bear resemblances, consult Rebecca Chopp, *The Praxis of Suffering: An Interpretation of Liberation and Political Theologies* (Maryknoll, N.Y.: Orbis, 1986).

[6] A. Scott Moreau, 'Option for the Poor', in A. Scott Moreau (ed.), *Evangelical Dictionary of World Missions* (Grand Rapids, Mich.: Baker, 2000), 711. According to Moreau, Gutierrez first coined this much-used phrase in a lecture given in Spain in 1972.

challenges First World dominance, capitalism, and imperialism. '[Liberationists] believe that there can be authentic development for Latin America [only] if there is liberation from the domination exercised by the great capitalist countries.'[7] These four basic liberation tenets shook the theological foundations of the Church as they challenged Christians of all stripes to radically rethink their role in alleviating the suffering of the poor, the oppressed, the discriminated and the forgotten of the world.

Contemporary liberation theology started in Latin America, but it certainly did not limit itself there.[8] Indeed it has encompassed the world; Robert Schreiter has identified it as one of the four 'global theological flows' that exist today.[9] In his excellent study of liberation theology as a social movement, sociologist Christian Smith substantiates the fact that a liberationist orientation diffused from Latin America to other parts of the Two Thirds World largely through international conferences.[10]

Smith points out in a footnote that Filipino theologians found the new perspective emanating from Latin America particularly appealing, most probably because of the Philippines' similar colonial encounter with the Spanish.[11] Liberation theology in the Filipino context expressed itself as the 'theology of struggle'. According to Eleazer Fernandez, the 'theology of struggle' has naturally manifested distinct Filipino features as it has formed out of the unique experience of revolutionary struggle in the Philippines.[12] The emphasis on the *struggle* toward liberation, in contrast to the end result of liberation, reflects one of the more salient features of the Filipino version of liberation theology, i.e., theology of struggle.[13]

---

[7] Gutierrez, *A Theology of Liberation*, 88.

[8] Forms of what could have been called liberation theology before its modern emergence obviously existed. See Martyn Newman, *Liberation Theology is Evangelical* (Victoria, Mallorn, 1990), especially his treatment of liberation themes throughout Protestant history (27-67).

[9] Schreiter, *The New Catholicity*, 16-18.

[10] C. Smith, *The Emergence of Liberation Theology*, 209. For a fairly recent sampling of theologies of liberation from the various regions of the world, see Virginia Fabella and R.S. Sugirtharajah, *Dictionary of Third World Theologies* (Maryknoll, N.Y.: Orbis, 2000).

[11] C. Smith, *The Emergence of Liberation Theology*, 263. The Philippines, for example, has been referred to, amusingly but certainly with an element of truth, as the 'Latin America of Asia'.

[12] Eleazer S. Fernandez, *A Theology of Struggle* (Maryknoll, N.Y.: Orbis, 1994), 2, 19-32.

[13] Eleazer S. Fernandez, 'Theology of Struggle', in Virginia Fabella and R.S. Sugirtharajah (eds.), *Dictionary of Third World Theologies* (Maryknoll, N.Y.: Orbis, 2000), 201.

Liberation Missiology?

Scholars of liberation have certainly established the movement's impact upon
theology proper, some even comparing it to the impact of the Reformation of
the sixteenth century.[14] Likewise ethicists have certainly noted its contribution
to the study of social ethics.[15] But because the roots and fruits of liberation
theology find their true home in Two Thirds World situations, because it deals
with the oppressed poor in relation to post- and/or neo-colonial international
relationships past and present, and because it deals with the Church's role in the
world of the oppressed poor, liberation theology has spoken to missiology in a
way unmatched by any other academic and practical field of study. Indeed,
liberation theology is primarily missiological reflection.

Its methodology also reveals its true missiological nature. It not only
depends upon classical theological categories - Christ, Church, mission,
sacrament, and so on - it also depends upon the tools of social analysis.
Whereas classical theology bases itself in philosophy and metaphysics,
operating primarily with spiritual/secular and believer/nonbeliever categories,
liberation theology has introduced the significance of the social sciences,
operating primarily with justice/injustice and person/nonperson categories.[16]
Most if not all liberation theologians, at least early on in the movement, have
found the Marxist tools of social analysis - more specifically, the domination
theory, dependence theory, and the class struggle - as the most useful.[17]

So the issues with which it deals, as well as the interdisciplinary way in
which it does it, place liberation theology squarely and primarily within the
inter-discipline of missiology. It seems odd, therefore, that some advocates of
liberation theology, at least in North America, have dismissed missiology as an
ideologically laden obsolete field of study, as if the very tenets of liberation
render it invalid. Why for instance have the more liberal seminaries, where
liberation theology has been hailed as the next reformation, essentially
discarded missiology in their curricula? This curious and unfortunate dismissal,

---

[14] Newman, *Liberation Theology is Evangelical*, 27-45. See also Richard Shaull, *The
Reformation and Liberation Theology* (Louisville, Ky.: Westminster/John Knox, 1991),
1-12.

[15] See Thomas L. Schubeck, *Liberation Ethics: Sources, Models, and Norms*
(Minneapolis, Minn.: Fortress, 1993).

[16] Gustavo Gutierrez, *The Power of the Poor in History* (Maryknoll, N.Y.: Orbis, 1983),
92.

[17] Liberation theology continues to evolve. Whereas Marxist tools of analysis were the
rule of the day in the early stages of the movement, they no longer occupy such a
prominent place. In Samuel Escobar, 'Beyond Liberation Theology: A Review Article',
Themelios 19/3 (May 1994), 16, Escobar cites Gutierrez as mentioning the liberationists'
'need to refine [their] analytical tools and develop new ones'.

however, does not negate the fact that liberation theology is inherently missiological.

Bosch considers liberation theology 'as one of the most dramatic illustrations of the fundamental paradigm shift that is currently taking place in mission thinking and practice'.[18] It has impacted the missionary enterprise in at least four ways. First, it has emphasized the necessity of action, and not just any action but action for justice with, among, and on behalf of the poor. Missionaries tend to be activists, so for the most part, they simply felt affirmed by liberation theology's revitalized 'faith without works is dead' challenge to the worldwide Church. The type of action that this new theological orientation called for needed specifically to address the hope of justice, dignity and freedom among the poor. That the Old Testament Book of Exodus figures prominently in liberation theology should not come as a surprise, for it illustrates Yahweh God *acting* in history to free the Hebrew slaves from Egyptian oppression.[19] In light of God's liberating actions, liberationists call not just for action for action's sake, but for action in the cause of social justice. This specific challenge, as a central non-negotiable aspect of church mission, has forever transformed missiology across ecclesial traditions.

Second, liberation theology has challenged missiology to renew its commitment to contextualization or inculturation.[20] Deane Ferm rightly points out the two inseparable sides of liberation theology as 1) desiring 'liberation from all forms of human oppression' and 2) insisting 'that theology must be truly indigenous'.[21] We should not overlook the fact that the proliferation of contextual theologies corresponded time-wise with the emergence of liberation theologies in the late 1960s and early 70s. As liberation themes gained an audience, the voiceless found their voice and the powerless found power to determine their own destiny.

Furthermore, it forced missionaries to take seriously the culture to which they were sent, especially the 'culture of poverty' within the larger host culture. Much credit goes to liberation theology for bringing to the mainstream of missionary thought and practice the process of contextualization that has profoundly affected both the self-identity of indigenous churches and the sensitive role of cross-cultural workers.

The third point of impact that liberation theology has had upon missiology follows the second in that it heightened the suspicion of the role of foreign missionaries altogether. It helped to bring to the fore the undeniable link

---

[18] Bosch, *Transforming Mission*, 432.

[19] Gutierrez, *A Theology of Liberation*, 155-160.

[20] There was a time when Protestants preferred the term 'contextualization' and Catholics 'inculturation'. but that is no longer the case as these interchangeable terms are used across traditions.

[21] Ferm, *Third World Liberation Theologies*, 1.

between colonialism and Christian missions. So in trying to overcome the effects of colonialism and neo-colonialism, liberation theologians naturally questioned the validity of foreign missionary endeavours. The disturbing link between the evils of colonialism and missions, made largely by the conscientization process brought on by liberation theology, undoubtedly played a role in catalyzing the Moratorium Debate of the mid-1970s.[22] The Moratorium called for an end to the flow of missionary personnel and funding that Two Thirds World church leaders claimed were hindering the indigenous development of the Church in the Two Thirds World.[23] The debate went on for a decade on both theological and practical levels, and though the idea finally lost steam, it forced the missionary enterprise to rethink the nature of the cross-cultural relationship; it forced missionaries to acknowledge their 'visitor status' and to submit to national church leadership accordingly.[24] Again, credit must go to liberation theology for profoundly changing the nature of the cross-cultural relationship between missionaries and national church leaders.

And fourth, liberation theology forever changed the course of missiology by questioning the goodness of the development aid paradigm implemented by the North and West in the Two Thirds World. As Chapter 1 established, an increasing number of critics began to challenge the assumptions that drove development aid, namely, that poorer nations simply needed some assistance in order to catch them up to modern industrial global society. The missionary enterprise across traditions jumped on the development aid bandwagon and went about its mission accordingly.

But as these critical voices began to gain a hearing, theologians and practitioners alike sought for an alternative approach to development, and the theme of liberation, with its signature emphasis on the indigenous and its anti-capitalistic, Marxist leanings, fit the bill. Liberation theology steered church social mission away from Western development practices that were based on the modernization theory and toward Two Thirds World solutions to context

---

[22] The concept of conscientization, popularized by Freire, originally meant the pedagogical objective of raising awareness among the poor concerning their condition. But in James Cogswell, 'Relief and Development: Challenges to Mission Today', *International Bulletin of Missionary Research* 11.2 (April 1987), the author suggests in addition that 'the term might well be used for the educational task to be done in the life of the church in the United States [and other affluent nations]. He writes, 'The conscience of the church must be awakened to the kind of world, which we have helped to create, in which hundreds of millions go hungry' (76).

[23] For a concise description of, and commentary on, the Moratorium Debate, see Emilio Castro, 'Editorial', *International Review of Mission* 64.254 (April 1975), 117-121. Other articles on the Moratorium also appear in the same *IRM* issue.

[24] Bernard Adeney, *Strange Virtues: Ethics in a Multicultural World* (Downers Grove, Ill.: InterVarsity, 1995), 51.

specific social problems based on dependency theory, thus profoundly changing the direction of missiology across the board.

A Radical Evangelical Response

Evangelicals did not escape the compelling challenges of liberation theology, as the many conferences and publications among them in the 1970s and 80s demonstrated.[25] Of course, responses to liberation theology varied. Those who categorically rejected it on the basis of unacceptable hermeneutics and Marxist sympathies were able to dismiss its challenges fairly easily. At best, they credited liberation theology for pricking the Church's social conscience; but beyond that, they branded it as the tool of Marxist based socialism (an enemy of the Gospel) and opposed it at every turn.[26]

Radical evangelicals, however, represented by regional groups like ISACC in the Philippines, the LATF based in Argentina, ESA in the USA, Concerned Evangelicals in South Africa, and others, responded differently. The challenges posed by liberation theology affected them deeply. To be sure, within the evangelical constituency, liberation theology found its most sympathetic ear among the radicals. As they allowed the challenges of liberation to re-orient them theologically to the misery of the suffering poor, radical evangelicals experienced a profound tension between their socio-political contexts and their traditional evangelical way of doing theology. The latter did not seem to have anything significant or relevant to say to the very real social, political and economic problems of the poor.

This tension acted as an external catalyst for radical evangelicals to attempt to address the social, political and economic questions of the day. They felt compelled 'to participate in the revolutionary struggle', as Gutierrez, Miguez-Bonino and others called the Church to do, as part and parcel of missionary faithfulness to the Gospel of Jesus Christ.

Contrary to charges made against them of succumbing to the latest theological fad from the conservative constituency, radicals saw their vision for social justice as fundamentally biblical and historically orthodox. On biblical fidelity, Sider counters the conservative charge against liberationists of disregarding scripture and writes, 'By largely ignoring the central biblical teaching that God is on the side of the poor, evangelical theology has been

---

[25] For example, see Carl E. Armerding (ed.), *Evangelicals and Liberation* (Phillipsburg, N.J.: Presbyterian and Reformed, 1977), which compiles papers on liberation theology from an evangelical perspective presented at the 1976 Annual Conference of the Evangelical Theological Society of Canada.

[26] See for example Richard John Neuhaus, 'Liberation Theology and the Captivities of Jesus', in Gerald H. Anderson and Thomas F. Stransky (eds.), *Mission Trends 3: Third World Theologies* (New York; Grand Rapids, Mich.: Paulist; Eerdmans, 1976), 41-61.

profoundly unorthodox'.[27] On historic Christianity, Martyn Newman argues that socio-political renewal constitutes a basic feature of historic evangelicalism; 'as such, the evangelical tradition has been one of the clearest precursors to many of the themes developed by liberation theology.'[28] With such convictions, radical voices like Escobar, Padilla, and Costas from Latin America, Maggay and Lim from the Philippines, Samuel and Sugden from India and the UK, Sider and Wallis from the USA, Bediako and Gitari from Africa, and many others have taken every opportunity to challenge fellow evangelicals to rethink the missionary task from the perspective of the underside.

Now having just established the deep affinity of radical evangelicals to the aspirations of liberation theology, it may seem contradictory now to claim that most of them could not ultimately identify with the movement. Despite being deeply moved by the genuine heart plea of liberationists on behalf of the poor, radical evangelicals felt compelled to look for an alternative methodology to address poverty and injustice in their respective contexts. Their critiques, however, differed qualitatively from their conservative brethren. With this qualification in mind, radicals (albeit in varying degrees even amongst themselves) offered at least four points of departure from liberation theology.

First, its beginning point of the concrete situation of the poor often led to what radical evangelicals considered an inadequate theological hermeneutics. For them, anything short of Jesus Christ as the starting point for theology indeed fell short of being Christian. Whereas conservative evangelicals insisted that the scriptural text serve as the only viable starting point for theology, radicals looked to the person of Christ that the text of scripture reveals. This difference may sound hair-splitting, especially in light of the fact that both conservatives and radicals believed that biblical authority did not play an adequate enough role in liberationist thinking. But in making the biblical person of Christ the basis of their critique - his birth, teaching, death, resurrection and promised return - radicals distinguished themselves from conservatives, who dismissed liberation theology on the basis of its lack of respect for the 'inerrant text of scripture'. Padilla argues that 'if theology is to be faithful to scripture ... [then] it cannot simply be 'theology of the Word'; it has to be 'theology of the Word *made flesh*.'[29]

---

[27] Ronald J. Sider, 'An Evangelical Theology of Liberation', in Kenneth Kantzer and Stanley Gundry (eds.), *Perspectives in Evangelical Theology* (Grand Rapids, Mich.: Baker, 1979), 132.

[28] Newman, *Liberation Theology is Evangelical*, 20.

[29] C. Rene Padilla, 'Liberation Theology: An Appraisal', in Daniel Schipani (ed.), *Freedom and Discipleship: Liberation Theology from an Anabaptist Perspective* (Maryknoll, N.Y.: Orbis, 1989), 43.

Radicals criticized liberationists not so much because they did not begin with the text of scripture,[30] but because they did not begin with Jesus Christ to which the text of scripture points. Andrew Kirk understands Christ and the events surrounding him as 'a particular historical praxis', and he champions these events as 'the first reference point for theological reflection' that is Christian.[31] It should not come as a surprise that the organizers of the first INFEMIT consultation chose Christology and its implications for mission to begin the string of consultations that occurred in the years that followed. For radical evangelicals, the living God in Jesus Christ, as revealed in scripture and enlivened by the Holy Spirit through an obedient Church, sparks genuine theology, not the static text of scripture or the historical, concrete situation of the poor. Jim Wallis explains: 'Biblical politics takes, as their starting point, the manner of God in Jesus Christ ... thus exemplify[ing] the political authority of the Incarnation'.[32]

Of course, to affirm Christ assumes a high view of scriptural authority, as Wallis' statement implies by speaking of biblical politics and the person of Christ in one breath. Nevertheless, the distinction made between the literal word of Scripture and the living Word of Christ as starting point for theological reflection remains an important one. Whereas conservatives tended to hope for the demise of liberation theology on the grounds that it did not begin with the biblical text, radicals wanted to strengthen liberation theology by reminding its proponents of the centrality of the biblical Christ. Hoping for its survival, Kirk writes, 'To pay more careful attention to its biblical hermeneutic is not an invitation to abandon its concerns for liberation ... but to lay a more solid foundation for future reflection.'[33]

A second radical evangelical critique of liberation theology during its early years dealt with the tendency toward a socio-political reduction of Christian salvation. This tendency in liberationist literature showed up frequently, like Jose Miranda's statements, 'To know Jaweh is to achieve justice for the poor' and 'God ... clearly specifies that he is knowable *exclusively* in the cry of the

---

[30] Of course, there is a wide range of approaches to scripture corresponding somewhat along Catholic and Protestant differences. Keeping in mind that early liberationists primarily came from Catholic ranks, the criticism from evangelicals that scripture does not hold a prominent enough place in liberation theology basically continues the *sola Scriptura* conviction of the Reformation. Liberation theology's overt claim to begin not with the text of scripture but with the context of poverty is the target of evangelical criticism on the contemporary scene.

[31] J. Andrew Kirk, *Liberation Theology: An Evangelical View from the Third World* (Atlanta, Ga.: John Knox, 1979), 145.

[32] Jim Wallis, 'Liberation and Conformity', in Gerald H. Anderson and Thomas F. Stransky (eds.), *Mission Trends 4: Liberation Theologies* (New York; Grand Rapids, Mich.: Paulist; Eerdmans, 1979), 56.

[33] Kirk, *Liberation Theology,* 207.

poor and the weak who seek justice'.[34] Sider bemoaned precisely this kind of reductionism in that it enabled many evangelicals to dismiss the liberationist social vision too easily.[35]

Conservatives tended to reject the notion of socio-political salvation as they pitted it against the notion of individual-spiritual salvation. Radicals, on the other hand, took liberation theology to task on the grounds that it failed to include the personal dimension of salvation. They also felt compelled to challenge the conservatives for failing to include the political dimension. An untrained observer may detect theological schizophrenia on the surface, but the genius of the radical evangelical vision is precisely in the broad scope of salvation that includes the totality of life. The Gospel of salvation in Jesus Christ cannot be an either/or affair. The Mission Statement of ISACC in the Philippines summarizes it well:

> The Gospel is for the whole person. Witness to it has both a verbal and visible dimension as expressed in prophetic proclamation of the Word as well as in the Spirit's work of transformation in the life of the individual and of nations. We believe that Christ is King, not just over the church, but over nations and peoples. His kingdom makes no distinction between the secular and the sacred; He rules over all of life.[36]

Based on such a vision, radical evangelicals challenged liberation theology to include a personal dimension both to its notion of salvation and to its practice of mission. They remained uncompromisingly committed to the need of every person to come to a saving knowledge of Jesus Christ, thus taking to task liberation theology's socio-political reductionism. Padilla articulates well this ongoing critique of the limitation of liberation's political salvation:

> It is not by accident that liberation theology is extremely inadequate when it comes to the questions that have no immediate bearing on politics or point to the supra-historical and personal dimensions of the Gospel. It has nothing to say, for instance on the question of the ultimate meaning of a person's life. The fact is that if the life of the individual person has meaning only in relation to the world of public, historical events, then it has no meaning beyond death. According to biblical teaching, however, the meaning of human existence is not exclusively found in relation to the historical process, but also in the ultimate destiny of the individual.[37]

---

[34] Jose Miranda cited in Ronald J. Sider, *Christ and Violence* (Scottdale, Pa.; Kitchener, Ont.: Herald, 1979), 119. Italics are mine.

[35] Sider, *Christ and Violence,* 119.

[36] See Appendix 3 for ISACC's 'Who We Are'.

[37] Padilla, 'Liberation Theology', 44.

Over-reliance upon Marxist social theory triggered the third radical evangelical critique of liberation theology. But again, their critique in this regard differed qualitatively from the conservatives who easily deemed liberation theology wrongheaded because of its overt association with Marxism. From knee-jerk reactions to well thought-out arguments against 'Christian Marxism', conservatives issued their cautions and warnings against liberation theology.[38] But radicals found these criticisms hard to swallow. Wallis prophetically assails his evangelical brethren in America when he writes,

> It is ... difficult to grant the integrity of ... critiques of liberation theology from an evangelical theology which has spent much of its energy justifying the privilege of the powerful and the poverty of the poor. ... Denunciations of the abuses of socialism ring quite hollow when being offered by the affluent and the loyal beneficiaries of American capitalism.[39]

In essence, radicals challenged conservatives first to take out the log of the ideological trappings of capitalism out of their (our?) own eye before trying to take out the speck of Marxist sympathies out of the liberationists' eye. Radicals, for the most part, tended to view Marxism as not any more or any less evil than other political, economic structures in the world today.[40]

Their critique of liberation theology with regard to Marxism emerged from the belief that its proponents often went beyond using Marxist tools of social analysis and increasingly looked to it as the solution to humanity's problems. Padilla articulates it this way: 'The question is ... whether liberation theology has not, by and large, gone beyond an acceptance of Marxist insights ... and fallen into a sociological captivity'.[41] Radicals sought to transcend ideological lines and remain faithful to the holistic transformation of the biblical kingdom vision that goes well beyond the limited class based, economic vision of Marxism. It also goes well beyond the limited prosperity based, materialistic vision of capitalism. 'Jesus' words are anathema to Marxists and capitalists alike', Sider contends, 'To Marxists because they worship Mammon by claiming that economic forces are the ultimate causal factors in history; to

---

[38] See for example Ronald Nash (ed.), *Liberation Theology* (Milford, MI: Mott Media, 1984). This entire volume contains well thought-out critical arguments against liberation theology, but see especially Dale Vree's chapter 'A Critique of Christian Marxism' (203-214).

[39] Wallis, 'Liberation and Conformity', 53.

[40] Samuel Escobar and John Driver, *Christian Mission and Social Justice* (Scottdale, Pa.; Kitchener, Ont.: Herald, 1978), 65-66.

[41] Padilla, 'Liberation Theology', 45.

capitalists because they worship Mammon by idolizing economic success as the highest good'.[42]

Lastly, liberation theology's early romance with revolution often led its proponents to sanction violence, and radical evangelicals, especially those of the historic peace churches, had fundamental trouble supporting this. In fairness, liberationists did not take the issue of violence lightly. After struggling with the obvious tension between the undeniable Christian commitment to peace and the 'institutional violence' of unjust social structures, liberationists found themselves justifying revolution as a form of 'counter-violence'. They held this 'institutional violence' responsible 'for the death of thousands of innocent victims', and to counter this with armed revolution as a last resort constituted a just form of violence.[43]

John Driver outlines four liberationist criteria for determining the legitimate use of revolutionary violence: '1) if oppressors have already utilized violence; 2) if all of the possibilities for legal action and protest have already been exhausted without success; 3) if the existing situation causes more human suffering than will probably result from revolutionary counter-violence; and 4) if there is reasonable assurance of success.'[44] Interestingly enough, such thinking aligns liberationists with the long church tradition of the just war theory, to which many, if not most, evangelicals adhere.[45]

For radical evangelicals, however, especially those steeped in the Anabaptist tradition, armed revolution ultimately violated the very essence of the Gospel. 'The Achilles' heel of the liberation justification of violence', C. Arnold Snyder argues, 'is the appeal to the incarnate Christ as example.'[46] In his excellent treatment of Christ and violence, Sider establishes Jesus as the suffering servant who, through the non-violent way of the cross, showed the way of victory over enemies of God's justice, peace and righteousness. He reasons, 'Because Jesus commanded His followers to love their enemies and then died as the incarnate Son to demonstrate that God reconciles His enemies by suffering love, any rejection of the nonviolent way in human relations involves a heretical doctrine of the atonement.'[47]

---

[42] Sider, *Rich Christians,* 118.

[43] Gutierrez, *A Theology of Liberation,* 109.

[44] John Driver, 'The Anabaptist Vision and Social Justice', in Daniel Schipani (ed.), *Freedom and Discipleship: Liberation Theology in Anabaptist Perspective* (Maryknoll:, N.Y.: Orbis, 1989), 105.

[45] Robert G. Clouse, 'Introduction', in Robert G. Clouse (ed.), *War: Four Christian Views* (Downers Grove, Ill.: InterVarsity, 1981), 25.

[46] C. Arnold Snyder, 'The Relevance of Anabaptist Nonviolence for Nicaragua Today', in Daniel Schipani (ed.), *Freedom and Discipleship: Liberation Theology in Anabaptist Perspective* (Maryknoll, N.Y.: Orbis, 1989), 121.

[47] Sider, *Christ and Violence,* 34.

Radical evangelicals, however, went about their critique of liberation 'counter-violence' with extreme qualification. In the face of very real injustice and oppression, platitudes of idealistic pacifism rang hollow. To the radicals, Christians enjoying the fruit of institutional violence, referring primarily to believers living in affluent nations, could not preach non-violence to liberationists. Speaking in the American context, Wallis asserts boldly, 'It is very hard to accept the scathing attacks on the violence of liberation movements from evangelicals who have defended every American military, political, and commercial aggression for decades.'[48] Related to this, radical evangelicals believed that Christians not participating in the struggle with, for, and among the oppressed poor had not earned the right to demand nonviolence from liberationists. Sider writes, 'Biblical non-violence can be lived and taught only in a context of genuine identification and involvement with the oppressed.'[49] Nonetheless, the radical evangelical commitment to non-violence remained steadfast, thus challenging liberation theology's (and conservative evangelical theology's) traditional position of just revolution.

Wheaton '83: Toward an Evangelical Theology of Liberation

As creative tensions often do, the combination of the internal tensions within the worldwide evangelical missionary community and the external tension applied by the challenge of liberation theology produced significant relevant fruit. It constrained radical evangelicals to articulate the Christian mission in a way that maintained fidelity both to biblical evangelical faith and to a contextual theology that truly served the oppressed poor. The Wheaton '83 Statement on Transformation served as that articulation, capping almost ten years of wrestling with these tensions and thus forging a new way of doing mission. Harking back to Lausanne '74, Samuel and Sugden write, 'At that Congress ... Padilla and ... Escobar from Latin America gave public expression to a missiological understanding that focused on the whole Gospel for the whole person in their social, political, economic, cultural and religious contexts.'[50] Nine years later in Wheaton, the time proved right to summarize in a definitive way the progress made on the radical evangelical journey toward holistic mission.

Three-in-One Consultation

Convened by WEF's Theological Commission and sponsored by approximately fifty churches, denominations, and mission groups (including the LCWE),

---

[48] Wallis, 'Liberation and Conformity', 53.
[49] Sider, *Christ and Violence*, 93-94.
[50] Samuel and Sugden, 'Introduction', *Mission as Transformation*, ix.

Wheaton '83 gathered three hundred and thirty six participants from fifty nine different countries to deliberate upon the theme, 'I Will Build My Church'. The participants, of whom sixty percent came from the Two Thirds World, met for two weeks at the Billy Graham Center of Wheaton College in Wheaton, IL from June 20 to July 1, 1983. Padilla links Wheaton '83 to Wheaton '66 on the 'Church's Worldwide Mission'.[51] Between the two meetings in Wheaton almost twenty years apart, missiologists point to Berlin '66, Lausanne '74 and Pattaya '80 as obvious antecedents to this small but significant international gathering.

Its thirty staff planners organized the consultation into three autonomous tracks that explored separate sub-themes. Track I explored 'The Church in Its Local Setting', Track II, 'The Church in the New Frontiers in Mission' and Track III, 'The Church in Response to Human Need'.[52] Thematically, the role of the local church served as the common denominator for the three tracks; functionally, plenary sessions and common Bible studies throughout the three-in-one consultation united the participants. For the hard work of delving deeply into their respective foci at hand, participants of the three tracks met separately for the first week, knowing that the task for the second week entailed integrating the three sub-themes.

To many observers in retrospect, due to the complexities of the issues before them in the limited amount of time given, Wheaton '83 did not achieve the hoped - for integration, except for the issuance of the 'Wheaton '83 Letter to the Churches'. This letter put in one document some of the key findings of each track and tried to end with a united note, appealing to the *missio Dei* and to the Church sent out into the world as an outflow of it.[53] If the letter served as the official binder of the three tracks, Peter Kuzmic's plenary presentation, which laid a solid foundation for holistic church mission based upon the Gospel of the kingdom, served as an unofficial but inspirational point of unity.[54]

---

[51] Padilla, 'Evangelism and Social Responsibility', 27.

[52] Track II presentations were eventually published in Patrick Sookhdeo (ed.), *New Frontiers in Mission* (Exeter; Grand Rapids, Mich.: Paternoster; Eerdmans, 1987) and Track III presentations in eds. Samuel and Sugden *The Church in Response to Human Need*. To my knowledge, no compilation volume for Track I was ever published.

[53] 'Wheaton '83 Letter to the Churches', *Evangelical Review of Theology* 9/1 (January 1985), 32-37.

[54] Mark Lau Branson, 'Special Coverage: Assemblies of the World Council of Churches and the World Evangelical Fellowship', *TSF Bulletin* 7.1 (September/October 1983), 22; William Cook, 'I Will Build My Church: Reflections on the Wheaton '83 Conference on the Nature and Mission of the Church', *Evangelical Review of Theology* 9.1 (January 1985), 28.

Track III: The Church in Response to Human Need

Regardless of not achieving the anticipated level of integration between the three tracks, observers have applauded the overall accomplishments of Wheaton '83, especially the feats of Track III. According to later assessments of the consultation, Track III organizers came to the event the most prepared of the three tracks, with a pre-published book containing papers for discussion at the consultation.[55] As a result, Track III bore the most fruit in terms of generating reflection and action in the post-Wheaton '83 period.

It did not proceed without wide disagreement as in the other two tracks, given the diversity of backgrounds and orientations, but it did accomplish the goal of producing a final summary report within the two weeks of the consultation. The drafting committee, made up of Arthur Williamson, Andrew Kirk, Tito Paredes, Paul Schrotenboer, David Bosch and Max Chigwida, worked under the leadership of Rene Padilla, the chairmanship of Vinay Samuel, and the coordination of Tom Sine, but the entire body of participants at Track III took an active part in finalizing the document.[56]

This document, the Wheaton '83 Statement on Transformation, marked a number of significant accomplishments in evangelical missiology, perhaps more than the participants expected. First, the Statement culminated for many the ten year journey toward holistic mission since Lausanne. Padilla asserts that 'Wheaton '83 completed the process of shaping an evangelical social conscience, a process in which people from the Two Thirds World played a decisive role.'[57] The second half of his assertion reflects the second accomplishment of the Statement, namely, the realization of the gradual but now certain influence of Two Thirds World evangelicals upon mission theology. Third, the Statement brought the biblical reality of the kingdom of God into prominence for the advancement of holistic mission thinking. 'It represents', writes Samuel and Sugden, 'a commitment to the ministry of the Gospel of the kingdom to bring change at all levels among every people.'[58] Fourth, the Statement reflected a non-dualistic approach to the thorny issue of the relationship between evangelism and social responsibility, perhaps for the first time since the fundamentalist-modernist controversy. In this way, it went beyond the accomplishment of the CRESR, which failed to overcome a dichotomous framework. Samuel and Sugden perhaps overstate the case when

---

[55] Tom Sine (ed.), *The Church in Response to Human Need* (Monrovia, Calif.: MARC, 1983) This book, aptly titled after the Track III sub-theme, served as a rough draft to a later version of the book, edited the second time around by Samuel and Sugden. Sine's edition and Samuel and Sugden's edition serve as a convenient 'before and after' look at the issues. Additional papers were also included in the revised edition.

[56] 'Wheaton '83 Statement', *Transformation*, 23.

[57] Padilla, 'Evangelism and Social Responsibility', 31.

[58] Samuel and Sugden, 'Introduction', *The Church in Response to Human Need*, xi.

they write, '[It] put to final rest for many evangelicals ... the argument between evangelism and social action.'[59] It nonetheless demonstrated the significant move toward genuine integration. Fifth, the Statement brought together the efforts of both theologians and practitioners, thus reflecting an integrated approach to the relationship between theory and practice. The desire for more 'reflective practitioners' and 'active theologians' increased among evangelicals as a result of the Statement. The way the leaders of the emergent movement of Transformation proceeded after the consultation demonstrates this desire, as they produced study guides, a video and eventually a book in order to facilitate holistic missionary reflection and action in churches, development organizations and mission agencies. Sixth, the Statement reflected openness to dialogue with the ecumenical Protestant mission tradition, thus assuming a reconciliatory posture toward ecumenicals, even though ecumenicals did not ultimately reciprocate.[60] For their part, evangelicals affirmed the WCC document, 'Ecumenical Affirmation: Mission and Evangelism', as planners of Wheaton '83 handed out copies to participants at the consultation.[61]

From Development (and Liberation) to Transformation

The seventh accomplishment deserves its own separate section since it is here that the term 'transformation' obtained its present usage. The very word choice 'transformation' did not come easily for the participants of Track III as they wrestled with the advantages and disadvantages of the more commonly used word 'development'. Actually, as Ralph Covell points out, the Track III participants settled at first for the term '*social* transformation'.[62] Later on, the word crafters among the proponents of this new understanding dropped the word 'social' and found the word 'transformation' to be rich enough by itself.[63]

---

[59] Samuel and Sugden, 'Introduction', *Mission as Transformation*, x.

[60] In an email correspondence dated 11 June 2007, Chris Sugden writes, 'The convergence between evangelicals and ecumenicals was never brought to fruition. This was for two reasons. First, when the convergence became serious, the ecumenicals would not engage with the real evangelical leaders but chose their own evangelicals to dialogue with; and second, when evangelicals started working seriously with the World Bank and enterprise solutions to poverty, the socialist ideology of the ecumenicals won out over their Christian convictions and they actively worked against this aspect of Mission as Transformation'.

[61] Ralph Covell, 'Wheaton '83', *Missiology* 11.4 (October 1983), 533. For the WCC Statement itself, see Scherer and Bevans, *New Directions in Mission and Evangelization I*, 36-51.

[62] Covell, 'Wheaton '83', 533.

[63] Compare, for example, the first publication of the Wheaton '83 Statement entitled 'Social Transformation: The Church in Response to Human Need' in the premiere issue of *Transformation*, 23, with its second publication as 'Transformation: The Church in

Whereas Roman Catholics and ecumenical Protestants preferred the term 'liberation' to replace the ideologically laden term 'development', radical evangelicals adopted 'transformation' not only to avoid those same ideological trappings, but also to align closer with their understanding of biblical teaching regarding deep-seated change from the human heart to human society. Furthermore, they also adopted it to distinguish itself from the ideological baggage that came with the term 'liberation', i.e., Marxist socialism, political revolution, and so on. Despite the absence of any direct 'transformation vs. liberation' language in the literature surrounding Wheaton '83, this claim is more than conjecture. In light of the radical evangelical critique of liberation theology established earlier, we can safely assume that indeed a search for an alternative term took place; for if the radicals were content with 'liberation', why did they not simply accept the term and join the ranks of liberation theologians? The very existence of an alternative term suggests strongly that the adoption of the term 'transformation' took place as a result of finding the term 'liberation' also replete with ideological baggage.

If Track III deliberations only implicitly chose 'transformation' over 'liberation', they *explicitly* chose it over and against the term 'development'. The five year study process on development, which began in 1978, revealed in the end that the very term 'development' posed insurmountable problems. Samuel and Sugden's *Church in Response to Human Need*, which made available the definitive papers of Track III, suggests just by the sequence of the chapters the intentional moving away from the term 'development' and officially adopting the term 'transformation'. Tom Sine's paper, which questioned the assumptions of the concept and practice of development, started the book, followed by Wayne Bragg's 'From Development to Transformation', which made the case for the term 'transformation' to replace development on the grounds that it far better conveys the biblical notion of complete change.[64] After thirteen more substantial chapters dealing with aspects of Transformation, the book climaxes with the Wheaton '83 Statement on *Transformation* - not Development, but Transformation.[65]

Response to Human Need' appearing Samuel and Sugden, *The Church in Response to Human Need*, 254.

[64] Tom Sine, 'Development: Its Secular Past and Its Uncertain Future', in Vinay Samuel and Chris Sugden (eds.), *The Church in Response to Human Need* (Oxford; Grand Rapids, Mich.: Regnum; Eerdmans, 1987), 1-19 and Wayne Bragg, 'From Development to Transformation', 20-51.

[65] Of course, not everyone agreed upon the wisdom of doing away with the term 'development'. The argument to retain it was more on pragmatic grounds. The Wheaton '83 Statement on Transformation itself reflects this sentiment. It states, 'Some of us still believe ... that 'development', when reinterpreted in the light of the whole message of the Bible, is a concept that should be retained by Christians. Part of the reason for this choice is that the word is so widely used. The Statement read, 'A change of terms,

The content of the Statement revolves around the central definition of Transformation, which again 'is the change from a condition of human existence contrary to God's purposes to one in which people are able to enjoy fullness of life in harmony with God'.[66] The filling out of this definition in the form of the Wheaton '83 Statement not only culminated a decade of internal and external tensions after Lausanne, it decisively advanced the course of the Transformational movement.

This brief review of both the internal and external tensions that gave birth to Transformation tells an important part of the holistic journey of radical evangelicals after Lausanne '74. The next chapter tells another important part, namely, the development of Transformation after Wheaton '83.

---

therefore, would cause unnecessary confusion' (256). Such sentiment probably accounts for the fact that the term continues to be used among evangelicals. In fact, Bryant Myers' influential work *Walking with the Poor* (Maryknoll, N.Y.: Orbis, 1999) has popularized the term 'transformational development', which has been picked up even by Sugden and others (see *Transformation* 20.2 [April 2003] where Sugden's article, 'Transformational Development: Current State of Understanding' appears). The term seems redundant to me, in light of the history of Wheaton '83, but it nevertheless demonstrates not only the continued use of both terms, but also that terms in general die hard.

[66] 'Wheaton '83 Statement', *The Church in Response to Human Need*, 255.

CHAPTER 4

After Wheaton '83:
Structural and Theological Developments

A name gives an entity or a phenomenon an identity, a right to exist with purpose and to develop in its own way. So when a group of radical evangelicals at Wheaton '83 adopted the name 'Transformation' to the missiological understanding that emerged out of the context of creative tensions between 1974 and 1983, the evangelical holistic missionary movement began to take on a life of its own.

The adoption of the term 'Transformation' at Wheaton '83 and its subsequent development as a missiology in its own right have occasioned the use of the label 'Transformationist' for radical evangelicals associated with the movement. As proponents of liberation theology are often referred to as 'Liberationists', so too these radical evangelical missiologists can be called 'Transformationists'. They themselves do not necessarily don the label, but it nonetheless conveniently describes the people associated with Mission as Transformation. So from this point on, I will refer to radical evangelical mission theologians and practitioners *after* Wheaton '83 as Transformationists.

Wheaton '83 not only culminated post-Lausanne holistic thinking, it also accelerated holistic practice throughout the world as Transformationists began to assert themselves more confidently. They built several key structures in order to facilitate the development and implementation of Mission as Transformation.

Implementing Structures

The International Fellowship of Evangelical Mission Theologians (INFEMIT)

The International Fellowship of Evangelical Mission Theologians (INFEMIT) stands tall among these structures. Officially formed in 1987, INFEMIT has encouraged Transformational praxis on local, regional and international levels, thus serving as one of the primary keepers of Mission as Transformation from its inception.[1]

---

[1] See 'INFEMIT News' *Transformation* 8.3 (July/September 1991), 32, for a list of the various theologians serving as its officers and compare it to the leadership of Track III

Although 1987 marks the year when INFEMIT officially formed, 1980 claims its true beginnings. As established earlier, radical evangelicals at Pattaya in 1980 reacted strongly against what they considered a regrettable return to pre-Lausanne mission thinking. In fact, the reaction at Pattaya that gave impetus toward the formation of INFEMIT registered enough of an impact that even INFEMIT's official Internet homepage claims 1980 as the year of its founding.[2]

Transformationists began to come to terms with the fact that the brand of holistic theology they espoused will probably never flow into the mainstream of evangelical missionary consciousness as long as 'managerial missiology', as Escobar has described it, dictated the current.[3] A turning point occurred at Pattaya; there Transformationists resolved to create avenues for theological reflection and action that took seriously the social, economic and religiously pluralistic realities of their respective contexts with or without the official backing of establishment evangelicalism, or as Costas put it, 'without strings attached ... organizational, financial, or ideological.'[4]

In light of their Statement of Concerns drafted at Pattaya, the resolve to do theology on their own terms strengthened in the context of grief and disappointment. Sugden observes that,

> In many evangelical circles the Two Thirds World was only interesting as a case study, a demonstration area of practical mission. The Two Thirds World Church was not expected to articulate its own missiology, its own theology or make a contribution to classical theological study of biblical interpretation or systematic theology. The theologians of INFEMIT understood this to be an assault on their dignity and on the integrity of their cultures.[5]

However, Sugden also points out that their resolve did not ultimately reflect a rejection of Western theologizing so much as it did the desire to affirm Two Thirds World theologizing.[6] The resolve ultimately had, in other words, a more intentional proactive thrust to it rather than a divisive reactionary one. In fact, not only did Transformationists *not* echo, for example, the extreme voices

---

of Wheaton '83 listed under 'Committees and Key Supporting Staff' in the *Wheaton '83 Conference Notebook* (20 July-1 July 1983), B-2:4-5, which was distributed at the conference in Wheaton, IL.

[2] 'INFEMIT', http://www.infemit.net/ (accessed 29 November 2002).

[3] Samuel Escobar, 'A Movement Divided', *Transformation* 8.4 (October 1991), 11-13 and 'Evangelical Missiology: Peering into the Future at the Turn of the Century', William Taylor (ed.), *Global Missiology for the 21ˢᵗ Century* (Grand Rapids, Mich.: Baker, 2000), 109-112.

[4] Costas, 'Proclaiming', 4.

[5] Sugden, 'Wholistic Evangelism', 39.

[6] Sugden, 'Wholistic Evangelism', 38-39.

clamoring for a Moratorium on Western missionaries, they actually called for partnership with non-Two Thirds World theologians based on equality and mutuality.[7] After all, if the enterprise of contextual theology proceeds fairly, it must ultimately acknowledge theologies from the North and West as legitimate contributors. The signers of the Statement of Concerns at Pattaya 'wanted a partnership with Western Christians and churches that expressed a relationship of reconciliation and mutual sharing in place of dominance and subservience'.[8] So this yet unofficial and loose network of Two Thirds World missiologists in 1980 officially recognized itself as INFEMIT in 1987, and it sought to provide not only avenues for authentic contextual theology from the Two Thirds World, but also opportunities for East-West, South-North, intercontextual partnership for the sake of the Gospel.

The network's first attempt at creating these avenues and opportunities occurred in 1982 at Bangkok in the form of an international consultation on Christology. Made possible by Partnership in Mission Asia (PIM Asia), twenty five theologians mostly from Africa, Asia, and Latin America gathered together to discuss 'the emerging Christologies in the Two Thirds World'.[9]

As much as the conference findings themselves contributed to the Christological question, the fact that for the first time Two Thirds World evangelical theologians met on their own initiative made this conference especially significant as it catapulted non-Western theological contributions onto centre stage.[10] To be sure, the Two Thirds World Christology forged at

---

[7] Sugden, 'Wholistic Evangelism', 38. Extreme proponents of the missionary moratorium called not only for an end to sending personnel and funds to foreign lands, but also to sending home those who were currently serving as missionaries. To understand the issues surrounding the Moratorium, see Gerald H. Anderson, 'A Moratorium on Missionaries?' in Gerald Anderson and Thomas Stransky, *Mission Trends 1,* (New York; Grand Rapids, Mich.: Paulist; Eerdmans, 1974), 133-141. For a more recent analysis, see F. Albert Tizon, 'Remembering the Missionary Moratorium', *Covenant Quarterly* 62.1 (February 2004), 13-34.

[8] Sugden, 'Wholstic Evangelism', 38. See also an extended footnote concerning this in Chris Sugden, *Seeking the Asian Face of Jesus* (Oxford.: Regnum, 1997), 206-207, f.n. # 49.

[9] David Gitari, 'Preface', in Vinay Samuel and Chris Sugden (eds.), *Sharing Jesus in the Two Thirds World* (Grand Rapids, Mich.: Eerdmans, 1984), vii. Gitari was one of the founding members of INFEMIT and chairman of the conference. Also, what is now INFEMIT was called at this conference as the Fellowship of Evangelical Mission Theologians of the Two Thirds World.

[10] These conference findings are published in Vinay Samuel and Chris Sudgen, 'Towards a Missiological Christology in the Two Thirds World', Vinay Samuel and Chris Sugden (eds.), *Sharing Jesus in the Two Thirds World* (Grand Rapids, Mich.: Eerdmans, 1984), 277-279. This same volume contains many of the papers presented at this first INFEMIT sponsored conference.

this first INFEMIT sponsored consultation impacted Wheaton '83 a year later, as reflected in the resultant Statement on Transformation. Part IV of the Statement, entitled 'Culture and Transformation', speaks redemptively of culture, and then declares that the goal of mission is to 'bring people and their cultures under the Lordship of Christ'.[11]

Representatives of the LATF hosted the second INFEMIT international consultation in 1984 at Cuernavaca, Mexico on the theme of the Holy Spirit, while representatives of the African Theological Fraternity (ATF) hosted the third consultation in 1987 at Kabare, Kenya with the theme, 'The Living God in Contemporary Life'.[12] It was at this third conference that INFEMIT officially formed as a network comprising the three continental fellowships of PIM-Asia, LATF and ATF, all of which continued to conduct their own regional conferences as well. The fourth meeting convened in 1991 at Osijek, (former) Yugoslavia under the theme, 'Freedom and Justice in Church State Relationships'.[13]

INFEMIT underwent an organizational restructuring at this fourth conference that entailed inviting Samuel to act as its full-time executive director.[14] He accepted and moved to England shortly thereafter in order to better implement INFEMIT's global objectives.[15] David Lim joined Samuel as one of the two members from Asia that made up INFEMIT's Board. Lim also agreed at that time to serve as chairman of INFEMIT's Literature and Publications Commission.[16]

From 1991 and on, INFEMIT preferred to work more in conjunction with its regional and local counterparts than solely sponsoring international conferences. This did not necessarily introduce anything novel, because INFEMIT partnered with like-minded regional and local institutions from the beginning. For example, it partnered with ISACC in Manila in 1986 for a conference on the Holy Spirit and politics. It also linked with PIM-Asia and WEF for a conference on Church and State in 1988. These gatherings merely sample the many collaborative efforts of INFEMIT with like-minded regional institutions.

Since 1991, however, no international conference findings sponsored solely by INFEMIT graced the pages of *Transformation,* which was unusual as

---

[11] 'Wheaton '83 Statement on Transformation', *The Church in Response to Human Need,* 260.

[12] To my knowledge, none of the papers were published from this second consultation. But several of the papers presented, as well as the Findings Report from the third consultation are published in *Transformation* 5.2 (April/June 1988), as well as in G.P. Benson and David Gitari (eds.), *The Living God* (Nairobi: Uzima, 1986).

[13] 'Declaration of Osijek', *Transformation* 8.3 (July/September 1991), 1-6.

[14] 'INFEMIT News', *Transformation,* 32.

[15] Chris Sugden, *Gospel, Culture and Transformation* (Oxford: 2000), viii.

[16] 'INFEMIT News', *Transformation,* 32.

Transformation regularly published INFEMIT conference reports. This indicates that INFEMIT underwent a subtle shift in strategy with regard to accomplishing its objectives. Based upon the published articles and conference reports in *Transformation,* INFEMIT chose primarily to join forces with, or simply lent support to, regional and local initiatives for missiological reflection in meetings sponsored by institutes like the Kairos Centre in Argentina, the Akrofi-Kristaller Memorial Centre for Mission Research in Ghana, ISACC in the Philippines, the Centre for Community Transformation also in the Philippines, and other institutions. As an international forum, the Oxford Centre for Mission Studies (OCMS) in the UK gained more prominence as the emerging centre of global theological reflection for the INFEMIT network. Because of its central place, OCMS warrants more detailed attention in the next section. Suffice it to say here that OCMS study programs and consultations for the most part seemed to take the place that INFEMIT had primarily held in sponsoring international conferences.

In keeping with the original vision that formed INFEMIT, its leaders kept the door open for partnership with theologians from Europe and North America, but the question of how wide to open that door generated serious disagreement among them. Some believed that it should extend full membership to 'One Third World' theologians while others, especially constituents from Latin America, expressed reservations, arguing that if these One Third World theologians became full members their voices would inevitably dominate the fellowship, thus undermining INFEMIT's primary reason-for-being.[17] But somewhere along the line, INFEMIT Europe and INFEMIT USA formed. Samuel confirms that these latter groups formed on non-permanent bases to serve specific functions.[18] INFEMIT USA, for example, recently completed a study project on evangelicals and politics in the Two Thirds World.[19] For the most part, North American and western European theologians continue to participate within INFEMIT on an invitation basis.

INFEMIT currently describes itself

> as a facilitating organization 1) providing support services to mission groups to foster the development of leadership, 2) enabling study and research in the theology and practice of mission, and 3) equipping regional and continental networks to undertake research into contextually relevant issues, develop an

---

[17] Laurel Gasque and Ward Gasque, '"Third World" Theologians Meet', *Christianity Today* 27 May 1991, 59-60.

[18] Vinay Samuel, interview by author, 26 July 2003, St. Davids, Pa., tape recording, Eastern University.

[19] See 'News from the International Fellowship of Evangelical Mission Theologians: INFEMIT USA', *Transformation* 18.1 (January 2001), 60.

internationally recognized corpus of research, and contribute significantly to evangelical scholarship globally.[20]

From its inception to the present, INFEMIT has served as 'structural keeper', the umbrella organization of Mission as Transformation, as well as the monitor for maintaining the centrality of the role of culture, particularly the culture of the Two Thirds World, for theological reflection.

Oxford Centre for Mission Studies (OCMS)

The Oxford Centre for Mission Studies (OCMS) stands as another major structure through which Mission as Transformation developed. Although we can distinguish them from each other, OCMS and INFEMIT are essentially one. OCMS in fact identifies itself as the research and study centre of the INFEMIT network. INFEMIT News of 1991 describes the relationship this way: 'OCMS is a project of INFEMIT and is sponsored by INFEMIT. It functions as a commission of INFEMIT in its relation to the INFEMIT board.'[21] The fact that the two institutions have also liberally shared their leaders attests to their oneness. As of 1991, Padilla occupied the Board Chair of both INFEMIT and OCMS. Moreover, four other people sat on both boards.

The organic connection between them notwithstanding, they have served different agendas within the same movement: INFEMIT has represented while the cultural agenda of Mission as Transformation, a constant reminder that this holistic understanding emerged from the Two Thirds World and continues to develop intercontextually, OCMS has emphasized the theological scholarship necessary to advance this understanding.

Founded in 1983, OCMS initially offered short summer courses, as well as sponsored or jointly sponsored consultations, in which internationally recognized voices served as resource persons. By offering intensive summer courses - like 'Missions and Social Transformation' taught by Rene Padilla, Vinay Samuel, and Ed Dayton in 1984[22], and by sponsoring consultations like the one on alternative churches in totalitarian societies featuring presenters like Jonathan Chao in 1985, OCMS was pioneering a cutting edge and daring form of theological reflection for evangelicals. Whether as summer schools or as consultations, these educational opportunities served the same purpose, namely, to tackle a range of contemporary theological and socio-political issues in a distinctively Transformational key for the worldwide missionary community,

---

[20] 'INFEMIT', http://www.infemit.net/ (accessed 7 February 2007).

[21] 'INFEMIT News', *Transformation*, 32.

[22] Bishop Stephen Neill was supposed to co-teach this class as well, but he died before the Summer School began.

but especially for Two Thirds World churches engaged in mission in their particular contexts.

OCMS offered these summer intensives and consultations regularly, but by their very nature their impact had limits. It seemed inevitable that OCMS had to develop programs that could analyze missional and ethical issues in a more in-depth and formal way. The January/March 1985 issue of *Transformation* announced an OCMS sponsored one-year diploma course in mission studies, for which Oxford University would make available its theological holdings.[23] Eventually, OCMS obtained its validation (or accreditation) through the UK Council for National Academic Awards (CNAA) and then through the Open University upon the closure of the CNAA. Then in 1992, it offered two courses through the Oxford University post-graduate Certificate in Theology Program, for the first time validating its courses through a recognized university. By 1996, OCMS began to offer masters' and doctoral degrees not only through the Open University but also through the University of Wales.[24] It also later affiliated with the University of Leeds in 1997 and then with the University of Utrecht in Holland in 1999.

Moreover, it began to create partnerships around the world with institutions like the Evangelical Theological Seminary in Osijek, Croatia, the Association for Theological Education by Extension (TAFTEE) in Bangalore, India, and Vanguard University in California, USA, in order to provide a truly international theological education for Christian leaders.[25] Samuel celebrates, 'This is one of the strengths of OCMS - it is international scholarship, not just local scholarship', a trait in theological education for which the twenty first century calls.[26]

The successful validation process with the British University system as well as the partnerships made with educational institutions all over the world occurred under the creative leadership of the first two Executive Directors Vinay Samuel and Chris Sugden. Lim served at OCMS as associate dean and chaplain between 1992 and 1994. With such a structure in place, OCMS has played a chief role in facilitating the creative scholarly development of Mission as Transformation since 1983.

---

[23] It was not until October 1989, however, that OCMS offered for the first time a nine month certificate course in Christian Theology and Development Studies.

[24] Abstracts for doctoral theses written for OCMS were first listed under 'Recent Theses', *Transformation* 13.3 (July/September 1996), 31-32.

[25] To get a full and current list of affiliated institutions, go to http://www.ocms.ac.uk/research/ (accessed 7 February 2008).

[26] Vinay Samuel, 'Christian Scholarship in the Twenty-first Century: A Non-Western Perspective', *Transformation* 19.4 (April 2002), 231.

Publishing Initiatives: Transformation, Regnum Books, and Others

The INFEMIT/OCMS network needed avenues through which to share Transformational perspectives with the international missionary community in order to challenge it, as well as to contribute to it. It created a publishing arm that produced (and continues to produce) a quarterly journal appropriately named *Transformation* in 1984 and a book company called Regnum Books in 1987.

The maiden issue of *Transformation* included introductory remarks by the editors concerning the new journal.[27] They explained in the first editorial that the renewal of evangelical commitment to social concern, the facilitation of a truly global discussion among socially-concerned evangelicals and the development of the holistic understanding of Transformation adopted at Wheaton '83 defined the journal's *raison d'etre*.[28] The new journal's subtitle, 'An International Dialogue on Evangelical Social Ethics', expressed as much.[29] Its change in 1991 to 'An International Evangelical Dialogue on Mission and Ethics',[30] as mentioned before, reflected a realization on the part of Transformationists that the dialogue on social ethics lies at the heart of the larger discussion on the Church's holistic mission in the world.

WEF served as *Transformation*'s first sponsoring institution; which made sense since WEF convened the Wheaton '83 Consultation that catalyzed Transformational thinking. But in the July/September 1988 issue of *Transformation*, the editors announced a new home for the journal: the Oxford Centre for Mission Studies. They explained what happened:

> For three years, there has been ongoing discussion about whether the World Evangelical Fellowship, as an international fellowship of national evangelical alliances located in diverse socio-political settings was the best parent organization for a journal of opinion which by its nature is sometimes controversial. Things that need to be published may sometimes feel uncomfortable to some person or group within the WEF network and the larger evangelical family. In April 1988, the WEF Executive Council decided that

---

[27] Tokunboh Adeyemo, Vinay Samuel and Ronald Sider served as the journal's original editors. In *Gospel, Culture and Transformation*, Sugden notes that it was Samuel and Sider who started the journal (23).

[28] 'Editorial', *Transformation* 1.1 (January/March 1984), 1-2.

[29] Ronald J. Sider, interview by author, 25 July 2003, St. Davids, Pa., tape recording, Eastern University. According to Sider, the journal's name was going to be something like the *Evangelical Review of Social Ethics* - to correspond with WEF's existing *Evangelical Review of Theology* - or the *Journal of International Christian Social Ethics*.

[30] The October 1991 issue showed for the first time this subtitle change. In the 'Editorial' of this issue, it says that 'the name change signifies an increased emphasis on wholistic mission'.

Transformation should find a new home. That new home is the Oxford Centre for Mission Studies.[31]

The WEF minutes for the meeting, wherein the decision no longer to publish *Transformation* occurred, explained the reasoning in similar ways. While affirming 'the valid and needed service' of *Transformation*, the WEF Executive Board thought *Transformation* would be more effective as an independent journal, free from 'any agency that exercises a censoring or inhibiting role.'[32] Some level of politicking on the part of WEF leaders undoubtedly influenced the decision as they strove to avoid misunderstanding among its worldwide constituents. But the decision to part ways occurred more or less on cordial terms between WEF and the editorial board of *Transformation*.[33] In fact, Tokunboh Adeyemo, then a member of WEF's Executive Council, remained one of the three editors for *Transformation* until 1994. As *Transformation* settled into its new home, the consolidation between INFEMIT, OCMS, and *Transformation* made the structures that much more effective in advancing Mission as Transformation.

Transformation has served the INFEMIT/OCMS network as its journal of international dialogue on mission and ethics. Regional Transformational fellowships also published journals that reflected their respective contexts, such as *Patmos* in the Philippines published by ISACC, *Mision* in Argentina published by the Kairos Centre, *Prism* in the USA published by ESA, *Unterwegs (On the Way)* in Germany by Rolf Zwick, and many more. These publications on both the international and regional levels sparked (and continue to spark) stimulating dialogue and creative practice as they tackled a wide range of issues from a Transformational perspective.

In addition to *Transformation* and regional journals, the INFEMIT/OCMS network also published full length books in order to make available extensive missiological research that journals could not accommodate. It accomplished this by creating its own publishing company called Regnum Books. An advertisement for Regnum first appeared in the back cover of the January/March 1987 issue of *Transformation* with the following description:

---

[31] 'Editorial', *Transformation* 5.3 (July/September 1988), no page number.

[32] Cited in David M. Howard, *The Dream That Would Not Die: The Birth and Growth of the World Evangelical Fellowship, 1846-1986* (Exeter: Paternoster, 1986), 172. Howard reports that the decision no longer to publish *Transformation* occurred at a meeting in the Netherlands in June 1985 (172). The editors of *Transformation* report this decision occurred in April 1988. In my 2003 interview with Sider, he recalled vaguely that it did take a while for the decision to be made and implemented. The discrepancy can probably be explained by process. A decision was made, but it took several years of discussion (as well as some possible waffling) to finalize it.

[33] Sider, interview.

[Regnum Books is] a new Two Thirds World publishing company on behalf of the African Theological Fraternity, the Latin American Theological Fraternity, and Partnership in Mission Asia [the three main continental fellowships that constituted INFEMIT at the time] in cooperation with major evangelical western publishers and based at the Oxford Centre for Mission Studies.[34]

The major evangelical western publishers mentioned in the description include WEF's Paternoster Press based in the UK and Eerdmans in the USA. In cooperation with these, Regnum Books has published the proceedings of various conferences and consultations, such as Samuel and Sugden's enduring *The Church in Response to Human Need*, Bruce J. Nicholls and Bong Rin Ro's *Beyond Canberra,* and others.[35] It also co-published a series of books with Lynx Publications in the UK, including Melba Maggay's *Transforming Society*.[36]

In an effort to balance regional representation, as well as to distribute its publications more effectively, Regnum Books began to link with other institutions around the world, thus broadening its base beyond Oxford and creating Regnum Books International (RBI).[37] As an imprint of Paternoster Press, RBI describes its current mission as making available 'quality missiological studies for theologians and missiologists, to emphasize research from the Two Thirds World, to ensure academic excellence and integrity from both younger and senior scholars, and to provide balanced regional representation'.[38]

Bridges: Participation in Lausanne-Sponsored and WCC Gatherings

INFEMIT, OCMS and the publishing arms of *Transformation*, regional journals, and RBI have provided interlocking structures for the advancement of Mission as Transformation primarily for the international evangelical community but certainly not limited to this constituency. One other structure deserves mention, namely, the bridges maintained that have kept dialogue open with the greater Christian community. Transformationists did not cloister together and cut themselves off from other fellowships; on the contrary, they participated outside of their own network, thus engaging the greater missiological world from a Transformational perspective.

---

[34] 'Regnum Books announcement', *Transformation* 4.1 (January/March 1987), back cover.

[35] Bruce J. Nicholls and Bong Rin Ro (eds.), *Beyond Canberra: Evangelical Responses to Contemporary Ecumenical Issues* (Oxford: Regnum; Lynx, 1993).

[36] Melba Maggay, *Transforming Society* (Oxford: Regnum and Lynx, 1994).

[37] RBI consists of satellites in Oxford (UK), Irvine (USA), Akropong-Akuapem (Ghana), Buenos Aires (Argentina), and New Delhi (India).

[38] 'About Us', www.regnumbooks.com (accessed 12 December 2002).

They continued to participate for example in Lausanne sponsored gatherings like the second International Congress in 1989 held at the Philippine Cultural Centre in Manila. Not surprisingly, their main involvement had to do with the social concern aspect of the Congress, Samuel serving as the coordinator of the Social Concern Track. The January/March 1990 issue of *Transformation* committed most of its pages to reflections on Lausanne II, naturally emphasizing the importance of integrating evangelization with social concern and vice versa. Other important presenters at the Congress, who contributed influentially from a Transformational perspective, included Tokunboh Adeyemo, Peter Kuzmic, and Os Guinness.

The fact that Filipino evangelicals hosted Lausanne II in Manila demonstrated an overall endorsement of the Lausanne movement among them, and it allowed for the participation of a substantial number of Filipino delegates. Moreover, welcoming speeches by then President Corazon Aquino and Senator Jovito Salonga helped to endorse the Lausanne movement for Filipino Christians as a whole.[39]

Critical reflections on the Congress, however, from several Filipino Transformationists, counterbalanced the tendency toward triumphalism. For example, Maggay lamented after the event:

As I suspected, the theme that for the last fifteen years [referring back to Lausanne '74] had turned the tide of worldwide evangelism towards greater sensitivity to culture and the poor had been turned into a platitude that grated more and more as the days went by. Worse, it seemed to have been domesticated into a bleeding-heart concern removed from the hardness of structural realities and the lack of radical suspicion towards ideological and cultural presuppositions. ... Lausanne II is a sign that it is a spirit that has spent itself; it is a tired horse that ought not to be ridden to death.[40]

Due to critiques such as these, along with positive contributions to the Congress in general and to the Social Concern Track in particular, Transformationists had an overall prophetic impact at Lausanne II (and at other lesser known Lausanne sponsored gatherings) that continued to challenge the greater evangelical missionary community to remember the Two Thirds World in all of its complexity, beauty, and contextual issues, not just in words (evangelism) but also in deeds (social concern).

While Transformationists continued to challenge fellow evangelicals concerning their commitment to social concern, they also challenged non-

[39] These addresses from Filipino officials are available in James D. Douglas (ed.), *Proclaim Christ Until He Comes* (Minneapolis, Minn.: World Wide Publications, 1990), 45-47.

[40] Melba Maggay, 'Lausanne II: In Remembrance of Things Past', *Isip-Isak* 2.3 (3rd Quarter 1989), 1, 7.

evangelicals not to forget evangelism as they increased their involvement in gatherings sponsored by the WCC. For example, Transformationists contributed greatly to the Stuttgart Consultation on Evangelism in March 1987, which convened for the purpose of pre-processing and thereby providing direction for the 1989 Conference on World Mission and Evangelism of the WCC. In spite of the diverse perspectives at this conference on how Christians should share the Gospel, the participants concluded that 'evangelism always means that - in one way or another - people are called to faith in Christ'.[41] Transformationists, including Evelyn Miranda-Feliciano and Isabelo Magalit from the Philippines, gave definitive voice at Stuttgart to what they identified as 'integral evangelism', which understands the evangelistic invitation contextually and inseparably from works of justice.[42]

A letter entitled 'A Jubilee Call', written to the WCC at the eighth Assembly in 1998 at Harare, also exemplified the commitment to evangelism and mission with which Transformationists challenged the ecumenical movement.[43] Drafted in the context of numerous meetings called by INFEMIT leaders Vinay Samuel, David Gitari, and others, 'the Jubilee Call' affirmed that 'evangelism, as [a] call to [a] personal turning to God, must be at the heart of the Church's mission of social transformation'.[44] The letter lamented that, 'while the theme "Turn to God: Rejoice in Hope" should have led to a strong emphasis on mission, evangelism and the church, this was largely missing'.[45] Fifty evangelicals from around the world at the Assembly, including Maggay, signed and presented the letter to the WCC.

The broad scope and holistic nature of Mission as Transformation, wherein evangelism and social concern flowed together, enabled Transformationists to challenge both evangelical and ecumenical mission traditions by way of creating bridges of participation and dialogue between them.

---

[41] 'Statement of the Stuttgart Consultation', in Vinay Samuel and Albrecht Hauser (eds.), *Proclaiming Christ in Christ's Way* (Oxford: Regnum, 1989), 213.

[42] A full list of the participants is included in Samuel and Hauser, *Proclaiming Christ in Christ's Way*, 224-225.

[43] 'A Jubilee Call', *Transformation* 16.2 (April/June 1999), 67-68. This letter was in line with other letters written by evangelical participants at other WCC gatherings. See for example 'Evangelicals at Vancouver: An Open Letter', *TSF Bulletin* 7.1 (September/October 1983), 18-19, written for the delegates of the sixth Assembly, and 'Evangelical Perspectives from Canberra', in Bong Rin Ro and Bruce Nicholls (eds.), *Beyond Canberra* (Oxford: Regnum; Lynx, 1993), 38-43, written for the delegates of the seventh Assembly.

[44] 'A Jubilee Call', *Transformation*, 67-68.

[45] 'A Jubilee Call', *Transformation*, 68.

Theological Developments in Mission as Transformation

The community of Transformational scholars and practitioners matured remarkably within and through the structures of INFEMIT, OCMS, journals and books, and bridges to other mission bodies, demonstrating depth and breadth of insight and covering a wide range of relevant missiological issues since Wheaton '83. The wideness of range, on the surface, can suggest the absence of cohesion to the Transformational agenda. However, at least four traceable, interrelated, theological developments, amidst the many issues that they covered, suggest otherwise. These four developments have provided a theological structure for the makings of a coherent missiology: 1) the importance of culture both local and global, 2) the impact of faith on economics, 3) the practice of holistic mission, and 4) the power of the Holy Spirit in mission (the contribution of radical Pentecostalism).

Local and Global Culture: Mission in Context as Transformation

Culture, both local and global, has played such a significant role in this missiology that to overlook its impact would cripple any effort to grasp the core of Mission as Transformation. 'Mission *in Context* as Transformation' actually reflects a more accurate description. The very existence of INFEMIT attests to the commitment of Transformationists to take seriously the local context - its religious, ethical, symbolic, socio-political, economic and other cultural aspects - for missiological reflection. By theologizing on their own terms, Transformationists opened the local contextual door wider than ever with an agenda that went well beyond understanding contextualization as a glorified form of cross-cultural adaptation. For them, contextualization meant taking seriously the culturally specific nature of the Gospel itself, which carried at least two implications.

First, missionaries from the North and West had to come to terms with the fact that the theology they brought with them could no longer serve (and perhaps never should have served) as the universal plumb line with which all other theologies had to level. Maggay observes that 'theology as it has developed in the West is just as culture-bound and as subject to the sort of suspicion that western theologians cast upon current indigenous attempts at contextualizing the Gospel.'[46]

Second, Christians from the South and East had to do their own theologizing in order to engage in relevant mission within their respective contexts. The second followed the first in that if Two Thirds World churches began to view with suspicion the notion that 'classical' theologians of the North and West held the measuring stick, then the burden to create their own measuring sticks

---

[46] Melba Maggay, *Filipino Religious Consciousness: Some Implications for Missions* (Quezon City: ISACC, 1999), 8.

was laid upon the 'younger' theologians of the Two Thirds World. 'Mission in Context as Transformation' called all local faith communities, Western and non-Western - to do their own biblical hermeneutics, to practice their own liturgical expressions, and to utilize their own mission approaches in light of their own contextual realities.

For Transformationists, however, the idea of contextualization has gradually meant more than just paying attention to local contexts. In a globalized world, 'Mission in Context as Transformation' has also come to mean grappling with an emerging global culture, i.e., the interacting realities of modernity, postmodernity and the phenomenon of globalization. These realities make up a discernable interrelated global culture that Transformationists have taken seriously.

Words like modernity, postmodernity and globalization elude clear, agreed-upon definitions, but to begin to understand how Transformationists have interacted with this global culture necessitates a basic understanding of these terms.

Modernity

The editors of the book that came out of the INFEMIT/OCMS sponsored Conference on Faith and Modernity in 1994 at Uppsala, Sweden define modernity as 'the intellectual and cultural heritage of the Enlightenment project, namely, the rejection of traditional and religious sources of authority in favour of reason and knowledge as the road to human emancipation'.[47] It refers to an optimistic faith in human ingenuity, rationality, and technology to determine social progress and ultimate reality.

Sociologist James Hunter identifies three institutional carriers of this worldview: industrial capitalism, the modern [bureaucratic] state, and the knowledge sector of universities and media that promote skepticism and humanism.[48] The confidence of the 'enlightened' in these institutions justified the colonization of 'lesser lands', of which the missionary movement played a part. For who, reasoned many missionaries and other well-meaning Westerners, would not want to avail of the benefits of a superior civilization? Chiefly through sustained colonialism (and ongoing neocolonialism), modernity has defined the rules of the world; it has constituted what Guinness has described as

---

[47] Philip Sampson, Vinay Samuel and Chris Sugden, 'Introduction', in Philip Sampson, Vinay Samuel and Chris Sugden (eds.), *Faith and Modernity* (Oxford: Regnum, 1994), 7.

[48] James D. Hunter, 'What is Modernity?' in Philip Sampson, Vinay Samuel and Chris Sugden (eds.), *Faith and Modernity* (Oxford: Regnum, 1994), 18-20.

'the first truly global culture in the world and the most powerful culture in history so far'.[49]

Postmodernity

Postmodernity comes onto the scene as a loss of faith in the ability of the modernist outlook to emancipate humanity and the world.[50] But contrary to the notion that postmodernity has replaced modernity, these two outlooks co-exist; which leads some to understand postmodernity as simply a later stage of modernity - 'another twist in its spiral' - rather than a radical break from it.[51] Nevertheless, it refers to a different way to understand the world.

Postmodernity claims that the Enlightenment project, upon which Western civilization was founded, has failed. It claims that human rationality, ingenuity, industrialization and determination have led not to a better world, but to an unjust world, in which elitist, hegemonic, and dehumanizing forces have created new kinds of cultural, economic, and socio-political inequities. In announcing the failure of modernity this worldview holds suspect any and all claims to universality and absolute truth, that is, grand narratives; for these grand narratives do not in fact represent the world but in reality only represent the West, which has imposed itself upon the rest of the world.[52] To deconstruct the imposed philosophical, religious, economic, cultural, and socio-political frameworks of the modernist West and to rediscover and affirm local constructs, therefore, define the postmodern project.

This challenge to the foundations of modernity certainly deserves some level of affirmation. In general, by exposing the false universality of the West, postmodernity has opened the door for non-Western contributions in the pursuit of truth, justice, and peace in the world. For religious discourse in particular, postmodernity has restored the validity of traditional religious outlooks, which were debunked by the doctrinaire worldview of modernity; but of course, it has also legitimized the existence of non-traditional, religious, 'New Age' perspectives as well. Even more particularly for the missionary work of the Church, postmodernity has brought the Western church to its knees, so to speak, calling it to repent of its undeniable cooperation with colonization and conquest. However, as David Paton admonishes, 'A call to repentance is not a call to drop important work, but to do it otherwise'.[53] Postmodernity has

---

[49] Os Guinness, 'Mission Modernity: Seven Checkpoints on Mission in the Modern World', in Vinay Samuel and Chris Sugden (eds.), *Mission as Transformation* (Oxford: Regnum, 1999), 296.

[50] Sampson, Samuel and Sugden, 'Introduction', 7.

[51] Sampson, Samuel and Sugden, 'Introduction', 8-9.

[52] Philip Sampson, 'The Rise of Postmodernity', in Philip Sampson, Vinay Samuel and Chris Sugden (eds.), *Faith and Modernity* (Oxford: Regnum, 1994), 36-38.

[53] Cited in Bosch, *Transforming Mission*, 365.

compelled the Church to go about its mission differently, with more cultural sensitivity, humility, and an emphasis on relationships over impersonal programs.

Despite its potentially affirming effects, however, postmodernity has yet to provide humanity a viable alternative to modernity. To point out modernity's failure obliges the postmodern project to provide something in its stead; which it has not yet adequately done. The unfortunate tendency among postmodernists is that many of them do not think such a task is possible or even necessary. Philip Sampson's characterization of postmodernity as 'nihilism with a smile' reflects both the shortcoming and the danger of the postmodern outlook.[54]

Globalization

At the risk of overgeneralization, acceptance of globalization characterizes the outlook of modernity, while resistance to it points to postmodernity. Sociologists David Held and colleagues provide a general definition of globalization as a 'widening, deepening and speeding up of global interconnectedness', which has an all-encompassing impact upon the world.[55] As a process, globalization offers exciting possibilities 'for the exchange of knowledge and ideas, for the expression of solidarity among peoples, for the sharing of human and material resources, and for fostering intercultural communication'.[56]

Far from being just a process, however, globalization can easily take on ideological dimensions, which demand the participation, the commitment, and even the loyalty of all. As an ideology, globalization offers nothing less than salvation - a unifying future for humankind - in accordance with a capitalist-based consumerist vision. Terms like 'McDonaldization' or 'Coca-colonization' capture in a popular way this particular kind of *eschaton*. In this light, ideological globalization competes with the salvation offered in Jesus Christ. I will say more about this in Chapter 9 as well as in the Conclusion. For now, it is helpful to distinguish between globalization as process and ideology, for the process (though certainly not morally neutral) can result in good if used for good. This fact should prevent any tendency to demonize the entire globalization phenomenon. However, in most cases throughout this book, I respond to globalization as ideology.

Whether as process or ideology, one irrefutable fact holds true about globalization - it affects all of life. While neo-liberal economics define the base, it moves well beyond it. Economist Rob van Drimmelen defines globalization as

---

[54] Sampson, 'The Rise of Post-Modernity', 30.
[55] Held, McGrew, Goldblatt and Perraton, *Global Transformations*, 14-15.
[56] 'The People of God Among All God's People', *The People of God Among All God's People*, 14.

the process of growing and intensifying interaction of all levels of society in world trade, foreign investment and capital market. It is abetted by technological advances in transport and communications and by a rapid liberalization and deregulation of trade and capital flows, both nationally and internationally, leading to one global market.[57]

As such, scholars can speak justifiably of globalization as a 'market culture'. Samuel somberly notes that 'it affects all our daily lives, our jobs, our children, our education and our future'.[58]

Together, modernity, postmodernity, and globalization have provided the makings of a complex global culture. And conferences like the one on faith and modernity and the many articles dealing with the phenomenon of globalization by Transformationists attest to how seriously they have addressed this global culture as part of the Church's mandate to interpret and transform the world. Samuel contends that the Christian response to ideological globalization has to do with intercontextual participation in the globalization of the Gospel. 'The continuing task of proclaiming the Gospel to every person and every community', he declares, '[requires bringing] ... the experience of people in the mission of the Church around the world together to share and so shape our common understanding of mission.'[59]

Whether analyzing local or global culture, however, Transformationists set limits to the role that cultural context plays for missiology; for divine revelation in Jesus Christ - not human culture - primarily determines the agenda for mission. As Samuel and Sugden say it, 'At the heart of Christian mission is our understanding of Jesus Christ, his person and mission.'[60] Nevertheless, God reveals in context; which makes the revelation versus contextualization debate in missiology ultimately artificial from a Transformational perspective. Communicating the divine revelation of Christ through a thorough understanding of culture, both local and global, defines both the privilege and challenge of Christian mission.

Faith and Money: Toward Transformational Economics

The sophisticated way, in which Transformationists have dealt with context, formulating theological responses to both local and global cultures, constitutes an integral part of the way in which Mission as Transformation has developed since Wheaton '83. The same can be said about their attempt at developing a

---

[57] Rob van Drimmelen, *Faith in a Global Economy: A Primer for Christians* (Geneva: WCC, 1998), 7-8.

[58] Vinay Samuel, 'Evangelical Response to Globalization: An Asian Perspective', *Transformation* 16.1 (January/March 1999), 4.

[59] Samuel, 'Evangelical Response', 7.

[60] Samuel and Sugden, 'Introduction', *Mission as Transformation*, ix.

Christian economics. Their efforts, beginning in 1987 at the first conference on Christian Faith and Economics in Oxford, could not have been more timely as the walls that perpetuated the Cold War in Eastern Europe literally came crashing down in 1989. Schreiter, along with many others, points to the rubble of those walls as the beginning point of the contemporary age of globalization, when democratic capitalism declared victory over communism.[61] Before, during, and after the historic end to the Cold War and the beginning of contemporary globalization, Transformationists have viewed economics as all-encompassing a hermeneutic of life as culture has served. As the editors of *Transformation* asserted in a special double issue dealing with economics in 1987, 'Economic life touches - no, substantially moulds - our lives.'[62]

Because of this view, Transformationists have spent much time since Wheaton '83 at the intersection of biblical faith and economics, praying, reflecting, debating and informing the views and practices of many Christian development organizations. The aforementioned 1987 conference in Oxford catalyzed a process to examine relevant issues in economics from a Christian perspective. The thirty-six participants of Oxford I, coming from fourteen countries spanning five continents, 'from many different areas of expertise including banking, business, economics, theology and social ethics' set the agenda for the first set of study processes.[63] Despite the fundamental differences represented among the participants, they were able to say at the end,

> We are grateful to God for growing in mutual trust and feel called to continue the dialogue across the lines of diverse disciplines, geographical locations, and socio-political perspectives. We also agree unanimously that we must work hard to integrate our biblical and economic analyses.[64]

Conference participants appointed a steering committee to facilitate regional study groups to explore biblical perspectives on the stewardship of creation, work and leisure, a definition of justice, freedom, government and economics, all of which they hoped to inform a comprehensive Christian perspective on the

---

[61] Schreiter, *The New Catholicity*, 4-14. Of course, global theorists differ on the periodization of globalization. For many, what is being presented as a 'new age' of globalization today is simply more of the same, but in accelerated mode. For others, the fall of communism has truly ushered in a new era. In *Global Transformations*, Held and colleagues identify periodization as one of the five sources of contention in the globalization debate (12-13).

[62] Tokunboh Adeyemo, Vinay Samuel, and Ronald J. Sider, 'Editorial', *Transformation* 4.3-4 (June-September/October-December 1987), no page number.

[63] 'The Oxford Conference on Christian Faith and Economics', *Transformation* 4.2 (June-September/October-December 1987), 22.

[64] 'The Oxford Conference on Christian Faith and Economics', *Transformation*, 23.

economy. In addition, micro-enterprise development among the poor required its own study process, which the steering committee also facilitated.

The culmination of these study processes occurred at the second follow up conference in 1990 also in Oxford. The number of participants tripled at Oxford II in order to represent the wide diversity within the evangelical community. The relentless desire for unanimity, which continued from the first conference, however, enabled the participants to achieve a genuine level of consensus. 'At this event', write the Editors of *Transformation* reporting on Oxford II, 'liberation oriented theologians affirmed free market strategies and conservative market economists demanded a special focus on justice for the poor.'[65] The papers written and circulated during the intervening years between the two conferences and the continuing deliberations at Oxford II eventually resulted in the Oxford Declaration on Christian Faith and Economics, a document that indeed reached an important level of consensus in understanding how biblical faith can evaluate, challenge, and inform economic life.[66] Organized under four headings: a) Creation and Stewardship, b) Work and Leisure, c) Poverty and Justice, and d) Freedom, Government and Economics, the Declaration managed to bridge divergent views while avoiding a reductionist unity. The *Transformation* Editors summarize the ways in which the Document manifested this bridge-building:

- Economic systems must be judged by their ability both to create wealth and to distribute it justly.
- Both freedom rights and sustenance rights are important and are grounded not in societal fiat but in God's creation of persons in the divine image.
- The God of the Bible demands special attention to the weak, especially the poor members of the community, because of their vulnerability; in this sense justice is biased.
- But civil arrangements rendering justice dare not go beyond what is due to the poor and the rich; in that sense justice is ultimately impartial.
- Biblical values and historical experience call Christians to work for democracy while recognizing that racism, materialism and concentrated economic power often lead to democracies to marginalize the poor and act unjustly.[67]

---

[65] Tokunboh Adeyemo, Vinay Samuel, and Ron Sider, 'Editorial', *Transformation* 7.2 (April/June 1990), no page number.

[66] For an extended discussion on the Declaration, see Herbert Schlossberg, Vinay Samuel, and Ronald J. Sider (eds.), *Christianity and Economics in the Post-Cold War Era* (Grand Rapids, Mich.: Eerdmans, 1994). There was serious doubt, even among the planners, whether any level of consensus could be reached with such a diverse group of people. See Ronald J. Sider's 'Introduction', (4ff.) to get a sense of the pleasant surprise among many of the level of consensus that was reached.

[67] Adeyemo, Samuel and Sider, 'Editorial'. I have taken the liberty to put these summary points in bullet form.

Oxford II also produced the Statement on Income Generation Programs among the Poor in Developing Countries.[68] Point #64 (under 'Mediating Structures') in the Oxford Declaration mentions the practice of micro-enterprise, but its importance warranted a separate statement in order to stress the need for credit based income generation among the poor as one of the keys for poverty alleviation around the world. Indeed since the Oxford Conferences, Christian micro-enterprise development (CMED) has become a - if not *the* - primary way in which Transformational reflections on economics have manifested concretely in the world. The IGP Statement of 1990 issued a call 'to the world Christian community as well as governments, aid donors, financial institutions and non-government organizations who are concerned with poverty alleviation, to make the promotion and support of credit based income generation programmes a high priority for development assistance', and then went on to recommend more specific actions for each of these sectors.[69]

The third Oxford Conference convened in 1995 at Agra, India to focus specifically on the market economy on the poor. In preparation for Oxford III, regional conferences in North America, Austria, Latin America and Russia convened, as Transformationists in these regions analyzed the effects of the post-Cold War market economy in their respective contexts.[70] Oxford III produced the Agra Affirmations, intended to supplement the Oxford Declaration as well as the IGP Statement in an essential way, namely, to 'develop biblical criteria for assessing economic life and strategies to enable the Church to fulfil its commission to help the poor in each society'.[71]

Then at the turn of the century, Transformationists once again revisited the faith and economics issue in light of the changes around the world to ask a set of questions primarily regarding the role of churches in economic development.[72] Under the editorship of Deryke Belshaw, *Transformation* covered a 'journal based colloquium' that spanned three issues from April 2000 to July 2001. The papers from this colloquium covered issues that ranged from the role of the church in Transformational development[73] to the dialogues that

---

[68] 'Statement on Income Generation Programmes among the Poor in Developing Countries', *Transformation* 7.2 (April/June 1990), 10-11.

[69] 'Statement on Income-Generating Programmes', *Transformation,* 11.

[70] See several reports from some of these conferences in 'Christian Faith and Economics', *Transformation* 11.2 (April/June 1994), 6-11.

[71] 'Agra Affirmations on Christian Faith, Market Economics and the Poor', *Transformation* 12.3 (July/September 1995), 5.

[72] Deryke Belshaw, 'Editorial', *Transformation* 17.2 (April/June 2000), 49.

[73] Bryant Myers, 'The Church and Transformational Development', *Transformation* 17.2 (April/June 2000), 64-67.

occurred between African evangelical churches and the World Bank[74] to Christian micro-enterprise development.[75]

Regarding the latter, again representing the most concrete way in which Transformational economic reflections have manifested, CMED has only matured and become more sophisticated since the Oxford Conferences, as Christian organizations such as Opportunity International, Food for the Hungry, World Vision, other lesser known development and mission agencies have essentially implemented the recommendations of the 1990 IGP Statement. In fact, according to a recent survey, over 1200 Christian organizations are involved in micro-enterprise development in the Two Thirds World.[76] As these IGP programs proliferated among the Christian missionary community in the last twenty years, the need for wise guidance on the theology and practice of CMED became acute. David Bussau, considered by many to be the father of the contemporary CMED movement, wrote *Reflections on Christian Micro-enterprise Development,* and also teamed up with Vinay Samuel to write *How Then Shall We Lend?* both in 1998,[77] and then collaborated with Russell Mask in 2003 to provide an introductory handbook aptly titled, *Christian Micro-enterprise Development: An Introduction.*[78] The reminder in these resources to keep poverty alleviation via CMED rooted in the Gospel comes through as a clarion call. As Bussau and Mask assert plainly, 'The ultimate concern of Christian MED is to open the community to experience the kingdom of God'.[79]

This brief overview of the Oxford Conferences and subsequent developments, especially and concretely in CMED, does not do justice to the sophisticated ways in which Transformationists have handled key economic issues of our time. It should demonstrate, however, how seriously they have taken economic life since Wheaton '83 as an arena that the Gospel must inform. Indeed a proper understanding of the stewardship of the resources of

---

[74] Robert Calderisi, 'The World Bank and Africa', *Transformation* 17/4 (October/December 2000), 132-141. See also Deryke Belshaw, Chris Sugden, Robert Calderisi (eds.), *Faith in Development* (Washington, D.C.; Oxford: World Bank; Regnum, 2001) for a full report on the conference involving the World Bank and African churches held in 2000 in Nairobi.

[75] Raj Patel, 'Micro-Finance Development in the Service of the Kingdom', *Transformation* 18.3 (July 2001), 142-145.

[76] Survey cited in David Bussau and Russell Mask, *Christian Microenterprise Development: An Introduction* (Oxford: Regnum, 2003), xi.

[77] David Bussau, *Reflections on Christian Micro-enterprise Development* (Sydney, AU: Opportunity International, 1998) and David Bussau & Vinay Samuel, *How Shall We Lend? A Biblical Validation of Microenterprise Development* (Sydney, N.S.W.: Opportunity International, 1998).

[78] David Bussau and Russell Mask, *Christian Microenterprise Development* (Oxford: Regnum, 2003).

[79] Bussau and Mask, *Christian Microenterprise,* 6.

God's creation, the divine pattern of work and leisure, justice especially for the poor, and the stress on human dignity in social structures have constituted the makings of a Transformational economics.

Or perhaps it is more accurate to say that these constitute the makings of a Transformational theology or ethics of economics, for Transformationists have dealt with economic issues just as they have with cultural issues, in a profoundly theological way. Just as they have primarily formulated a theology of culture and not necessarily ethnographies of culture; so too they have primarily formulated a theology of economics and not an economic system per se. One criticism of the Oxford Conference, for example, states that it 'bills itself as a discussion of economic principles from a Christian perspective, but its final document [the Oxford Declaration] shows more unity on theology than on economics'.[80] This may be true; but seen another way, this very truth articulates the strength of the Oxford movement, for what better contribution could an international, interdisciplinary group of followers of Christ offer than well thought out theological principles that guide the economic decisions of churches, development organizations, and policy makers?

(W)Holistic Mission: Toward a Truer Integration[81]

Mission as Transformation has developed a theology of culture on both the local and global levels. It has also developed what could be called a Transformational theology of economics. A third core theological development since Wheaton '83 has to do with biblical holism. While definitions vary for the missiological use of the term 'holistic', discussions about it 'often start by asking if evangelism and social action are present and how they connect'.[82] As established in Chapter 1, Mission as Transformation emerged in large part from working out the missiological tension between evangelism and social concern. Wheaton '83 marked a significant step forward for many evangelicals, as it attempted once and for all to discount the unbiblical, Enlightenment-ridden dichotomy between these two missionary approaches.

---

[80] Lawrence Adams and Fredrick Jones, 'Stewardship in the Nineties: Two Views', in Herbert Schlossberg, Vinay Samuel, and Ronald J. Sider (eds.), *Christianity and Economics in the Post-Cold War Era* (Grand Rapids, Mich.: Eerdmans, 1994), 165.

[81] The terms 'wholism' and 'holism' are interchangeable. Some prefer the former perhaps to dissociate Christian notions of integration from the New Age use of 'holism', or perhaps for some it better conveys the notion of including the whole of everything with regard to the scope of God's mission. But since 'wholism' never really gained widespread acceptance, I decided to use 'holism' for this study in order to avoid any confusion.

[82] Thomas H. McAlpine, *By Word, Work and Wonder: Cases in Holistic Mission* (Monrovia, Calif.: MARC, 1995), 2.

While mainstream evangelicals continued to proceed cautiously in the post-Lausanne era, making sure that evangelism remained primary, Transformationists embarked on a missionary agenda after Wheaton '83 that rendered the language of primary/secondary invalid for how kingdom ministries interrelate, declaring the need for Transformation on all levels of life.

As the affirmation of the legitimacy of both evangelism and social concern defined holistic mission after Lausanne I, all those who believed in the importance of social concern, including those who kept evangelism primary, felt like they had a right to identify themselves as holistic. This 'social responsibility is needed but evangelism is more important' brand of holistic mission correlated with the 'Two Mandates' approach to mission - the evangelism mandate and the cultural mandate - which basically affirmed both the proclamation and demonstration of the Gospel but within a dualistic worldview that necessarily held evangelism as primary.[83] Nevertheless, insofar as these evangelicals affirmed social concern along with, or even in the service of, evangelism, they could deem themselves as holistic.

Transformationists, however, took the meaning of holistic mission to new depths; they not only affirmed both evangelism and social concern, they melded them inseparably together as two aspects of the same call. Sugden notes that 'the Wheaton Consultation of 1983 coalesced the two [mandates] into one.'[84] Transformationists proceeded with this strong sense of integration, developing a deeper, truer holistic missiology; not just theoretically, but practically as well, as their holistic commitment to the poor remained central.

In 1985, *Transformation* began running a series of articles entitled 'Wholistic Models of Evangelism and Social Responsibility' wherein local churches and development organizations involved in this type of integration told their stories and shared their models. These stories attest to the practical outworking of Mission as Transformation. Analyzing these stories as case studies, Thomas McAlpine has drawn important conclusions about holistic mission since Wheaton '83. He concludes his work by identifying the emerging shape of holistic mission, using three categories and nine points, which I conveniently put in simple table form (Table 1).[85]

Samuel celebrates these theological developments and writes, 'Contextualization and wholistic mission [are] the success of the mission movement of the last thirty years [referring back to Lausanne '74] ... in getting involved and reshaping the whole of life - this is the real development in mission'.[86]

---

[83] Vinay Samuel cited in Sugden, *Gospel, Culture and Transformation*, 21-22.

[84] Sugden, *Gospel, Culture and Transformation*, 23.

[85] McAlpine, *By Word, Work and Wonder*, 121-139.

[86] Samuel cited in Sugden, *Gospel, Culture and Transformation*, 20.

Table 1: Features of Holism

What is holism?	1. church as sign of the kingdom 2. church as ministering in word, deed and sign and recovering the whole
Where is holism seen?	3. with the poor
How is holism expressed?	4. through a rehearsing of Scripture 5. through an orientation of process over program 6. through a commitment to continual conversion or learning 7. through the local-global tension 8. through small groups 9. through leadership that serves this mission

Mission as Transformation and the Holy Spirit:
A Radical Pentecostal Contribution

A fourth and arguably the most noteworthy theological development of Mission as Transformation since Wheaton '83 has to do with a renewed sense of the power of the Holy Spirit in Mission as Transformation, as a group of radical Pentecostals joined the conversation.[87]

Long time INFEMIT leader Peter Kuzmic articulates well the emergent thinking of radical Pentecostals:

> Twentieth century Pentecostalism is a recovery of full-fledged apostolic Christianity, of the whole gospel. The whole/'full' gospel means total commitment to all the demands of Jesus, including the entire spectrum of ethical (personal and social) requirements that are inherent in the gospel message. The whole gospel implies joyful celebration of God's gifts of salvation and continuous openness to the Holy Spirit to confirm the word by signs and wonders. The whole

---

[87] The term 'radical Pentecostal' should elicit a question mark, because the very people it seeks to identify do not necessarily use the term for themselves. But it is useful for two reasons. First, this study has credited the radical evangelical constituency for shaping Mission as Transformation. So to describe Pentecostals who have contributed to this missiological understanding as 'radical' aligns them with other 'radicals' who are not Pentecostal. Second, a growing diversity characterizes the worldwide Pentecostal communion. So using the label 'radical Pentecostal' distinguishes a particular group, which is committed to the integration of evangelism, social concern, and signs and wonders, from other groups within the movement, which continue in forms of fundamentalism that remain suspicious of social justice ministries. For these two reasons, I utilize the term 'radical Pentecostal' to describe Pentecostals who have joined the worldwide community of Transformationists.

gospel covers proclamation of truth and exhibition of love, manifestation of power and integrity of life. [The whole gospel] is in word, deed, and *sign.*[88]

With the one significant exception of Kuzmic's involvement with INFEMIT from the beginning, serious dialogue between the INFEMIT/OCMS network of scholars and radical Pentecostals did not occur until 1988 at the Words, Works, and Wonders Consultation in Pasadena, California, USA. Planned by a committee that included Samuel and Sugden and coordinated by Sider and Anglican Charismatic Michael Harper, the consultation brought together on the one hand 'evangelicals especially known for their emphasis upon social action' and on the other hand, evangelicals known 'for their emphasis upon Pentecostal and charismatic renewal ... to learn from each other, share respective emphases and engage in mutual questioning'.[89] The positive exchange between the two groups caused the planners of the consultation to commit to more ongoing dialogue, resulting in two more follow up meetings in 1990 and 1994 respectively.

The second meeting in 1990 in London under the theme, 'Spirit, Kingdom, Church and Creation' solidified the common theological base of both groups, namely, a theology of the kingdom of God. Brian Hathaway presented 'The Kingdom Manifesto', a document drafted by the Evangelical Fellowship of New Zealand after the 1988 Consultation, which articulated this common theological base.[90] The document showed such promise that planners of this series of consultations on the Holy Spirit and mission formed a committee in order to facilitate the study of the Manifesto on both the international and regional levels.

The third consultation, held in 1994 at Malacca, Malaysia convened under the theme 'Word, Kingdom & Spirit', served to bring these many reflections together, resulting in an integration of three documents: 'The Kingdom Manifesto on the Whole Gospel', 'A Kingdom Prayer', and 'Kingdom Affirmations and Commitments'.[91] Of the eighty five participants in Malacca, ten of them came from the Philippines.[92] Moreover, Maggay was one of the major speakers at this third consultation.

The international dialogue that began in 1988 with the desire to see what evangelical social activists and Pentecostal/Charismatics could learn from one

---

[88] Peter Kuzmic, 'Pentecostals Respond to Marxism', in Murray W. Dempster, Byron Klaus, and Douglas Petersen (eds.), *Called and Empowered: Global Mission in Pentecostal Perspective* (Peabody, Mass.: Hendrickson, 1991), 160. Italics mine.

[89] 'Conference Findings Report', *Transformation* 5.4 (October/December1988), 1.

[90] Brian Hathaway, 'The Kingdom Manifesto', *Transformation* 7.3 (July/September 1990), 6-10.

[91] 'Word, Kingdom & Spirit', *Transformation* 11.3 (July/September 1994), 1-6.

[92] 'Word, Kingdom & Spirit', 11, 33. I was privileged to be a part of the Filipino delegation at this consultation.

another resulted by the time of the third consultation in a kingdom missiology that brought together the three missionary streams of evangelization, social concern, and renewal in the Holy Spirit. This integrated consciousness shed new light on the meaning of holistic mission. Instead of the discussion beginning and ending with the relationship between evangelism (word) and social concern (work), it now included for many a power dimension, the supernatural power of the Holy Spirit (wonder), in order to bear witness to the whole Gospel.

In addition to the findings of these three consultations, several key Pentecostal voices contributed significantly to the development of Mission as Transformation. Three names in particular - Murray Dempster, Byron Klaus and Douglas Petersen - had not only contributed articles in *Transformation*, they also edited two important volumes that promoted holistic mission in the Pentecostal tradition. *Called and Empowered* has served as a standard text for courses in Pentecostal mission theology since its publication.[93] And *The Globalization of Pentecostalism*, the result of a conference held in 1996 at San Jose, Costa Rica that brought together Pentecostals and the likes of Jose Miguez Bonino, Vinay Samuel, and Harvey Cox, showcases the emerging scholarship among radical Pentecostals in dialogue with others concerning cutting edge missiological issues.[94] Petersen also turned his doctoral thesis, which he earned at OCMS, into a book entitled *Not By Might Nor By Power: A Pentecostal Theology of Social Concern in Latin America*, a book that has contributed to the progressive thinking occurring within his own denomination, the Assemblies of God, especially in Latin America where the book is available in Spanish.[95] During the writing of these various publications, Dempster, Klaus and Petersen held teaching posts at Vanguard University in the USA.[96] Undoubtedly, the connection between these three radical Pentecostals and the INFEMIT/OCMS network facilitated Vanguard's eventual role as a USA satellite centre for OCMS as well as the clearing house for the journal *Transformation's* USA subscribers.

Dempster, Klaus and Petersen (in addition to Kuzmic) have advanced a radical version of Pentecostalism that has contributed to the development of Mission as Transformation since Wheaton '83. The inclusion of articles written

---

[93] Dempster, Klaus, Petersen (eds.), *Called and Empowered: Global Mission in Pentecostal Perspective* (Peabody, Mass.: Hendrickson, 1991).

[94] Murray Dempster, Byron Klaus and Douglas Petersen (eds.), *The Globalization of Pentecostalism: A Religion Made to Travel* (Oxford: Regnum, 1999).

[95] Douglas Petersen, *Not By Might Nor By Power: A Pentecostal Theology of Social Concern in Latin America* (Oxford: Regnum, 1996).

[96] Petersen continues to teach there as the Margaret S. Smith Professor of World Missions and Intercultural Studies, Dempster is its President, and Klaus moved on to become the President of the Assemblies of God Theological Seminary in Springfield, Missouri, USA.

by Dempster and Petersen, as well as the 'Brussels Statement on Evangelization and Social Concern' of the Assemblies of God, in Samuel and Sugden's *Mission as Transformation* demonstrates the significance of their contribution to this missiology.[97] Taken together, these works by radical Pentecostals point to the emphasis upon the operative supernatural power of the Holy Spirit for holistic mission today, a power evident in the holistic mission of Jesus as well as the early church. Non-evangelical scholars, like Harvey Cox and Walter Hollenweger, have noted and praised this brand of Pentecostalism, in which the Holy Spirit informs holistic mission in the radical evangelical tradition.[98]

Conversely, Mission as Transformation has influenced Pentecostalism (at least its Assemblies of God expression). The Brussels Statement, the result of a consultation of the Division of Foreign Missions of the Assemblies of God in 1998, illustrates this mutual influence. While the Brussels Statement affirms the rich history of Pentecostal involvement in both evangelism and social concern, it also expresses the need today to enunciate the integration theologically.[99] The missiology of Transformation, as Kuzmic, Petersen, Dempster and Klaus have advocated it within their denomination, has provided resources for Pentecostals to accomplish this important theological task. In this way, radical Pentecostals have served as a two-way conduit through which Pentecostalism and Mission as Transformation have profoundly impacted each other.

The implementing structures and theological developments of Mission as Transformation since Wheaton '83 have shown the growing maturity and sophistication of the missionary journey among radical evangelical theologians and practitioners. These Transformationists around the world share convictions that unify their missionary vision. Part II seeks to discern these common convictions, which, when taken together, constitute the global dimensions of Mission as Transformation.

---

[97] See Samuel and Sugden, *Mission as Transformation* for a convenient compilation of the following: Murray Dempster, 'A Theology of the Kingdom - A Pentecostal Contribution' (45-75), Douglas Petersen, 'Pentecostals: Who Are They?' (76-111), and 'Brussels Statement on Evangelization and Social Concern' (112-117).

[98] Harvey Cox, *Fire from Heaven: The Rise of Pentecostal Spirituality and the Reshaping of Religion in the Twenty-first Century* (Reading, Mass.: Addison-Wesley, 1995), 295-296; Walter Hollenweger, *Pentecostalism: Origins and Developments Worldwide* (Peabody, Mass: Hendrickson, 1997), 206-208.

[99] 'Brussels Statement on Evangelization and Social Concern', *Mission as Transformation,* 117.

PART II

Global Dimensions

Introduction to Part II

This historical overview, from the failure/neglect of evangelical social concern to its relative recovery after World War Two to its developing maturity at the hands of evangelicalism's more radical constituents, provides the necessary backdrop to attempt now a theological analysis of Mission as Transformation.

As we have already discussed in Part I, in light of modernity, postmodernity and globalization, contemporary missiology (along with many other disciplines) requires a negotiation between global and local realities, since the world that the Church seeks to serve has both an emerging global culture and increasingly assertive local cultures. To quote Robert Schreiter again, who has done much in paving the way for doing theology between the global and the local, 'One thing seems clearly to have emerged out of [the movement from modernity to postmodernity]: any theology needs to attend both to its contextual and to its universalizing dimensions.'[1] Sugden claims a similar idea when he explains Samuel's missiology as particular to the Asian context, but 'the themes of mission that he deals with ... are of universal relevance: they are rooted in the mission of the kingdom of God.'[2] Part II seeks to understand the global dimensions of Mission as Transformation, as it interacts with the biblical reality of the kingdom of God in Transformational perspective.

As the truth of the contextual nature of theology has gained more acceptance, theologians have responded diversely to the notion of a global theology. Consistent with the postmodern turn in philosophy, the humanities, the social and even the natural sciences, some ultra liberal theologians simply and categorically reject the very idea of it, not only for informing local Christian theologizing, but also for challenging other faith claims. Within this response, no truths or values or norms apply to all.[3] Other theologians affirm

---

[1] Schreiter, *The New Catholicity*, 3.

[2] Sugden, *Gospel, Culture and Transformation*, vii.

[3] See for example John Hick and Paul F. Knitter (eds.), *The Myth of Christian Uniqueness*, (London: SCM, 1987) and Pui Lan Kwok, 'Discovering the Bible in the Non-Biblical World', in R.S. Sugirtharajah (ed.), *Voices from the Margins* (London; Maryknoll, N.Y.: SPCK; Orbis, 1995), 303.

the importance of global/universal formulations but re-configure them in light of postmodern or 'post-colonial' realities.[4] I argue decidedly along the lines of the latter, relying heavily on Schreiter's idea of 'a new catholicity', a new way of conceiving universality that sees specific contexts (the local) making up an intercultural 'pan-local' phenomenon (the global). The mark of this new catholicity, he claims, is 'a wholeness of inclusion [the affirmation of local theologies] and fullness of faith [the global applicability of the universal Gospel] in a pattern of intercultural exchange and communication'.[5]

As Part II seeks to identify the global dimensions of Mission as Transformation, it does not mean to suggest that worldwide uniformity of belief and practice exists among Transformationists. On the contrary, Transformationists include missiologists and missionaries who come from many different cultural as well as denominational backgrounds including Anabaptist, Reformed, Anglican, and Pentecostal/Charismatic. Such diversity on various important levels virtually ensures lively debate on any given theme, as any single issue of the journal *Transformation* would illustrate. Nevertheless, a common evangelical faith out of which flows a shared passion for both personal and social change holds this diversity of perspective together.

Chapter 5 seeks to understand the biblical basis, more specifically, the biblical reality of the kingdom of God for mission as Transformationists have understood it. Some may question discussing a biblical basis for Mission as Transformation under the 'global dimensions' section, fearing that contextual readings of scripture will not get their due. To be sure, a biblical basis of the kingdom in global perspective does not and must not negate local readings. It simply attempts to identify shared beliefs worldwide among Transformationists about the biblical kingdom.

The recent recovery of kingdom theology among radical evangelicals has unfolded at international gatherings within the INFEMIT/OCMS network. This at least means that a diversity of socio-cultural perspectives has informed it. This fact alone should enable the biblical theology of the kingdom, which under girds Mission as Transformation, to survive post-colonial scrutiny. Western theologians did not systematize, universalize, and then disseminate a 'One Third World' ivory tower conception of the kingdom; rather, theologians from

---

[4] I hesitate to use the term 'post-colonial' because there is an entire school of thought, which includes the likes of Edward Said, Homi Bhabha, and Gayatri Spivak, that claims the term. Despite the existence of this school of thought, the meaning of postcolonial continues to lack precision. Its use among scholars ranges from a strictly historical description of the post-World War II de-colonization process of many countries to critical theories surrounding that process after the colonial period in and across various disciplines including literary studies, linguistics, history, sociology, and anthropology. I use it in line with the former. And in order to indicate the description rather than the theory, I will simply employ the hyphen, thus 'post-colonial' and not 'postcolonial'.

[5] Schreiter, *The New Catholicity*, 132.

all over the world (including from the West) have forged it and then have held themselves accountable to it in their respective contexts. To see how Transformationists worldwide understand and interpret the biblical kingdom missiologically defines the task of Chapter 5.

Chapter 6 follows this Transformational understanding of God's reign by developing the eight missiological components identified by Samuel within the framework of the biblical kingdom. Related to the concern regarding discussing the Bible in the 'global dimensions' section, some may also ask at this point, 'Why begin with Samuel's framework to understand Mission as Transformation globally? What makes Samuel's formulation (and Sugden's expansion of it) the global one? I have identified Vinay Samuel and Chris Sugden as leading authorities on the global understanding of Mission as Transformation, but are not their voices as local as any other? Samuel and Sugden do not consider themselves as anything other than contextual theologians, and considering them as the primary guiding voices of global Mission as Transformation does not violate this fact. It simply acknowledges the work these two theologians have accomplished in advancing this missiology since Lausanne '74 and even more so since Wheaton '83. They spearheaded the establishment of Transformational institutions - INFEMIT and OCMS. They have initiated and coordinated international consultations and conferences to grapple with relevant issues from a Transformational perspective. They served as original editors (along with Tokunboh Adeyemo, Ronald Sider, Mark Lau Branson, and Andrew Kirk) of *Transformation,* which, as established earlier, facilitated (and continues to facilitate) international dialogue among Transformationists. And they themselves wrote (and continue to write) many articles and edited many books that have made Two Thirds World scholarship accessible to the international missionary community.

Other Transformationists have certainly contributed to the advancement of this missiology via similar efforts, but it has been Samuel and Sugden who have primarily sought to systematize these efforts into a cohesive missiology. Their book *Mission as Transformation* exemplifies this; they describe the edited volume as bringing 'together in one place material that has been developed since 1983 on the understanding and practice of Mission as Transformation'.[6] They have achieved this feat while remaining true to form as contextual theologians, not neglecting to tackle context specific issues from a Transformational perspective.

Because of such efforts to systematize definitive works of this missiology, including their own reflections, fellow Transformationists have recognized them as leading voices. In a personal email from Douglas Petersen, for example, when asked about the history of INFEMIT and OCMS, he states, 'The person who would easily be the most accurate is Chris [Sugden]', and then a

---

[6] Samuel and Sugden, 'Introduction', *Mission as Transformation,* ix.

few lines later, 'Vinay is so influential that likely in the end [the history] will be how Vinay remembers it.'[7] In a personal interview with Ron Sider, to cite another example, he qualified his responses to questions of an historical and theological nature concerning Mission as Transformation by saying, 'You should really be talking to Vinay [Samuel].'[8] For someone like Sider, who is himself a pioneer of the movement, to defer to Samuel as the definitive word on Mission as Transformation should persuade anyone who may question Samuel (and Sugden) as leading voices for this missiology as it has developed globally. They represent the best of contextual theology, as they seek 'the Asian face of Jesus', but understand that face to be 'at home everywhere in the world. It is particular to a culture, yet always at home in each culture. It is able to rise above cultures to draw cultures together.'[9]

Their efforts to frame Mission as Transformation, as it has developed globally, have led them to propose eight missiological components. But Samuel simply lists them with all too brief commentary, as if to dare others to develop them further.[10] Sugden's expansion of the components notwithstanding,[11] this chapter takes the dare; for if these components truly define the global features of Mission as Transformation, then each of them deserves a careful articulation.

---

[7] Douglas Petersen, email correspondence to author, 15 June 2003. For a list of publications that summarize and interpret Samuel's work, see the bibliographical section entitled 'Discussions and Summaries of Vinay Samuel's Work' in Sugden, *Gospel, Culture and Transformation,* 138.

[8] Sider, interview.

[9] Sugden, *Gospel, Culture and Transformation,* 130.

[10] Samuel, 'Mission as Transformation', 229-231.

[11] Sugden, *Gospel, Culture and Transformation,* 23-27.

CHAPTER 5

The Biblical Kingdom

The recovery of the dynamic biblical reality of the kingdom of God among radical evangelicals has inspired, framed, and unified Mission as Transformation. The Wheaton '83 Statement says it plainly: 'We have come to see that the goal of transformation is best described by the biblical vision of the kingdom of God'.[1] Such an assertion at that time demonstrated a level of courage since much of 'the evangelical constituency were very hesitant to embrace the theme of the kingdom of God for Christian social involvement'.[2] As a residue of the era of the Great Reversal when they sought to dissociate themselves from the kingdom - now advocates of the Social Gospel, evangelicals remained suspicious of kingdom language for mission. Refusing to see the biblical notion of the kingdom of God as relevant to current issues, evangelicals relegated it either to the inner life or to a far away future.

By way of contrast, Transformationists rediscovered the biblical story of the kingdom of God in the quest to minister effectively to the poor and oppressed. Sixteen years after the adoption of the Wheaton '83 Statement, Samuel and Sugden continue to affirm that, 'the kingdom of God is the organizing biblical and theological concept', thus indicating that the kingdom has remained the primary guiding force behind Mission as Transformation.[3] This chapter seeks to understand the kingdom basis of this missiology, thus providing its biblical theology of mission.

The Role of the Bible in Mission as Transformation

This task begs the prerequisite question of how Transformationists use the Bible missiologically. Irrespective of Catholic-Orthodox-Protestant and conservative-liberal divides, Scripture continues to (and always will) hold a central place in the fundamental areas of 'Christian identity and self-understanding, and it remains as an enduring source of authority, faith and

---

[1] 'Wheaton '83 Statement', *The Church in Response to Human Need*, 257.

[2] Vinay Samuel and Chris Sugden, 'Introduction to Part I', in Vinay Samuel and Chris Sugden (eds.), *Mission as Transformation* (Oxford: Regnum, 1999), 5.

[3] Samuel and Sugden, 'Introduction to Part I', 3.

inspiration for mission'.[4] This common affirmation of the Bible's place, however, has not prevented the divergent ways in which mission traditions have gone about using the scriptures. J.N.J. Kritzinger attempts to simplify this diversity within Protestantism by suggesting a continuum whose opposite poles consist of a 'conversionist approach', in which the Bible is used to fulfil a primarily evangelistic mission agenda, and a 'liberationist approach', in which the Bible is used to fulfil a primarily social justice agenda.[5] Where would Transformationists land on this continuum? This question has two parts: 1) How Transformationists view the Bible, and 2) How they use it for mission.

The Bible: The Inspired Story of the Kingdom of God

Transformationists have claimed all along that they stand stalwartly in the Protestant evangelical mission tradition, which affirms the enduring Reformation principle of *sola Scriptura*. Kritzinger asserts that this principle has remained central to Protestant mission thinking in general.[6] The Lausanne Covenant, the definitive statement that speaks for the evangelical wing, articulates the *sola Scriptura* principle in this way:

> We affirm the divine inspiration, truthfulness and authority of both Old and New Testament Scriptures in their entirety as the only written Word of God, without error in all that it affirms, and the only infallible rule of faith and practice. We also affirm the power of God's Word to accomplish his purpose of salvation. The message of the Bible is addressed to all mankind. For God's revelation in Christ and in Scripture is unchangeable. Through it the Holy Spirit still speaks today. He illumines the minds of God's people in every culture to perceive its truth freshly through their own eyes and thus discloses to the whole church ever more of the many-colored wisdom of God.[7]

According to John Stott, this statement, 'concentrates on three features of the Bible - its authority, its power, and its interpretation'.[8] Its authority and power for church mission lie in the fact that it alone contains the good news of Jesus Christ, if in fact the Church defines its mission as bearing witness to this good news. By virtue of what it conveys, the Gospel, the Bible informs the

---

[4] 'The People of God Among All God's People', *The People of God Among All God's Peoples,* 17.

[5] J.N.J. Kritzinger, 'The Function of the Bible in Protestant Mission', in Philip L. Wickeri (ed.), *Scripture, Community, and Mission* (Hong Kong; London: Christian Conference of Asia; Council for World Mission, 2002), 21-22.

[6] Kritzinger, 'The Function of the Bible', 20.

[7] 'Lausanne Covenant', *Making Christ Known,* 13.

[8] John R.W. Stott, 'Lausanne Covenant', in John R.W. Stott (ed.), *Making Christ Known* (Grand Rapids, Mich.; Cambridge: Eerdmans, 1996), 13.

vision, strategy, experience, and goal of the Church's mission like nothing else. In that sense, the Bible 'is the only written Word of God' on which the Church must rely as its final authority. Moreover, the good news of Christ to which the scriptures testify 'is the power of God for salvation' (Rom. 1:16).

As for its interpretation, the Covenant statement makes it clear that evangelical missiologists strive to live in the tension between the unchanging, powerful, and authoritative revelation of God and the rich diversity of human cultures through which they engage and interpret the scriptures. This tension creates a bi-focal lens through which evangelical interpreters first, out of high respect for the Bible's contents, strive to understand the issues with which the original authors wrestled; while through the second lens, they commit to viewing contemporary issues contextually and locally. Stott asserts, 'The *whole [worldwide] church* is needed to receive God's whole revelation in all its beauty and richness.'[9]

In answer then to how the evangelical mission tradition (which is itself thoroughly and healthily diverse) views the Bible, it sees it as nothing less than the written Word of God freshly and relevantly communicated by the Holy Spirit. As such, it conveys the saving Gospel of Jesus Christ like no other source, and thus carries with it a finality in authority, a power to convey salvation, and a translatability that speaks to all cultures.

Transformationists walk in step with their fellow evangelicals with regard to this view of the Bible but with an added distinction, namely, their emphasis upon the dynamic reality of the kingdom of God. For them, the Bible does not just contain the theme of the kingdom along with other themes; it constitutes and frames the whole of the Bible as the *overriding* theme, which makes sense of all other themes. The story of the kingdom of God, which has a beginning, an end and a middle, constitutes the Bible, and it binds and coheres the Bible's diverse pages.

John Bright's classic *The Kingdom of God*, which many Transformationists have affirmed, still has no parallel in aiding students to grasp the biblical notion of the kingdom in narrative historical form.[10] In it, he writes that the kingdom 'involves ... the total message of the Bible. Not only does it loom large in the teachings of Jesus, it is to be found in one form or another through the length and breadth of the Bible.'[11] Wishfully, Bright even suggests as a title for the

---

[9] Stott, 'Lausanne Covenant', 15.

[10] John Bright, *Kingdom of God* (Nashville, Tenn.: Abingdon, 1953). Bright's historical treatment of the kingdom has indeed influenced Transformational thinking. For example, his book was required reading in a missiological course taught by Douglas Petersen entitled 'The Kingdom of God and Third World Mission', which I took as a graduate student in 1985 at Vanguard University (then Southern California College).

[11] Bright, *The Kingdom of God*, 7.

collection of the sixty-six *biblios*, 'The Book of the Coming Kingdom of God'.[12]

Understanding the Bible as story serves as a welcome alternative to viewing it as say, a handbook or a book of creeds and doctrines. *As* story, the Bible humanizes and personalizes God's truth, thus making it potentially relatable to other human stories across generations. In relating the Bible as story to development work, for example, Bryant Myers sees Transformational development as the stories of the poor converging with the biblical story. In that convergence,

> The biblical story provides a very helpful framework for seeking answers to [what our stories are for, where they are going, and whose story is the true story]. [It] explains how every community's story began and why its story is full of pain, injustice, and struggle at the same time that it is full of joy, loving relationships, and hope. [It] provides the answer to how the stories of the community ... may reorient themselves to that intended by their Creator and describes, *in the metaphor of the kingdom of God*, what the best human story is like. [It] also tells us how all our stories will end. Most important, we can learn what our stories are for: the worship of the one true God.[13]

From this view of the Bible as the inspired authoritative story of the kingdom of God, several important aspects of the Bible come to the surface among Transformationists. First, they view the Bible in its entirety. No one passage, such as Matthew 28:18-20 around which conversionists gravitate or Luke 4:18-19 around which liberationists gravitate, nor any one sub-story such as Paul's church planting journeys or Luke's story of Jesus as friend of the poor and outcast, will do. If Bible interpreters want to understand the story, they must take the whole of it seriously.

Second, Transformationists view the Bible as a unity in the midst of diversity. This view obviously overlaps with the first, but this angle emphasizes not the necessity to have the whole Bible in view, but rather the necessity to see it in its unity.[14] It holds together all of the diverse thoughts, perspectives, sub-plots, and emphases of the biblical writers by the all pervasive narrative of the kingdom of God. While its narrative nature unifies the scriptures, however, it does not deny the diversity found in them. On the contrary, Transformationists appreciate the diversity in perspective found in the Bible, but understand all of the sub-stories as strengthening the one story - the story of the kingdom of God informing, guiding and challenging the stories of the kingdoms of humankind.

---

[12] Bright, *The Kingdom of God*, 197.

[13] Myers, *Walking with the Poor*, 11-12. Italics mine.

[14] Samuel Escobar, 'Our Hermeneutic Task Today', in Mark Lau Branson and C. Rene Padilla (eds.), *Conflict and Context: Hermeneutics in the Americas* (Grand Rapids, Mich.: Eerdmans, 1986), 5.

Third, Transformationists see the Bible as 'dead letter' without the Holy Spirit breathing life, relevance and understandability to it. The Holy Spirit, who has continued Christ's kingdom ministry on earth, enables the truth of the text to transcend the limitations of language and to speak to all generations. Samuel asserts, 'The Spirit enables biblical narrative to be both applicable to a given context and maintain its universality and integrity throughout history.'[15]

Fourth, Jesus Christ emerges as the central figure in a Transformational view of the Bible. The life, teaching, example, death, resurrection, and return of Christ constitute the core of the kingdom theology that drives Mission as Transformation. Transformationists confess in their important Kingdom Affirmations and Commitments Statement that 'We believe that the Kingdom of God and Jesus Christ the King are inseparable' and 'We believe that the Kingdom of God becomes evident where people confess the King and do his will.'[16]

The Bible: Kingdom Text for Holistic Mission in Context

The Bible, the comprehensive, unified in the midst of diversity, Spirit-breathed, and Christocentric story of the kingdom of God, serves as the defining, shaping, and motivating text for Mission as Transformation in at least four basic ways.

First, the biblical kingdom defines the mission of the Church as bearing witness to Jesus Christ in the world by the power of the Holy Spirit. This definition at once narrows and broadens missionary engagement with the world. It narrows it by dictating the content of the Church's proclamation, namely, Jesus Christ and no one and nothing else. On the other hand, it broadens it by allowing the creative, unpredictable Spirit to determine the strategy. Verbal proclamation (evangelism), demonstration (social concern), lifestyle (example), music and the arts (beauty), and healing and miracles (signs and wonders) only begin to express church mission activities when it submits itself to the Holy Spirit. In light of the Spirit who blows where it wills (Jn. 3:8), the evangelism versus social concern debate is much too limited! Insofar as the Church submits its mission strategy in the world to the creative power of the Holy Spirit, the shape of mission defies limits and formulas.

Second, the biblical kingdom reveals a God who cares about the whole person - physical, psychological, social, and spiritual. This holistic perspective challenges the polarization between conversionist and liberationist approaches on Kritzinger's continuum. The Transformational approach holds firmly to an

---

[15] Vinay Samuel, 'The Holy Spirit in Word and Works: A Study in John 14 to 16', *Transformation* 11.3 (July/September 1994), 12-14; Sugden, *Gospel, Culture and Transformation,* 50-53.

[16] 'Kingdom Affirmations and Commitments', in Vinay Samuel and Chris Sugden (eds.), *Mission as Transformation* (Oxford: Regnum, 1999), p.15.

integrative 'both/and' that refuses to see soul and society (and everything in between such as family and other social groupings) as entirely separate human domains. For Transformationists, to say that God, whose concerns range from social structures to human hearts, cares about one domain over the other violates the biblical record. On Lim's continuum of mission approaches, in which he identifies five positions (three more than Kritizinger's), the Transformational approach occupies the centre, affirming both conversionist and liberationist emphases.[17] In light of the story of the intervention of God in human affairs - the kingdom of God - all levels of human existence encounter God and are thereby changed.

Third, the biblical kingdom reveals a God who communicates through human cultures and societies. In light of the mixed cultures of the Hebrew people turned (the nation of Israel), and in light of the mission to Gentiles that occupied the early church, Transformationists view the kingdom of God as knocking down the dividing walls between races, cultures, and classes (Eph. 2:13-22). This conviction compels Transformationists to commit to contextualization, as well as to multiculturalism in its missionary engagement with, for and in the world.

And fourth, the biblical kingdom reveals a God who cares about the whole world. The very language of 'kingdom' conveys not just the idea of the rule of God, but also the realm over which God rules, which ultimately covers the whole world throughout time. The Church most certainly plays a special role as 'the realm within the realm' where God has gathered the redeemed and empowered them to accomplish God's will in the world. Indeed the Church serves as God's primary model and agent of change. But God's dealings ultimately go through and beyond the Church; for the *missio Dei* involves the salvation of the whole world.

Having addressed the issue of the use of the Bible in mission, we can now undertake the task of highlighting the key themes in the biblical story of the kingdom of God as Transformationists have articulated them. Samuel and Sugden provide a helpful framework for a Transformational understanding of the New Testament material concerning the kingdom by framing it with the categories of Christological, Pneumatological, and Eschatological.[18] However,

---

[17] David S. Lim, *Transforming Communities* (Mandaluyong: OMF, 1992), 29. Lim explains the various approaches on his continuum in narrative form; which in addition to conversionist, liberationist and transformationist categories are spiritualist on the extreme right and humanist on the extreme left. For this continuum in chart form, see Al Tizon, 'Mission as Wonder: A Pentecostal Theology of Mission for an Age of Postmodernism in Dialogue with David Bosch', *Missionalia* 29.3 (November 2001), 417.

[18] Samuel and Sugden, 'Introduction to Part One', 3-5.

to grasp the significance of these New Testament categories necessitates first a brief overview of kingdom theology in the Old Testament.

The Kingdom Story in the Old Testament

The phrase 'kingdom of God' does not appear in the Old Testament, which offers at least a surface explanation as to why most kingdom expositions begin with the New. Based on a survey of biblical works by Transformationists, three basic themes - *shalom* and fall, redemption through peoplehood, and messianic hope - have outlined their understanding of the kingdom story in the Old Testament.

Shalom and Fall

Only a shallow translation of the Hebrew word *shalom* would limit its definition to the idea of the absence of conflict or peace.[19] Although it certainly includes peace, *shalom* also conveys the justice and righteousness that produces that peace (Jer. 6:13, 28). *Shalom* denotes a state wherein God rules, resulting in a harmonious relationship between God and humankind.[20] And flowing from that relationship come: 1) the wholeness of persons, physical, psychological, spiritual and emotional well-being, 2) the wholeness of human interactions - love and family, social justice, righteousness and peace, and 3) the wholeness of the relationship between humankind and the rest of creation - ecological sustenance and environmental stewardship.

God created such a world, and humankind shone as the crown jewel of that creation, being made in the image of God to facilitate *shalom* existence (Gen. 1:26-31). The creation story in the book of Genesis depicts God creating the world in six days, and at the end of the sixth day, 'God saw everything that He had made, and indeed it was very good' (Gen. 1:31). God's affirmative evaluation of the entire created order reflects the biblical theological fact that

---

[19] Walter Brueggemann, *Living Toward a Vision: Biblical Reflections on Shalom* (New York: United Church Press, 1982). Brueggemann suggests that no one biblical word captures the well-being of all of existence, but *shalom* comes close (15-16). A biblical word study in Gerhard Kittel and Gerhard Friedrich, *Theological Dictionary of the New Testament* (Grand Rapids, Mich.: Eerdmans, 1985), 207-211, attests to the richness of the word. Coupled with the Greek word *eirene*, the Hebrew word *shalom* covers the widest sense of well-being ranging from peace with God and self to peace between persons and nations to peace with animals and the whole created order. While *shalom* conveys primarily a social reality, *eirene* builds upon the social and describes the well-being of the whole person.

[20] David Gitari, *In Season and Out of Season: Sermons to a Nation* (Oxford: Regnum 1996), 45-47, 88.

the world began in a state of *shalom*. *Shalom* existed because God ruled the universe.

The account of the fall of humanity in Genesis 3 conveys the tragic disruption of that *shalom*. Through Adam and Eve's disobedience via the serpent's deception, sin entered into the world. A closer look at the nature of the serpent's temptation reveals the fundamental genesis of sin, namely, the desire to know enough to be like God, to know enough to be the masters of the universe (Gen. 3:5ff). 'Wanting to be gods and taking life into their own hands, [Adam and Eve with the aid of the serpent] mounted an insurrection.'[21] In essence, the act challenged God's rule, and consequently *shalom* existence collapsed.

In place of it, humanity, alienated from God, attempted to rule, which has resulted in 'widespread deception, distortion, and domination in all forms of human relationships - with God, within one's self (and family), within the community ... and with the environment'.[22] An all-encompassing, holistic deprivation manifesting in injustice, poverty, war, immorality and environmental debasement as a result of humanity's rule replaced the *shalom* of God's rule. 'Thus', explains Maggay in simple enough terms for a Sunday school class, 'We became sad and mad and bad.'[23] The theme of *shalom* and the subsequent fall from *shalom* runs through Transformational literature.

Redemption through Peoplehood

God's redemptive response to the fallen condition constitutes the rest of the biblical kingdom story. God first subjected the earth and its inhabitants to a thorough cleansing, a removing of the curse, and thus renewing the creation, which the story of Noah and the flood represents (Gen. 6:11ff). With a cleansed and renewed creation, God then initiated the long-term project of redemption by forming a people, beginning with the call of Abra[ha]m in Genesis 12, through whom God sought to restore God's rule. Such an arrangement with the seed of Abraham assumed then the possibility of *shalom* reappearing upon the earth among a people, a kingdom, which would represent life under the rule of God - the kingdom of God.

But the promise to Abraham that God will make of him a great nation was not an end in itself, but a means 'to bless all the families of the earth' or said a little differently, to restore the whole world of nations under the rule and reign of God (Gen. 12:1-3).[24] For Transformationists, herein lies the biblical seed of

---

[21] Melba Maggay, *A Faith for the Emptiness of Our Time* (Mandaluyong: OMF, 1990), 30.

[22] Myers, *Walking with the Poor*, 27.

[23] Maggay, *Emptiness of Our Time*, 38.

[24] Waldron Scott, *Bring Forth Justice* (Grand Rapids, Mich: Eerdmans, 1980), 46-48.

understanding God's global mission in terms of God's kingdom. Through the particularity of a people with whom God has entered into a covenant relationship, a kingdom community, God invites all into right relationship with him so that all can experience the restoration of *shalom* - forgiveness of personal sin and social reconciliation.

From the events surrounding Abraham and his descendants Isaac and Jacob, a people or a nation began to take shape in the form of the twelve tribes of Israel (Gen. 49, 50:24-25). But their sense of peoplehood did not really solidify until the time of Moses and the events surrounding him. Enslaved under severe Egyptian oppression, Abraham's descendants cried out to their God, and God heard them (Exo. 3:7-9). God used Moses to liberate the Hebrew people from Egypt (Exo. 3-12). Three months later on Mt. Sinai, God invited the people to enter into a covenant relationship, wherein they would be God's people and Yahweh would be their God (Exo. 19:1-8). The peoples' acceptance of God's invitation realized and set in motion God's plan of universal redemption via the particularity of a people.

Bound then by covenant, God began to set the boundaries of the new nation in the form of laws that provided the structure for religious, political, economic, military, and judicial institutions, thus did the Hebrew people attain nationhood, its identity shaped by its experience with the God who mercifully heard their cry, powerfully liberated them, and willfully determined to lead them as their king.

Israel maintained its identity intentionally without a human king for nearly two hundred years under the leadership of charismatic judges on an 'as needed basis', for in the minds of the early Israelites God reigned as their only king (Jud. 8:22-23). Israel's request for a human king in I Samuel 8, therefore, signaled a major turning point in the development of its sense of peoplehood. In rejecting God as king (I Sam. 8:7), the people of Israel said in essence that they preferred to govern themselves, yet another manifestation of the original sin of Adam and Eve.

Although much of the tragic failures of the nation can be traced to the corrupt monarchial rule of the Israelite kings as the Lord had warned through the prophet Samuel (I Sam. 8:10-18), the monarchy further defined the notion of the kingdom of God, primarily in the person and rule of David. During his reign, Israel experienced its finest years as it subdued enemy nations, prospered in material wealth, and strengthened its religious and political identity in Yahweh God. In the eyes of many, the era of David's rule fulfilled the promise made to Abraham that from his seed God would forge a great nation. Israel would not forget the prosperity experienced under King David. And as the kings that followed fell into moral and political failures and Israel split into northern and southern kingdoms only to be taken into captivity by foreign powers, the memory of the person of David determined Israel's hope for a coming Messiah who will save them from corruption, subjugation and evil.

Messianic Hope

Transformationists at this point focus upon the ministry of the prophets, whose dual message of uncompromising judgment and messianic hope further defined the notion of the kingdom. As the human kingdoms of Israel and Judah all but caricatured the kingdom of God, the prophets and apocalyptics looked to God's future of a coming kingdom to be inaugurated by a Messiah figure (Isa. 9:6-7; Dan. 7:13-14). The hope of the coming 'day of the Lord', while enduring the shame of captivity, kept Israel from total despair and annihilation.

But beyond the solace and challenge that the prophetic message brought to their present situation, it more significantly defined their future hope in the coming kingdom of God via a messiah in the line of David. 'The prophets promised that some day the Messiah would come to bring God's actual rule on earth in a new [and] powerful way.'[25] This Messiah will usher in a new era where he will put an end to tears, make premature death non-existent, implement justice and prosperity as standard experiences, and cause God's peace and harmony to characterize all relationships; even 'the wolf and the lamb will feed together' (Isa. 65:17-25).

In sum, God's new era, God's kingdom, will constitute a new heaven and a new earth. This 'wild hope', as Tom Sine calls it, set the stage for the ministry of Jesus who began with the announcement that 'the time is fulfilled and the kingdom of God is at hand' (Mk. 1:14-15).[26] The themes of *shalom* and fall, redemption through peoplehood, and messianic hope provide a basic outline of the Transformational understanding of the kingdom in the Old Testament, which also set the historical and theological stage for Jesus' inaugural announcement of the kingdom's arrival in the New Testament.

The Kingdom Story in the New Testament

Samuel and Sugden have arranged selected articles and statements in their recent compilation of Transformational material into Christological, Pneumatological and Eschatological categories, which correspond with their understanding of the flow of kingdom theology in the New Testament.

---

[25] 'Kingdom Affirmations and Commitments', *Mission as Transformation*, 13.

[26] Tom Sine, *Wild Hope: Crises Facing the Human Community on the Threshold of the 21st Century* (Dallas, Tex.: Word, 1991), 235-237. I cite Sine's phrase 'wild hope' to summarize the prophetic ministry of the Old Testament, but he uses the term much more broadly to include not only the hope of the New Testament, but also the hope of the Church's mission today. Sine's 'wild hope' is synonymous with the very notion of the kingdom of God.

Jesus Christ: The King Has Come/The Kingdom has Dawned

At the centre of Christian belief is the claim that the Creator of the Galaxies became flesh in a particular carpenter [named Jesus] in a tiny colony of the Roman Empire ... Christians believe that this carpenter became a wandering preacher who announced the news that the Messianic kingdom long predicted by the prophets and eagerly awaited by the oppressed Jews was breaking into history in his own person and work.[27]

This simple description succinctly sums up for Transformationists where the Jesus of the New Testament fit into God's redemptive outworkings, namely, as the fulfilment of the messianic hope and the personification of God's ultimate intentions for the human future (*shalom*).

The Gospels not only portray Jesus in this way, they also portray him as being fully cognizant of this fact. Luke, for example, has Jesus beginning his public ministry with a scene in the Nazareth synagogue. He first quoted from the prophet Isaiah: 'The Spirit of the Lord is upon me, because he has anointed me to bring good news to the poor; He has sent me to proclaim release to the captives and recovery of sight to the blind, to let the oppressed go free, to proclaim the year of the Lord's favour' (Lk. 4:18-19; Isa. 61:1ff). Then, 'Today this scripture has been fulfilled in your hearing' (Lk. 4:21). Not grasping the full implications of this statement, the congregants continued to speak well of him until he further explained that the fulfilment of which he spoke resided in his person, and furthermore, that his hometown Nazareth would reject this. The peoples' rage exploded upon him, driving him to the edge of a cliff to do away with him, but he managed to escape the mob. Such a violent reaction to Jesus' self acknowledgement portended the tribulations that led Jesus to the cross, the enduring symbol of the kingdom of God as Jesus and the early Church preached it (Lk. 4:22ff).

Indeed the theology of the cross and resurrection of Christ represents the original contribution of the New Testament to the notion of the kingdom of God. In light of Israel's history, Jesus' use of 'kingdom of God' certainly struck a familiar chord, but Graham Cray rightly points out that Jesus' teaching concerning the kingdom took it from the realm of future hope to present reality. He taught that, 'The kingdom ... the future rule of God was in some sense present now'.[28] But it had only dawned; its fulfilment or consummation would come at an even further future.

---

[27] Ronald J. Sider, 'Christian Ethics and the Good News of the Kingdom', in Vinay Samuel and Albrecht Hauser (eds.), *Proclaiming Christ in Christ's Way* (Oxford: Regnum, 1989), 122.

[28] Graham Cray, 'A Theology of the Kingdom', in Vinay Samuel and Chris Sugden (eds.), *Mission as Transformation*, (Oxford: Regnum, 1999), 28.

Transformationists have fully adopted the idea of the already-and-not-yet kingdom of God as they have built upon the classic works of New Testament scholars who include Oscar Cullman and especially George Eldon Ladd.[29] 'The presence of the future', as Ladd has coined it, conveys the profound New Testament conviction that God's future *shalom* has invaded the present.[30] And only the person of Jesus made such a reality possible. Jesus, the very embodiment of God in the incarnation manifested the kingdom of God in his person. The long awaited Messiah King had arrived in the God-Man Jesus Christ according to the New Testament witnesses, and with him, the kingdom had dawned. The connection between the person of Jesus and the biblical reality of the kingdom of God figures prominently among Transformationists. For them, to proclaim Jesus also announces the kingdom and vice versa: To announce the kingdom also proclaims Jesus.[31]

The birth, life and teachings of Jesus climaxed at the cross and empty tomb; all of these constitute what Maggay refers to as 'the Jesus events'.[32] The cross and resurrection of Christ symbolize the new perspective of the kingdom. Although the prophetic literature hinted at a Messiah that will come as a suffering servant (Isa. 53), most of the Jews of the day could not fathom the idea that their long awaited Messiah would end up on a cross - Rome's most gruesome form of capital punishment reserved for its worst criminals. But there he eventually hung and died. His followers thought it the end of the 'Jesus movement' (Lk. 24:13-21), but on the third day, Jesus rose again, thus validating all that he had said about himself as the fulfilment of the hope of Israel and of the whole world (Lk. 24:22-53).

The cross of Christ paved a new way of entering into the kingdom of God and the resurrection validated that new way (Maggay 1990:74). Sin, sorrow, hatred, injustice, oppression, war, and even death itself have no permanent power over humankind because of the cross and resurrection of Christ. Indeed as the overall witness of the New Testament declares, when the Church proclaims the good news to the world, it proclaims Christ crucified and risen, and the coming of his kingdom.

---

[29] Oscar Cullman, *Christ and Time* (Philadelphia, Pa.: Westminster, 1951); George Eldon Ladd, *The Presence of the Future* (Grand Rapids, Mich.: Eerdmans, 1974). See, for example, Cray, 'A Theology of the Kingdom', 28-33; Kuzmic, 'Eschatology and Ethics', 148-149; Ken Gnanakan, *Kingdom Concerns: A Biblical Exploration toward a Theology of Mission* (Bangalore, India: Theological Book Trust, 1993), 119-125; and C. Rene Padilla, *Mission Between the Times* (Grand Rapids, Mich.: Eerdmans, 1985), 186-189, who all refer to, and build upon, Cullman, Ladd, and others.

[30] Ladd's clever title, *Presence of the Future*, sums up perfectly the idea of the now and not yet nature of the kingdom of God.

[31] Mortimer Arias, *Announcing the Reign of God* (Minneapolis, Minn.: Fortress, 1984), xvii.

[32] Maggay, *Emptiness of Our Time*, 51-76.

Ken Gnanakan points out that the theology of the cross and resurrection of Christ developed on the ancient mission field primarily by the pen of the apostle Paul.[33] Paul taught that Jesus' death propitiated, as a final act, for the sins of the world and that his resurrection demonstrated God's power over the ultimate consequence of sin, namely, death (Rom. 5:15-21). Furthermore, this forgiveness of sin and victory over death applied not just to those of Jewish descent but to all (Rom. 3:21-26). Such provision and power ultimately demonstrated God's love for all humankind that 'while we were still sinners, Christ died for us' (Rom. 5:8). As Myers concludes, 'Any work of human transformation that does not announce this incredibly good news is fatally impoverished. The cross and resurrection are the very best news that we have'.[34] At base, Mission as Transformation unequivocally and unashamedly proclaims Jesus Christ and the dawning kingdom.

The Holy Spirit: Life and Power While the Kingdom Community Awaits

Transformationists can only preach Christ and the kingdom by the power of the Holy Spirit, a missiological truth only recently emphasized, as radical Pentecostals have joined the holistic mission conversation. The people of God in the New Testament - the Church, made up of both forgiven Jews and Gentiles who had committed their lives to Jesus Christ in faith - had a calling: to represent the kingdom of God with its full implications as an alternative community amidst the communities of the world and to signal the coming kingdom. God once called Israel as a geo-political nation to witness to the kingdom (Isa. 42:6; 49:6). But since the time of Jesus, God has called all who call upon the name of Christ to gather together into communities of faith where gender, racial, cultural, economic, social and political walls have broken down (Gal. 3:27-29) and where the world can see justice in the midst of injustice, peace in the midst of war, righteousness in the midst of wickedness, mercy in the midst of cruelty, joy in the midst of hardship, and life in the midst of death. This, according to a Transformational understanding of the New Testament, characterizes how the Church should live in 'the last days'.[35]

---

[33] Gnanakan, *Kingdom Concerns,* 139-158. This assertion more broadly affirms the inherently missionary character of the New Testament. See also Bosch, *Transforming Mission,* 16, where the author invokes an earlier missiologist, Martin Kahler, who referred to mission insightfully in 1908 as 'the mother of theology'.

[34] Myers, *Walking with the Poor,* 37.

[35] Life and mission in 'the last days' require further elaboration, which Chapter 5 takes up; for precisely at that juncture does Mission as Transformation take shape. For now, suffice it to point out that in Transformational thought the idea of 'last days' represents the period between Christ's ascension and Christ's return, or between the now-and-not-yet of the kingdom. Such an understanding of the 'last days' maintains the continuity between the New Testament Church and the Church of the twenty first century.

Such talk would smack of idealistic drivel without the biblical reality of the Holy Spirit, whom God has lavishly poured out in these last days (Acts 2:17-21). Jesus' instruction to his disciples to wait in Jerusalem for the coming of the Holy Spirit had behind it the implication that to represent the kingdom as a redeemed community *now* as it awaits God's final future requires a power beyond the human (Lk. 24:49; Acts 1:8).

This radical and courageous recovery of the role of the Holy Spirit for holistic mission, particularly as it is expressed in the biblical tandem of *Luke-Acts*, pinpoints one of the significant contributions of radical Pentecostals in the development of Mission as Transformation. Transformationists of the Pentecostal persuasion believe that the same Spirit who empowered Jesus himself (Lk. 4:18) also empowered the early church that immediately followed (Acts 2). Murray Dempster establishes the connection between Jesus' ministry and the early church's ministry by virtue of the Holy Spirit's ministry.[36] When the Holy Spirit fell upon the disciples in Acts 2 in fulfilment of Jesus' promise in Acts 1:8, the fearful band of closet believers were transformed into Spirit-filled, zealous missionaries throughout the known world.

The rest of the book of Acts simply records the Spirit-empowered acts of the apostles, or 'the acts of the Holy Spirit *through* the apostles', as many Pentecostals describe the book. As the Church continues to live in the last days, Pentecostal Transformationists audaciously believe that this same Holy Spirit continues today to empower believers in the same way that the Spirit did in the New Testament to proclaim and demonstrate the good news of the kingdom of God to the ends of the earth.[37]

From a Transformational perspective, the New Testament basically testifies in at least four ways as to the role of the Holy Spirit in the last days. First, the Spirit authenticates the truth of Jesus (Jn. 14:17, 26) through ecstatic personal experience commonly referred to today as the baptism in the Holy Spirit (Acts 1:5). By authenticating the truth via experience, the Spirit empowers believers to live out the faith in confidence, hope, and exuberance often despite external circumstances.[38] Spirit baptism - and all of its biblical synonyms, such as filling, infilling, outpouring, and so on – 'suggests a total experience of the presence of the Holy Spirit'.[39] Specifically concerning Pentecostals, Petersen

[36] Demptster, 'A Theology of the Kingdom', 48-51.
[37] 'Brussels Statement on Evangelization and Social Concern', *Mission as Transformation*, 42.
[38] Petersen, *Not By Might Nor By Power*, 85-88.
[39] J. Rodman Williams, 'Baptism in the Holy Spirit', in Stanley M. Burgess and Gary B. McGee (eds.), *Dictionary of Pentecostal and Charismatic Movements* (Grand Rapids, Mich.: Zondervan, 1988), 42.

asserts, '[They] have always emphasized experiential Christianity as the way to validate the authenticity of their doctrinal confession.'[40]

Pentecostal or not, however, experiencing the faith, in contrast to merely accepting theological propositions intellectually, has that existential authenticating effect that makes the faith worth dying for. One would hardly die for a set of propositional truths; the *experience* of these truths in real life, on the other hand, accounts for Christian martyrdom throughout the ages beginning with Stephen in Acts 7:54-60.

The New Testament, especially *Luke-Acts*, declares that this profound kind of experiencing God results from the work of the Holy Spirit. Indeed the kingdom of God - the rule of God - includes the inner life.[41] The claim that the baptism in the Holy Spirit happens today in the same profound manner distinguishes Pentecostals from other Christian traditions. But the difference between Pentecostals and non-Pentecostals among Transformationists with regard to the role of Holy Spirit led experience seems more a matter of degree than of substance. Pentecostal or not, Transformationists underscore the importance of a personal, experiential relationship with Christ by the power of the Holy Spirit that catapults them to engage in Spirit filled holistic ministry.

Second, flowing out of this authenticating personal experience, the Spirit enables the corporate experience, the Church, to live the life worthy of the call to represent Jesus Christ as the visible, earthly community of the kingdom of God. As the Spirit leads the Church into all truth (Jn. 14:17, 26) and believers begin to yield to the sway (or fruit) of the Spirit, the Church demonstrates the Spirit's transforming power.

---

[40] Petersen, *Not By Might Nor By Power*, 78. Petersen discusses the tendency to err among some Pentecostal groups regarding Spirit baptism. He writes, 'Rather than equipping the believer for supernatural empowerment on behalf of others, [Spirit-baptism] becomes an obsession in one's concern for more and more personal and extraordinary experiences' (87).

[41] Howard Snyder, *Models of the Kingdom* (Nashville, Tenn.: Abingdon, 1991), 52-54. Snyder summarizes via models the various ways in which the Church has viewed the kingdom of God throughout history. The 'kingdom as inner spiritual experience' is but one of eight models he presents. The other seven are the kingdom as future hope, mystical communion, institutional church, countersystem, political state, christianized culture, and earthly utopia. In an earlier article by Snyder entitled, 'Models of the Kingdom: Sorting out the Practical Meaning of God's Reign', and reprinted in Samuel and Sugden, *Mission as Transformation*, he states that 'no one of these models is fully biblical and fully adequate. But several of them do embody key truths of the kingdom as taught in Scripture that need to be reflected in a usable contemporary biblical theology of the kingdom' (131-132). In this light, Snyder offers, as a biblically warranted strength of the 'kingdom as inner spiritual experience', the fact that it accents the intimate, personal, and spiritual nature of the kingdom.

Third, which also flows out of the authenticating experience of Spirit baptism, the Spirit empowers believers to engage the world in mission with accompanying signs and wonders. Few would argue that the day of Pentecost in Acts 2 marked the beginning of the Church's missionary fervour that changed the world. From that point on, the early disciples began zealously proclaiming the Gospel, setting in motion works of evangelization (Acts 2:14-41), compassion (Acts 11:27-30) and miraculous signs (Acts 2:43), not only through the early Church, but also, according to a Pentecostal Transformational perspective, through the Church ever since. None other than the Holy Spirit, who testifies to Jesus Christ (Jn. 15:26; 16:14), has empowered the Church throughout the ages to proclaim the Gospel by word, deed and sign.[42]

Fourth, the Holy Spirit convicts the world regarding sin, righteousness and judgment (Jn. 16:8-11). This function features the Holy Spirit's work outside of the Church, but certainly not without reference to it. Sugden interprets Samuel's pneumatology and explains, 'The Holy Spirit exposes the ideas and structures of the world as sinful against the backdrop of a community of Jesus' disciples who live out his teachings.'[43] The Spirit exposes the sin of the world, the inadequacies of human rule that have resulted in alienation, corruption, injustice, immorality, poverty and so on, while simultaneously pointing the world in the direction of a visible people, the Church, which experiences forgiveness of sin in Christ and lives victoriously by the Spirit over sin's personal, as well as social consequences. The Spirit in essence reveals to the world its own chaos, while at the same time, inviting it to gaze upon the Church with a holy envy as the Church visibly lives out the kingdom in *shalom* relationships.

In sum, the Transformational understanding of the New Testament witness concerning the kingdom of God sees the long awaited Messiah King arriving in the person of Jesus, who through 'the Jesus events' reintroduces the firstfruits of God's *shalom* upon the earth. Since Christ's ascension, the Holy Spirit continues to minister among and through the newly formed people of God - the Church - made up of both Jew and Gentile who profess faith in Christ, authenticating the truth, sanctifying and empowering the believers, and convicting the world of sin, thus continuing the long term historical project of God to bring universal salvation via a particular people.

---

[42] I cite only one biblical reference for each of the early church's word, deed and sign ministries, but the entire book of *Acts* is replete with these ministries working together as the Church's holistic proclamation of the Gospel.
[43] Sugden, *Gospel, Culture and Transformation*, 51.

Eschatology: The Certainty of God's Future/The Practice of Hope

A well rounded view of eschatology encapsulates in another way the notion of the kingdom of God from beginning to end. Samuel and Sugden sum up as much when they assert that 'the theme that relates God's intentions in creation to its final fulfilment is the kingdom of God, which will be completed with the establishment of a new heaven and a new earth in which the righteousness of God will reign through the lordship of Christ'.[44]

Kuzmic rightly views eschatology as 'both the *finis* (the destination) and the *telos* (the journey toward that destination) of history'.[45] It concentrates not only on what the future holds, but also on the historical and present march *toward* that future. In this sense, eschatology pervades the whole discussion on the biblical kingdom. The succinct thought, 'God's people living out God's intentions by God's power as a reflection of God's certain future' can easily serve as the Transformational thesis statement for the whole of the eschatological story of the Bible.

The biblical Christ once again provides the substance for this Transformational view of eschatology, particularly the theology of the first and second advents. 'The keystone of ... New Testament eschatology', Kuzmic explains, 'is the double advent of Christ, and there is a unique relation between the event of the first coming which predetermines the second coming and makes it inevitable, as that which has already come will be ratified and perfected by what is yet to come.'[46] The kingdom had arrived in Jesus Christ at his first coming, but only at his second coming will the kingdom come in its fullness. To remain faithful to the complexity of the biblical record requires this kind of negotiating of the tension between the realized (past and present) and the yet to be realized (future) natures of the biblical kingdom.

Responding to those who tend to interpret the kingdom exclusively in the future, Kuzmic writes, 'Looking forward to the future coming without looking backward to the implications of the past coming of Jesus is a distortion of the biblical perspective.'[47] But conversely, Transformationists also critique those who view the kingdom exclusively in the realized as an equally inadequate biblical perspective. Only affirming both the realized and the yet to be realized natures of the kingdom of God in creative tension will do justice to the biblical, eschatological vision.

First then to the *finis,* the last things, the End: Transformational eschatology rightly begins with the future, for the New Testament testifies to the certainty

---

[44] Vinay Samuel and Chris Sugden, 'God's Intentions for the World', in Vinay Samuel and Chris Sugden (eds.), *The Church in Response to Human Need* (Oxford; Grand Rapids, Mich.: Regnum; Eerdmans, 1987), 128.

[45] Kuzmic, 'Eschatology and Ethics', 135.

[46] Kuzmic, 'Eschatology and Ethics', 149.

[47] Kuzmic, 'Eschatology and Ethics', 149.

of God's coming *shalom*. In Jesus Christ, the kingdom *will* come in its fullness. Obviously influenced by Isaiah's beatific vision (Isa. 65:17-25), the writer-seer of the Book of Revelation caught a clear glimpse of God's future in Christ:

> See, the home of God is among mortals. He will dwell with them as their God; they will be his peoples, and God himself will be with them; he will wipe away every tear from their eyes. Death will be no more; mourning and crying and pain will be no more, for the first things have passed away'. And the one who was seated on the throne said, 'See I am making all things new'. Also he said, 'Write this, for these words are trustworthy and true' (Rev. 21:3-5).

Only this certainty makes it possible to begin theological reflection with the future. Otherwise, to begin with the present as determinative of the still uncertain future would make up the only reasonable way to proceed. But in light of the assured reestablishment of the *shalom* of God in Christ, it is the future that wills the present to conform to it. Sugden writes, 'We start with the future to develop vision for the present.'[48]

According to Transformationists, this certainty in God's coming *shalom* gives biblical eschatology its credence in the Christian faith. They warn the Church that when it seeks a detailed clarity of the End and not simply to be comforted and motivated by the certainty of the End, it undermines the true value of biblical eschatology; not to mention that it often also falls into embarrassing, laughable error. In the hands of misguided evangelicals, idle speculations, conspiracy theories, and mathematically calculated predictions of times and events, what Kuzmic pejoratively calls 'biblical arithmetic', have made a spectacle of the whole eschatological enterprise.[49]

Although not as worthy of dismissal as pop, end-times prophecies, heated controversies that occur among scholars concerning the details of the millennium, the tribulation, and so on, also bring down eschatology to embarrassing depths. Kuzmic posits that there is probably no other doctrine on which evangelicals are more divided and even opposed to each other as the doctrine of 'the last things'.[50] Although these debates occur often in scholarly fashion, they still distract the Church from the primary purpose of biblical eschatology, namely, to assure and instil confident hope in God's people in light of God's future in spite of hard and dark times.

Transformationists deem discussions of the end-times that detract from this essential faith as useless. As tempting as it is to assign specific numbers and places and personalities to biblical prophecies, the Church must not forget that future visions had a primarily *pastoral* function for God's people who were

---

[48] Chris Sugden, 'Transformational Development: Current state of understanding and practice', *Transformation* 20.2 (April 2003), 73.
[49] Kuzmic, 'Eschatology and Ethics', 136.
[50] Kuzmic, 'Eschatology and Ethics', 136.

being persecuted.[51] A persecuted people did not have the luxury of speculating on the details of God's future; rather, they needed to hear the promise of God to bring the kingdom in its fullness in order to persevere and have hope amidst tribulation. Furthermore, the promise of God's future inspired them to take the Gospel with confidence and boldness to the ends of the earth. Sugden develops a theology of resurrection (eschatology), which he claims has always had a vision for the here and now in contrast to an escapist vision.[52] Indeed the biblical theology of the assured future in God has always had present implications for new life and justice. Sugden asserts, 'The resurrection is the announcement that this purpose of the fulfilment of creation will finally be achieved, that those who have lived lives in conformity with the resurrection life - lives of faith, righteousness and holiness through God's grace - will be vindicated.'[53]

In light of the assured future, the Spirit filled Church perseveres and hopes as it engages the world in bold, holistic mission according to the love, justice, righteousness and peace of the coming kingdom. In light of the End, the Church participates with God to accomplish the *missio Dei,* God's mission, which is 'the reconciliation of all things, on earth and in heaven with Christ as the head (Col. 1:19; Eph. 1:10)'. Sine at once issues both an affirmation and a challenge: 'The God who ... promised to make all things new will be faithful in bringing us to [God's] future. And we have the privilege of collaborating with that God in bringing that future to fruition.'[54] Kuzmic calls this 'the practice of hope';[55] Maggay calls it 'the practice of radical hope'.[56]

This collaboration with God as a reflection of, and a movement toward, that future defines the *telos* aspect of biblical eschatology. If 'last things' brings into focus the nature of the *finis,* then life and mission in the 'last days' bring into focus the nature of the *telos.* Since Mission as Transformation emerged in the context of an evangelicalism that often emphasized the *finis* at the expense of the *telos,* it should not come as a surprise that Transformationists developed the latter more fully to balance the eschatological scale.

Keeping the *finis* always in view, how then have Transformationists understood the nature of the *telos,* the goal of history and the Church's participation with God to accomplish that goal? In light of the story of the biblical kingdom, the basic answer lies in the Spirit empowered mission of the

---

[51] Kuzmic, 'Eschatology and Ethics', 136.
[52] Chris Sugden, 'Death, Injustice, Resurrection and Transformation', *Transformation* 22.2 (April 2005), 69.
[53] Sugden, 'Death, Injustice, Resurrection and Transformation', 69.
[54] Sine, *Wild Hope,* 243.
[55] Kuzmic, 'Eschatology and Ethics', 158-160.
[56] Maggay, *Transforming Society,* 101-103.

Church to share Jesus holistically and contextually. Chapter 6 seeks to flesh this out in more detail.

CHAPTER 6

Kingdom Mission in between the Times

In light of Christ's first coming, how should the Church act in the world as it anticipates his second coming? In light of the 'presence of the future', how does the Church that represents the kingdom live today within the kingdoms of the world? In light of the travail of these 'last days', how does the Church live out its calling as it awaits the certainty of God's 'last things?' Reflections on these types of questions explore the relationship between the kingdom of God, eschatology, and church mission, i.e., mission in between the times, i.e., the theological heart of Mission as Transformation.

For Transformationists, the concept of 'last days' (*telos*) does not allow the Church to wait idly; rather, it inspires God's people to active engagement with a needy world in preparation for the 'last things' (*finis*). The *telos* aspect of eschatology spells out the kingdom mission of the Church as it actively awaits the *finis*. This chapter seeks to understand how Transformationists have worked out the Church's mission worldwide in these 'last days'. Samuel's eight components of Mission as Transformation provide the basic outline:

1. An integral relationship between evangelism and social change
2. Mission as witness and journey in the world
3. Mission in context
4. Practice and theory: praxis
5. The local nature of theology
6. Freedom and power for the poor
7. Reconciliation and solidarity
8. Building communities of change.[1]

Consistency and clarity call for some rewording of these headings, trying of course not to alter their essential thrusts. I *do* seek to develop these components; that is, to enhance and clarify them. Based upon the findings of the biblical, now-and-not-yet, eschatological kingdom of God in the previous chapter, at least three basic themes of kingdom theology - integration, incarnation, and commitment to the poor - come to the fore, and these can help to organize the eight components.

---

[1] Samuel, 'Mission as Transformation', 229-230.

Kingdom Integration

The biblical reality of the kingdom of God has served as a theological integration point for Mission as Transformation in a variety of indispensable ways; for the very idea of a realm in which God rules inherently covers the full range of existence. Dichotomies, prioritizations, and ultimate divisions make increasingly less sense in light of the universal, integrating kingdom. On Samuel's list, numbers 1, 7 and 8 substantiate this kingdom theme of integration.

Word, Work and Wonder

The recovery of the biblical kingdom among radical evangelical missiologists broadened the scope of salvation to include compassion and justice ministries, while avoiding the liberal tendency to replace the biblical mandate to *tell* the good news. Contrary to criticisms aimed at Transformationists from certain sectors of the evangelical community that they have compromised on Gospel proclamation, evangelism has always remained a priority. Padilla asserts in the movement's early stages that 'the widest and deepest human need is a personal encounter with Jesus Christ through whom the Kingdom is mediated.'[2]

Such a commitment to the verbal proclamation of the Gospel has never wavered, but Transformationists saw the need to realign it with the larger picture of the kingdom of God. Mortimer Arias laments that much of the Church's evangelistic activities have ignored the kingdom of God to its bane. He admonishes the heralding Church to recover the kingdom; for if God has called the Church to continue Christ's ministry, then it must preach nothing less than the Gospel of the kingdom.[3] Sharing the saving knowledge of Jesus with others amounts to inviting them to enter into the kingdom and to join a community that purposes to live out that kingdom in the context of a needy world. The kingdom, which in Transformational thinking has both personal and social ramifications, serves as the theological integration point that binds the missionary activities of social concern and evangelism.

For Transformationists, however, the kingdom integration of evangelism and social concern does not begin and end with simply affirming the merits of both activities. Not going beyond such an affirmation can lead to the misunderstanding that evangelism and social concern can somehow stand on their own. The profound challenge of kingdom integration from the perspective of Transformationists strikes precisely at this juncture, for in their thinking, evangelism and social concern need each other in order to fulfil the holistic demands of the kingdom. They must maintain their respective distinctions from each other, but they must also acknowledge each other's worth in an

---

[2] Padilla, *Mission Between the Times*, 198.
[3] Arias, *Announcing*, 1-12.

interdependent relationship. Maggay considers it erroneous to 'confuse evangelism for social action and social action for evangelism'.[4] But the kingdom of God demands both activities operating interdependently with each other for the sake of the Gospel.

Maggay opts for the word 'witness' to unify the two aspects; the Church bears 'witness to the kingdom in the world by both "proclamation and presence"'.[5] If the Church defines its witness by proclamation at the expense of presence or by presence at the expense of proclamation, then it violates kingdom integration. But confusing the two creates an unhealthy mix that weakens both. Authentic kingdom witness means an integration of these two missionary activities that inseparably unifies them without losing their respective and distinct characteristic functions. This kind of kingdom integration renders the evangelism versus social concern, as well as the primary versus secondary debates, null and void without reducing the degree of conviction for both. This integral nature between evangelism and social concern constitutes a vital component of Mission as Transformation.

As kingdom integral thinking has matured among Transformationists, another piece to the holistic mission puzzle has come into place as radical Pentecostals have joined the discussion. Due to their missiological contributions, Transformationists worldwide have begun to see the invading kingdom of God as the sphere in and through which the Holy Spirit empowers the Church to bear witness to the Gospel with 'signs and wonders'. Healings, exorcisms, resurrections, and miracle feedings pervaded the kingdom ministries of Jesus and the early Church; they signaled the coming kingdom that is not of this world (Jn. 18:36), thus making the kingdom a present reality that miraculously touched the sick, the poor, the broken, and even the dead. The list of 'Signs of the Kingdom' in the Kingdom Affirmations and Commitments Statement of 1994 includes, 'deliverance from the forces of evil' and 'the Holy Spirit working in power ... transforming people, performing miracles and healings today, and sustaining people in their suffering'.[6]

Transformationists understand the kingdom of God, not just for social ethics and community development, not just for evangelism and church planting, not just for supernatural Holy Spirit power and miraculous healings, but for all of these. Mission as Transformation defies the convenient but erroneous associations of evangelism with conservatives, social concern with liberals, and power ministries with fanatics. The important Kingdom Affirmations and Commitments Statement testifies to the kingdom integration of 'the three streams of world evangelization, social action and renewal in the Spirit', or as Thomas McAlpine conveniently phrases it, the integration of 'word, work and

---

[4] Maggay, *Transforming Society*, 16.

[5] Maggay, *Transforming Society*, 22.

[6] 'Kingdom Affirmations and Commitments', *Mission as Transformation*, 16-17.

wonder'. This kingdom integration constitutes the first global dimension of Mission as Transformation.

Reconciliation/Solidarity and Stewardship[7]

Number 7 on Samuel's list 'reconciliation/solidarity and stewardship' refers to another type of kingdom integration, namely, the commitment to the unity of humankind, to the 'one new humanity' in Christ and ultimately of all creation. From beginning to end, the eschatological kingdom of God has represented God's desire for '*all* the families of the earth to be blessed' (Gen. 12:3). So although God indeed had a special relationship with his people (Israel in the Old Testament and the multicultural Church in the New), God's plan of redemption has always intended to encompass the whole world. God has always desired to see all persons, peoples, and indeed the whole creation under the lordship of Christ (Jn. 3:16; Rom. 8:18-21).

This Transformational perspective of God's desire for universal salvation fundamentally differs from other forms of Christian universalism that either believes all are already saved or that all will be saved. Tokunboh Adeyemo lists a number of Christian voices throughout the ages who espoused various forms of universalism including Clement of Alexandria, Gregory of Nyssa, and more recently Karl Barth, John A.T. Robinson, and fellow African John Mbiti.[8] He then proceeds to make a biblical case against this brand of universalism on several grounds: 1) God's love requires God's justice - 'The universalists forget that God's perfection of righteousness and justice is equally ultimate [to God's radical love]'; 2) the God-given freedom for human choice - 'The universalist claim that people are saved against their will is erroneous'; and 3) a God-ordained call to preach the Gospel to the ends of the earth - 'If everyone is saved automatically ... then the Lord's commission ... to preach the Gospel ... is a mockery'.[9]

Adeyemo caps his argument with, 'Though God does not desire any to perish, men [sic] rebelliously turn away from Him'.[10] This statement further demonstrates the distinction between universalism and 'a salvation that is universally accessible'.[11] An integral kingdom perspective simply points to

---

[7] Samuel, 'Mission as Transformation', 230-231. Samuel lists this component as 'Reconciliation and Solidarity', but in the personal interview, he expanded upon it and added the concept of stewardship. Hence, the expansion to 'Reconciliation/Solidarity and Stewardship'. Vinay Samuel, interview by author, 26 July 2003, St. Davids, Pa., tape recording, Eastern University.

[8] Tokunbuh Adeyemo, *Salvation in African Tradition* (Nairobi: Evangel, 1979), 98.

[9] Adeyemo, *Salvation in African Tradition*, 101-102.

[10] Adeyemo, *Salvation in African Tradition*, 103.

[11] John Sanders, *No Other Name: An Investigation into the Destiny of the Unevangelized* (Grand Rapids, Mich: Eerdmans, 1992), 107-108.

God's desire for all to come to a saving knowledge of Christ, as well as God's plan to give all persons the opportunity to experience salvation irrespective of gender, color, ethnic identity, religious background, social status and so on. Not all will respond, but all will have the opportunity as the Church holistically proclaims the Gospel to the ends of the earth.[12]

This perspective of God's desire and plan for universal human emancipation also differs from any horizontal talk of a new humanity. For all of the possible good that came out of human wrought utopian visions, they have also resulted in unjustifiable forms of savagery, oppression and poverty. The concentration camps of Nazism to build the new Arian Germany, the failed worldwide experiments of communism at the expense of untold millions of Eastern European, Asian, and African peoples to build the classless society, and the killing fields of Cambodia to return to agrarian bliss are bloody, tragic spectacles of humanity's failed attempts to reconcile itself.

What then, if not these, *does* the 'reconciliation of all things' mean in Transformational thought? It means that ultimate reconciliation comes from God, and out of that truth flow ministries of penultimate reconciliation. Transformationist Miroslav Volf, in his powerful theological treatise on reconciliation, cautions that salvation 'ought not to be taken out of God's hands'.[13] From the outset Volf assumes that the horizontal reconciliation between peoples hinges upon the vertical as he differentiates between 'non-final and final reconciliation'. He writes, '[The question] is not how to achieve the final reconciliation, but what resources we need to live in peace in the absence of the final reconciliation. ... I will advocate here for a non-final reconciliation based on a vision of reconciliation that cannot be undone.'[14]

As an outflow of the sovereign final reconciliation between God and humanity through Christ comes the demand of the integral kingdom for a 'non-final reconciliation' between nations and between people. Such a theology can act as a catalyst for a powerful affront to violence between warring factions, like between the Serbs and the Croats in the 1990s, who in the absence of this

---

[12] Some zealous evangelical missionaries take Matt. 24:14 literally, which states, 'And this good news of the kingdom will be proclaimed throughout the world, as a testimony to all the nations; and then the end will come'. A literal interpretation of this places the full burden upon the missionary enterprise to take the Gospel to the ends of the earth in order to usher in the End. Others look primarily to Romans 2, where an 'exception clause' seems to exist for those who may not get the direct opportunity to hear the Gospel, thus understanding the role of world mission in more realistic terms, that is, it has a role to play, but it is not solely responsible to bring about the End.
[13] Miroslav Volf, *Exclusion and Embrace: A Theological Exploration of Identity, Otherness, and Reconciliation* (Nashville, Tenn.: Abingdon, 1996), 109. Volf writes from the perspective of his own war-torn country of what was once Yugoslavia, which makes his case for reconciliation that much more powerful.
[14] Volf, *Exclusion and Embrace*, 109-110.

kind of radical reconciliation, violently broke up Volf's homeland of former Yugoslavia.

Solidarity with 'the other' inseparably relates to this non-final reconciliation in that solidarity expresses reconciliation concretely and practically. Samuel expounds upon Galatians 2:11-21, where Paul confronted Peter who dissociated himself from the Gentiles for the sake of the circumcised.[15] Samuel interprets Paul's action against the more prestigious, established Peter as an act to protect the integrity of the all inclusive Gospel. Peter had an opportunity to demonstrate solidarity with Gentiles, 'the other', as a testimony to the Gospel, but bungled it by refusing to eat at the same table with them in order to maintain his safe status among Jewish Christians. Paul decried such a stance, Samuel stressed, for solidarity with 'the other' lies at the very heart of the Gospel.

This type of solidarity comes with a price, which should not surprise anyone, since from a Transformational perspective, it flows out of a theology of the cross. With the cross of Christ as the backdrop, the Church stands in solidarity with 'the other' regardless of the consequences. The Church's role in genuine, effective reconciliation between peoples can only happen if the Church commits itself to being in solidarity with 'the other', those marginalized and poor in society, as a testimony to the Gospel. Samuel asks rhetorically, 'Who are we in solidarity with?'[16] Those faithful to the Gospel answer with 'the other'.

The idea of stewardship takes reconciliation/solidarity to the next level. Whereas reconciliation/solidarity attempts to put an end to the cycle of violence between peoples, the idea of stewardship has with it a sense of proactive responsibility that demonstrates care for 'the other' as persons made in the image of God. Reconciliation/solidarity opens the door to genuine healing; stewardship proactively walks through it. For Samuel, to understand the work of the Church in bringing persons and peoples together as fulfilling the biblical call to stewardship completes the picture of reconciliation/solidarity.[17]

The Church has typically understood stewardship in relation to creation and therefore to environmental concerns, and rightfully so. But the 'reconciliation of *all* things' in Christ leads to the necessary connection between creation care and people care. Samuel concedes that Transformational thinking regarding a full-orbed understanding of stewardship has yet to mature.[18] But scriptures that

---

[15] Vinay Samuel, sermon on Galatians 2:11-21, 24 July 2003, St. Davids, Pa., Evangelicals for Social Action Thirtieth Anniversary Celebration, Eastern University. Samuel provided the morning Bible studies, which began the activities of each of the three days of the event.

[16] Samuel, 'Mission as Transformation', 231.

[17] Samuel, interview.

[18] Samuel, interview.

speak of reconciliation with both creation and people together in one breath demand it, such as Paul's words, 'We know that the whole creation has been groaning in labor pains until now; and not only the creation, but we ourselves ...' (Rom. 8:22-23). In fact, Samuel argues that stewardship should begin with persons and peoples in mind and then broadened to include the whole creation.[19] In Christ as peoples begin to confront and then embrace their differences, it does not take long to extend the care of persons made in the image of God to the care of the environment and to the rest of God's creation. 'An activity of the kingdom of God,' Sugden claims as he interprets Samuel, 'are right relationships between God and people, among people, and in all of creation'.[20]

These three aspects - non-final reconciliation, solidarity, and stewardship - in interaction with one another foreshadow the final reconciliation of all things in Christ, where the one new humanity will enjoy a new heaven and a new earth. Integrated together by a theology of the kingdom, these three aspects have directed Transformationists to work toward the reconciliation of all things in Christ. Indeed together they constitute a shared conviction, a global dimension, that propels the Church to engage the world integrally as it awaits the *finis,* the end of time.

Communities of Integration: Where the Present and Future Meet

The Wheaton '83 Statement on Transformation asserts, 'We affirm that the kingdom of God is both present and future, both societal and individual, both physical and spiritual.'[21] Number 8 on Samuel's list, building up communities of change, integrates these various levels of reality by locating them in the particularity of human communities. This constitutes the third global dimension of Mission as Transformation.

From the perspective of this missiology, the future of God meets present humanity in the context of concrete local communities. These communities provide the world stage upon which God acts transformatively on both societal and individual levels, as well as physical and spiritual levels. Viewing human communities in this way leads to understanding the missionary task as 'building communities of change' toward God's future. 'On this point, I was thinking of the eschatological dimension of Mission as Transformation', confirms Samuel, 'We must build communities toward God's future.'[22]

Tom Sine sheds more light on this idea when he encourages development practitioners to 'know what the end game is'. When asked to define

---

[19] Samuel, interview.

[20] Sugden, *Gospel, Culture and Transformation,* 18.

[21] 'Wheaton '83 Statement', *The Church in Response to Human Need,* 264.

[22] Samuel, interview.

Transformation, he poses a question that he believes churches, development organizations and mission agencies need to ask in order to understand the nature of Transformation: 'In the end', he asks, 'What does a community look like that has been transformed in Christ?'[23] A contextual end vision of the justice, righteousness, and peace of the kingdom of God drives Transformational ministries. This point of kingdom integration from the perspective of Mission as Transformation brings together the concrete historical present and God's future in the particularity of human communities, thus dictating the mission of the Church as building communities of change.

In light of the kingdom of God, the present-future integration brings together the societal and the individual. This point overlaps significantly with Number 1 on Samuel's list of components, namely, the integration of evangelism and social concern, and therefore does not need too much elaboration here, except to say that the kingdom of God demands no less than transformed communities made up of transformed individuals. The fallacy that if one emphasizes the transformation of individuals, then social transformation will automatically follow is equal only to the fallacy that if one emphasizes the transformation of society, then individual transformation will automatically follow. Mission as Transformation demands working on both the societal and individual levels. 'It is important', Samuel explains, 'to centre the whole process on what God has done in Christ by opening individuals *and* communities to the transcendent and to the intervention of God in contemporary life.'[24]

The present-future integration of the kingdom of God also brings together the physical and the spiritual. The concrete, historical circumstances of poverty, violence, political instability, injustice and oppression demand a physical response from the Church, for God most certainly cares about the affairs of this present world. The Church, of course, must take precautions to keep the affairs of this world in perspective; for addressing them at the expense of a vital spirituality can surely threaten the very distinct character of the Church of Jesus Christ. Social ministry without the Spirit can reduce the Church to a mere social service organization with an ornamental cross on top of it! The Church must maintain the spiritual side of mission - the sense of the Transcendent - in light of the coming of God's certain future and invite any and all to a living relationship with God through Christ and the Spirit.

Evangelicals have held up this aspect of mission by their signature emphasis upon personal evangelism. However, in maintaining the spiritual side of mission, the physical needs of people and the community have notoriously fallen by the wayside, as we established in Part I of this study. Conversely, ecumenicals have boasted in responding to the social and physical needs of

---

[23] Tom Sine, interview by author, 25 July 2003, St. Davids, Pa., tape recording, Eastern University.

[24] Samuel, 'Mission as Transformation', 233. Italics mine.

people, but often at the expense of the spiritual side of mission. Kingdom integration from the perspective of Mission as Transformation demands holistic engagement on both the physical and the spiritual levels in human communities.

The missiological integration of the societal, the individual, the physical and the spiritual within the theological integration of humanity's present and God's future intersect in the concrete historical locus of human communities. To build up these communities according to the now-and-not-yet kingdom, therefore, should define the *telos* mission of the Church, as it gets involved in evangelism and church planting, as well as in social change and political engagement. Community building of this nature makes up another crucial component, another global dimension, of Mission as Transformation.

Kingdom Incarnation

The recovery of the biblical reality of the kingdom of God among Transformationists has indeed led to important missiological integrations, which has drawn out the first three global dimensions. While the kingdom integrates the many facets of human communities, unifies missionary activities, and ultimately reconciles all things in Christ, it also specifies and particularizes life. To understand this aspect of the kingdom, we need not look any further than the incarnation of God in Christ.

Jesus Christ embodied in his person all that God desires for humanity. In other words, with him came the presence of the kingdom in bodily form. Indeed the incarnation of God in Christ demonstrates 'how seriously God takes the material world' and how much God loves it (Jn. 3:16).[25] Kingdom incarnation serves as the basis for ongoing missiological reflections on contextualization and local theologies. Transformationists have demonstrated their deep missiological understanding of the incarnation by their uncompromising commitment to culture as a hermeneutical key. Numbers 3, 4, and 5 on Samuel's list reflect this commitment and serve as the basis for three more global dimensions.

---

[25] Myers, *Walking with the Poor*, 46. Roman Catholic missiologists invented a synonym for contextualization—inculturation—which attempts to synthesize the anthropological process of acculturation or enculturation with the theological concept of incarnation to convey the nature of the communication process between God, Church and cultures. See also Schreiter, *Constructing Local Theologies*, 5 and Eduardo C. Fernandez, *La Cosecha* (Collegeville, Minn: Liturgical Press, 2000), 100-101.

Mission in Context

This aspect of Transformation, mission in context, emphasizes the process by which Transformationists strive for an authentic localized translation of the trans-cultural Gospel. As we have already seen, Mission as Transformation is more fully 'Mission in Context as Transformation'. Since the beginning of serious holistic reflections among radical evangelicals, the commitment on their part to view context hermeneutically continues to define their missiology. As Bediako contends, 'Theology is called to deal always with culturally rooted questions.'[26] Culture - the language, worldview, beliefs, values, art forms, customs, laws, socio-economic structures, social relationships, and material things[27] - provides the initial structure and boundaries within which the Gospel takes on contextual form.

As the Son of God became Jesus the Jew in Greco-Roman culture, so too the representative Church of God today must become the Church of urban Manila, of suburban Midwest America, of a rural village in Mexico, of a tribe in Nigeria, and so on. Ed Lapiz' comment that 'every tribe and nation must be allowed to evolve a brand of Christianity whose spirit is biblical but whose body is indigenous' says it succinctly.[28] The tension between the attempt to take culture seriously and the attempt to maintain fidelity to the biblical Gospel has led at least to three unavoidable issues for the missiological task: 1) honesty in biblical hermeneutics; 2) an appreciation of culture; and 3) the call to take part in the transformation of culture.

Honesty in biblical interpretation means to realize from the outset that no one reads the text of scripture without the biases of his/her own culture. This idea holds true everywhere and at all times, but it surfaces most overtly in the cross-cultural situation,[29] for in such a situation missionaries soon discover that their theological constructs do not readily fit the sensibilities and thought patterns of the receptor culture.[30] Maggay brings out the complexity of the cultural task, for example, as she refers to American Protestant mission efforts in the Philippines. She writes,

> [It] involves a communication situation where a multi-cultural Filipino receives a largely western missionary who has come to preach a Semitic Gospel which through the centuries has been domesticated within the conceptual boundaries of

---

[26] Bediako, *Theology and Identity*, xv.
[27] 'Wheaton '83 Statement', *The Church in Response to Human Need*, 259.
[28] Ed Lapiz, 'Filipino Indigenous Liturgy', *Patmos* 14/2 (February 1999), 26.
[29] Vinay Samuel, 'Gospel and Culture', in Vinay Samuel and Albrecht Hauser (eds.), *Proclaiming Christ in Christ's Way* (Oxford: Regnum, 1989), 83.
[30] Charles H. Kraft, *Christianity in Culture* (Maryknoll, N.Y.: Orbis, 1979), 3-22.

Greek thought and interpreted through the exigencies of Nordic and Anglo-Saxon cultures.[31]

Needless to say, to understand the Gospel purely, i.e., outside of culture, is wishful thinking.

Hermeneutical honesty entails releasing any notion of purity or superiority in the exact way in which one has understood the Gospel in his/her particular context. Moreover, it entails releasing the propensity to apply that understanding directly in another culture. This kind of releasing (which is easier to write about than to practice!) opens the door to humility, vulnerability and teachability, as missionaries attempt to live out the Gospel in a different way. It fosters a cross-culturally friendly environment where fellow Christians can decipher together the core truths of the Gospel. 'Mission in Context as Transformation' requires this kind of honesty in approaching the sacred text for the sake of the context.

'Mission in Context as Transformation' also requires an affirmation of culture; for 'culture is God's gift to human beings'.[32] The number of definitions and approaches to culture testifies to its complexity. A Transformational approach understands it as the product of the inherent creativity of human beings as they are made in the image of the creative God. Culture reflects human creativity, which reflects divine creativity.

Furthermore, this same creativity should lead to an appreciation of the diversity of cultures that exist in the world. Maggay argues compellingly that cultural diversity comes from God. Part of her argument reads,

> Clearly, cultural diversity is part of God's design for the world. We know this from the fact that he does not make anything twice - even the flowers of the field are not exactly alike. His diverse creation is to be matched by the splendour and richness of the nations coming into the city of Jerusalem [Rev. 21:24]. At the end of time there will be this great throng from every tribe and people and nation, praising the Lamb with a multitude of tongues [Rev. 7:9-10]. Ethnicity, or even nationality, is not obliterated but enhanced as people of various cultures come to God. We do not cease to be Jew and Greek, male and female, when we come to Christ. These identities remain part of who we are and what we are, and [they] form the context of our obedience to what it means to belong together in Christ.[33]

In touch then with the creative edge of God in human cultures, Transformationists affirm not only culture in general as a reflection of the Creator, but also affirm the diversity of cultures as an expression of the Creator's will.

---

[31] Maggay, *Filipino Religious Consciousness*, 7.

[32] 'Wheaton '83 Statement', *The Church in Response to Human Need*, 259.

[33] Melba Maggay, *Jew to the Jew, Greek to the Greek* (Quezon City: ISACC, 2001), 13.

Postmodern extremists, who interpret appreciating culture as leaving it well alone, would applaud this approach to culture thus far.[34] From the perspective of Mission as Transformation, however, the other necessary side of appreciating culture is transforming culture. For along with reflecting the beauty and creativity of created humanity and Creator God, culture also reflects the depths of human depravity and demonic activity. The Wheaton '83 Statement plainly asserts that 'people have sinned by rebelling against God; therefore the cultures we produce are infected with evil.'[35]

Despite postmodern dismissals at this point, the evangelical heritage that Transformationists affirm cannot turn a blind eye on manifest sin and its personal and social consequences. The list of sins, which ranges from forced slavery of children to ethnic cleansing governmental graft and corruption, bribery, environmental degradation, domestic violence, drug trafficking and prostitution, etc., has no end. In light of overt social evils such as these, the 'affirm and leave alone' approach to culture is, at best, misguided cultural romanticism and at worst, ethical irresponsibility.

From a Transformational perspective, appreciating culture while also understanding the need to transform it are only superficially contradictory, for the reality of the kingdom of God holds together the affirmation of the *shalom* of God while also taking seriously the fall of humanity and humanity's cry for holistic redemption. Transformational activities serve as signposts to the powerful vision of the kingdom of God - as Jesus Christ embodied and taught it - where creation will enjoy the justice, righteousness, peace, and joy of God.

In sum, through a culturally honest approach to Scripture, an appreciation of culture, and participation in the transformation of culture! Mission in Context as Transformation seeks to incarnate the trans-cultural Gospel authentically into local cultures. Therefore in this missiology, biblical interpretation, cultural analysis and Transformational ministries synergistically define the mission of the Church.[36] This three-pronged view of contextualization constitutes another vital global dimension of Mission as Transformation.

Full Contextual Engagement

The theme of kingdom incarnation in Transformational thinking goes the second mile with regard to contextualization by providing the impetus for full

---

[34] Kraft, *Christianity in Culture*, 49-52. Kraft expounds upon the 'cultural validity model', which is more commonly known as cultural relativism. He basically affirms this anthropological model and in fact builds upon it to develop what he calls biblical cultural relativism (124-128). It is only when proponents go extreme with it and declare an 'absolute relativism' that Kraft objects.

[35] 'Wheaton '83 Statement', *The Church in Response to Human Need*, 259.

[36] Sugden, *Gospel, Culture and Transformation*, 3-4.

contextual engagement with the local situation. If God became flesh and proceeded to occupy the seat of power as the meta-Human above all humanity, the very truth of the incarnation would still stand alone as the greatest event in human history.

But God in Christ did not take a transcendentally high position far above and away from ordinary human existence; on the contrary, God in Christ demonstrated personal, relational solidarity with human beings. From taking on rural village existence as the son of a labourer (Lk. 2:39) to calling the twelve disciples his friends (Jn. 15:15) and 'eating with tax-collectors and sinners' (Mt. 9:10ff), Jesus immersed himself fully in human community.

In light of this deep level of incarnation, long-distance, short-term, and separated involvement with the local culture falls short of authentic mission. In Samuel's estimation, 'If Christians have no involvement in the world they become cardboard figures',[37] meaning they become something less than authentic (artificial or superficial) when they engage in mission activities that are not completely immersed in the life of a local culture. Cross-cultural missionaries who do not bother to learn the language and/or who cloister themselves inside walled compounds in the midst of the host culture exemplify this sort of artificiality. Wealthy Christians of the same culture who may give to the poor via the church offering plate but who avoid the 'seedier' poorer side of town also exemplify this lack of authenticity. The truth of the incarnation of God in Christ challenges such disengaged mission.

Some Transformationists go as far as to take full engagement to mean actually living in the slums to which they feel called. Viv Grigg's experience in *Tatalon*, a squatter community in Metro Manila, serves as one of many examples among Transformationists of the 'incarnational model', which he documents in the volume *Companion to the Poor*.[38] When Grigg lived in *Tatalon*, he served under the auspices of a mission agency called Servants Among the Poor, which has the distinction of requiring its personnel to apply the incarnational model in their missionary engagement with the poor.[39]

When Vinay Samuel and family moved to a slum area on the outskirts of Bangalore, India to pastor a church, they exercised full contextual

---

[37] Samuel, 'Mission as Transformation', 230.

[38] Viv Grigg, *Companion to the Poor* (Monrovia, Calif.: MARC, 1990).

[39] Jenni M. Craig, *Servants Among the Poor* (Manila; Wellington: OMF: Servants, 1998), 326. Servants' ministry ethos is printed as the Appendix in Craig's narrative account of the Servants missionaries' experience in the Philippines. Evelyn Miranda-Feliciano adds an epilogue wherein she writes, 'Following the incarnational example of Christ, [Servants missionaries] have allowed their lives to be intertwined with those Filipinos commonly labeled, "*mga eskwaters*"-words often uttered with a sneer, if not fear by the more comfortable folk' (322). See also Servants missionary Michael Duncan, *Costly Mission: Following Christ into the Slums* (Monrovia, Calif.: MARC, 1996), which is Duncan's personal story.

engagement.[40] When a community development staff team from ISACC in the Philippines moved into the town of Nasugbu in Batangas province, it also exemplified full contextual engagement.[41] Such missionaries indeed take incarnational mission to inspiring levels and therefore have the strongest right to preach full contextual engagement. This understanding and application of deep incarnation constitutes another essential component of Mission as Transformation.

Behind the practice of this kind of full contextual engagement lies a theological process that involves three aspects - *theoria* or truth, *praxis* or practical commitment and *poiesis* or imagination.[42] Regarding the relationship between theory and practice, Transformationists claim that only as the Church fully engages human communities practically and concretely can it arrive at any substantial and meaningful truth. On this point, Transformationists stand with liberationists who insist that theology is a second act, a reflection upon concrete acts among the poor and oppressed. This dynamic methodology for theology challenges the traditional model of theologizing, which understands reflection (or theorizing) as leading to action in a more linear fashion, not giving the action step any power to inform further reflection. Liberationists point out that this traditional model results in static doctrines of truth that are ultimately rendered unserviceable in the here and now.

In contrast, this new way of theologizing, where theory comes second, leads to *the liberation of theology*.[43] Juan Luis Segundo develops this unconventional methodology for theology by popularizing 'the hermeneutic circle', which he describes as 'the continuing change in our interpretation of the Bible [that] is dictated by the continuing changes in our present day reality.'[44] Petersen sees this methodology as a way for evangelicals 'to keep their theological reflection integrally tied to concrete human experience, to the meaning of scripture, and to pastoral action'.[45] After demonstrating the compatibility of the hermeneutic circle to Pentecostal theology, he also affirms it as the approach that can truly establish a viable, effective Pentecostal social theology in Latin America.[46]

Furthermore, only the church-in-praxis, a church fully engaged in human communities moving toward the kingdom, can experience and appreciate

---

[40] Ronald J. Sider, *Good News and Good Works* (Grand Rapids, Mich.: Zondervan, 1994), 53-69.

[41] ISACC, *Sambahaginan: An Experience in Community Development* (Quezon City: ISACC, 1992).

[42] Bosch, *Transforming Mission*, 431-432; Samuel, 'Mission as Transformation', 229-230; Sugden, *Gospel, Culture and Transformation*, 24.

[43] Taken from the title of Segundo's book, *The Liberation of Theology*.

[44] Segundo, *The Liberation of Theology*, 8.

[45] Douglas Petersen, 'Praxis', in A. Scott Moreau (ed.), *Evangelical Dictionary of World Missions* (Grand Rapids, Mich.; Carlisle: Baker; Paternoster, 2000), 781.

[46] Petersen, *Not By Might Nor By Power*, 193-209.

genuine contextual worship, art, symbolism, piety, spirituality and mystery. The term 'imagination' tries to capture the fullness of this aspect - the affective, trans-logical, creative element of the human person. Bosch draws out this aspect of imagination as a necessary piece to the contextualization discussion; for even if one achieves a balanced reconciliation between theory and practice, theology remains incomplete without the element of beauty. Bosch then goes on to equate truth, justice and beauty with some familiar categories. He writes, 'The best models of contextual theology succeed in holding together in creative tension *theoria, praxis* and *poiesis,* or if one wishes, faith, hope and love'.[47] Samuel asserts, 'This [three-way integration] is the way the Spirit acts.'[48] The Spirit empowered Church that fully engages a particular cultural context in theological reflection, *shalom* action, and creative imagination lives out the incarnation of Christ; or said slightly differently, the fully engaged Church *re-incarnates* Christ into the world. Transformationists all over the world have affirmed this deep, extensive way of immersing into culture as a way to continue the incarnational way of Christ on earth. In this way it constitutes another global dimension of Mission as Transformation.

Local Faith

If the global dimensions of mission in context and full contextual engagement emphasize the incarnational translation of the Gospel into a local culture, then the next dimension of local faith emphasizes the result of that process. A contextual, fully engaged outworking of the Gospel produces a truly local church that does theology, worship and mission locally. The Gospel remains in the abstract if it does not finally take on bodily form into a visible, concrete local Christianity.

The creation of INFEMIT bears witness to the commitment of Transformationists to affirm, develop and celebrate the local nature of the Christian faith, thus constituting another vital dimension of Mission as Transformation. In fact, as we will see later on, any notion of a global Mission as Transformation owes its very inspiration to theologies forged out of local situations. We can only talk of Mission as Transformation as a global missiology if we acknowledge the local missiologies that make it up.

Samuel distinguishes the local nature of theology from 'systematic theologies [which] are of little use to help change a local church [or situation]. They help people write exams. A systematic theology, however wonderful, has to be localized'.[49] By systematic theology, Samuel refers to the unquestioned missiological approach most commonly applied during the 'era of

---

[47] Bosch, *Transforming Mission,* 431.
[48] Samuel, 'Mission as Transformation', 230.
[49] Samuel, 'Mission as Transformation', 230.

noncontextualization' in which the dominant Western Church understood its beliefs and practices as universally normative and therefore unalterable.[50] The missionary enterprise of that era expected local cultures to conform to this systematic (Western) version of the faith, resulting, for example, in Sunday mass conducted in Latin for tribal communities, theological education requiring scholarly knowledge of Augustine, Aquinas, Luther, Calvin and Wesley before graduating ministerial students in Asian, African, and Latin American seminaries, and so on.

With this era essentially behind the Church (late anthropologist Paul Hiebert places this era as occurring between 1800 and 1950[51]), thanks in large part to the advances made by the discipline of contextual theology, non-Western local churches doing local theologies, appropriating local worship practices, and developing local missiological approaches to evangelization and social justice have enjoyed increasing respect in the worldwide Christian community. Bosch, for example, points out that 'a generation or so ago, no theological institution in the West would have deemed it necessary to offer courses on theological developments in the Third World; today more and more of them have integrated such courses into their curricula - not as interesting oddities but as an essential dimension of theological education.'[52] Bosch said this in 1991; his assertion has proven increasingly true over time.

Having said this, the phenomenon of importing one cultural form of the faith to other contexts still exists today. Lapiz points out, for example, many South Korean missionaries, who come to the Philippines with a seemingly predetermined agenda and the money to implement it, as the latest example of subjecting the Filipino Church to imported, and therefore inappropriate, forms of theology, worship, and mission.[53] The only difference may be that the importing process does not happen under the guise of paternalistic dominance like the West once held over the rest of the world. But whether out of a sense of dominance or a general ignorance of advances made in contextualization, the local nature of the faith is undermined if the local church does not allow itself

---

[50] Paul Hiebert, 'Critical Contextualization', *International Bulletin of Missionary Research* 11.3 (July 1987), 104-106.

[51] Hiebert, 'Critical Contextualization', 104.

[52] Bosch, *Transforming Mission,* 428.

[53] Ed Lapiz, *Paano Maging Pilipinong Kristiano* (Makati City: KALOOB, 1997), xii-xiii, 143-144. Of course, there are examples of Korean missionaries in the Philippines who are quite aware of issues of contextualization. For example, the husband/wife tandem of Wonsuk and Julie Ma spent many years on the faculty of the Asia Pacific Theological Seminary in Baguio City, encouraging students to take context seriously for theology and ministry. Byung-yoon Kim at Philippine Baptist Theological Seminary also in Baguio also exemplifies contextual sensitivity. For some of their (and others') thoughts on contextualization, see Wonsuk and Julie C. Ma (eds.), *Asian Church & God's Mission* (Manila; West Caldwell, N.J.: OMF; Mountain World Mission, 2003).

to develop according to the traditions, customs and art forms of its own local context.

When Samuel wrote, 'Context says that theology, Christian mission and understanding are always local', he put proper emphasis on the local/particular, but not ultimately over and against any global/universal notions of theology.[54] Emphasizing the local simply brings out the fact that the work of the Gospel happens not ethereally in the clouds but on the ground. '[Theology] is both local and global, but local theology is critically important because that is where we find the truth, embody it, and live it out.'[55]

Samuel discusses the integral relationship between theory, practice, and imagination under this component too, demonstrating that numbers 3, 4 and 5 on his list are ultimately inseparable. They together put forth a missiological understanding of the incarnation of God in Christ, the very embodiment of the kingdom of God among the kingdoms of the world.

Kingdom Commitment to the Poor

The biblical reality of the kingdom of God generates at least one other essential theme upon which Transformationists have built their missiology, namely, the kingdom's commitment to the poor. By 'poor', Transformationists generally understand this broadly and holistically, that is, not just in economic or spiritual terms, but in economic, spiritual, social, psychological and physical terms.

Bryant Myers uses 'a family of definitions' that creates a multi-dimensional view of poverty. Drawing from several sources, he outlines poverty 1) as deficit - lack of basic necessities like food, water, housing, and so on; 2) as entanglement - disadvantage due to physical, family, and social situations; 3) as lack of access to social power - no means to avail of state, political, social and economic resources; 4) as disempowerment - entrapped in webs of personal, social, cultural, physical and spiritual relationships that render persons powerless; and 5) as a lack of freedom to grow - captivity to mental, physical, spiritual and social strongholds.[56] He concludes 'that poverty is a complicated social issue involving all areas of life - physical, personal, social, cultural and spiritual'.[57] Real people, in contrast to abstract, faceless masses, live out these dimensions of poverty. The missionary Church needs this reminder regularly so that the issue of poverty does not get reduced to dispassionate theories and

---

[54] Samuel, 'Mission as Transformation', 230; Sugden, *Gospel, Culture and Transformation*, 24.

[55] Samuel, interview.

[56] Myers, *Walking with the Poor*, 61-81.

[57] Myers, *Walking with the Poor*, 81.

useless romanticism. 'The poor are not primarily a class', reminds development practitioner Ruby Barcelona, 'the poor are people.'[58]

The sick, deprived, downtrodden, marginalized, voiceless, powerless, penniless and oppressed, the poor, occupy a special place in the biblical kingdom. 'The legislative material [that] opposes exploitation, the cry of the poor in the Psalms, the prophets' declaration that God is on the side of the poor, the good news to the poor in the Gospels, and the poor in the community of the faithful in Acts, Paul, James and Revelation' testify to the fact that from beginning to end of the biblical kingdom story, God especially cares for the poor.[59] Jesus himself defined his mission in terms of the poor when he declared in the Nazareth synagogue, 'The Spirit of the Lord is upon me because he has anointed me to bring good news to *the poor*' (Lk. 4:18). He then backed up his words throughout his ministry by identifying with the tax-collectors, sinners, prostitutes, lepers and the oppressed masses.

The *shalom* toward which the kingdom moves involves justice for all, which precisely warrants the special attention due to the poor. Some have interpreted special attention to the poor as a violation of the justice for all principle, but as the Oxford Declaration on Christian Faith and Economics states, 'Justice requires special attention to the weak members of the community because of their greater vulnerability.'[60] Stephen Mott explains further that 'justice must be partial in order to be impartial. Only by giving special attention to the poor ... can one be said to be following the principle of equal consideration of human interest.'[61] If all should have access to God's blessings, then it stands to reason that those who do not have access need special attention to restore their rightful place as God's image-bearing children.

This special attention, however, does not mean that the poor have a claim on the Gospel simply on the basis of their condition. God loves both the rich and the poor, and God's justice applies to all. Indeed all are redeemed by the same Gospel of grace in Jesus Christ. Precisely because of this truth, the

---

[58] Ruby Barcelona, 'The Face of the Poor', *Patmos* 11.2 (2nd Quarter 1995), 3.

[59] Vinay Samuel and Chris Sugden, 'Evangelism and the Poor: An Introduction', in Vinay Samuel and Chris Sugden (eds.), *Evangelism and the Poor* (Bangalore: Partnership in Mission-Asia, 1983), 3. See also Ronald J. Sider (ed.), *For They Shall All Be Fed* (Dallas, Tex.: Word, 1997), for a comprehensive compilation of biblical references pertaining to justice and the poor.

[60] 'Oxford Declaration on Christian Faith and Economics', *Christianity and Economics in the Post-Cold War Era*, 22.

[61] Stephen C. Mott, *Biblical Ethics and Social Change* (New York: Oxford University Press, 1982), 66. For a more detailed discussion of the impartiality/partiality of biblical justice, see also Mott's 'The Partiality of Biblical Justice: A Response to Calvin Beisner', in Herbert Schlossberg, Vinay Samuel, and Ronald J. Sider (eds.), *Christianity and Economics in the Post-Cold War Era* (Grand Rapids, Mich.: Eerdmans, 1994), 81-99.

impoverished warrant the special attention of the Church in order to ensure that the impoverished have access to all that God has for them. Transformationists have affirmed statements like 'God is on the side of the poor' precisely to reflect this understanding, which essentially agrees with the liberationist notion of 'the preferential option for the poor'.[62] Irrespective of phrasing, the truth of God's commitment to the poor stands on solid, biblical ground. Numbers 2 and 6 of Samuel's list of the components of Mission as Transformation reflect this kingdom commitment.

Mission as Journey (with, for and among the Poor)

Mission requires an attitude of humility, openness to change and invitation, an attitude that is more described by the image of journeying with others than of judging others from a higher place.[63] Of the eight components on Samuel's list, this one could have easily stood alone, for it says something about mission itself, that mission reflects an ongoing, mutually transforming experience between fellow human beings who have submitted to the One who alone can and will consummate all things. Mission as journey conveys the human experience of God's mission.

Keeping in mind that Mission as Transformation was originally inspired by theologians and practitioners who served in contexts of poverty, this notion of mission as journey in Transformational thought means journeying with the poor. It points to the fact that the poor transform mission as much as mission transforms the poor. So even though this component of mission as journey can stand alone as a word about the overall missionary enterprise, it becomes specific to the kingdom's commitment to the poor when seen from the perspective of Transformationists. It is more accurate therefore to describe this global dimension of Mission as Transformation, journey with the poor. At least three key ideas flow from this understanding.

Mission as journey with the poor first of all means humility, or what Bosch calls the 'vulnerability of mission'. This vulnerability assumes equality between persons and cultures. Bosch distinguishes between what he calls 'exemplar missionaries' and 'victim missionaries'.[64] Exemplar missionaries

---

[62] Sider, 'An Evangelical Theology of Liberation', 117. See also Gustavo Gutierrez, 'Option for the Poor', in Ignacio Ellacuria and Jon Sobrino (eds.), *Mysterium Liberationis: Fundamental Concepts of Liberation Theology* (Maryknoll, N.Y.; Victoria: Orbis; CollinsDove, 1993), 235-250, in order to see how liberationists themselves explain this idea.

[63] Samuel, 'Mission as Transformation', 229.

[64] David J. Bosch, 'The Vulnerability of Mission', in James A. Scherer and Stephen B. Bevans (eds.), *New Directions in Mission and Evangelization 2* (Maryknoll, N.Y.: Orbis, 1994), 80-83.

engage culture and society as examples of holiness and spirituality. They arrive on the scene as if they have somehow overcome the struggles of the human condition. They come as teachers of the only right way to understand the Gospel. Nathan Price, the fictitious Baptist missionary in Barbara Kingsolver's best-selling novel *The Poisonwood Bible* provides a picture of what humility is not. Unbending, unteachable and missionizing under an aura of self-reliance and superiority, missionary Price bungles the very message of the Gospel by a correctable mispronunciation. Wanting to say in the people's language, 'Jesus is precious', he preaches instead, 'Jesus is poisonwood'. As an exemplar missionary, he not only embarrasses his family, he also alienates the very people he seeks to serve.[65]

By way of contrast, mission as journey with the poor calls for an attitude more akin to 'victims' or servants afflicted by their own weaknesses and vulnerabilities and who seem always to have before them the absolute necessity of the grace of God for their own lives. It calls for meekness strong enough to break the superior/inferior default relationship between the missionary and the indigenous of the missions-colonial era. The missionary victim posture enables the poor and non-poor to walk side by side toward God's intentions.

Related to this humility, mission as journey with the poor also means openness to change. Sugden writes, 'The concept of journey relates well to transformation since it always leaves open the possibility of change.'[66] A study such as this (or any systematic work) poses a danger in that it might convey finality or come across as a definitive, unalterable word on Mission as Transformation. The fact is, Mission as Transformation itself continues to transform. Missiological formulations at best mark specific places on the journey. Referring to the official Wheaton '83 Statement on Transformation for example, Samuel and Sugden write, '[It] is itself not a goal but a landmark.'[67] Twenty years later after the official adoption of the Statement, Samuel states that 'Transformation is always an ongoing journey, always something that assesses more the stages [of the process] rather than the results.'[68]

In Transformational perspective, the journey means learning together and partnering with the poor to bring about lasting change for everyone and everything involved, even mission itself. For Servants missionaries in the Philippines, for example, testimonies of changes in the way in which they understand God's mission as a result of 'incarnating' among the poor include the elements of relinquishing control, depending more on God, formulating a more adequate theology of suffering, and a deep sense of family and

---

[65] Barbara Kingsolver, *The Poisonwood Bible* (New York: HarperCollins, 1998).
[66] Sugden, *Gospel, Culture and Transformation*, 23.
[67] Samuel and Sugden, 'Introduction', *The Church in Response to Human Need*, xi.
[68] Samuel, interview.

community.[69] On the personal level, Fr. Benigno Beltran, a Transformational Catholic priest who has spent over twenty years living and ministering among the twenty five thousand plus residents of Manila's garbage dump community (infamously known as Smokey Mountain) writes, 'I would like to thank [the poor] for making me less the theologian I was and more the human being I dream of becoming.'[70]

Lastly, mission as journey with the poor means invitation. 'Mission is mission on the way', writes Samuel, 'inviting people to take part in a journey.'[71] The journey toward God's intentions constrains travellers to let fellow travelers know of the blessings ahead, for God's intentions of justice, peace, righteousness, love, forgiveness, and joy are meant for all. In light of humility and openness to change, missionaries must also poise themselves to be invited into the journey of others, more specifically into the journey of the poor. And this mutual inviting creates the space for Transformation to occur for all involved in the process. Servants missionary Judy Marsh testifies,

> For the first couple of years living with our neighbours in the slums, they offered us space to be ourselves. We determined not to change them but to offer them space where change could take place. By sharing our lives together, we create space where our neighbours can see what is happening in their journey with God, and how they can have access to God's strength to change. It's in this open, receptive space that change has occurred in my neighbours, and in me too.[72]

Mission as journey means humility, openness to change, and invitation with, for and among the poor. To the extent that the Church understands Mission as Transformation as this kind of journey, it reflects the kingdom's commitment to the poor.

Freedom and power through Personhood

Transformationists understand the Gospel as liberating and empowering people, as restoring identity and dignity to persons, especially the downtrodden and poor. Freedom and power through personhood constitute another vital component of this missiology, a dimension that Transformationists share worldwide. This dimension testifies to the power of the Gospel to release people to their full potential as human beings made in the image of God. All have access to the power of this Gospel to liberate and empower, but the scriptures testify to God's proactive pursuit of the poor to make available to

---

[69] Craig, *Servants Among the Poor*, 171-176.

[70] Benigno Beltran, *Christology of the Inarticulate: An Inquiry into the Filipino Understanding of Jesus Christ* (Manila: Divine Word, 1987), ix.

[71] Samuel, 'Mission as Transformation', 229.

[72] Cited in Craig, *Servants Among the Poor*, 177.

them the freedom and power that the Gospel generates. It is under this component that Samuel speaks positively of the liberationist notion of the 'preferential option for the poor'. He asks rhetorically, 'The Gospel is power and freedom - for whom? Who needs it most, who deserves it most?'[73] The categories of freedom and power serve as mere beginning points to bear witness to the vision of the Gospel to fulfil the full potential of human beings. Sugden finds identity and dignity as useful categories to convey similar, if not the very same, ideas.[74] Myers sees recovering true identity and discovering true vocation as other ways to draw out the same dynamics.[75]

From these various categories, a concept emerges that ties them together, the concept of personhood. Samuel makes the connection between freedom, power and personhood and asserts that the first two categories come into clearer focus as the discussion moves to the third category.[76] The transformation of the human person lies at the heart of Mission as Transformation.[77]

According to Samuel, the idea of personhood needs more attention among missiologists and social activists. He writes,

> Very few people talk about ... character among the poor. We have such romantic ideas about the poor. If you live with them you begin to realize that they know they need character as much as anyone else, especially as their situation has distorted their potential to love, forgive and ability to cope with stress and sacrifice. They need their personhood to be restored.[78]

Samuel then develops ten aspects of personhood. A person first has a body, which is located in a community. In other words, personhood comprises a physical self as it interacts in a community of selves. Second, personhood also has an inner self that has to do with one's own psyche, emotions, and internalizations. Third, personhood comprises a vocational self that defines one's role in family and community. Fourth, personhood expresses itself as a moral self, which defines one's beliefs, convictions, code of conduct, standards and so on. Fifth, personhood has everything to do with integrity, which holds all that a person is in his/her commitment to truth (honesty), faithfulness and excellence. Sixth, the ability to love others, to show compassion and to demonstrate tolerance defines maturing personhood. Seventh, the ability to identify and resist evil also defines maturing personhood. Eighth, personhood has the freedom to develop and grow, to undergo a process of maturity, to be a

---

[73] Samuel, 'Mission as Transformation', 230.

[74] Chris Sugden, 'What is Good about the Good News to the Poor?' in Vinay Samuel and Chris Sugden (eds.), *Mission as Transformation* (Oxford: Regnum, 1999), 238-239.

[75] Myers, *Waking with the Poor*, 115-118.

[76] Samuel, interview.

[77] Sugden, 'Transformational Development', 72-73.

[78] Samuel, 'Mission as Transformation', 244-245.

self in development. To stifle this aspect diminishes one's personhood. Ninth, personhood expresses itself in a responsible self, which enables one to determine his/her own life course, to manage and to choose. And tenth, which Samuel emphasizes, personhood reaches its pinnacle when the praying and worshipping self emerges.[79] Insofar as mission strives to build up these aspects of personhood, according to Samuel, true transformation occurs. While the poor develop as whole persons in Christ, taking on a new identity as well as a greater sense of dignity, they are set free to develop and flourish and they are empowered to pursue the peace, justice, love and joy of the kingdom of God and to serve others in Christ's name.

We have attempted here to gain a better understanding of the eight components of Mission as Transformation put forth by Samuel, as we have organized them under the three kingdom themes of integration, incarnation, and commitment to the poor. They constitute the *telos*, the way in which Transformationists understand the Church's missionary engagement with the world in 'the last days' as it awaits 'the last things'.

These components in unity make up the global dimensions of Mission as Transformation, that is, they make up the shared values of Transformationists worldwide as they are informed by an intercontextual evangelical understanding of the biblical reality of kingdom of God. As this chapter has reorganized, developed and identified these components as this missiology's global dimensions, the list now looks like this:

1. word, work and wonder
2. reconciliation, solidarity and stewardship
3. communities of integration
4. mission in context
5. full contextual engagement
6. local theology
7. mission as journey with the poor
8. freedom, power through personhood.

While these eight global dimensions constitute a holistic missiology that has emerged among radical evangelicals, they remain true to the theme of mission as journey in that they do not claim finality or comprehensiveness. They represent instead a missiology in progress. As such, large issues remain that need further and deeper reflection, such as religious pluralism and interfaith dialogue, religious persecution, mission spirituality and so on. These issues do not easily fit into any of the eight global dimensions, and yet articles pertaining to them in the journal *Transformation* attest to the fact that Transformationists

---

[79] Samuel, 'Mission as Transformation', 245-246. I have again taken the liberty to reword these aspects for the sake of consistency and clarity.

have not ignored them.[80] Indeed the journey of mission certainly continues as Transformationists seek to grow in their response to relevant issues such as these in an ever changing world.

Gaining a global perspective of Mission as Transformation only goes so far in understanding this missiology. Its very nature necessitates a local perspective, which defines the task of Part III.

---

[80] For example, with regard to doing mission in the context of religious pluralism, INFEMIT's first consultation on Christology in 1982 tackled this issue head-on. See Samuel and Sugden, *Sharing Jesus in the Two Thirds World*, wherein many articles deal with other religions and their implications for Christian mission. For more recent Transformational reflections on religious pluralism, see *Transformation* 20.4 (October 2003), which has as its theme, 'Hinduism, Islam and Mission Challenges Today'.

With regard to mission spirituality, see Susan S. Phillips, 'Garden or Circus: Christian Care in the Face of Contemporary Pressures', *Transformation* 22.3 (July 2005), 158-165, which was a paper presented at OCMS on 14 September 2004. It challenges life and mission conducted like a circus (juggling many activities, walking a tightrope, balancing all of life's demands, etc.) and invites Christians to go the Garden of Gethsemane where Jesus taught his disciples to stay alert, be watchful, and to pray.

PART III

Local Filipino Dimensions

Introduction to Part III

The inherently contextual nature of Mission as Transformation requires a local rendering if we are going to understand this missiology at all. We cannot ultimately succumb to the temptation to restrict our study to the global 'grand narrative' of Mission as Transformation; for it is on the local level that this missiology grows and flourishes.

Schreiter defines a local theology as the dialectic, dynamic interaction of the three principal roots of Gospel, church, and culture.[1] As such, 'local theology' can simply join a list of synonyms that conveys the indispensability of the value of context for theology. Schreiter himself in fact describes 'local theology' as his term of choice over 'contextual theology', 'inculturation', and other terms, but ultimately they all point to the same phenomenon.[2] Eduardo Fernandez concurs; after discussing several theologians' terms of choice with reference to Schreiter, he writes, 'Whether we use the term "inculturation", "local theology" or "contextual theology", what is being implied is a dynamic interaction between Gospel, church, and culture.'[3]

By mild contrast, I prefer to describe the relationship between contextualization and local theology as causal; the former leads to the latter, while affirming their inseparability. An authentic contextualization of the Gospel leads to a truly local church doing theology, worship, and mission according to its local culture. The term 'local theology', therefore, specifically refers to what results from the process of authentic contextualization. Part III attempts to gain an understanding of how a particular brand of missiology that has been articulated globally as Mission as Transformation has emerged specifically in a local context.

The colonial experience and the predominantly Christian population of the country have made the Philippines a prime context in which to study the local dimensions of Mission as Transformation. Moreover, my own missionary experience in the Philippines has inspired this study in the first place and

---

[1] Schreiter, *Constructing Local Theologies*, 21.
[2] Schreiter, *Constructing Local Theologies,* 5-6.
[3] E. C. Fernandez, *La Cosecha*, 111.

therefore serves as the most logical context on which to focus. In Chapter 7, we will explore Filipino Mission as Transformation first, in global theological context, i.e., how the local Filipino expression and the global dimensions relate to each other, and second, in local historical context, i.e., how it emerged out of the historical events of the times, particularly the events surrounding the People Power Revolution of 1986.

Chapter 8 then goes deeper into the local Filipino dimensions of Mission as Transformation, as it seeks to gain an understanding of this missiology in the context of the nation's larger historical struggle for freedom. For Filipino Mission as Transformation did not occur in a vacuum; indeed it has developed consistently along recognizable historical and theological lines in the Philippines. The works of Melba Maggay, Evelyn Miranda-Feliciano, David Lim and others associated with the Institute for Studies in Asian Church and Culture (ISACC) figure prominently here.[4]

Unlike with the global dimensions, where Samuel's eight components of Mission as Transformation served as that discussion's starting point, the discussion concerning local Filipino dimensions has no such preliminary list. As we peer inductively therefore through the lens of Filipino history, we seek in Part III to discover the local Filipino dimensions of Mission as Transformation from scratch.

---

[4] Drawing extensively upon those associated with ISACC reflects my understanding of ISACC as leading the way of holistic mission for the Filipino evangelical church. Drawing extensively upon those associated with ISACC reflects my understanding of ISACC as leading the way of holistic mission for the Filipino evangelical church. It does not, however, intend to devalue of the contributions of others.

CHAPTER 7

Filipino Mission as Transformation in Global and Historical Context

Global Theological Links

To gain a better understanding of the relationship between global and local realities gets at the heart of this book. Therefore, as our focus now shifts to how Mission as Transformation emerged locally in the Philippines, we must first ask, how does the Filipino expression of Mission as Transformation relate to its global expression? How do we even know that we are talking about the same thing? The answer lies in theology, which reveals the same missiological DNA in both local Filipino and global manifestations. Filipino Mission as Transformation shares the basic kingdom themes of integration, incarnation, and commitment to the poor, which serve as the global framework for Mission as Transformation. Before exploring the innards of Filipino Mission as Transformation then, we need first to understand its connection to the global reality of this missiology.

Kingdom Integration

Transformational kingdom integration unifies missionary practice (in word, work and wonder), engages society in mission in light of the reconciliation of all things in Christ (reconciliation, solidarity and stewardship), and works for transformation in all realms of life in light of God's future (communities of change). The rediscovery of the biblical reality of the kingdom of God has compelled Transformationists to think integrally in these ways against a largely Enlightenment ridden, dichotomous worldview. The very need to put Church mission back together speaks primarily to the realization on the part of Western missiologists of the wholeness that characterizes God, humanity, church mission, and the world.

Such integral thinking has generally enjoyed a home among Two Thirds World peoples. In fact, Western theologians have rediscovered the notion of kingdom integration due largely to challenges that have come from the Two

Thirds World.[1] Nevertheless, it also rings true that many Two Thirds World churches have fallen captive to the dominant Western theological orientation of colonial missions, thus defining their self-identity in foreign terms.[2] So what has served as a rediscovery of wholeness for Western churches has served as a reawakening for Two Thirds World churches to the affirmative values of their own cultures to inform their own theologizing.

For example, Maggay states that 'Filipinos make no sharp distinctions between the natural and the supernatural, the sacred and the secular, public and private realms.'[3] This holds true in most if not all Two Thirds World cultures; their respective worldviews naturally tend toward an integrated perspective of life. Therefore insofar as Filipino theology reflects a Filipino worldview more than the worldview of Western culture (brought in by foreign missionaries), it tends to interpret reality in a more integrated way in contrast to a more Enlightenment, either/or, *dis*-integrated way. Despite being quite aware of the North American born fundamentalist-modernist debate that raged in mission circles, Filipino Transformationists have not allowed the debate's residual wedging effect to dictate the way in which they have engaged society in mission.

Early on amidst a sea of evangelical suspicion, Maggay defined ISACC, the institutional vanguard of Filipino Mission as Transformation, as

a fellowship of evangelical believers who seek to see the Kingdom revealed in its many aspects. We earnestly pray, as Jesus taught us, that the Kingdom would come, that its presence be felt ever more strongly in the church, the arts, the academic community, the media, and in the conduct of our political and social institutions.[4]

Fifteen years later, this holistic vision showed no signs of waning as she wrote, 'It is the church in academia, the church in politics, the church in the marketplace. ... Witness to the kingdom requires more than preachers; it demands the whole body of Christ to be visibly present in all areas of human

---

[1] Padilla, 'Evangelism and Social Responsibility', 27-33.
[2] See, for example, Bediako's *Theology and Identity,* 234-252, where the author documents the adverse effects of the European missionary enterprise on the African Church's search for self-identity. He writes, 'It is unfortunate that the quest for an African Christian identity in terms which are meaningful for African integrity and also adequate for Christian confession, should become so pervasively bedeviled by the missionary enterprise that was instrumental in bringing African Christianity into being'... (252).
[3] Maggay, *Filipino Religious Consciousness,* 29.
[4] Melba Maggay, 'Notes from the Editor: Tidings from the Fisher-King', *Patmos* 1.1 (1st Quarter 1979), 24.

life.'[5] In the hands of the likes of Maggay, Lim and others, natural Filipino tendencies toward integration and the courage to challenge Western, either/or, missionary thinking have resulted in a holistic, integrative theology of mission in the Philippines that corresponds with the global Transformational notion of kingdom integration.

Kingdom Incarnation

The Transformational notion of kingdom integration unifies humanity and the world, but not at the expense of human diversity. It calls the Church to do mission on all levels (holistically), but not at the expense of either cultural sensitivity (mission in context) or deep cultural involvement (full contextual engagement). In fact, holistic mission and contextualization go hand in hand in Transformational thinking. 'Holism', writes Evelyn Miranda-Feliciano, 'puts the living Christ in the midst of wiping noses and swabbing wounds; amidst miracles of healing and tooting of tricycles'[6] The theme of integration, where the unity of all things informs mission, has an inseparable complement in Transformational kingdom thought, namely, the incarnation, which leads to missionary engagement that takes cultural distinctions and deep relationships seriously and that has as its goal the development of localized faith. In the Transformational kingdom vision, the integration of all things in Christ does not oppose cultural distinction, and cultural distinction does not oppose integration.[7]

Filipino Transformationists have stood upon the theological truth of the incarnation of God in Christ in order to stress the importance of contextualization, missional immersion, and the Filipinization (or localization) of the faith. ISACC's self-descriptive mission statement includes,

> Jesus in saving us became a human being just like us. He identified with a particular culture at a particular time; He was a Jew. In the same way, we believe that the gospel must be in context, immersed in the culture and story of a people. We seek to speak sensitively, according to a people's ways of thinking and feeling, and in a way that truly brings good news to the places where they fear and hurt.[8]

With this kind of commitment to incarnation, Filipino Transformationists have modeled the discerning of God's will from a Filipino perspective. Articles

---

[5] Maggay, *Transforming Society*, 21-22.

[6] Evelyn Miranda-Feliciano, 'Pagbubukid at Pangitan: Finding the Roots of Development', in ISACC (ed.), *Hasik-Unlad: An Experience in Community Development Training* (Quezon City: ISACC, 1998), 323.

[7] Maggay, *Jew to the Jew, Greek to the Greek*, 55-56.

[8] 'Who We Are?' See 'Appendix Three' of this book.

in ISACC's regular periodical *Patmos,* like 'The Gospel in Our Context' and 'The Text in Context' and regular columns like the 'Word for the World Today', demonstrate for its readers a way to understand biblical truth with Filipino eyes and to appropriate them relevantly for Filipino life. These types of articles also demonstrate an explicit affirmation of Filipino culture long repressed by centuries of colonial rule, as they interweave biblical faith and Filipino lifeways positively.

In affirming Filipino culture, however, Transformationists keenly avoid a 'contextualism' that undermines the power of the Gospel to transform culture. Miranda-Feliciano's *Pinoy Nga, Biblikal Ba?* for example, attempts to take an honest look through a scriptural lens at some cherished values and practices of Filipinos and challenges them in light of the culture of the kingdom of God. [9] This simultaneous affirmation of, and challenge to, Filipino culture come from the biblical reality of the incarnation of God in Christ when Jesus became a Jew in order to call not only Israel but the whole world to transformation. 'The vigor and the wonder of the Incarnation', according to Maggay, 'have yet to excite the Filipino imagination,'[10] implying that if it ever does, Filipinos would see God *among* and *for* them, affirming who they are as well as challenging them to become what God desires them to be. This kind of application of the incarnation links Filipino Transformationists with the worldwide Transformational fellowship whose self-definition includes the incarnate Son Jesus Christ, the very embodiment of God and God's kingdom.

Kingdom Commitment to the Poor

Kingdom commitment to the poor, the third basic theme that has united Transformationists around the world, has compelled these radical missionary theologians and practitioners to journey, or to be in solidarity, with the marginalized, the powerless, the voiceless, the oppressed, the hopeless and the lost, struggling with them for the sake of their personhood in Christ.

This Transformational kingdom theme basically echoes the liberationist language of God's 'preferential option for the poor', affirming that God pays special attention to the poor in line with the compassionate sheep farmer who leaves the safe ninety-nine in search of the one which was lost (Lk. 15:3-7). Jesus told this parable to members of an elite religious community who would have identified themselves with the safe ninety-nine. But in the Two Thirds World, the inverse would prove truer: leaving the one safe sheep (the few

---

[9] Evelyn Miranda Feliciano, *Pinoy Ba, Biblical Ba?* (Mandaluyong City: OMF, 1995). A literal translation of the title would read, *It's Filipino, but is it Biblical?* But the English title of the same volume is entitled *Filipino Values and Our Christian Faith* (Mandaluyong City: OMF, 1990).

[10] Melba Maggay, *The Gospel in Filipino Context* (Mandaluyong: OMF, 1987), 9.

privileged elite) in order to find the lost and needy ninety-nine (the masses of the poor) would better describe faithful mission in the Two Thirds World.

For Transformationists in the Philippines, where poverty abounds, the kingdom's commitment to the poor compels the Church to engage in ministries among, with and for them. Maggay couches this call rather softly at first and ponders, 'In the Philippines ... it does not seem possible to speak without hearing the cry that rises from the poor' and then declares it more forcefully as she interacts with the story of Lazarus and the rich man in Luke 16. She warns, 'We are not allowed to find rest until the sight of Lazarus at the gate ceases to be ever before us.'[11]

The Centre for Community Transformation (CCT), which began in 1992, exemplifies a biblically inspired and practically driven organization among Filipino Transformationists. Co-founded by development guru Ruth Callanta,[12] CCT provides practical assistance to the poor primarily through a micro-enterprise development strategy that creates 'fellowships of entrepreneurs'. These fellowships provide venues for aspiring entrepreneurs among the poor (mostly women) to keep members accountable to one another and to encourage them to practice biblical values. Lim, a co-founder of CCT, has served as its resident theologian and has provided biblical tenets for working among the poor.[13]

The fact that the poor have faces and names, that they are made in the image of God in which they attain personhood and dignity, stands out in Filipino Transformational literature. Poverty is not first and foremost an issue to debate but a situation that involves real human suffering. Herman Moldez, General Secretary of Inter-Varsity Christian Fellowship in the Philippines (IVCF-Phil), drives home this point by defining poverty as, 'the poor living in slums, children begging and risking their lives in the streets ... while selling food and flowers just to survive, [and] the exploited and oppressed tribal minorities who are helpless to defend themselves. They are those who remain ignorant and illiterate, who live by scavenging, and who die of hunger.'[14] The poor have faces and names in the sight of the God of salvation and justice. Filipino Transformationists do not forget this truth as they continue to live out locally

---

[11] Maggay, *Transforming Society,* 12.

[12] See Ruth Callanta, *Poverty: The Philippine Scenario* (Manila: Bookmark, 1988), a widely used volume in both Christian and secular organizations seeking to be of practical assistance to the poor.

[13] David S. Lim, *Transforming Communities* (Mandaluyong: OMF, 1992), 7. In this short volume, Lim discusses eight biblical tenets to establish the Church's mission to the poor. He discusses humanity as: 1) created by God, 2) created with dignity, 3) created with a body, 4) created with a habitat, 5) created with a duty, 6) created with a community, 7) marred by the Fall, and 8) redeemed in hope.

[14] Herman A. Moldez, 'Taking Sides with the Poor: Biblical Basis and Demands', *Patmos* 7.2 (2ⁿᵈ Quarter 1991), 9.

and on the ground the global/universal Transformational understanding of the kingdom's commitment to the poor.

Filipino Mission as Transformation in Local Historical Context

The kingdom themes of integration, incarnation and commitment to the poor link the local and global dimensions of Mission as Transformation. With this established, we are ready to gain a local perspective of Mission as Transformation, i.e., to understand it in local Filipino historical context. Of the need for Filipino Christians to theologize contextually, church historians De la Costa and Schumacher write, 'Local churches ... must reflect not only on the historical perspective of the *universal* Church, but *on that of their own people. Only in this way will they be able to evolve a truly indigenous theology which can provide principles of action [for] Filipino Christians today.*'[15] How did Mission as Transformation emerge out of Filipino soil?

Beginnings: From IVCF-Phil to ISACC

The roots of Transformational thinking in the Philippines go back to individuals associated with the IVCF at the University of the Philippines. According to Maggay, in the late 1960s and early '70s, IVCF-Phil provided many students the opportunity to come to personal faith in Christ (which she herself did at that time) and to experience community with like minded Christians in an intellectually free, socially aware environment.[16] Its clear and distinctly Christian perspective served as a viable, faith based activism that better appealed to the religious sensibilities of Filipinos. As such, IVCF-Phil served as an alternative to radical Marxism on campus for many Christians.[17] Under the leadership of Maggay and others, IVCF-Phil conducted regular, contextually relevant Bible studies, and it circulated a university paper called *Silahis* that developed a considerable readership on campus between 1969 and 1972.[18] These regular outputs sought to appropriate the scriptures for both personal and social transformation among the university population, thus serving as a conduit through which evangelical Christians addressed the burning social issues of the day from the perspective of personal faith.

---

[15] Horacio de la Costa and John N. Schumacher, 'Preface', in Horacio de la Costa and John N. Schumacher (eds.), *Church and State: The Philippine Experience* (Quezon City: Loyola School of Theology, 1976), iii-iv. Italics are mine.

[16] Melba Maggay, interview by author, 19 June 2004, Techny, IL, tape recording, Divine Word International.

[17] Maggay, interview.

[18] Maggay, interview.

Against the pressure to dichotomize individual salvation and social relevance, many evangelical student movements throughout the world continued to cultivate a holism that helped shape Mission as Transformation.[19] These student movements defied the widespread stereotype among non-evangelicals that all evangelicals ignore social issues.[20] In the Philippines, IVCF represented such a movement, and Maggay served as a principle player to advance this type of holism. As a result, many young Filipino evangelicals began to define their Christian faith in this integrated holistic way.

The passion from this campus movement guaranteed a life after the university for many of them. That life took on institutional shape in 1978 in the form of the Institute for Studies in Asian Church and Culture or ISACC. As Wheaton '83 announced the official birth of a global notion of Mission as Transformation, the formation of ISACC in 1978 announced the official birth of an earlier local Filipino version of it.[21] The magazine *Patmos*, whose maiden issue came out in early 1979, succeeded *Silahis*, and the wider evangelical community began to get wind of this brand of holistic Christian mission. Maggay, Lim, Magalit and others - including Americans Mac Bradshaw and Bill Dyrness formed the Institute, and together they spearheaded Transformational praxis in the Philippines.[22]

Undoubtedly, ISACC's courageous leadership in mobilizing evangelicals to take part in the People Power Revolution of 1986 played a key role in establishing Filipino Mission as Transformation. To the role of radical evangelicals in the Revolution, which demonstrated Mission as Transformation at its contextual finest, we now turn.

---

[19] This kind of integration was occurring throughout many different campuses around the world among evangelical university students, many of which were affiliated with the International Fellowship of Evangelical Students (IFES). To learn more about the history and ethos of IFES, see www.ifesworld.org. Familiar names of Transformationists, like Samuel Escobar, David Lim, Miroslav Volf, David Gitari, and others have appeared in IFES literature, particularly in the organization's journal *Themelios*, and they have been involved in different IFES functions.

[20] Because the IVCF is evangelical, many have lumped it along with the rest of the evangelical stereotype of social non-involvement. But in reality, IVCF has always had as part of its objective to speak relevantly and effectively to current issues. See, for example IVCF-USA, 'Core Commitments', www.intervarsity.org/aboutus/commitments.php (accessed 27 September 2004), where it states as one of its core values, 'We pursue ethnic reconciliation by practicing mutual empowerment, grace and truth and by promoting personal and systemic justice'.

[21] Note that the local Filipino version was born five years before its global birth. The global has no existence without the local; I elaborate on this idea in Chapter 9.

[22] Mac Bradshaw was also one of the founding members of INFEMIT.

Filipino People Power[23]

Few would argue that the defining seed of the 1986 Revolution germinated in a prison cell where Senator Ninoy Aquino Jr. spent seven and a half years. Imprisoned for allegedly sympathizing with Communists and then later charged with subversion, murder and illegal possession of weapons, Aquino became for Filipinos the political symbol of suffering during the Martial Law years. Before the declaration of Martial Law, Aquino did in fact voice strong, relentless opposition to Marcos' policies as the country went from bad to worse. Inflation rose to unprecedented heights, corruption in government reached new levels, and poverty abounded while Marcos and his cronies amassed untold wealth.

In this context, Aquino dared to dissent. But as a result, he eventually took on the dubious honour as Marcos Enemy Number One, while at the same time becoming the convenient political figure with whom the disgruntled masses identified. Consequently, the day after Marcos declared Martial Law on September 22, 1972, Aquino was arrested along with other political dissidents. 'The major charges against me', Aquino later wrote from prison, 'turn on alleged violations of Republic Act No. 1700, the Anti-Subversion Law. There are four separate charges; a total of nine specifications. In the face of all these charges I say: I am not guilty!'[24]

Aquino remained in prison until 1980 when Marcos finally allowed him to go to the United States to receive heart surgery. Marcos' primary motive, according to journalist Stanley Karnow, smelled every bit the political manoeuvre that it was; allowing Aquino to receive the best medical treatment in the US would 'get rid of him while appearing altruistic'.[25] The Aquinos stayed in America, settling in Newton, MA for what Mrs. Aquino called 'the three happiest years of [their] life'.[26] Senator Aquino's conscience, however, continued to haunt him concerning the state of affairs in his homeland. He once again resumed his open criticism of Marcos in the American media and eventually 'evoked General MacArthur's famous World War Two dictum, "I

---

[23] 2001 witnessed two People Power uprisings - People Power II (January 16-20) and People Power III (April 25-May 1) - related to the impeachment of then President Joseph Estrada. In both instances, evangelicals were highly visible and relatively influential given their minority status in the country. For detailed accounts of evangelical involvement in these people power movements, see David S. Lim, 'Consolidating Democracy: Filipino Evangelicals in Between People Power Events, 1986-2001, 2002', Unpublished paper sent by Lim to author, 2003.

[24] Benigno S. 'Ninoy' Aquino Jr., *Testament from a Prison Cell* (Los Angeles, Calif.: Philippine Journal, Inc., 1988), 111.

[25] Stanley Karnow, *In Our Image: America's Empire in the Philippines* (New York: Ballantine, 1989), 400.

[26] Cited in Karnow, *In Our Image,* 400.

shall return"'.[27] Attempting to make good on his promise, Aquino left for the Philippines. But upon stepping off the plane at the Manila International Airport on August 21, 1983, he was shot dead.[28]

The assassination, as well as the bogus trial that found the Marcos government innocent of it, provided the final straw for the Filipino people. Less than three years after the assassination, the collective indignation of the people turned into an unstoppable force that simultaneously toppled the twenty year rule of President Ferdinand Marcos and catapulted Mrs. Corazon 'Cory' Aquino, the martyred Senator's quiet housewife, turned empowered widow, to the presidency. The collective force of the people first compelled Marcos to call a snap election in November 1985. Pressured by the increasing unrest of the people, Marcos wanted desperately to demonstrate, especially to then US President Ronald Reagan who saw the tide turning and began encouraging Marcos to step down peacefully, that he still had the peoples' support. When he realized his error in judgment during the actual election in early February, overt undermining of the democratic process began to occur in the poll stations, 'almost all of it [being conducted] by Marcos' thugs'.[29] When the snap election declared Marcos the winner, the people's outrage came to boiling point. Aquino denounced the election results as fraudulent, which everyone basically knew already, and called the people to boycott crony-run establishments, withhold paying taxes, and engage in other forms of civil disobedience.

But that call became moot when then National Defense Minister Juan Ponce Enrile and then Armed Forces Chief of Staff (and future President) Fidel Ramos defected in final protest of Marcos injustice. As Marcos moved in to quell the rebellion, the masses - women and men, young and old, rich and poor, urban and rural, clergy and lay, Catholic, Protestant and Muslim - rallied to the streets in their support. Realizing that he had truly lost the support of the people (not to mention the support of US political allies), Marcos, his family, and sixty of his loyal followers fled to Hawaii to take the United States' offer of political asylum. The swearing in of Cory Aquino, as the Republic's new President on February 25, 1986 euphorically marked the victory of the People Power Revolution.

Evangelical Participation and Emerging Mission as Transformation

Catholics and ecumenical Protestants certainly contributed to the ferment of revolution before and during the actual events, as we shall see in more detail in the next chapter. But what contribution, if any, did evangelical Protestants

[27] Karnow, *In Our Image,* 400.
[28] As President, Cory Aquino re-named the airport the Ninoy Aquino International Airport in honor of her martyred husband.
[29] Karnow, *In Our Image,* 413-414.

make during this time? True to its reputation, the institutional Filipino evangelical community, as represented by the Philippine Council of Evangelical Churches, did not at first take sides for or against Marcos. Interpreting in a literal way the Romans 13 injunction to submit to the governing authorities, the PCEC issued a 'Call to Sobriety' as the country waited for the results of the snap election. The Call urged 'people to uphold the soon to be announced election results', meaning that the PCEC encouraged its constituents to take a wait-and-see posture and to pledge their support to the winner of the snap election.[30]

Something happened, however, between February 14th, the day PCEC issued the Call, and the actual events of February 22-25: evangelicals declared war on Marcos with their feet and their actions. Shining examples of evangelical involvement (seemingly in defiance of the Call) certainly include the Far East Broadcasting Company (FEBC), an evangelical run radio station, airing the events, along with discussions regarding civil disobedience led by the director of the station Fred Magbanua. The FEBC in fact played a vital role in keeping the people informed when the government blocked the airwaves at Catholic run Radio Veritas. Other examples include prominent leaders like Jun Vencer, then General Secretary of PCEC, and Eddie Villanueva, then an anchorman for FEBC and who of course eventually became the voice of the growing Pentecostal/Charismatic community, encouraging their constituents to join in the action. Vencer, in fact, utilized his authority as PCEC General Secretary and had 'tents, food, and medicines sent to the evangelical groups manning the barricades at EDSA'.[31]

On February 24th, just ten days after issuing the Call to Sobriety, the PCEC announced a different statement that still displayed hesitancy but nevertheless clear movement on the part of its leaders. It said in part, 'After much prayer, we have arrived at the moral conclusion that the legitimacy of the present administration should be questioned.'[32] Then three days later in the aftermath of the Revolution, it issued yet another statement that credited God in ordering the events 'in such a way that Mrs. Aquino and Mr. Laurel were placed at the actual helm of government'.[33]

While the official voice of mainstream evangelicalism waffled, however, a significant minority did not. Leading the way in basically ignoring the Call to Sobriety and going boldly to the streets was a minority evangelical constituency, among them Magalit then pastor of Diliman Bible Church, Maggay founder of ISACC, and others, who organized the *Konsensiya ng Febrero Siete* (KONFES, the Conscience of February 7th, referring to the

---

[30] Lim, 'Consolidating', section 3.3.1.

[31] Lim, 'Consolidating', section 3.3.1.

[32] Lim, 'Consolidating', section 3.3.1.

[33] Lim, 'Consolidating', section 3.3.1.

fraudulent snap election). Under the KONFES banner, evangelicals associated with ISACC, IVCF-Phil, Diliman Bible Church, and a few other churches issued an alternate call via Radio Veritas and FEBC's DZAS, a call to join the barricades particularly at Gate Two of Camp Aguinaldo at EDSA. Maggay reminisces that those who responded to KONFES' alternate call exceeded her expectations not just in quantity, but also in the quality of the turnout:

> Churches from faraway places came, whole busloads from Bulacan, Batangas, Tagaytay, and other nearby provinces. We had always thought that we had a following among more thoughtful and sophisticated churches, those with fairly large contingents of professionals who, like us, trace their roots to Inter-Varsity. Quite predictably, they all came. But it was a surprise to me to see so many other grassroots churches, simple folk who had come because they heard a call within them and knew it was right to come and be counted.[34]

Evangelicals joined the Filipino masses, which cried, '*Sobra na, tama na*', a street motto among the people that translates in English as, 'That's it! Enough!' A strong sense of spiritual, peaceful and purposeful solidarity propelled them to the streets. Magalit recalls,

> We had no intentions of toppling the Marcos government by force of arms. We did join to express our protest in the conduct and counting of the February 7th election, but we went mainly to add to the civilian buffer so that a shooting war could be averted or postponed. We knew that our lives were at risk. We also believed in the safety of numbers but our faith was in God. We were unarmed except for our Bibles and our hymnbooks![35]

When Marcos fled and government officials inaugurated Cory Aquino as the new President of the Republic, evangelicals rejoiced with the masses, praising God for his intervention in the life of the nation.

The first People Power Revolution opened the eyes of Filipino evangelicals wider than ever to view socio-political involvement as part of the mission of the Church. Lim's treatment of evangelical participation in People Power identifies how evangelicals on the whole have increased their social awareness, their sense of responsibility, and their concrete political action since 1986 in three areas: 1) electoral processes that include religious endorsement, electoral education and partisan involvement; 2) people power uprisings (Lim traces the increase of evangelical participation from its relative tentativeness during the first People Power in 1986 to its high visibility during the second one in 2001 to oust the corrupt President Joseph Estrada); and 3) civil society, which comprised non-governmental and non-business organizations that exist for

---

[34] Maggay, *Transforming Society*, 90-91.
[35] Isabelo 'Bel' Magalit, 'Church and State Today', *Phronesis* 7.2 (2000), 57-58.

specific causes like poverty alleviation, political advocacy, AIDS crisis and so on.[36] Evangelical involvement in civil society has increased exponentially since 1986. The fact that Lim begins with 1986 for his study of evangelical participation in Philippine political life tells of the watershed nature of the first People Power Revolution.

It turns out that those in the minor evangelical constituency that had led the way for evangelical participation in People Power I had been assertive several years before in its criticism of the Marcos presidency, publishing for example the 'Novaliches Letter' in June 1981 that critiqued governmental negligence, as well as publishing a public letter condemning the assassination of Senator Aquino in 1983. The leaders of this constituency were ready to lead the rest of the evangelical community in the Revolution because they already laid the groundwork for biblically sound and Gospel inspired socio political involvement. These leaders make up the key proponents of Mission as Transformation in the Philippines.

Transformationists in the Filipino Evangelical Community

ISACC, the visible representative of radical evangelical mission in the Philippines, had to endure years of heavy criticism from the evangelical mainstream. In a personal newsletter, Maggay penned that in the beginning years 'the evangelical establishment treated us like the plague' and it did so because of ISACC's 'advocacy of contextual theology and social responsibility.'[37] But nineteen years after ISACC's founding and subsequent accomplishments, the PCEC, which represents mainstream evangelicalism in the Philippines, presented ISACC the distinguished Evangelical Today Award in 1997 for its excellence in demonstrating the Gospel's relevance to Filipino society. Undoubtedly, ISACC's catalytic role in mobilizing evangelicals in People Power I helped to gain the eventual respect of the Filipino evangelical community.

What ISACC pioneered thirty years ago has resulted in many different streams of Transformational activity throughout the country. Indeed the number of evangelical development organizations and social action alliances has increased dramatically. 'I notice in the past 10 years', wrote Maggay in 1995, 'Christian development organizations have mushroomed.'[38] A short list of these organizations, members of the *SANGKOP* Alliance of Christian Development Agencies network (ACDA), would include Mission Ministries Philippines (MMP), Centre for Community Transformation (CCT), *Tulay sa Pag-Unlad*

---

[36] Lim, 'Consolidating Democracy', sections 2-4.

[37] Melba Maggay, Personal Newsletter (January 1996), 1-8 and 'Notes on This Issue', *Patmos* 11.2 (2nd Quarter 1995), 2.

[38] Maggay, 'Notes on this Issue', 2.

(Bridge of Progress), *Botica Binhi* (Peoples' Pharmacy), the National Coalition of Urban Transformation (NCUT), the Fellowship of Christians in Government (FOCIG), and many others.

This proliferation of evangelical development ministries, however, needs qualification, for not all socially active evangelical groups in the Philippines are Transformational, at least not in the narrow sense. For example, many of the Charismatic churches that have embraced political activism, including the ones that catapulted Charismatic leader Eddie Villanueva to run for the presidency in 2004, would not register on the Transformational radar. Indeed the diversity that has come to characterize evangelical social philosophy elsewhere in the world has also developed along similar lines in the Philippines.

Lim identifies three types of socially involved Filipino evangelicals. He begins with Transformationists, among which he properly places ISACC, followed by Conservatives represented by the relief and development arm of PCEC as a second type, and Charismatics represented by the growing number of Pentecostal/Charismatic churches associated with the Philippines for Jesus Movement (PJM) as a third type.[39]

Of these three types, Transformationists make up the smallest constituency, due most probably to four distinctives they possess that have not boded well for the Filipino evangelical populace: 1) an equal embrace of social concern and evangelism whereas most evangelicals would see evangelism as the higher priority; 2) a suspicion of foreign influence (more on this later under the discussion of the critical consciousness of Filipino Transformationists); 3) an ecumenism that enables them to hold hands with mainline Protestants and Roman Catholics for the sake of transformation (more on this later under the discussion of the Transformationists' understanding of the whole church in all of its denominational forms); and 4) a leaning toward a more radical politics.

So where are Transformationists located socially within the Filipino evangelical community?[40] They make up a small minority that has had a disproportionately large influence on Filipino evangelicalism as well as on the greater Filipino society. They catalyzed the burgeoning social concern movement among evangelicals, but they themselves have remained small in number. If theorists regard 'transformation' as simply a synonym for social action in general, then it is entirely plausible to see it differently; that is, to see Filipino Mission as Transformation as a much larger loosely knit movement of socially active evangelicals. But in a narrower historical sense, Filipino Transformationists remain small in number, but continue to exert remarkable influence from the margins.

---

[39] Lim, 'Consolidating Democracy', section 1.4.

[40] According to Lim, the number of evangelicals in the Philippines as of 2000 is five million strong or approximately seven percent of the entire population.

Other local versions of Mission as Transformation around the world can attest to this same kind of 'influence from the margins' phenomenon, like the ministry of ESA, ISACC's Transformational mirror in the USA. In a personal interview at the ESA Thirtieth Anniversary Celebration in 2003, Tom Sine bemoaned the still relatively unknown status of ESA among mainstream American evangelicals as he pointed out the meager few hundred in attendance.[41] And yet, its influence upon the American Evangelical Church, especially in the person of Ron Sider and his best-selling book *Rich Christians in an Age of Hunger*, cannot be denied.[42] John Dilulio Jr., University of Pennsylvania political scientist and former head of the White House Office of Faith-based and Community Initiatives, recently praised Sider's success in awaking the Church to its social responsibility and referred to him as the 'pope of evangelical social activism'.[43] This disproportionate influence (relative to its size) describes the Transformational voice in many parts of the world including the Philippines, embodied there in institutions like ISACC and individuals like Maggay, Lim, De Boer, and Miranda-Feliciano.

With the global connections of Filipino Mission as Transformation established, its historical background reviewed, and its social location grounded, we can now move on to understand the specific dimensions of Mission as Transformation's local Filipino version.

---

[41] Sine, interview.

[42] Sider's *Rich Christians,* now in its fifth edition at the time of this writing, was ranked seventh on *Christianity Today's* Top 50 Most Influential Evangelical Books in the 20th Century. Go to http://www.christianitytoday.com/ct/2006/october/23.51.html (accessed 23 August 2007).

[43] John Dilulio, Jr., Speech, 24 July 2003, St. Davids, Pa., Evangelicals for Social Action 30th Anniversary Celebration, Eastern University.

CHAPTER 8

Kingdom Mission beyond Colonialism

Unlike our discussion of the global dimensions of Mission as Transformation, where Samuel's list of the eight components served as a starting point, our discussion of its Filipino version has no such preliminary list. What source then can we consult to find the local dimensions of Filipino Mission as Transformation? If we want to understand its *local* Filipino dimensions, then it stands to reason that we must peer through the lens of local Filipino church history. How has the Church acted throughout the centuries in the Philippines? More specifically, how has it responded to the socio-ethical challenges of life under colonial rule? I contend that Filipino Transformationists acted in synch with the historical record of the church when they pioneered holistic mission in general and mobilized fellow evangelicals in the 1986 People Power Revolution in particular. Their actions resonated with the best of the historical Filipino church in mission, for in the Philippines the Church as in all God's people - Catholic, Independent and Protestant - played a definitive role in the peoples' historical struggle against foreign domination and domestic despotism through the centuries.

At least four basic historical threads stand out in church history that I believe have guided Filipino Transformationists (whether consciously or not) to engage with their culture and society in mission: 1) subversion and resistance to colonialism, 2) the development of a nationalist or local faith 3) a commitment to church unity with a purpose and 4) a catalyst for people movements as responses to oppression.

Resistance and Subversion from the Beginning

Resistance and subversion against colonialism constitute the first historical thread. Nationalist historian Renato Constantino claims that resistance is in fact 'the unifying thread of Philippine history'.[1] Eleazer Fernandez concurs and traces it back to the Battle of Mactan of 1521 when Magellan, who was there on behalf of the Spanish Church and Crown, was killed at the hands of Chief

---

[1] Renato Constantino, *Ang Bagong Lumipas I* (Quezon City: Foundation for Nationalist Studies, 1997), 13.

Lapu-Lapu. He writes, 'The resistance of Lapu-Lapu against the forces of Fernando Magallanes ... gave birth to an important tendency in Philippine history - resistance to foreign domination.'[2] Indeed resistance against the cruelty of Spanish tyranny began immediately among the people. Rodgrigo Tano notes that 'in the three centuries of Spanish rule more than 300 rebellions and uprisings are recorded', amounting to an astounding one or more revolts every year since the Spanish set foot on the islands.[3]

However, according to Mario Francisco, to say that resistance against colonialism is *the* unifying thread of Filipino history oversimplifies and romanticizes the past.[4] For example, conversion to Christianity and cooperation with missionary efforts of the colonizers describe a very different native response to foreign religious imposition. For no Church would have developed, Catholic or Protestant, if many people did not in some form genuinely accept the religion of the colonizers. Applying to church history William Henry Scott's idea of 'cracks in the parchment curtain', i.e., of obtaining glimpses of the people's perspective in between the lines of colonial archives, would reveal genuine conversion experiences and authentic Christian devotion among early native Filipinos.[5] Nevertheless, resistance against the injustices of the colonial project began immediately, and it has expressed itself in various forms ever since.

As to when exactly the Christian faith became a motivating factor in the people's resistance no one can say for certain. Guillermo and Win report the year 1585 as witnessing 'the first recorded rebellion by Christian Filipinos against Spain'.[6] But if the examples of early Spanish missionary defenders of the natives against colonial injustice figured into the development of the indigenous faith, which is likely, then we can intelligently speculate that Christian faith played an important part in the people's resistance. Early on, exemplary Spanish missionaries, like Bishop Domingo de Salazar, defended the rights of the natives against maltreatment.[7] They also committed Christian catechesis to the native vernacular, indicating a sincere religious motive amidst

---

[2] E. S. Fernandez, *Theology of Struggle*, 9.

[3] Rodrigo D. Tano, *Theology in the Philippine Setting* (Quezon City: New Day, 1981), 19.

[4] J. Mario Francisco, interview by author, 23 January 2004, Berkeley, Calif., tape recording, Jesuit School of Theology at Berkeley.

[5] William H. Scott, *Cracks in the Parchment Curtain* (Quezon City: New Day, 1982). This book represents an approach to historiography that looks for the perspective of the 'losers of history' amidst the records of the 'winners of history'.

[6] Artemio R. Guillermo and May Kyi Win, *Historical Dictionary of the Philippines* (Lanham, Md.; London: Scarecrow, 1997), xx.

[7] John N. Schumacher, *Readings in Philippine Church History* (Quezon City: Loyola School of Theology, 1987), 28.

the obvious political and commercial motives of the whole colonial enterprise.[8] Church historians attribute the eventual native reception of the Gospel to such actions.[9]

The Christian faith that formed out of Filipino soil, however, differed markedly from the version of Catholicism that the Spanish brought with them. As Filipino Christians infused indigenous elements to the faith, something other than Spanish Catholic Christianity resulted, creating what most people today refer to as 'folk Catholicism'. Many Christians in both Catholic and Protestant Filipino communities view this folk Christianity with disdain and dismissal.[10] But it would be misguided not to take it seriously, for contrary to folk religion characterizing an unsophisticated syncretism of some kind, Filipino folk Catholicism reflects remarkable tenacity on the part of the native population. Recent post-colonial historiography makes a strong case that this 'folk Catholicism' embodied a passive resistance against the evils of colonialism.

Nationalist historian Vicente Rafael's groundbreaking work *Contracting Colonialism* makes the case that early Filipinos interpreted, or rather intentionally *mis*interpreted, the Spanish missionaries' translated preaching and literature, at once as a form of submission to, and subversion of, the religious instruction they received.[11] Submission to the religious impositions of the colonizers undoubtedly characterized an aspect of Filipino folk Catholicism, thus enabling some to build a valid case that the hybrid faith served the colonial project. But its subversive, undermining nature proved just as real. Anthropologist Kathleen Nadeau writes,

> The indigenous Filipinos interpreted Christianity in terms of traditional Southeast Asian cultural practices and beliefs. Many articulated the language of Christianity as a means for expressing their own values, ideals, and hopes for liberation from their colonial oppressors. In effect, Filipinos developed their own version of folk

---

[8] Schumacher, *Readings in Philippine Church History,* 28-38. Concerns regarding maltreatment of the population, as well as the effective spread of the faith among them, were aired out between 1582 and 1586 by a Salazar-inspired synod-the Synod or Junta of Manila-which instituted rules of justice and evangelization.

[9] Schumacher, *Readings in Philippine Church History,* 55.

[10] Rodney L. Henry, *Filipino Spirit World* (Mandaluyong: OMF, 1986), 5-16. According to Henry, pre-Spanish Filipino religion was built on a basic animistic orientation, a worldview that perceived nature and the human events of birth, life, death, family, work, and harvest as in control of a hierarchy of spirits. The people sensed the presence of these spirits-be they the supreme god (holding the name *Bathala, Laon* or *Kabunian* depending on the region) or *anitos* (lower, more accessible gods) or ancestral beings. And accordingly, they lived life religiously; meaning 'secular life' and 'religious life' enjoyed a continuity alien to most Westerners.

[11] Vicente L. Rafael, *Contracting Colonialism* (Quezon City: Ateneo de Manila University, 1988).

Catholicism to contest and eventually transform Spanish rule. Folk Catholicism was largely an indigenous resistance to Spanish Christian colonialism.[12]

As an example of the way in which Filipino folk Catholicism subversively resisted the colonizers, we need only consider the *Pasyon*, a Filipino rendering of Christ's passion play originally written in 1704 and performed in provinces throughout the country ever since. According to nationalist historian Reynaldo Ileto, the *Pasyon* played an integral role in inspiring popular movements and revolts against Spanish colonial rule in general and the Revolution of 1896 against Spain in particular. He writes,

> Popular movements and revolts were far from being blind reactions to oppression. They became popular precisely because leaders were able to tap existing notions of change; the *pasyon* was freed from its officially sanctioned moorings in Holy Week and allowed to give form and meaning to the people's struggles for liberation.[13]

Constantino, Fernandez, and others are correct when they identify resistance and subversion as an historical Filipino constant. The people fused their religious orientations into Christianity, creating 'folk Christianities', which point to a kind of subversion of the imposed religion of the colonizers.

Indeed resistance and subversion against the colonial experience constitute a main thread in the fabric of Filipino church history. Filipino Transformationists have followed along this thread in at least two ways: 1) critical consciousness, or a cautious posture toward non-Filipino influences, albeit political or ecclesial and, 2) the ministry of prophecy, or a critical posture toward the state. These two ways constitute the first two local Filipino dimensions of Mission as Transformation.

Critical Consciousness

The dimension of critical consciousness emerges out of strong convictions regarding biblical justice, human dignity and cultural identity, all of which the colonial experience undermined in the Philippines. Miranda-Feliciano's *Unequal Worlds* roots the Transformational sense of justice and human dignity in the scriptures, primarily in the books of the prophets[14] And Maggay's *Jew to*

---

[12] Kathleen M. Nadeau, *Liberation Theology in the Philippines: Faith in a Revolution* (Westport, Conn.; London: Praeger, 2002), 4-15.

[13] Reynaldo Ileto, *Pasyon and Revolution* (Quezon City: Ateneo de Manila, 1979), 316.

[14] Evelyn Miranda-Feliciano, *Unequal Worlds* (Quezon City: ISACC, 2000). Each chapter of *Unequal Worlds* is formatted like a Bible study (with some commentary from Miranda-Feliciano), encouraging Christians to discover for themselves God's concern for the poor.

the Jew, Greek to the Greek roots cultural identity in the vision of the multicultural worship found in Revelation 7.[15] This strong sense of biblical justice, human dignity and cultural authenticity has translated into a confident critical consciousness among Filipino Transformationists toward foreign endeavors in the country in general and the foreign missionary enterprise in particular. As a result, some sectors within the Filipino evangelical community consider them somewhat hostile toward outsiders.[16]

As for the foreign missionary enterprise, Filipino Transformationists have cultivated and maintained a critical consciousness toward it, seeing its potential value in the hands of a global God, but also ensuring that it ministers with a proper attitude of humility and supportiveness. 'Please', Maggay pleads, 'no more missionaries with an awful teacher complex.'[17] Miranda-Feliciano offers a list of 'Do's' for missionaries wishing to serve in the Philippines: 'learn the language, learn our kinesics (non-verbal language), appreciate our way of greeting or initial contact, learn our way of hospitality and be sensitive to our lifestyle.'[18] Maggay offers a list of 'Do's *and* Don'ts'. Her Do's closely mirror her colleague's list; her Don'ts comprised stereotypes to avoid: 'the godfather' who doles out goodness from a position of power, 'the bull in the china shop' whose well-meaning overzealousness tramples on everyone's feelings and sensitivities, 'the trying-hard' whose over-eagerness to do things culturally correct makes a fool of him/herself, and 'the reluctant hero' who recognizes his ineffectiveness and becomes overly apologetic about even being there.[19]

Filipino Transformationists have not ever gone as far as their mainline Protestant counterparts who took seriously the call for a missionary moratorium in the mid-1970s,[20] but neither have they ever opened their arms uncritically to welcome foreign missionaries, like conservative and charismatic evangelicals

---

[15] Maggay, *Jew to the Jew, Greek to the Greek*,48-56.

[16] During my first year in the Philippines as I was considering who to work with, a well meaning fellow missionary said to me, 'Don't work with ISACC; they hate foreigners, and they're leftists'. His biases turned out *not* to be as uncommon within the conservative evangelical expatriate community as I had hoped.

[17] Melba Maggay, 'Some Do's and Don'ts', in Melba Maggay (ed.), *Communicating Cross-Culturally* (Quezon City: New Day, 1989), 27.

[18] Evelyn Miranda-Feliciano, 'Do's in the Philippines', in Evelyn Miranda-Feliciano (ed.), *All Things to All Men* (Quezon City: New Day, 1988), 43-47.

[19] Maggay, 'Some Do's and Don'ts', 27-31.

[20] Mariano Apilado, interview by author, 13 April 2004, San Anselmo, Calif., tape recording, San Francisco Theological Seminary. Apilado described a time in the mid-1970s when the pressure coming from the Filipino mainline Protestant community for a missionary moratorium sent home American missionary professors teaching at Union Theological Seminary in Dasmarinas, Cavite.

in the country have typically tended to do.[21] Over against total rejection and uncritical affirmation, Filipino Transformationists have taken an alternative, proactive posture of educating foreign missionaries. ISACC, for example, has attempted to share cultural insights to the wider expatriate missionary community by conducting regular cross-cultural orientation seminars covering topics like Filipino culture, communication skills, contextual biblical interpretation and culturally sensitive evangelism specifically to promote healthy cross-cultural relationships that can result in effective partnership in the work of the Gospel in the Philippines.[22] These seminars testify to the critical consciousness of Filipino Transformationists toward foreign missionaries without rejecting them. After her list of Do's and Don'ts, Maggay addresses the missionaries:

> While we say, 'Let there be no patronizing, no more domination', we also say 'We embrace you as brothers and sisters and receive you as gifts from the hand of Him who has sent you. Together we shall work and together we shall learn, and if by chance you wound us we shall love and cover it with the blood that bought us. So let there be no fear. Serve in freedom and sensitivity. If by chance you stumble on the way, pick yourself up and have a few good laughs. That is our way.[23]

This attitude among Filipino Transformationists toward foreign missionaries in particular, however, merely reflects a larger critical consciousness toward foreign presence in general. For example, ISACC launched an anti-US Bases campaign in April 1990, a little over a year before the Military Bases Agreement was due to expire in September 1991. The only organized effort among evangelicals to contribute to the nationwide debate concerning the US military bases, ISACC joined in public protests, sponsored lectures and open forums and wrote extensively against the renewal of the bases. After lamenting the neo-colonial control of the US over the nation, Miranda-Feliciano pleaded with her fellow Filipinos that together they have a chance 'to make a decisive stand against [America's] continual meddling in our nation's affairs ... by having its military bases removed - once and for all - from our soil'.[24] She strengthened her case by referring to the nonviolent revolution of 1986: 'To continue to host facilities and instruments of carnage', she argued, 'is a grim irony for a people who toppled down a dictatorship in a most peaceful,

---

[21] Lorenzo Bautista, 'The Church in the Philippines', in Saphir Athyal (ed.), *Church in Asia Today* (Singapore: Asian Lausanne Committee for World Evangelization), 180.

[22] In a personal email correspondence dated 13 October 2004, in reference to the impetus behind these seminars, Bill Dyrness wrote, 'Rather than griping about missionaries, they [ISACC leaders] decided they should do something constructive about them!'

[23] Maggay, 'Some Do's and Don'ts', 31.

[24] Evelyn Miranda-Feliciano, 'Beyond the Bases', *Patmos* 6.1 (1st Quarter 1990), 2.

bloodless revolution, now being copied by many countries.'[25] The debate surrounding the bases raged until the eruption of Mt. Pinatubo in May 1991, which decisively ended the era of US military presence in the Philippines.[26]

The phenomenon of ideological globalization represents the most current outside force to which Filipino Transformationists have responded critically. It should not come as a surprise that prophetic voices from many sectors of society have denounced the evils of ideological globalization as the most contemporary form of old-fashioned colonialism. Only the naïve and the benefactors of globalization avoid making the comparison. Constantino analyzes globalization practices in the Philippines and warns that 'the multilateral institutions are now performing the functions of the former colonial powers in behalf of the global corporations'.[27] Without critical awareness, Filipino values and identity blur once again in the face of an external force.

Filipino Transformationists have contributed to this critical awareness of the dangers of globalization as ideology. In the last several years, ISACC has dedicated whole issues of *Patmos* to this phenomenon, offering biblical, theological, sociological, psychological, political, historical and personal insights concerning the dangers and consequences of succumbing to its power, not only from *Patmos* regulars like Maggay and Miranda-Feliciano, but also from the likes of Fr. Ed de la Torre and Bishop Ben Dominguez. Like the colonialism of old, ideological globalization threatens Filipino identity as market forces flatten and homogenize cultures by promoting consumerist values and backing them up with dazzling technology and seductive products. It also leaves many behind, namely, the poor, who cannot keep up with the race to the top. 'It is predicted', Maggay reports, 'that two thirds of the world's population will get excluded from this process, [and] one third, formed mostly out of its professional elites, is on the way to becoming a "world middle class" whose lifestyle and consumption patterns are boringly the same.'[28]

Filipino Transformationists have demonstrated a critical consciousness not only toward the foreign missionary enterprise, but also toward foreign intervention in other arenas of social life. Based out of biblical conviction

---

[25] Miranda-Feliciano, 'Beyond the Bases', 14.

[26] Along with their surroundings, Clark Air Force Base in Angeles City and Subic Naval Base in Olongapo City were buried under sixty to seventy feet of volcanic debris. Because of this disaster, coupled with the volatile debate surrounding their presence, the U.S. military decided not to pursue renewing its contract with the government, thus ending fifty years of U.S. military presence in the Philippines. Depending on where one stood on the debate concerning the U.S bases issue, the volcanic eruption was seen by the religious as either God's vindication of Philippine sovereignty or God's wrath upon the Philippines lifting his blessing of protection out of the country.

[27] Renato Constantino, *The Invisible Enemy: Globalization and Maldevelopment* (Quezon City: Foundation for Nationalist Studies, 1997), 1.

[28] Melba Maggay, 'Finding Our Way into the Future', *Patmos* 16.2 (September 2001), 5.

concerning liberation (justice and freedom) and a wounded colonial past, Filipino Transformationists have modeled a critical consciousness against the spirit of colonialism that follows along the historical thread of subversion and resistance.

A Prophetic Ministry

Moving from critical consciousness against external imposition to a focus upon realities that are internal to the country defines the second dimension of Filipino Mission as Transformation, namely, the ministry of prophecy. Prophecy differs from the first dimension only in that it focuses 'in-house' or 'in-nation'. Whereas critical consciousness challenges non-Filipino colonial-like forces coming from the outside, prophecy challenges the national institutions, the powers that be, that run contrary to the demands of the kingdom of God.

Liberationists have coined the word 'conscientization' as a contemporary synonym for prophecy. While certainly not averse to using the term, Filipino Transformationists do not shy away from validating the biblical office of prophet by identifying it as such, despite the presence of reprehensible figures that give the term a bad name. Miranda-Feliciano dismisses so-called prophets who come as arrogant proclaimers of gloom and doom or as television personalities of prosperity or as star gazers of last days predictions.[29] For Filipino Transformationists, these carry on the tradition of the 'false prophet' in the scriptures. She then proceeds to feature Micah as an exemplary prophet in the truest biblical sense, as one who decries social injustice from a truly grieving heart and who calls people back to a life of holy obedience to God.[30]

This Filipino Transformational theme builds upon the biblical notion of the people of God acting as the social conscience of society. From the passionate prophets in the Old Testament to 'the obedience of a small band of earnest disciples [constituting] a challenge to secular powers' in the New Testament, the collective people of God make up that 'city on the hill' that other cities look upon with holy envy.[31] As a counter-cultural community, the people of God, empowered by the Spirit of God, pricks the conscience of its surroundings in order to redeem those surroundings.

Two natural venues for this authentic kind of biblical prophecy emerge: church and society. And Filipino Transformationists have done well to speak to both. With regard to the Church, they have challenged fellow evangelicals to be the salt and the light that God has called them to be. 'As salt', Maggay preaches, 'We penetrate society and act as a preservative against social

---

[29] Miranda-Feliciano, *Unequal Worlds*, 37-38.

[30] Miranda-Feliciano, *Unequal Worlds*, 38.

[31] Maggay, *Transforming Society*, 49.

putrefaction, restoring and affirming whatever is good and just and lovely in the things around us. As light, we stand before forces of darkness, a sign of the truth about the human condition and the meaning and direction of history and existence'.[32]

In the Filipino context, Transformationists have challenged the Church to fulfil this call first by rejecting the conservative evangelical missiology of the West that has discouraged socio-political engagement. Maggay laments, 'Because the Filipino Evangelical Church is for the most part a creature made in the pale image of the American Bible belt, it has remained alienated from the surrounding culture.'[33] The Church needs to reject this image.

But by doing so, by saying 'no' to the ideological power of Western colonial missions that has misshapen the Filipino people of God, the Church must re-imagine itself according to the kingdom as it is expressed in the Philippines where poverty, exploitation, injustice and misery abound. This means, among other things, passionately and powerfully engaging society with the Gospel for the sake of the poor and oppressed as integral to the Church's mission in the Philippines.[34]

These admonitions to the Church essentially lead to the second venue where Filipino Transformationists have exercised the office of prophet: the socio-political arena. The image of the Church as prophet among the secular powers - politicians, state institutions, social systems, etc. - has captured the Filipino Transformational imagination. If the Church is simply being the Church, then it already challenges its surroundings to conform to a realm wherein Christ rules - the kingdom of God. Maggay says it this way: 'The Church is an alternative centre of power when it is most truly itself. At its best', she continues, 'the Church is a constant sign to authorities that there is a new order, a kingdom that while not *of* this world is *in* the world and continually poses a threat to established arrangements of social reality.'[35]

In voicing well-informed public opinion and taking strong socio-political stands on issues that matter to the society-at-large, Filipino Transformationists have paved the way for fellow evangelicals to fulfil the biblical call to prophetic ministries of salt and light. They not only offer prophetic words to the Church, they also do the same to socio-political institutions, thus serving as a vanguard of the prophetic call for evangelicals as they engage the powers-that-be with the Gospel. 'Our faith', declares Miranda-Feliciano, 'is to salt society with kingdom values and perspective.'[36]

---

[32] Maggay, *Transforming Society*, 48.

[33] Maggay, 'Some Do's and Don'ts', 56.

[34] Maggay, *Transforming Society*, 16-22.

[35] Maggay, *Transforming Society*, 35-36.

[36] Evelyn Miranda-Feliciano, 'Introduction', in ISACC (ed.), *Courage to Live These Last Days* (Quezon City: ISACC, 1999), 10.

ISACC's *Courage to Live These Days*, which compiles social editorials that first aired as five minute radio commentaries, exemplifies the voicing of opinion and the taking of stands from a Transformational perspective. Written by an ISACC team, these editorials cover a range of issues including family, women, the economy, poverty, and national peace. Most, if not all, of these editorials contain that biblical prophetic edge in that they go against mainstream practice and/or against the political vision of current government. For example, in 'The Filipino Family Deserves to be Protected', Miranda-Feliciano challenges the motivation behind the support of government for the overseas contract workers system (OCW). She writes, 'We all know why government is very much interested in the economic effects of the OCW phenomenon. It provides a positive contribution to our gross national product.' 'Meanwhile', she continues, 'family life is slowly and steadily deteriorating due to the absence of one or both parents.'[37] In 'Golf Course Development or Rice Self-Sufficiency', Miranda-Feliciano laments the increased construction of golf courses in the country as the government's way of symbolizing the nation's economic boost at the expense of much needed rice lands.[38] In 'RP-US Ties', Barcelona-Lavarias challenged then President Estrada's support (as well as the US push) to renew the Visiting Forces Agreement, which would bring US military presence back into the country. The consequences, she prophesies, 'would be worse than having a couple of stationary bases in the country [referring to Clark Air Force Base and Subic Naval Base that were dismantled after the eruption of Mt. Pinatubo].'[39] These editorials merely sample the courageous public voice of Filipino Transformationists, a voice that has challenged the Filipino Church to be faithful to its call as prophet as well as to keep Filipino state and society accountable to God.

Continuous with the historical thread of subversion and resistance, Filipino Transformationists have not only cultivated a critical consciousness toward outside colonial-like forces that seek to impose their will upon the people, they have also exercised the ministry of biblical prophecy that has challenged both church and society in the service of the Gospel of Christ.

Nationalistic or Local Faith

Another significant historical thread, along which Filipino Transformationists have followed, features the Filipinos' self-assertion as a people, which of

---

[37] Evelyn Miranda-Feliciano, 'The Filipino Family Deserves to be Protected', in ISACC (ed.), *Courage to Live These Last Days* (Quezon City: ISACC, 1999), 24-25.

[38] Evelyn Miranda-Feliciano, 'Golf Course Development or Rice Self-Sufficiency?' in ISACC (ed.), *Courage to Live These Last Days* (Quezon City: ISACC, 1999), 52-53.

[39] Ruby Barcelona-Lavarias, 'RP-US Ties', in ISACC (ed.), *Courage to Live These Last Days* (Quezon City: ISACC, 1999), 120.

course cannot be rightly appreciated without the first thread of subversion and resistance. Indeed, the forging of a national identity that differed from the identity imposed by the colonizers flowed out of the resistance against them.

Both church and secular historians agree that the Church played a key role in the making of the Filipino nation. We cannot speak historically of the birth of the nation without discussing the role of the Church; and vice versa, we cannot speak of the Church without the efforts to localize or 'Filipinize' the Christian faith. It was in fact the parish centreed issue of 'secularization', i.e., the controversy surrounding the removal of Filipino priests from local parishes in the mid-nineteenth century, that marks the true beginning of Filipino national consciousness.[40] Along with many others, three native Catholic priests - Frs. Mariano Gomez, Jose Burgos, and Jacinto Zamora - spoke out against the discrimination that kept Filipino clergy from running their own parishes, and they paid the ultimate price.[41] Looking for someone to blame for instigating the Cavite Mutiny of 1872, the Spanish government pinned it on the three priests, and then hoping to deter future subversives, it publicly executed them.[42]

Their executions became the rallying point of the people's growing intolerance for discrimination and injustice.[43] The people had enough, and calls for structural reform led by the likes of Jose Rizal and other *ilustrados*[44] intensified between 1872 and 1895, a period that gave birth to the Propaganda Movement when members of the Filipino *ilustrado* class began to articulate and disseminate anti-government literature.[45] Although proponents of the

---

[40] The secularization controversy had to do with the removal of Filipino clergy from the parishes by a renewed effort to Hispanicize the churches in the mid-1800s, as Spanish clergy poured back into the country. For details of the secularization issue, see John Schumacher, *Revolutionary Clergy: The Filipino Clergy and the Nationalist Movement* (Quezon City: Ateneo de Manila, 1981), 1-32.

[41] Schumacher, *Revolutionary Clergy,* 1-23.

[42] The Cavite Mutiny of 1872 refers to an incident led by a Filipino sergeant that left the governor of Cavite province dead, as the sergeant and his soldiers seized the arsenal of Fort Felipe and held it overnight.

[43] The creative abbreviation of the last names of the three priests-'GOMBURZA'- embodied the increasing discontent among Filipinos of Spanish abuses, particularly against the friars who were seen as taking the parishes away or keeping them from Filipino clergy.

[44] An *ilustrado* was a member of the Philippine elite, i.e., wealthy and educated, during the Spanish period. Under the catalytic vision of Jose Rizal, the *ilustrados* organized a society called the *Liga Filipina,* which called for structural reform that would assimilate Filipinos justly into Spanish society in the Philippines.

[45] 'Anti-government' was virtually synonymous with 'anti-friar', as the friars' duties bled into the socio-political sphere. For more on the Propaganda Movement, see John Schumacher, *The Propaganda Movement, 1880-1895: The Creation of a Filipino Consciousness, the Making of the Revolution* (Quezon City: Ateneo de Manila, 1997), which continues to be one of the standard textbooks for this period.

movement did not intend for anything more than equal opportunity in a Spanish run society, it nevertheless provided the impetus that led to the Philippine Revolution of 1896, which clearly demonstrated the desire of Filipinos to assert themselves as an independent people, a nation free from foreign rule.

The story of the Philippine Revolution, first with the war against the Spanish and then with the war against the Americans, is a tragic one filled with intrigue, betrayal and deception. Historians have done well to document this, so there is no need to retell it here in detail.[46] For our purposes, however, we need only to remember that the Church continued to play an integral role in the Revolution, as clergy maintained prominent official positions in the transitional government. They also took part in armed resistance. But their most enduring impact was to serve as essential 'counselors and inspirers' of the Revolution, providing religious sanction for the fight against tyranny and injustice.[47] They continued in this role, as the war shifted from fighting the Spanish to fighting the Americans in 1899.

In spite of the defeat at the hands of the Americans in 1901, the sense of nationhood only strengthened among the people. This growing sense of 'Filipino being and becoming' enabled the people to cling tenaciously to the hope of independence despite the steady and thorough Americanization of the islands. As with the Spanish, Filipinos found ways to resist and undermine the new government while simultaneously acquiescing to it, and the Church, in its Catholic, Independent, and Protestant forms, was no exception, as it rode the wave of nationalism in developing the leadership and life of their respective religious communities.

American-style democracy created an interesting irony in the Filipino Church experience: as it enjoyed its new freedom to develop as it saw fit, thanks to the American political philosophy of the separation of church and state, it also used that freedom to express its resentment toward, and resistance against, American rule. Indeed the process of Filipinization that occurred in the churches constituted an important way in which nationalism expressed itself. It in fact defined the Church's primary contribution to the Philippines' historical struggle for justice and freedom during the years of American rule prior to World War Two.

Although the Propaganda Movement produced many books, articles, and pamphlets, Rizal's now famous novels *Noli Mi Tangere* first published in 1887 and *El Filibusterismo* in 1892 registered the most impact for the nationalist cause. These novels are available in many versions and in many languages. For a listing, go to www.filipinobooks.com.

[46] To name just a few, see Reynaldo C. Ileto, *Filipinos and Their Revolution* (Quezon City, Philippines: Ateneo de Manila, 1998) and Samuel K. Tan, *The Filipino-American War, 1899-1913* (Quezon City: University of the Philippines, 2002).

[47] Schumacher, *Revolutionary Clergy*, 48ff.

To be sure, the Catholic Church and the Philippine Independent Church continued to develop nationalistically. But for our purposes, we focus now on how Filipino Protestants took advantage of the nationalist spirit and developed their version of the faith according to it. As Protestant missionaries aggressively propagated the faith at the beginning of the American period, many thousands of Filipinos responded. Maggay claims that they had a ready audience among Filipinos, who increasingly placed all that was unjust about Spanish rule upon the convenient heads of the friars.[48] This anti-clericalism, which ultimately translated into contempt for both the church and state of Spain, indeed paved the way for Filipinos to receive American ways rather readily, including American Protestantism. In fact, the first decade of Protestantism in the Philippines continues to provide a rich case study in church growth. For example, by 1908, less than ten years in the country, the Methodists registered 16,569 members and the Presbyterians 10,000.[49]

But like Catholicism, a 'folk Protestantism' also formed,[50] speaking once again not only to the tenacity of the pre-colonial religion of the islands, but also to the peoples' simultaneous submission to, and subversion of, American rule in general and to Protestant religious instruction in particular. But this time, the new converts had a relatively fresh nationalism upon which to draw. Consequently, it did not take long before a truly Filipino Protestant Church emerged. By 1909 under the charismatic leadership of Nicolas Zamora, grandnephew of Fr. Zamora, who by then reached revolutionary cult hero status along with the other two martyred priests, the *La Iglesia Evangelica Metodista en las Islas Filipinas* (IEMELIF) officially formed. One Filipino senator in 1922 described the IEMELIF as 'an offshoot of the Filipino fight for freedom from American domination'.[51] Other Protestant churches followed suit and committed themselves to the Filipinization of the faith.

Filipino Mission as Transformation has been continuous with this historical thread of nationalism as it has long championed the indigenization or localization of the Church. Filipino Transformationists, from the beginning, have challenged the Church, particularly the evangelical Church, to be Filipino in its theology (*theoria*), its mission (*praxis*), and its worship (*poesis*). The affirmation of lifeways and values indigenous to Filipinos constitutes much of this process. And because these have been repressed by centuries of colonial

---

[48] Melba Maggay, 'American Protestant Missionary Efforts and Filipino Culture', *Patmos* 14.1 (July 1998), 5.

[49] Arthur Tuggy, *The Philippine Church: Growth in a Changing Society* (Grand Rapids, Mich.: Eerdmans, 1971), 100-122.

[50] Henry, *Filipino Spirit World*, 15-16.

[51] Cited in Ruben F. Trinidad, 'Nicolas Zamora and the IEMELIF', in Anne C. Kwantes (ed.), *Chapters in Philippine Church History* (Mandaluyong City; Colorado Springs, Col.: OMF: International Academic, 2002), 203.

and neo-colonial forces, affirming Filipino cultural orientations for Transformationists has also meant deconstructing American colonial values so deeply imbedded in the Filipino psyche. Lapiz urges that 'the worldwide church must be freed from the monolithic, intrusive, patronizing and colonialist Western Church culture that has been imposed over it.'[52] Regarding the Filipino Church in particular, he writes,

> The Filipino Christian is lost somewhere. To be a 'good Christian', does he have to abandon his cultural heritage and thus be a 'bad Filipino'? This sense of being lost is sometimes shared and often caused by his foreign mentors who taught him, and probably even sincerely believed it themselves, that being Christian means being Westernized.[53]

He goes on to outline special ways that Filipino Christians, by virtue of their Filipino-ness, contribute to the world, thus affirming their cultural values, traditions, family and social relationships.[54]

Anthropologist F. Landa Jocano uses the same approach of affirming Filipino culture via colonial critique, but then goes on to build a case for cultural affirmation based upon pre-colonial civilization on the islands. Using primarily archaeology, Jocano claims that pre-colonial Philippines easily met 'the criteria of civilization', which consist of 'efficient technology, predictive sciences, writing, art and religion, foreign trade, big population [urban centres], megalithic structures, government, laws and warfare'.[55] Wild 'what if' speculations aside of what the Philippines would be like today if it did not

---

[52] Ed Lapiz, 'Filipino Indigenous Liturgy', *Patmos* 14.2 (February 1999), 26.

[53] Lapiz, *Paano Maging Pilipinong Kristiano*, xiii.

[54] Lapiz, *Paano Maging Pilipinong Kristiano,* 1-26. Lapiz affirms that Filipinos: 1) are brown, which is beautiful and not to be shamefully contrasted with the superior whites; 2) are a touching people, demonstrative of their love for others; 3) are linguists, learning languages more easily than others and thus, able to bridge cultures; 4) are groupists, i.e. communal in nature; 5) are social weavers, constantly making connections with one another via 'smooth interpersonal relationships'; 6) are adventurers, making inroads in other lands often out of economic necessity but nevertheless become 'world savvy' in the process; 7) have *pakikiramdam,* or the ability to feel deeply and to discern what others are feeling; 8) are very spiritual; 9) are timeless, meaning they measure time not with precision but with feeling and event; 10) are spaceless, meaning they understand space as something to share and not own.

[55] F. Landa Jocano, *Filipino Prehistory: Rediscovering Precolonial Heritage* (Manila: PUNLAD, 1998), 189-200. Archeological discovery has uncovered metal tools, glass products, evidences of sophisticated dentistry, complex writing, highly developed art and religion, well-established trading practices, traces of urban centres, structural wonders like the rice terraces of Banawe, governmental and legal systems, and military defense systems, all of which point to a highly civilized society before the coming of the colonizers.

encounter the atrocities of sustained colonialism, Jocano urges his fellow Filipinos: 'We must exert deliberate efforts to make [our pre-colonial heritage] part of our consciousness or we will never recover from our cultural amnesia. Deprived of the past we can be proud of, we will continuously search for meanings of our destiny [everywhere else] but our native ground.'[56]

By simultaneously affirming indigenous Filipino ways of life and rejecting the colonial effects in the development of the Church, Filipino Transformationists have followed along the historical thread of a nationalistically inspired localization of the faith in discernible ways constituting the next three local Filipino dimensions of Mission as Transformation: 3) holistic ministry in accordance with Filipino worldview, 4) a theology of beauty, and 5) a spirit world cosmology.

Whole Being/Whole Ministry

The indigenous Filipino worldview that tends toward an integrated, whole life perspective of reality breeds holistic ministry, serving the whole person with the whole Gospel. Unlike the view arising from the Enlightenment, which has been dominant in much of Western culture in the last two hundred years, no clean breaks exist between natural and supernatural, physical and spiritual, body and soul, and individual and social in the Filipino's typical perception of reality. Transformational holistic ministry in the Philippines comes fundamentally from the holistic way in which Filipinos generally view the human person; which should shed some light on why I locate this particular dimension here under the historical missiological theme of nationalistic or localized faith. For to perceive Transformational holism in the Philippines as merely the product of the social reawakening that occurred within the worldwide evangelical mission community beginning in the 1960s does not present the whole picture.

· The importance of this point lies in the motive behind holistic ministry. The Western debate regarding the nature of mission as *either* evangelism *or* social concern no doubt made its mark in many churches in the Two Thirds World, including many of the evangelical churches in the Philippines. Indeed the Filipino evangelical community participated in the lively debates that tried to settle the issue of the place of social concern in the mission of the Church. And 'after almost two decades of debate', referring to the watershed effect of Lausanne '74, Maggay concludes, 'social concern is now entrenched as a part of the church's agenda.'[57] Credit should go mostly to the likes of Maggay and other Transformationists in bringing about this shift in the Philippines.

---

[56] Jocano, *Filipino Prehistory,* 209.
[57] Maggay, *Transforming Society,* 16.

But they did not just argue on theological and sociological grounds; they also argued forcefully on cultural grounds, affirming the generally holistic nature of the Filipino worldview. The evangelism versus social concern debate between fundamentalists and modernists exploded elsewhere, mainly in North America, and therefore has no historical or cultural basis in the Philippines. Missionaries brought the dichotomy with them, and insofar as Filipino Christians lend credence to it, they perpetuate the colonial legacy. According to Lorenzo Bautista, the evangelical missionaries, who inundated the country after World War Two, 'were part of the conservative side in America who were reacting to the modernists and social gospel advocates'.[58] The evangelistic fruit of their work therefore consisted of Filipino converts who viewed social concern as secondary to the evangelistic work of the Gospel at best and deceptively distracting of the real work of the Gospel at worst. Filipino Transformationists have challenged such dichotomous thinking on the ground that it is ultimately alien to the Filipino religious imagination.[59] For the Filipino, the Gospel addresses all of life. In order for Christianity to be truly 'good news' it must contain more than words, more than proclamation; it must also have a visible element, a presence that permeates the totality of life. Evangelists who grasp this Filipino cultural holistic outlook will present the Gospel holistically by both proclamation and presence.

Furthermore, besides a more integrated whole life perspective at play among Filipino Transformationists, the overwhelming social needs in the Philippines also warrant holistic ministry. Maggay insists that '[social action] needs to be done if the Gospel is to be heard at all, especially in the Third World'.[60] In the face of real poverty and fundamentally flawed social structures, the Church does not have the luxury of emphasizing personal needs over social ones or spiritual needs over physical ones. The needs are too intertwined to untangle and too great to pause and debate! So in addition to solid biblical and theological reflection, Filipino Transformationists have seriously taken into account both their indigenous holistic worldview as well as the dire socio-political context to stress holistic ministry as ultimately the only kind of ministry in the Philippines. In this way, they perpetuate the ongoing quest for a faith identity that is truly Filipino. Herein lies the connection between holistic mission and nationalism in Filipino Mission as Transformation.

Theology of Beauty

Another dimension that continues the historical thread of a nationalistic or localized faith, the fourth of nine dimensions of Filipino Mission as

---

[58] Bautista, 'The Church in the Philippines', 183.

[59] Maggay, *Filipino Religious Consciousness,* 16-17.

[60] Maggay, *Transforming Society,* 21.

Transformation, has to do with an appreciation of the witnessing power of the arts - music, dance, literature, visuals and so on. By placing the role of beauty or the aesthetic in a prominent place in the witness of the Gospel, Filipino Transformationists affirm the indigenous sense of the transcendent, the splendorous, the fascinating and the beautiful. According to Maggay, the use of parables and the revival of symbols would best tell the good news of Christ in this context since Filipinos, though literate, generally respond to life in fascination, not with critical inquiry.[61] In an unsigned editorial entitled, 'Art for God's Sake' in an issue of *Patmos,* a Filipino aesthetic writes, 'Beauty is essential, and though our sense of the beautiful has become muddled in recent times, there is everywhere a groping for things that would put a measure of it into our lives.'[62]

By understanding contextual art as witness, Filipino Transformationists do not mean using art for the purpose of evangelism in the narrow sense of the word, as if art makes for some manipulative kind of witnessing tool. Neither does it mean needing to be explicitly religious. The writer of 'Art for God's Sake', wonders rather facetiously if 'Jesus in his carpentry ever felt the need to put Bible verses on his tables and chairs!'[63] Rather, Transformationists understand authentic art in and of itself as a witness to the character of God. 'The source of ... beauty', declares Miranda-Feliciano, 'is Jesus Christ Himself, the Creator of all that is pleasing, artistic and beautiful. Let us then show forth His beauty.'[64]

Colonialism once again stands guilty as charged for the stifling of this indigenous sense of beauty as a form of Christian witness. Western values of utility and efficiency supplanted the significance of the beautiful and relegated it to secondary, optional, even frivolous status. The lingering effects of this process have produced a poverty of authentic symbols, stories, and other art forms in the Philippines. One can build a case that the Filipinizing of Spanish Catholic imagery on jeepneys (a common mode of public transportation), home altars, and storefronts as well as the Filipinizing of American pop culture icons of music and drama testify to Filipino creativity. But a Transformational perspective requires going beyond imitating or putting a Filipino spin upon imposed alien art forms in order to do justice to the indigenous Filipino sense of beauty.

Filipino Transformationists have taken the lead in pointing out this particular consequence of colonialism not only directly by educating church and society on these matters, but also by taking proactive, affirmative steps like incorporating poetry, fiction, and indigenous art in their literature as evidenced

---

[61] Maggay, *The Gospel in Filipino Context,* 16.

[62] 'Art for God's Sake', *Patmos* 2.2 (2nd Quarter 1990), 4.

[63] 'Art for God's Sake', 5.

[64] Miranda-Feliciano, *Unequal Worlds,* 42.

throughout regular issues of *Patmos*. Taking 'the lead by example' philosophy to another level, ISACC recently sponsored a major musical drama production in 2002 entitled *Bayan, Isang Paa Na Lamang*.[65] The narrative written by Maggay and the music composed by the late nationally renowned musical artist Lucio San Pedro, this 'zarzuela' dramatized 'a history from below' of the Philippine Revolution of 1896.[66] Its critical acclaim at both the Community Theatre of the University of the Philippines and the Cultural Center of the Philippines in 2002 encouraged its producers enough that at the time of this writing a 're-run is in the works'.[67]

Much of the work of Filipino Transformationists in the search for an authentic indigenous aesthetic has focused upon the worship practices of the Church - its music, its liturgy, its preaching, and so on. The *Himnaryong Pilipino Project* of ISACC has published several volumes of *Samba Hymnbooks*,[68] a collection of original Filipino choral pieces, which were the result of nationwide song writing contests in search of culturally sensitive composers. Several other ISACC publications like Maggay's *Diyata't Isang Sanggol*,[69] which is a Christmas cantata set to the indigenous sense of story and rhythm, Miranda-Feliciano's *Of Songs, Words and Gestures*,[70] which offers ways to Filipinize church liturgy, and Olga Cadiz' *Kakatok-Katok-Katok, at Iba Pa*,[71] which is a collection of dramatic sketches for churches and other Christian gatherings, all testify to the Filipino Transformational commitment to church reform via the dismantling of Western worship patterns and the restoring of the indigenous sense of beauty among God's people in the Philippines.

Other noteworthy examples of ministries of reform in church worship among Filipino Transformationists include KALOOB, 'an ensemble of musicians, dancers, researchers, and enthusiasts [that exists] to study, redeem, and promote Philippine music and dance for Christian worship'.[72] KALOOB's commitment to this vision has led its members to teach churches how to

---

[65] My own English translation of this is *People, Just One More Step*.

[66] I should note here that Maggay herself was the recipient of the nationally-renowned Palanca Literary Prize in 1998.

[67] See Appendix Three for ISACC's 'Who We Are' document.

[68] The English translation for 'samba' is 'worship'.

[69] Melba Maggay, *Diyata't Isang Sanggol* (Quezon City: ISACC, 2001). An English translation of this title (again my own) is, *This One Child: A Musical Drama for Christmas*.

[70] Evelyn Miranda-Feliciano, *Of Songs, Words and Gestures* (Quezon City: ISACC, 2000).

[71] Olga Cadiz, *Kakatok-Katok-Katok at Iba Pa* (Quezon City: ISACC, 1997). An English translation of this title is, *Knock, Knock and Other Riddles*.

[72] Lapiz, *Paano Maging Pilipinong Kristiano*, back flap.

incorporate native instruments and dance into their worship. KALOOB founder and pastor Ed Lapiz urges,

> Let the Filipino be a Christian, but let him be a Filipino Christian. Let him make music to the Lord Creator with his *agong, kulintang, kubing, gitara* and *sulibaw.* Let his choirs be garbed in *malong, kimona,* or *patadyong* whether in their archaeological authenticity or contemporary and avante garde reinterpretations. Let his Lord's Supper consist of *puto,* or among the hill tribes, *kamote.* Let him relive the passion of Christ the singing of ... the *Pasyon.* Let him pray sometimes not with words but with *Subli.* ... Let him celebrate his faith. Let him be what God created and meant him to be: Filipino![73]

Such Transformational efforts have led the way in the Philippines to experience God authentically and to witness to God's beauty and creativity as part of the mission of the Church in society. To affirm a theology of beauty as Filipino Transformationists have followed along 'beautifully' with the historical thread of the Filipinization of the faith.

Spirit World Cosmology

This particular thread can also be seen in yet another dimension of Filipino Mission as Transformation, namely, a revived sensitivity to the spirit world. In deconstructing the naturalistic, cerebral faith of Western colonial Christianity, churches of the Two Thirds World, of which Filipino evangelical churches are no exception, have begun to reclaim a lost cultural cosmology that does not draw a clear line between the natural and supernatural worlds. 'Instinct tells the indigenous Filipino', claims Maggay, 'that in some vague way disease or calamity is connected to a cosmic imbalance, a breakage in the fragile life system in which the world of the spirits and the world of human beings intersect and impinge on each other.'[74]

Contrary to the typical Western missionary response to this belief, relegating it to superstition or outright demonizing it, Maggay points out the dire need for Filipinos to understand 'Jesus as Lord of the Spirits', that faith in Christ requires transcending the rationalistic orientation of the West and affirming Jesus as one who subdues evil spirits and who ends demonic oppression.[75] Filipino Christians in general have never had to overcome unbelief in the spirit realm, but only the superficial acquiescence to Western dualistic Christianity. At the cultural core, awareness of an unseen realm has always occupied Filipino consciousness, strong enough in fact to transform the very systems of

---

[73] Lapiz, *Paano Maging Pilipinong Kristiano,* 150. Words in italics are native instruments, dress, foods, and chants.

[74] Maggay, *Filipino Religious Consciousness,* 22.

[75] Maggay, *The Gospel in Filipino Context,* 4-6.

the religion of the colonizers, creating unique 'folk Christianities' of both the Catholic and Protestant varieties.

The expansion of Pentecostalism in the Philippines (and throughout the world) testifies to the 'coming out' of a spirit world cosmology long repressed by Western colonial missions. Consistent with Walter Hollenweger's understanding that Pentecostalism around the world has its roots partially in the Western holiness movement and partially in the traditional and/or popular religion of a given context,[76] Filipino Pentecostalism combines spirit world cosmology, traditional healing, power encounters with evil, etc., with evangelical piety and missionary fervour. A God who cannot heal, intervene in state affairs, overcome evil elements, and communicate his will does not register in Filipino religious thought.

This is not to say that all Filipino Transformationists regard themselves as Pentecostal. In fact, some of them maintain a cautious posture toward Pentecostalism's tendency toward emotional hype, spiritual manipulation and misguided 'God-said' language.[77] Having said that, the congruence enjoyed between indigenous Filipino cosmology and a Pentecostal theological orientation undoubtedly explains, at least in part, the exponential growth of Pentecostalism in the Philippines.[78] By virtue of their Filipinoness, the world of the supernatural, the possibility of miracles, healings, signs, wonders, and

---

[76] Hollenweger, *Pentecostalism: Origins and Developments Worldwide*, 2. Hollenweger traces the roots of Pentecostalism to black oral, catholic, evangelical, critical and ecumenical roots. The black oral root has manifested contextually in different parts of the world, which can be generalized to say that characteristic of Pentecostalism is its adherence to traditional indigenous religious tendencies. The other four roots Hollenweger discusses-catholic, evangelical, critical and ecumenical-come together at some point and contribute to the Holiness Movement. These five roots, according to Hollenweger, which have grown through two distinct traceable origins, define Pentecostalism worldwide.

[77] The latest move of the Pentecostal/Charismatic community, of which many Transformationists have criticized, was the endorsement of one of its own-Eddie Villanueva-to run for President in the May 2004 elections. In a personal email correspondence to me dated 18 April 2004, Lim wrote, 'You should be here to feel the intensity and high hopes of these brethren [95% of Pentecostal and Charismatics]; I'm afraid we'll need a lot of counseling clinics for depressed Charismatics after May 10! It's just my 'fearless prophetic' opinion, of course!'

[78] The largest and fastest growing Church in the Philippines is the Pentecostal Jesus Is Lord Fellowship with Villanueva as its chief figure head. Also, the Philippines for Jesus Movement (PJM) represents an alliance of mostly Pentecostal and Charismatic churches that prays for both individual and social revival in the Philippines.

cosmic spiritual warfare naturally inform Transformational missiology in the Philippines.[79]

Some Filipino Transformationists have used the *Journal of Asian Mission* (*JAM*), one of the regular publications of the Asia-Pacific Theological Seminary of the Assemblies of God in the Philippines, as a venue through which to explore the socio-missiological implications of Filipino Pentecostalism.[80] Joseph Suico's thought provoking article published in *JAM* in 1999, for example, captures the essence of the movement with regard to its impact upon society. After discussing Filipino Pentecostal social activity, he concludes, 'The ability of the Pentecostals to create a Christian moral alternative that enables greater decision making power [on the personal and family levels] is probably the greatest impact Pentecostalism has had on Philippine society.'[81] He states this as an affirmation in that personal lives are being changed, as well as a hope in that a truly 'social doctrine', as Suico calls it, that challenges corruption in government, human rights abuses and the gap between the rich and the poor, needs to be developed among Filipino Pentecostals.[82] The affirmation of the indigenous Filipino spirit world cosmology among Transformationists combined with their radical social commitment has made them the key players in developing this Holy Spirit inspired 'social doctrine' for which the likes of Suico call.

A holistic ministry that involves at least evangelism and social concern, a theology of beauty and a spirit world cosmology partially make up a missiology that has taken indigenous Filipino culture seriously, thus extending the historical thread of the nationalization or localization of the Christian faith.

Church Unity with a Purpose

A third historical thread that holds Filipino Church history together comes from a deep sense of solidarity and community, namely, church unity. As keynote speaker at the 2004 Annual Meeting of the American Society of Missiology, Maggay pointed out an irony of Philippine reality. She said, 'Filipinos have trouble being a nation, but we have no trouble getting together as a

---

[79] See for example, Julie C. Ma, *Mission Possible: Biblical Strategies for Reaching the Lost* (Oxford: Regnum, 2005), especially 62-68, where she records power encounters among the Kankana-ey Tribe in the Philippines. I count Ma among what I have called 'radical Pentecostals' in this book.

[80] Although this journal covers Asia, many if not most of the articles speak to the Philippine context. This journal is is available on-line at http://www.apts.edu/jam.

[81] Joseph R. Suico, 'Pentecostalism: Towards a Movement of Social Transformation in the Philippines', *Journal of Asian Mission* 1.1 (March 1999), 19.

[82] Suico, 'Pentecostalism', 19.

community.'[83] Long before the Philippines declared independence as a nation in 1946 as a result of decolonization, there has existed among Filipinos 'an unrecognized sense of a shared identity, a solidarity deeper than mere political constructs like being a nation'.[84] Furthermore, this solidarity 'seems to be triggered, not by ideology, but by a collective feeling of outrage' when injustice manifests itself one too many times.[85] Whether it results from indigenous propensities toward a more communal existence or from the necessity of sticking together as a people in an oppressive colonial situation or a combination of both, Filipinos have held unity and community in high regard.

In line with this sense of community and solidarity amidst colonialism, the Filipino Church served as a strong unifying force among a people struggling to understand itself over and against the backdrop of Spanish colonial injustices. Mario Francisco's treatment of eighteenth and nineteenth century Christianity as church (institution) and story (popular indigenous expressions) demonstrates religious faith's unifying function, that is, its significant role in the making of a people. He writes, 'Christianity played a multifaceted role as church and story in what became the historical trajectory of nineteenth century native society, the birth of the Filipino nation.'[86]

Filipino Protestants followed suit in this sense of solidarity and community and sought church unity from the beginning. Fortunately, American Protestant missionaries also demonstrated a desire for unity early on, as evidenced in the formation of the Evangelical Union of 1901. From there, the Filipino Protestant Church formed various alliances including the National Christian Council in 1929, the Philippine Federation of Evangelical Churches in 1938, and the Federation of Evangelical Churches in the Philippines in 1942 just to name a few of the efforts at visible church unity.[87]

Protestants sought unity, however, not just for unity's sake, even though in light of the Filipino sense of community, the desire for it had merit in and of itself. But the unity that Filipino Protestants sought had a strong social concern purpose to it, especially after World War Two. It was church unity with a purpose. It was ultimately unity for the sake of the greater Filipino society. Filipino Protestant churches needed more than ever to unify together if they were effectively going to play a part in nation building efforts after the ravages of World War Two. Enrique Sobrepena, a renowned leader in Filipino

---

[83] Melba Maggay, 'Engaging Culture: Lessons from the Underside of History', *Missiology* 33.1 (January 2005), 66.

[84] Maggay, 'Engaging Culture', 66.

[85] Maggay, 'Engaging Culture', 66.

[86] Jose Mario Francisco, 'Christianity as Church and Story and the Birth of the Filipino Nation in the Nineteenth Century', unpublished manuscript (23). Photocopy given by Francisco to the author, March 2004.

[87] T. Valentino Sitoy, *Comity and Unity* (Quezon City: NCCP, 1989), 112.

ecumenism at that time, later offered this interpretation of the era immediately after the war: 'The churches realized that they must cooperate if they were to be effective in the rehabilitation of their corporate life and in the rebuilding of the nation, in which they were set to function under God.'[88]

With clear post-war nation building purposes in mind, Filipino Protestants set their sights upon a broader constituency that led to the formation of the United Church of Christ in the Philippines in 1948 (UCCP). Church historians agree that this union, which brought together smaller unions and some former denominational holdouts, represented a breakthrough in Filipino ecumenism.[89] Other church groups joined in the years that followed, making the UCCP the most inclusive Protestant union in the country. Richard Deats reports that by 1963, 1,146 organized churches and 142,405 members made up its constituency.[90]

Before the war, Filipino Protestants traditionally concentrated on the Church's moral and spiritual influence on individuals as the primary means to make an impact upon society.[91] But post-war developments, both on the social level as the country lay in ruins and on the missional level as 'humanization' increasingly defined the agenda of the global ecumenical movement, noticeably shifted in the direction of the Church's social responsibility. Deats applauds this shift and identifies it as a 'more profound contribution to the task of nation building [which] is being expressed through a variety of projects, pronouncements and publications that deal with such areas as rapid social change, economic development and social justice.'[92]

Large churches, like the Methodist Church, the Philippine Episcopal Church, and the Philippine Independent Church decided not to join the UCCP when it first formed. Multiple reasons factored into their decision, including nervousness of talk among zealous ecumenists about creating one united Protestant Church.[93] But this did not stop unity efforts. After several consultations due to the tenacity of the ecumenical vision among certain Protestant leaders, a cooperative union formed in 1963 called the National Council of Churches in the Philippines (NCCP) in order to bring churches together on the basis of common mission but with no official aspirations toward one united Protestant Church. This union based on cooperation brought together seven churches: UCCP, *Iglesia Evangelica Unida de Cristo*, IEMELIF, Philippine Methodist, Episcopal, Baptist and Philippine Independent

---

[88] Cited in Sitoy, *Comity and Unity,* 113-114.

[89] Sitoy, *Comity and Unity,* 117. See also Richard L. Deats, *Nationalism and Christianity in the Philippines* (Dallas, Tex.: Southern Methodist University, 1969), 110.

[90] Deats, *Nationalism,* 113.

[91] Deats, *Nationalism,* 113.

[92] Deats, *Nationalism,* 118.

[93] Sitoy, *Comity and Unity,* 119-128.

Churches, as well as two affiliate agencies: the Philippine Bible House and the Association of Christian Schools and Colleges.

Only a year after its formation, the first NCCP Director Isabelo De los Reyes, Jr., penned,

> The [NCCP] has already established a vital and visible relationship among its member churches. These seven churches today recognize each other as confessing Christ as God and Saviour according to the Scriptures, sharing the same baptism and participating in a common calling to the glory of the One God, Father, Son and Holy Spirit. All are expected to listen as well as to speak; to give as well as to receive; and all of them are happy to serve as fellow members in a small replica of the World Council of Churches, never looking for 'unity characterized by uniformity' and without any pretensions to establish or become a super-church.[94]

With the Filipino Protestant churches united more than ever, they participated in the rebuilding of the nation 'in terms of religious education, rural cooperative and agricultural projects, and other humanitarian programs'.[95]

Social concern activities among Filipino Protestants inevitably led to increased political involvement. In March 1965, for example, the NCCP brought together the Protestant constituency and became instrumental in overturning the Cuenco Bill, a bill that sought to impose specific kinds of religious instruction in public schools, which the NCCP interpreted as violating religious liberty and the constitutional rights of the people. The NCCP joined other civic organizations as entities exercised their right to protest. The corporate voice rose loudly enough that the Congress overturned the implementation of the Bill.[96]

The success of such pronouncements and protests strengthened the resolve among Filipino Protestants that they could indeed contribute to the welfare of the nation. Then in 1967 at the NCCP Annual Convention, influential lay people like Senator Jovito Salonga and University of the Philippines Professor Augustus Espiritu challenged the Church to take seriously the social institutions

---

[94] Isabelo De los Reyes, Jr., 'The Dawn of Christian Unity in the Philippines', *Philippine Ecumenical Review* 1.1 (1964), 3. One should not underestimate the influence of the WCC as well as the former East Asia Christian Conference (now called the Christian Conference of Asia [CCA]) upon the formation of the NCCP and other national councils all over Asia. The local national bodies also informed the larger bodies giving them practical expressions on the grassroots level. The spirit of ecumenism at that time was such that it produced bodies committed to unity on all levels from the local (national councils like the NCCP) to the regional (like the East Asia Christian Conference) to the global (like the WCC).
[95] Oscar S. Suarez, *Protestantism and Authoritarian Politics* (Quezon City: New Day, 1999), 41.
[96] NCCP, 'Report of the Administrative Secretary to the Second General Convention', *Philippine Ecumenical Review*. Special issue (1965), 13.

of the nation as an arena for Christian involvement. This Convention marked a turning point in Protestant political awareness.[97] By 1969, the NCCP issued the 'Statement of Social Concern' wherein Filipino Protestants articulated their commitment to social justice in a political climate that was becoming increasingly more volatile.

Church unity with a purpose indeed constitutes a consistent historical thread that has helped to hold together and define Filipino church and nation. The next two local Filipino dimensions of Mission as Transformation have continued this historical thread: 6) the emphasis that Transformation occurs through all church forms - local congregation, para-church, development organization, and 7) the emphasis that the whole Church across denominational traditions - evangelical Protestant, ecumenical Protestant, and Catholic - is needed in order to bring about the Transformation for which the kingdom of God calls.

Across Church Forms

Filipino Mission as Transformation affirms the whole Church, in its congregational, organizational and para-church forms, as a primary agent of change in society. Local churches, relief and development organizations, specialized para-churches, mission agencies, not to mention Christian presence in government, business, the arts, and all other areas of social life, work together to take part in the transformation of society. Maggay captures this idea when she writes,

> For the Word to have a body, the church and its entire gamut of gifts are needed. The whole body of Christ is to stand as a sign, a visual aid to the kingdom that has come. It is important to grasp that this body which makes the Word visible is not limited to the local church. The *ecclesia visibilis* is God's people making the presence of the kingdom felt in all areas of life, the leaven which permeates all of human activity. It is the church in academia, the church in politics, the church in the marketplace.[98]

Talk of the whole Church in this manner could have a weakening effect upon the significance of the local church as an agent of change, but it does not at all fade in Filipino Transformational thought and practice. In fact, *Hasik-Unlad*,[99] an effective mobile community development training program of ISACC in the mid-90s, came into being primarily for the sake of local churches and organizations that work with local churches. Two development courses that ISACC's Research and Training Department offered regularly - 'The Church as

---

[97] Suarez, *Authoritarian Politics,* 47-48.

[98] Maggay, *Transforming Society,* 21.

[99] The *Tagalog* name of this project had a sub-title that read, 'Sowing the Seeds of Development', which is also a loose English translation of the title.

an Agent of Change' and 'Skills Enhancement in Community Development in the Context of the Local Church'[100] - served as precursors to *Hasik-Unlad,* and their names are telling of the conviction that drove the effort, namely, the vital role of the local church in community transformation.[101]

This conviction has stood despite local churches that seem unwilling to engage in holistic ministries. In the book that has documented the *Hasik-Unlad* experience, I list various obstacles in working with local churches in the area of community transformation, including resistance from pastors who had received nothing in their theological training concerning ministry to the poor, an inadequate understanding and implementation of servant leadership that undermined the empowerment of the people and mismanagement or even criminal misuse of resources. 'But no matter how imperfect ... the church is God's. We therefore cannot simply abandon it when doing something as God-like as caring for ... the poor.'[102]

The *Hasik-Unlad* Program trained 'over a hundred churches ... in seven provinces' in a span of four years with the hope that these churches share the training with other churches in order to spread both the knowledge and the skill to conduct ministries with and for the poor.[103] A list of partners of *Hasik-Unlad* includes LIGHT Ministries, which in and of itself serves as an example of the Filipino Transformational belief in the local church.[104] LIGHT, located in the Mt. Pinatubo, ravaged province of Zambales, is a network of local churches for the purpose of community transformation. LIGHT's original motto, 'Empowering local churches to empower their communities in Christ's name', demonstrates, along with *Hasik-Unlad* and other Filipino Transformational efforts, the view of the local church as a crucial agent of kingdom change.

But the local church is but one functional form among other forms like para-churches, mission agencies, and Christian NGOs that make up the whole Church in mission. From setting up micro-enterprise projects to providing

---

[100] These two courses eventually expanded into a full blown curriculum for churches, consisting of seven modules that ranged from biblical basis to project and financial management. For a more detailed outline of the curriculum, see Vylma V. Ovalles, 'Pagpupunla at Paghahasik', in ISACC (ed.), *Hasik-Unlad: An Experience in Community Development Training* (Quezon City: ISACC, 1998), 49-55.

[101] Lucila V. Arboleda, 'Pagbubungkal ng Lupa', in ISACC (ed.), *Hasik-Unlad: An Experience in Community Development Training* (Quezon City: ISACC, 1998), 33.

[102] Al Tizon, 'Ang Pagyabong ng Komunidad at ang Iglesya', in ISACC (ed.), *Hasik-Unlad: An Experience in Community Development Training* (Quezon City: ISACC, 1998), 81.

[103] Florinda Toledo-Juarez, 'Introduction', in ISACC (ed.), *Hasik-Unlad: An Experience in Community Development Training* (Quezon City: ISACC, 1998), 1.

[104] I was privileged to work with evangelical church leaders in Zambales province in establishing LIGHT, which stands for Livelihood, Income-Generating, Help and Training.

alternatives for prostitutes, human rights advocacy and values education in government, these specialized efforts have undoubtedly played a vital role in holistic transformation.

Consistent with the historical constant of church unity with a purpose, Filipino Mission as Transformation has sought to bring these efforts together into a viable network for greater social impact. The *Samahan Ng mga Organisayong Pangkaunlaran* (SANGKOP),[105] which has brought together over thirty Filipino Transformational organizations, represents one such network. De Boer, who essentially founded SANGKOP, reminisces: 'At first it was just six of us back in June of 1988. We met in my office and the results from the brainstorming that emerged from that ad hoc committee are seen in an organization of thirty Christian groups which have consolidated their forces into an effective, holistic, and relevant body working with and for the poor.'[106] SANGKOP lost some momentum in the late 90s, but under new leadership, a reformed network re-emerged as the Alliance of Christian Development Agencies (ACDA). Founded in 1999, ACDA seeks to bring together the vision and the resources of Christ-centreed development organizations for the purpose of transforming poor communities through holistic ministries.

Filipino Mission as Transformation affirms and encourages the whole Church in all of its functional forms - local church as well as specialized para-church organizations - to work together in bringing about enduring social change. By doing so, it advances the historical continuity of church unity with a purpose.

Across Denominations

A more daring affirmation of the whole Church constitutes the seventh dimension of Filipino Mission as Transformation, namely, affirming the whole Church across denominations, even non-evangelical traditions in the task of social transformation. Some Filipino Transformationists have come to terms with the fact that the whole Church must include the faithful in both ecumenical Protestant and Catholic Churches if the transformation of society has a fighting chance.

Such a conviction did not bode well with many Filipino evangelicals, even some among those involved in SANGKOP. Indeed the divide between Catholics and Protestants in the Philippines goes far and wide, and many evangelicals (as well as many Catholics) consider it premature to attempt to

---

[105] An English translation of the name would read something like the Alliance of Christian Transformational (or Development) Agencies.

[106] Cited in F. Albert Tizon, 'Revisiting the Mustard Seed: The Filipino Evangelical Church in the Age of Globalization', *Phronesis* 6.1 (1999), 20.

bridge the gap at this time. But most Filipino Transformationists believe that this hostile division has originated from imported fundamentalist theologies of both the Catholic and the Protestant sectors; for divisions that run along these lines ultimately violate the Filipinos' sense of solidarity.

As suggested earlier, this sense of solidarity emerges most prominently during times of great need. Maggay, for example, explains that evangelicals experienced 'a crisis of paradigm' during the first People Power Revolution when, in the heat of the moment, Catholics, evangelicals and even Muslims prayed together. When Cardinal Sin instructed all to kneel as the Marcoses fled the country, Maggay recollects that 'some of the evangelicals ... [looked] at me and said, "What shall we do?" I said, "Let's kneel". Together with the rest we knelt.'[107]

The crisis of the Mt. Pinatubo eruption of 1991 presented another opportunity for Christians of different traditions to come together in one of the hardest hit provinces, Zambales. 'Testimonies from many church leaders in this area would attest to the fact that before the eruption of Mt. Pinatubo, they did not know of each other or of their ministries. It took a massive blast, the second most destructive in the twentieth century, to have the churches acknowledge one another's existence.'[108]

In light of the notion of crisis as unifier, one can surmise that Filipino Transformationists who felt strongly about collaboration with the non-evangelical sectors of the Church for the sake of the city of Manila viewed the city as a region in crisis and did not need the blast of a volcano or the cruelty of a dictatorial government to convince them. Under the Transformational leadership of De Boer, Lim, and American Mac Bradshaw and in partnership with Fr. Ben Beltran of the Risen Christ Parish Church located in the then infamous Smokey Mountain, the National Coalition of Urban Transformation (NCUT) was born. Formed in 1998, NCUT has led the way in affirming the whole Church across denominational traditions in the Philippines. 'I'm delighted', affirms De Boer, 'to see our brothers and sisters from across denominational lines extend their hand of fellowship to one another in exploring innovative ways of bringing the Gospel of Jesus Christ to our urban centres'.[109]

It is important to note that NCUT was formed in response both to biblical conviction and the great needs of the city, not primarily in reaction against those evangelicals who did not share the vision of cooperation with non-evangelicals. Although fundamental disagreements existed among them

---

[107] Melba Maggay, 'Signs of the Presence of the Kingdom in the February Revolution', in Douglas J. Elwood (ed.), *Toward a Theology of People Power* (Quezon City: New Day, 1988), 64.

[108] Tizon, 'Ang Pagyabong ng Komundad at ang Iglesya', 83.

[109] De Boer, 'Hope of the City', 6.

regarding this kind of unity, NCUT formed without much resistance, and it has maintained complementary relations with the likes of SANGKOP and later ACDA. While respecting those who could not yet see the virtue of working with non-evangelicals (especially Roman Catholics), NCUT visionaries dared to move forward with Evangelical-Catholic dialogues, collaborative consultations covering micro-financing, housing, environment, justice for the poor, theological education, etc., and cross-denominational community projects.[110] The Pacific Rim Urban Think Tank of 2001,[111] which brought together both local and international urban leaders from around the world, demonstrated the extent to which NCUT succeeded in bringing the whole Church together for the sake of the city. Hosted by NCUT at the Asian Theological Seminary in Manila, the participants were treated to a truly ecumenical experience as they listened to keynote speakers David Lim representing an evangelical Protestant perspective, Mariano Apilado representing a mainline Protestant perspective and Fr. Benigno Beltran representing a Roman Catholic perspective.

The *whole* Church, which crosses human drawn denominational lines and which utilizes all local church and para-church forms, defines important dimensions of Filipino Mission as Transformation, dimensions that extend the historical thread of church unity with a purpose.

Mass Movements: Mobilizing the Poor

One other historical thread that weaves throughout the Filipino Church experience has to do with the integral role that the Church has played in mobilizing the masses for action. In a Two Thirds World setting, the idea of 'the masses' does not just refer to numbers but more significantly to the numbers that *suffer*; thus do the terms 'mass' and 'poverty' go together. According to Catholic social ethicist Vitaliano Gorospe, 'The urban and rural poor, the labourers, the farmers and landless rural workers, the fisherfolk, the indigenous peoples, the street children, the prisoners, the victims of ... [disaster], the elderly, the handicapped, and other marginalized groups' make up eighty five percent of the population.[112] 'Appalling mass poverty', he

---

[110] De Boer, 'Hope of the City', 13.

[111] The Pacific Rim Urban Think Tank was an annual event of the International Urban Associates (IUA) that gathered Christian leaders in a city located in the Pacific Rim in order to discern what God was doing in that city through various ministries and churches. I participated in the event in Bangkok, Thailand in 2000 and Manila, Philippines in 2001.

[112] Vitaliano Gorospe, *Forming the Filipino Social Conscience* (Makati City: Bookmark, 1997), 5.

laments, 'is the most tragic aspect of Filipino life.'[113] He characterizes the social situation 'by two death-dealing realities, namely, "kahirapan" [suffering due to poverty] and "walang kaayusan sa bayan" [injustice and lack of peace and order]'.[114] In the Philippines therefore, when the Church has helped to mobilize the masses, it has helped to mobilize the poor.

Historians simply cannot overlook the Church's influence whenever the masses of the Filipino people have come together for the cause of freedom and justice. It was in fact the courage of native clergy in the mid-1800s, who fought for justice in the parishes, that sparked what finally burst into revolutionary flames against Spain in 1896. Just like the integral role that the Filipino Church (both Catholic and Protestant) played in the more recent uprisings, the Church did much to inspire and mobilize the fight for freedom against Spanish tyranny and oppression a hundred years earlier. Indeed, the uprising of 1896 can really be said to be the first People Power Revolution in the Philippines. Of the heavy influence of Filipino priests before and during the Revolution, Schumacher writes, '[They] were a capable moving force behind a Filipino nationalist movement among the masses.'[115] It is true that as the Revolution progressed, the power shifted from the clergy to legal and military strategists, but:

> Even though the intellectual leadership of the nationalist movement had passed from the clergy to the lay *illustrados,* the developed nationalism of the 1890s would have been able to move only a small portion of the people had not the influence of the clergy supported it.[116]

To be sure, however, the much more recent history of the People Power Revolution of 1986 and the events leading up to it highlight in an unprecedented way the thread of the Church's role in mobilizing the masses for action. As for the Catholic Church, we cannot describe its involvement in the People Power Revolution as anything but overt and upfront. It was after all the Cardinal himself, Jaime Sin, who persuaded Mrs. Aquino, herself a devout Roman Catholic, to run against Marcos in the snap election; it was he who convinced Salvador Laurel Jr. to run as Vice President alongside Aquino instead of opposing her in order to consolidate political opposition against Marcos; and it was he who primarily rallied the people Catholic and non-Catholic to the streets via Radio Veritas in defense of defectors Enrile and Ramos when Marcos threatened to squash the rebellion. American journalist Stanley Karnow described Cardinal Sin 'as the country's shrewdest politician' at that time.[117]

---

[113] Gorospe, *Forming*, 20.

[114] Gorospe, *Forming*, 19-20.

[115] Schumacher, *Revolutionary Clergy*, 64.

[116] Schumacher, *Revolutionary Clergy*, 64.

[117] Karnow, *In Our Image*, 411.

Cardinal Sin, however, claimed he only acted in accordance with the higher power of God, which the figure of the Virgin Mary ultimately embodied for Filipino Catholics. On the corner of EDSA and Ortigas Avenue, where much of the actual non-violent Revolution took place, the EDSA Shrine of the Virgin Mary stands commemorating for Catholics not only the events of February 1986, but more importantly, God's hand in bringing about the Revolution.

Filipino Ecumenical Protestants also participated. Richard Schwenk claims that Protestants participated significantly relative to their minority status.[118] First, they helped to prepare the way during the Martial Law years by sustained education and courageous political involvement. Petz Guerrero rightly points out that the Revolution came about in large part as 'the result of a continuous, protracted, long process of awareness-building and organizing among our people'.[119] Second, inseparably related to the first, ecumenical Protestants made official statements and took corporate stands against the Marcos dictatorship. From the Statement of Concern in 1974 to the Officers' Statement on the February Elections in 1986 to the Post-February 25 Statement, the NCCP utilized its prophetic office to question and denounce the injustices of the Marcos government. Third, ecumenical Protestants occupied and made the best of key political positions, like Ramos whose military defection triggered the Revolution and who succeeded Aquino as President in 1992. Fourth, they joined others in the streets leading the masses in prayer, food distribution, car-pooling, and worship services.[120] And fifth, they joined the Church at large in helping people afterward to interpret theologically the events of the God inspired Revolution.

In the same spirit, Filipino Transformationists were the vanguard for fellow evangelicals to join the peaceful overthrow. As established earlier, the short list of kingdom themes that unify Transformationists around the world includes a commitment to the poor. In the Filipino context, this commitment has expressed itself most dramatically in contributing to the mobilization of the masses for the cause of freedom and justice. The People Power Revolution in particular provided the context for Filipinos to rally together, and Filipino Transformationists took the lead on behalf of the evangelical community to participate in the historic uprising. By such leading, Filipino Transformationists followed along the historical thread of the Church's role in catalyzing mass movements. From this historical constant, the last two dimensions of Filipino Mission as Transformation come to the fore: 8) religious validation and inspiration, and 9) solidarity and empowerment.

---

[118] Richard L. Schwenk, *Onward Christians! Protestants in the Philippine Revolution* (Quezon City: New Day, 1986), 2.

[119] Cited in Schwenk, *Onward Christians,* 36.

[120] Schwenk, *Onward Christians,* 24-32.

Religious Validation and Inspiration

Filipino Transformationists have carried on the tradition of the Church's role in mobilizing the masses first by validating and inspiring social action primarily among evangelicals since the People Power Revolution of 1986. Insofar as the people believe the Church's claim that the fight is accomplishing God will, the Church's support of a given social change movement puts the divine stamp upon it, thus validating it and inspiring people to participate in it.

The fact that the Church has always played a key role in Filipino society corresponds to the indigenous mix of politics and religion throughout the nation's history. Such a mix harks back to the integrated worldview of the Filipino where natural and supernatural realms respectively make up an indivisible continuous whole. Thus, to understand God as intervening in political affairs, whether directly or indirectly through God's people, squarely lands within the bounds of a Filipino worldview. 'The experience at EDSA', states Maggay referring to the phenomenon of People Power, 'is continuous with the indigenous fusion of the political and the mystical in our historical situation.'[121] Sociologist Randy David concurs when he assesses the first People Power uprising as divinely led. Shortly after the event, he remarked, 'I have been a student of revolutions, but this is the first time I have seen a revolt led by the Virgin Mary.'[122]

This culturally grounded fusion explains in large part why the imposed separation of church and state has never really grabbed hold in the Filipino corporate psyche, despite the Constitutional language to the contrary. Lim observes that 'among the population ... it has always been felt that the Church's mission should include active participation in important national issues, since these are perceived to be important moral concerns related to love, righteousness, freedom, justice and peace.'[123] He aptly summarizes the hope of church state relations that is consistent with a Filipino worldview with a benediction like pronouncement: 'May the Philippines become a nation with the soul of a church.'[124]

Post-World War Two evangelicals in the Philippines were reawakened to their sense of social responsibility amidst the 1986 People Power Revolution due largely (perhaps solely) to the Filipino Transformationists among them who led the way. Through education, prophetic statements, prayer rallies, the provision of practical avenues for participation in the streets during the actual events and other various ways, Filipino Transformationists did their part in spiritually validating the mass cry for justice and inspiring evangelicals to join

---

[121] Maggay, 'Engaging Culture', 66.

[122] Cited in Maggay, 'Engaging Culture', 66

[123] David S. Lim, 'Church and State in the Philippines, 1900-1988', *Transformation* 6.3 (July/September 1989), 26.

[124] Lim, 'Church and State', 31.

many other fellow Filipinos against the Marcos regime. The godly success of that first People Power (by 'godly' I mean at least that it was bloodless and effective) contributed to the awakening of socio-political involvement among evangelicals; for it has undeniably become more a part of Filipino evangelical mission ever since.

Since 1986, four more People Power movements occurred. People Power II in January 2001, to impeach the corrupt and inept movie star turned President Joseph 'Erap' Estrada, and People Power III in April of the same year, to call for his return, make up the two other official mass movements in the spirit of People Power. But in 1997 and 1999 respectively, two other mass actions occurred that Lim also considers to have come from the same well, namely, when the people rallied against Ramos in 1997 and then Estrada in 1999 who both proposed to make fundamental changes in the Constitution in order to extend their respective terms of office.[125] These rallies protested the 'cha-cha' proposal (short for 'charter change') to enable the current President to run for a second term, which the 1987 Constitution written under the Aquino administration forbade. Led by Cardinal Sin and former President Aquino, people rallied against the proposed Constitutional amendment, and enough people pressure registered in both 'cha-cha' attempts that neither succeeded.

Whereas the Filipino Evangelical Church can largely credit its Transformational constituents for awakening it from its social slumber in 1986, it can cite varied influences in the four other People Power movements. Indeed, the diversity that exists among Filipino evangelicals began to surface in the political arena. While some evangelical leaders like Eddie Villanueva pleaded with their constituents to support the 'cha-cha' proposals, Transformationists largely espoused an 'anti-cha-cha' stance and encouraged their spheres of influence to join Sin and Aquino to prevent the Philippines from becoming another 'banana republic' that changes the Constitution at every turn.[126]

In People Power II, a more unified Filipino evangelical voice arose for Estrada's impeachment. While more conservative and moderate evangelicals hesitated at first to join the masses, Transformationists forged ahead unwaveringly in supporting efforts to impeach the President. Immediately after the Singson revelations in October 2000, which undeniably implicated Estrada in a major illegal gambling operation called *jueteng*, through which Estrada was gaining personal and family wealth,[127] ISACC issued an open letter, which

---

[125] Lim, 'Consolidating', section 3.3.2.

[126] Lim, 'Consolidating', section 3.3.4.

[127] In a TV-radio press conference at Club Filipino on 8 October 2000, Governor Luis "Chavit" Singson, a former friend of then current President Estrada, stunned the nation with his shocking revelation that the President had been receiving monthly payoffs from centralized *jueteng* collections since taking office. Singson was involved as well, which further strengthened the fact that his revelations were true.

urged its members 1) to pray everyday that Estrada would be removed from office, 2) to urge other government officials to abandon Estrada, and 3) to join prayer and protest rallies whenever possible.[128] They also organized a forum in November on moral leadership and governance as well as a special Christmas worship service in December, both of which clearly called for the President to step down. And in January 2001 in the heat of the second People Power, it was ISACC, under the auspices of 'Evangelicals for Justice and Righteousness', who was leading the prayer service at the EDSA Shrine when the military defected to the side of the people.[129] To be sure, these actions on the part of Filipino Transformationists helped to mobilize the masses for the events of January 2001, which ousted Estrada from office.

As for People Power III, where many people once again rallied this time to reinstate Estrada perhaps as an overreaction to what many considered a disrespectful arrest of the former President on plunder charges in April 2001, Filipino Transformationists took a stand, along with many other evangelicals, this time *against* the uprising and urged their constituents not to participate.[130] Whether by endorsing or rejecting a people movement, Filipino Transformationists have demonstrated continuity with the historical thread of the Church's role in mobilizing the masses by way of spiritual validation and inspiration.

Solidarity and Empowerment

Affirming the strong unity that forms among the people for the cause of social justice, a solidarity that cultivates a sense of empowerment to shape the future makes up the second way. Taken together, solidarity and empowerment constitute the last dimension of Filipino Mission as Transformation that we derive from history.

While Filipinos cannot claim uniqueness among the nations in rallying together in times of crisis, the depth of unity reached in response to injustice that the first and second People Power Revolutions demonstrated has earned for itself a worldwide reputation. Their non-violent, spiritual, swift and massive natures have captured the attention of international scholars, activists and critics alike. Remembering the first People Power, Maggay states that people came in droves from all sectors and classes of society; 'a people known to be fractious stood in solidarity together.'[131] As a result, a unique power swept the land, accomplishing what years of diplomatic attempts from the moderate side and armed attempts from the radical side could not. It only took four days in the

---

[128] Cited in Lim, 'Consolidating', section 3.3.2.

[129] Lim, 'Consolidating', section 3.3.2.

[130] Lim, 'Consolidating', sections 3:1 and 3.3.2.

[131] Maggay, 'Engaging Culture', 64.

first People Power to force a seemingly invincible dictator to seek political asylum in Hawaii, and another four days in the second People Power to replace a corrupt incompetent leader, thereby rendering impeachment proceedings unnecessary. The Filipino people achieved a remarkable level of solidarity and empowerment during those revolutionary events. Centuries of struggle against colonial rule, a maturing of Christian faith and the Filipinos' sense of community and unity came together to catalyze a revolution. And when Filipino Transformationists joined in, they acted continuously with the historical thread of the Church's contribution to the mobilization of the poor for freedom and justice.

The Gospel at work in between People Power events, however, deserves some credit. For the Church to get in position to walk in solidarity and empowerment with the masses during these historic times, it would have had to have stood in solidarity and empowerment with them during the 'non-historic', 'normal' times. In the end, People Power must be truly about people, not about ideals or principles or strategies. For true People Power advocates, therefore, the daily grind of the poor compels a daily response to stand in solidarity with them in their suffering and to facilitate processes among them that foster a sense of human dignity, responsibility, and contextual (on the ground) solutions to their problems, i.e. empowerment. Barcelona points out that poverty too often becomes a mere issue to be dissected. She writes, 'Social scientists have discovered its anatomy. Researchers and statisticians have put numbers to it. No less than the President of the Philippines has vowed to fight against it.'[132] But who stands with them in their [daily] struggles?

Attempting to remain in touch with this human side of poverty, Filipino Transformationists have engaged the poor incarnationally during non-crisis times (if we can say that daily poverty is a non-crisis). Maggay shares some 'side notes', as she describes them, from her experience of joining a church in the slums in the early 1990s. She writes, 'I decided to move from my middle class church and started to root a part of myself among a people whose grimy claim to existence I had mostly written about rather than lived with.'[133] Her side notes include the need for development practitioners to relinquish control, the concreteness of God among the poor, and the importance of the people themselves giving shape to both their personal and social transformations.[134]

This kind of solidarity cultivates an empowerment that truly serves the poor; for in such a relationship, the poor can realize the ability to direct their own future. Lim describes it this way in practical terms:

---

[132] Barcelona, 'The Face of the Poor', 3.
[133] Melba Maggay, 'Crossing the Cultural Divide: Reflections from Down Under', *Patmos* 11.2 (2nd Quarter 1995), 14.
[134] Maggay, 'Crossing the Cultural Divide', 15-16, 21.

Transformational missiology ... historically ... has developed into a strategy that aims to facilitate the discipling process of empowerment of the members of a community or people-group from being passive recipients to becoming active participants in tackling issues (both local and global, as well as physical, social, or religious) that affect their lives, primarily through the 'community development - community organization' approach.[135]

The combination of the kingdom themes of incarnation and commitment to the poor have led Filipino Transformationists to identify deeply with the poor on a daily, practical basis, thus earning them the right to stand in solidarity and empowerment with the people when unjust times call for mass action.

These historical threads, as we have called them throughout this chapter, have drawn out and organized at least the following nine local dimensions of Filipino Mission as Transformation:

1. critical consciousness
2. prophetic ministry
3. whole being/whole ministry
4. theology of beauty
5. spirit world cosmology
6. across church forms
7. across denominations
8. religious validation and inspiration
9. solidarity and empowerment

These nine local dimensions, which we have organized under four historical constants, make up Filipino Mission as Transformation. They reflect the uniqueness of a missiology that has emerged in a particular historical context. They obviously differ from Samuel's list of the eight global dimensions, upon which we expanded in Chapter 6, but the two lists obviously overlap as well. To grasp how the local and global understandings of Mission as Transformation relate to one another and create 'glocal' dimensions defines the task of Part IV.

---

[135] Cited in Santos Yao 'David Lim', in Charles van Engen, Nancy Thomas and Robert Gallagher (eds.), *Footprints of God: A Narrative Theology of Mission* (Monrovia, Calif.: MARC, 1999), 166.

PART IV

Missiological Glocalization

Introduction to Part IV

Today's increasingly interconnected interdependent world calls for an understanding of the mission of the Church in terms of the global and the local. The simultaneously expanding and compressing, ever-changing areas of economics, technology, politics and culture - the four sets of the 'logics of globalization' according to sociologist Philip Kelly - have made the negotiation between the global and the local a fundamental imperative for many, if not all, disciplines.[1]

For missiology, the globalization phenomenon has created the newest way of discussing context. Schreiter claims that 'world events - some of which have been occurring over a period of time, others of which have happened more abruptly with still not clearly seen consequences - are producing new contexts for theology'.[2] The world events of which he speaks make up the complex of social processes known today as globalization, and the new contexts for theology emerge out of the interplay between global culture and local cultures. To understand more fully, therefore, the missiology of Transformation requires a negotiation of its global and local understandings. How does the local understanding of a particular missiology, Filipino Mission as Transformation, contribute to the shared global understanding of Mission as Transformation? And conversely, how does its shared global understanding contribute to local understandings of Mission as Transformation all over the world, especially the one expressed in the Philippines?

We have thus far, at least implicitly, assumed a harmony between the global and the local, an inseparable, interdependent, mutually benefiting relationship - a symbiosis. This assumption is partially based upon sociologist Roland Robertson's 'globalization paradigm' that has come, according to Donald Lewis, 'to dominate discussion of 'globalization' in the field of sociology of

---

[1] Philip E. Kelly, *Landscapes of Globalization* (London; New York: Routledge, 2000), 3-8.
[2] Schreiter, *The New Catholicity*, 4, 26-27.

religion'.[3] The fact that Robertson's understanding of globalization not only includes the local, but actually sees it as constituting the global, is one of the salient features of his view. 'The global is not in and of itself counterposed to the local', he contends, 'Rather, what is often referred to as the local is essentially included with the global. In this respect, globalization, defined in its most general sense as the compression of the world ... involves the linking of localities'.[4] Others have developed this idea as well, such as political scientist David Held and colleagues, who speak of the processes that make up globalization as 'a deepening enmeshment of the local and global such that the impact of distant events is magnified while even the most local developments may come to have enormous global consequences'.[5]

This view does not eliminate the tension between local and global realities. Indeed the complex processes of globalization carry with them the frightening possibility of infighting between global forces and local reactions. Held and colleagues claim that the benefits and consequences of globalization are uneven, 'generating new patterns of inclusion and exclusion, new winners and losers'.[6] Robertson adds to this thought and states as a matter of fact that 'cultural clashes and tensions are an inevitable feature of globalization.'[7] He warns further that 'nothing about globalization should lead people to believe that globalization is leading to a more peaceful world'.[8] That said, the fact that these sociologists have established the organic link between the global and the local at least qualifies the polarity - the global *versus* the local idea - that dominates all too many globalization discussions. Although the tension between the two realities is real, to pit them against each other as inevitable enemies ultimately misleads the conversation. In fact, it is the dynamic creativity of that tension that helps to prevent both 'globalism' - the unbridled

---

[3] Donald M. Lewis, 'Globalization: The Problem of Definition and Future Areas of Historical Inquiry', in Mark Hutchinson and Ogbu Kalu (eds.), *A Global Faith: Essays on Evangelicalism and Globalization* (New South Wales: The Centre for the Study of Australian Christianity, 1998), 29.

[4] Roland Robertson, 'Glocalization: Time-Space and Homogeneity-Heterogeneity', in Mike Featherstone, Scott Lash and Roland Robertson (eds.), *Global Modernities* (London: Sage, 1995), 35.

[5] Held, McGrew, Goldblatt, and Perraton, *Global Transformations*, p.15. Held and colleagues go further in an Appendix in their book and list five 'indicators of international enmeshment', i.e., how exactly the global and the local relate in the key arenas of: 1) politico-legal, 2) military, 3) economic, 4) socio-cultural, and 5) environmental (453-454).

[6] Held, McGrew, Goldblatt, and Perraton, *Global Transformations*, 27.

[7] Roland Robertson, 'Globalization and the Future of "Traditional Religion"', in Max L. Stackhouse and Peter J. Paris (eds.), *God and Globalization, Vol. 1: Religion and the Powers of the Common Life* (Harrisburg, Pa.: Trinity Press International, 2000), 61.

[8] Robertson, 'Globalization', 61.

promotion of modernity, capitalism, and the values that flow out from these at the expense of local cultural ways of life, and 'localism' or 'contextualism' - the reactive (sometimes violent) assertion of post-modernity, of local identity and local knowledge at the expense of contributing to the global good.

The global-local symbiotic view of globalization has necessitated for Robertson the invention of a new term, or rather a new appropriation of an existing marketing term, namely, 'glocal' and its noun form 'glocalization'. Derived primarily from a Japanese business technique called 'dochakuka', glocalization has meant for Japanese economics 'the tailoring and advertising of goods and services on a global ... basis to increasingly differentiated local and particular markets'.[9] Robertson believes that this terminology, appropriated generally to global social theory, conveys better what he has been saying all along about globalization, namely, that the global and the local are organically and therefore inseparably intertwined. Moreover, globalization involves 'the creation and the incorporation of locality, processes which themselves largely shape, in turn, the compression of the world as a whole'.[10] Therefore, not only are the global and the local inseparably intertwined; they also determine each other's respective forms. From a sociological perspective then, glocalization means generally the organic and symbiotic relationship between the global and the local.

The development of worldwide evangelicalism in general demonstrates this idea of glocalization. Sociologist Paul Freston, who has led the way in research concerning evangelicalism on a global scale particularly with regard to its political influence, writes that 'the current moment of globalization of Christianity requires a recognition of the 'priesthood of all cultures', a creative play on the Protestant doctrine of the priesthood of all believers, which conveys the integral role that each and every Christian plays for Christianity.[11] The 'priesthood of all cultures' then conveys the idea of each and every culturally defined local faith contributing to a global faith. He explains further that 'Christianity is ... a universalism which affirms the particular, unlike modernity (a universalism which denies the particular) and post-modernity (a set of particularisms which do not attain universality). ... Evangelicalism's combination of universalism and particularity may be uniquely powerful in creating global community.'[12] Although Freston himself does not use the term

---

[9] Robertson, 'Glocalization', 28.

[10] Robertson, 'Glocalization', 40.

[11] Paul Freston, 'Evangelicalism and Globalization: General Observations and Some Latin American Dimensions', in Mark Hutchinson and Ogbu Kalu (eds.), *A Global Faith: Essays on Evangelicalism and Globalization* (New South Wales: The Centre for the Study of Australian Christianity, 1998), 72. See also Freston's *Evangelicals and Politics* for an overview of his research.

[12] Freston, 'Evangelicalism and Globalization', 72.

'glocal', his treatment of the global-local relationship clarifies the concept as it applies to the worldwide evangelical movement.

The glocalization of Mission as Transformation can be seen as a subset of the larger glocalization of evangelicalism, a subset that has done its part in ensuring that the globalizing evangelical movement includes holistic voices from the Two Thirds World. Out of the ruins of the period wherein a Western colonial missiology dominated, a global intercontextuality that has become greater than the sum of its parts - a gestalt effect - has emerged. Rather than taking one contextual version of the Gospel and imposing it as *the* Gospel throughout the world via the missionary enterprise, the shapers of Mission as Transformation have recognized the plurality of localities that has created an intercontextual, 'pan-local', *global* phenomenon in theology. They have seen churches of the Two Thirds World shape the very idea of global Mission as Transformation. As this intercontextuality matures through communication, exchange and partnership, it comes into its own and reflexes back to inform and reshape local theologies. If Parts II and III have expanded upon the global and local dimensions of Mission as Transformation respectively, then Part IV considers its *glocal* dimensions.

CHAPTER 9

Glocal Dimensions: Partnership in Mission in the Twenty First Century

Chapter 6 reorganized and expanded upon the eight components of Mission as Transformation that originated with Samuel and Sugden and identified here as this missiology's global dimensions (Table 2), and Chapter 8 drew out nine local Filipino dimensions from the history of the Filipino Church-in-mission in the national struggle for freedom and justice (Table 3). As we can see, the two charts make up very different lists. I contend, however, that the two lists relate to, and in fact, need each other.

Table 2: Global Dimensions

Biblical Kingdom Themes for Church Mission	Global Dimensions of Mission as Transformation
Integration	1. word, work and wonder 2. reconciliation/solidarity and stewardship 3. communities of change: where the present and future meet
Incarnation	4. mission in context 5. full contextual engagement 6. local faith
Commitment to the Poor	7. mission as journey with, for, and among the poor 8. freedom and power through personhood

We have two distinct goals in this chapter. First, we must understand the nature of the global-local relationship, i.e., their theoretical connections with and reliance upon each other. What part does locality play in globalization and what part does globality play in localization? Indeed, 'the complex web and networks of relations between communities, states, international institutions, non-governmental organizations and multinational corporations which make up the global order' reveal some kind of relationship between local and global realities.[1] What exactly is the nature of that relationship in the worldwide Transformational network?

Table 3: Local Filipino Dimensions

Missiological Themes from a History of the Filipino Church-in-Mission	Local Filipino Dimensions of Mission as Transformation
Subversion and Resistance	1. critical consciousness 2. prophetic ministry
Nationalistic or Local Faith	3. whole being/whole ministry 4. theology of beauty 5. spirit world cosmology
Church Unity with a Purpose	6. across church forms 7. across denominations
Mass Movements: Mobilizing the Poor	8. religious validation and inspiration 9. solidarity and empowerment

The second goal flows from the first: we need to discover the *glocal* dimensions of Mission as Transformation, i.e., how the whole Church in its mosaic of cultures has engaged, and must continue to engage, the whole world in a *glocal* partnership for mission.

Mission as Transformation Between the Global and the Local

The Local in the Global: Globalization from Below

As I shared the global dimensions of Mission as Transformation with Melba Maggay in a personal interview, she interrupted me at one point and said, 'Actually, all of these things were being done on the local level. We were living them out in our own situation long before they were articulated globally.'[2] This sentiment reflects an important truth, namely, that missionary initiatives within a given locality are not dependent upon outside influences; that contextual expressions of the Gospel spring up in response to particular socio-cultural situations. This truth may be obvious now in the face of advances made by contextual liberation theologies around the world in the last thirty five years, but missiologists cannot overstate it. Filipino radical evangelicals were

---

[1] Held, McGrew, Goldblatt and Perraton, *Global Transformations,* 15, 27.

[2] Maggay, interview. The quote above is my loose English translation of our conversation that was in 'Taglish', a style of talk that creatively combines Tagalog and English.

responding holistically to injustices occurring in the country, not because of any external driver. Maggay, Lim, Magalit, Miranda-Feliciano and others engaged in culturally relevant Mission as Transformation before there *was* Mission as Transformation.

Or perhaps it is more accurate to say it this way: The local Transformational initiatives occurring in the Philippines and many other places around the world created the global notion of Mission as Transformation. As once of many local Transformational initiatives, Filipino Mission as Transformation has helped to make a global missiology of Transformation possible. Together these local initiatives have created an intercultural phenomenon that reveals a set of shared convictions, which constitute the making of a global missiology. The eight global dimensions that this study has identified have attempted to define these pan-local convictions of Transformationists worldwide. Global Mission as Transformation essentially showcases the idea of the 'linking of localities',[3] 'the priesthood of all cultures',[4] a 'globalization from below'.

Of these interesting phrases, the 'globalization from below' captures most saliently the globalized end product of the sum of localities, despite the varied uses of the phrase among global theorists. Brecher, Costello and Smith's volume by that title use the phrase to convey an alternate global movement of grassroots social activists to challenge the 'globalization from above', which refers to the onslaught of elite, hegemonic, Enlightenment based Western modernity (what I have been calling ideological globalization).[5] Ben Knighton, Dean of the Research Program at OCMS, sees it as a way to describe one of the responses to globalization, namely, the localizing of global values, thus reflexively changing the face of globalization.[6] Paul Freston describes worldwide evangelicalism as a 'globalization from below' to convey the lay people driven nature, as well as the social underside nature (particularly when referring to Pentecostals) of the worldwide movement.[7] David Smith applies the 'globalization from below' idea to missiology and hopes for the possibility of a globalization 'not driven by the search for profit but by a spirit of human solidarity and compassion'.[8]

Our use here seeks to complement these other perspectives as we employ the idea of the 'globalization from below' to emphasize the polycentric nature of

---

[3] Robertson, 'Glocalization', 35.

[4] Freston, 'Evangelicalism and Globalization', 72.

[5] Jeremy Brecher, Tim Costello and Brendan Smith, *Globalization from Below: The Power of Solidarity* (Cambridge, Mass.: South End, 2002).

[6] Ben Knighton, 'Globalization and Christian Mission in Africa', *Transformation* 18.4 (October 2001), 210-211.

[7] Freston, 'Evangelicalism and Globalization', 72.

[8] David Smith, *Mission After Christendom* (London: Darton, Longman and Todd, 2003), 101.

Mission as Transformation, to stress the fact that its global understanding was built from the bottom up out of local Transformational theologizing happening all over the world. The eight global dimensions did not fall from the sky; or if they did, they fell and rooted in contextual soil before missiologists could discern and interpret them. Or a less palatable theory: elitist Western theologians concocted them in their ivory towers and proceeded to use technologies available to them to impose their new fangled theology upon the rest of the world. Neither of these explanations accurately describes the process by which the eight global dimensions of Mission as Transformation have emerged. They identify instead the common streams of observable, holistic initiatives flowing locally out of faithful evangelical church communities all over the world.

The Wheaton '83 Statement on Transformation reports in its introduction that 'local churches and Christian mission and aid agencies ... *from 30 nations*' contributed to its articulation.[9] Padilla claims that the Statement 'completed the process of shaping an evangelical social conscience, a process in which people from the Two Thirds World played a decisive role.'[10] Indeed the global notion of Mission as Transformation has come about as a result of the process of a 'globalization from below'. No global dimensions to speak of would exist if it were not for Transformational activities happening on the local level all over the world.

Filipino Transformationists in particular have contributed to global Mission as Transformation in a variety of ways. Direct participation in definitive international conferences during the last twenty five years, including Wheaton '83, obviously points to Filipino Transformational input. Melba Maggay and Jun Vencer, who served as President of the World Evangelical Fellowship (WEF) for many years, in fact took part in Track III of Wheaton '83 that produced the Statement on Transformation. Filipino involvement at the important Word, Kingdom & Spirit Consultation in 1994, where the kingdom theme of integration advanced significantly, also points to the contextual influence of Filipinos as ten of the eighty five international participants had come from the Philippines. Miranda-Feliciano served on the convening committee and Maggay delivered one of the keynote addresses at the consultation.

In addition to direct participation in conferences and consultations, Filipino Transformationists have published articles in the international journal *Transformation* (and elsewhere) - nineteen to be exact between 1984 and 2000 - that report and define Transformational activities for the greater missionary community. Book length treatises from Filipino Transformationists have also

---

[9] 'The Wheaton '83 Statement', *The Church in Response to Human Need*, 254. Italics mine.

[10] Padilla, 'Evangelism and Social Responsibility', 31.

contributed to the international dialogue. Samuel in fact describes Maggay's *Transforming Society* as 'the most comprehensive overview of the missiology and theology of wholistic Christian involvement in social change as espoused by the INFEMIT movement'.[11]

But the most distinct contribution of Filipino Transformationists to the global understanding lies not in their direct participation at conferences or in their scholarly research *per se*, but rather in what they have brought to the global table from their local participatory experience of People Power. Their courageous leadership for the Filipino evangelical community in the two major People Power Revolutions (1986 and 2001 respectively) has contributed more to the worldwide shaping of Mission as Transformation than anything else that they may have written or done.

Their participation in People Power has testified to the power of Transformation as a genuine kingdom mission activity. Despite the fact that the People Power phenomenon as a whole in the Philippines has developed 'a dark underside' as it has been used 'by demagogues to foment disorder and hold the government hostage to their narrow interests and demands', People Power, when used in the true service of justice truly bears the signs of the kingdom.[12] Referring specifically to the first People Power Revolution, Maggay asserts, 'There are a few moments in history when the kingdom does seem to come down. This is one of them.'[13]

The manner in which Transformationists paved the way for the Filipino evangelical community to take part in the fight against great odds in 1986 and 2001 respectively has indeed inspired that community to grow in its Christ-centreed socio-political involvement. It has furthermore surely strengthened and encouraged the development of Mission as Transformation globally, especially in the area of church-state relationships. Maggay, Lim, Miranda-Feliciano and other Filipino Transformationists played key roles, for example, in the Church, State and Nation Building Conference, which convened in Hong Kong in 1988, just two years after the first People Power. Lim presented a paper there in which People Power figured prominently.[14] The official conference report also mentioned the participation of Filipino evangelicals in the Revolution as a point of encouragement for the international gathering.[15] Indeed the leadership of Filipino Transformationists during the two People Power Revolutions has testified to the notion that Christians can take part in the

---

[11] Cited in Sugden, *Gospel, Culture and Transformation*, 20.

[12] Maggay, 'Engaging Culture' 64.

[13] Maggay, 'Engaging Culture', 65.

[14] Lim, 'Church and State', 27-32.

[15] 'Church and State and Nation Building: A Conference Report', *Transformation* 6.3 (July/September 1989), 33.

genuine transformation of society. And not only that, they can do it worshipfully, prayerfully and non-violently.

These profound local Filipino expressions of Mission as Transformation have joined other Transformational expressions happening in other localities around the world to determine the nature of an intercultural phenomenon - global Mission as Transformation. The local's relationship to the global reflects at once a simple and complex arrangement: it is the very constitution of the global - the global does not, *cannot*, exist without the local - but the coming together of localities creates a global reality that becomes greater than the sum of its parts; it creates a gestalt entity to which localities make themselves accountable. We now turn to this side of the global-local relationship in Mission as Transformation where the global informs the local.

The Global in the Local: Pan-Localization from Above

What exactly transpired when those radical evangelicals from over thirty nations (primarily from the Two Thirds World) wrote the Statement on Transformation at Wheaton '83? The previous section just established the fact that Transformational activities were happening locally all over the world before Wheaton '83. For example, the official announcement of the birth of Mission as Transformation in the Philippines, the formation of ISACC in 1978, occurred five years before. So missiologists certainly cannot credit Wheaton '83 for catalyzing local activities. Two Thirds World churches did not (and do not) wait with bated breath for some kind of global permission to engage their local contexts holistically with the Gospel! Even the best of international bodies simply do not function that way. Specifically, the Wheaton '83 Statement on Transformation did not and does not determine whether local Transformational activities happen. Rather, Wheaton '83 and subsequent consultations along with their resultant statements have merely helped to recognize a global version of Mission as Transformation. Maggay suggests that the process itself of corporate grappling with a given issue at these international, multi-cultural gatherings is equally, if not more, valuable than the end product of carefully drawn up statements.[16]

Both process and statement from these international gatherings give credence to a powerful global reality that derives its authority from the locales themselves. Participants are drawn to these international gatherings first, in search of global validation as they interact with others from different parts of the world who are experiencing mission in similar ways, and second, in search of global guidance as they seek next steps in the work of the kingdom in their respective locales. I argue that the validation and guidance experienced at these international gatherings give a global version of Mission as Transformation its

---

[16] Maggay, interview.

reason for being. The other side of the idea of 'globalization from below', where the local informs the global, is the idea of 'pan-localization from above', where the global informs the local.

How exactly does the global inform the local? This 'pan-localization from above' nature of global Mission as Transformation results in an invisible, but very real power: an 'aura' of positive accountability, 'positive' in that it seeks to guide, encourage, and support, not to impose, standardize, and judge. This aura of positive accountability once again derives its life on the strength of international conferences where participants from all over the world have voluntarily come together precisely to share with one another how they are discerning the movement of God in their particular locales for the purpose of finding common strands.

These common strands usually end up synthesized and articulated into statements, which serve as the most tangible proof of this powerful aura. They do not produce this aura; rather, they merely serve as evidence that there exists a level of international agreement about the truth and/or a strategy of Christian mission by which local regions are expected to abide. Of course, even the very thought of a 'Mission as Transformation police' to make sure locales implement the conference findings is ludicrous. The responsibility lies primarily upon the locales themselves to adapt and apply the intent of international statements as they see fit in their particular contexts. Nonetheless, grassroots Transformational theologians and practitioners feel a real sense of accountability on the local level, a sense that emanates from the presence of the intercultural reality of global Mission as Transformation.

In order for the global to provide this kind of accountability for the local, it must necessarily transcend the local. Localities together have granted authority to the global, but then they turn right around and voluntarily submit to this authority. The very act of gathering together at international conferences to address missiological issues conveys the desire on the part of local Transformationists to transcend or to go outside of their respective local situations in order to gain a larger perspective. By this process, the global becomes more than the sum of its intercultural parts; it transcends the local in order to speak into the local.

This 'pan-localization from above' type of global authority, however, has its limits. Generally speaking, Robertson claims that 'insofar as globalization incorporates locality, it necessarily limits itself.'[17] In other words, because the local creates the global and gives it its authority, a given global reality - in this case, global Mission as Transformation - needs to remember its fragile existence, its interdependence with the local and its subservience to the local. Such a notion of the global resembles Schreiter's idea of a 'new catholicity' in that it seeks a positive universality through difference. Avoiding

---

[17] Robertson, 'Globalization', 64.

homogenization at all cost, Schreiter's new catholicity calls for a kind of 'humble globalization' that seeks not to control, oppress and homogenize peoples. He writes, 'The oppressive dimensions of the global ... must be analyzed, deconstructed and dismantled'.[18] This 'humble globalization' should seek to affirm, serve, and enhance cultural identities and contextually relevant movements of social change while not allowing them to drive into the theological cul-de-sac of localism.

Localism or contexualism, which we can define as an extreme postmodern overemphasis upon the local while rejecting all global or universal notions, can lead to a number of disastrous results related to cultural and theological relativism, which at least includes isolationism and fundamentalism. Isolationism occurs when a locale looks only to itself for guidance. This form of cultural and theological relativism claims that what happens on the local level has meaning only for that particular locale. This idea prevents a local theology from contributing to a global understanding as well as receiving input from outside sources. In other words, that locale has no religious or ethical accountability except to itself - isolationism. Furthermore, it becomes marginalized and largely irrelevant. The old order Amish subculture in America comes to mind. In its attempt to protect itself from modernization, the Amish community has isolated itself from the dominant culture, and its people have essentially relinquished their rights as American citizens to influence the mainstream.

Cultural and theological relativism can also devolve into arrogance, which not only believes that what happens on the local level has meaning only for that locale, it also believes that what happens on the local level *belongs* to that locale, and it must resist any threat to diminish its cultural and/or religious identity. This form of relativism is called fundamentalism. Robertson makes this point when he first of all defines relativism (or 'relativization' as he seems to prefer) as referring 'to the ways in which adherents to cultural traditions come to feel threatened by existence alongside rival or alien identities or traditions in an increasingly interdependent world'.[19] He then says outright that 'relativization has been largely responsible for what has come to be called 'fundamentalism.'[20] A positive, intercultural or pan-local view of the global as a powerful aura of accountability would prevent isolationism, fundamentalism and any other misguided form of localism related to cultural relativism.

Inspired by the aura of accountability that emanates from the global reality of Mission as Transformation, Transformationists from all over the world encourage, support, partner and consult with each other, thus strengthening local efforts globally. In the Philippine context, Transformationists have

---

[18] Robertson, 'Glocalization', 26.

[19] Robertson, 'Globalization', 61.

[20] Robertson, 'Globalization', 60.

welcomed the support of the growing missiological fraternity of Transformationists worldwide from the very beginning. Founding members of ISACC, for example, include Americans Mac Bradshaw, who was at that time working with World Vision Philippines, and Bill Dyrness who taught theology at the Asian Theological Seminary (ATS).[21] Original funding for ISACC came through Partnership in Mission (PIM), which at that time was under the leadership of Vinay Samuel from India. Of all non-Filipino influences in the forming of the vision of ISACC, Maggay singles out Wayan Mastra from Indonesia who exemplified for her the practice of contextual theology. She remembers Mastra's determination to be truly Indonesian with regard to theology and church practice and how not to depend on foreign funding and personnel to engage Indonesian society with the Gospel. His example gave Maggay the courage to develop ISACC in a genuinely Filipino way.[22]

Besides the international influences in its early stages, ISACC has since developed an international board of reference that includes Wayan Mastra and Goh-Keat Peng from Asia, John Stott from the UK, Miriam Adeney and Ronald Sider from the USA, Samuel Escobar and Rene Padilla from Latin America, and other key figures associated with the global Transformational mission community. Issues of *Patmos* throughout the years have also published articles and creative pieces from international friends like Bill Dyrness, Miriam Adeney, Rhoda Bradshaw, Neville Carr, and others who had lived and worked in the Philippines at various points. Furthermore, international friends were often invited to national conferences as participants and speakers. One conference entitled 'At Such a Time as This', which took place a few months before the first People Power Revolution, particularly highlights international collaboration. Sugden reports that Samuel led a team from INFEMIT to Manila, and coupled with ISACC - they together discussed the role of responsible Christians 'at such a time as this'.[23] Samuel called Filipino evangelicals to prayer and to invoke the power of the Holy Spirit to change politicians. The conference undoubtedly contributed to the spiritual courage displayed by ISACC-led evangelicals during the four momentous days in February 1986. So as contextually and indigenously as Filipino Mission as Transformation has

---

[21] Maggay, interview. Maggay also emphasizes the integral roles that both wives Rhoda Bradshaw and Grace Dyrness played in the nurture of the vision of ISACC.

[22] Maggay, interview. Maggay obviously knows Mastra personally and received the valuable input to which she refers through direct mentorship of some kind. Others must settle for Mastra's works, which include a book he co-authored with Douglas G. McKenzie entitled *The Mango Tree Church: The Story of the Protestant Christian Church in Bali* (Brisbane: Boolarong Publications and the Joint Board of Christian Education, 1988). See also Chris Sugden, *Seeking the Asian Face of Jesus* (Oxford: Regnum, 1997), which commits the first four chapters to understanding Mastra as a contextual theologian.

[23] Sugden, *Gospel, Culture and Transformation,* 122.

proceeded to develop, it has always listened to international voices that have sensitively contributed to the unfolding of the kingdom of God in the Philippines.

Beyond ISACC, ATS also developed into an environment of intercultural reflection on Transformational thought and activity. The likes of David Lim who served as academic dean from 1978 to 1992, Isabelo Magalit who has served as President of the Seminary since 1989, Corrie De Boer and Lorenzo Bautista who both teach there, have assured a Transformational Filipino presence at ATS. But important non-Filipino voices have also helped to shape Filipino Mission as Transformation there. Dyrness, who taught at ATS between 1974 and 1982, certainly helped to cultivate the ground for Transformational growth. Filipino Transformationists appreciatively look to Charles Ringma from Australia, who taught there between 1991 and 1997, as doing much to shape and promote Filipino Mission as Transformation from a non-Filipino perspective, primarily through a required class he taught, appropriately entitled 'Transformational Theology'.[24] In fact, when the time came for ATS to invite a presenter for its First Annual Lecture on Holistic Mission in December 2002, it beckoned Ringma to make a return trip to the Philippines.[25]

Taken together, these examples demonstrate the global reality of Mission as Transformation informing the local Filipino experience of it by way of support, encouragement, dialogue and partnership, inspired by an essential powerful sense of global accountability that has prevented the valuable works of God's grace in Filipino society from falling into the postmodern trap of theological and cultural localism.

Glocal Dimensions of Mission as Transformation

The global-local interplay just described sets the stage for proposing *glocal* dimensions of Mission as Transformation. Glocalization once again basically points to the organic and symbiotic nature of the relationship between the global and the local. The previous section set out to explain this relationship essentially by attempting to answer the theoretical question, 'How do the global and the local relate with, and rely upon, each other?' With this plausibly answered, the time has come to understand glocalization missiologically, that is, to gain glocally informed insights for relevant and effective missionary engagement.

More specifically for our study, we must understand glocalization with reference to holistic mission. Evangelicals enthusiastically embraced the

---

[24] For more on this course, see Charles Ringma, 'Transformational Theology: Some Curriculum Issues', *Phronesis* 2.1 (1995), 77-91.

[25] The paper he presented has been published as 'Holistic Ministry and Mission: A Call for Reconceptualization', *Missiology* 32.4 (October 2004), 431-448.

missionary formula, 'the whole Church to take the whole Gospel to the whole world', at the second Lausanne World Congress in 1989 in Manila. The notion of glocalization emphasizes the 'whole Church' aspect of this formula in that it generates missiological principles that promote unity for all God's people across cultures to engage in mission together. While the global and local dimensions of Mission as Transformation emphasize the Transformational commitment to the whole Gospel for the whole world, the glocal dimensions emphasize the whole Church together for the task.

We can identify four glocal dimensions of Mission as Transformation. The first dimension (1) to be at once orthodox and contextual, is more theological in nature as Transformationists refuse to compromise either. And the next three dimensions (2) incarnational dialogue (3) post-colonial reconciliation, and (4) collaborative action, reflect the more practical side of missiological glocalization as they flesh out the essentials of genuine intercultural partnership in mission.

Orthodox and Contextual

A mission theology that is glocal upholds the two sides of biblical faith: its transcultural or universal nature on the one side and its contextual, culturally rooted nature on the other. If historical mission models erred on the side of imposing a false universal notion of the faith upon the world, then the reactionary swing of contextual mission models in the last thirty five years has tended to err to the other side. The discipline of contextual theology deserves due recognition for helping the Church correct itself; for through it the Church has realized that what had been regarded as *the* universal faith and practice for all peoples, at least during the Enlightenment era of Western dominated missions, was in fact just another contextual theology imposing itself upon the rest of the world. It imposed itself because it could, as the European and North American churches exerted their dominance over 'the younger churches' during the colonial period. The realization that Western theology had the same properties as those theologies labeled 'contextual' or 'exotic' loosened the grip of the West upon the Two Thirds World. This loosening led to the absolute necessity of taking each context seriously in order to do theology responsibly. Schreiter asserts, 'It has gradually become unthinkable ... to engage in any theological reflections without first studying the context in which it is taking place. Without such an initial analysis, a theology ... can become either irrelevant or a subtle tool of ideological manipulation.'[26]

However, contextual theology goes too far if it does not recognize the role that contextual theologies play in formulating a global theology, which reflects the universal nature of the faith. Schreiter also writes that 'theology cannot

---

[26] Schreiter, *Constructing Local Theologies*, 4.

restrict itself only to its own and immediate context; if the message of what God has done in Christ is indeed Good News for all peoples, then the occurrence of grace in any setting has relevance for the rest of humanity.'[27] Neither globalism nor localism will do for mission in today's world. To engage a world that first had been subjected to the inadequate false 'universal Christianity' of the modernist colonial era and then now subjected to the more recent confusion of the backlash of postmodern 'Christianities' necessitates not more of either; but rather a theology that embraces both an authentic global/universal and a sensitive local/particular. The Church needs a *glocal* theology of mission. It needs a transcendent but grounded vision that affirms 'constants in context', i.e., a theology of mission that is glocal.[28]

The person of Jesus Christ provides the primary biblical resource for such a theology. Jesus Christ is the God of the universe who incarnated as a Jew in Greco-Roman society for the sake not just of Israel's salvation but for the salvation of the whole world (Jn. 1:1-14; 3:16). Insofar as the Church's mission continues Christ's mission in the power of the Spirit, it proclaims by word, deed and sign the historic biblical message of salvation for all peoples while affirming the diverse ways in which this good news has incarnated within the many cultures of the world. Maggay asserts, 'Christianity is a global religion that is at the same time incarnational... There is a sense in which we are "global Christians", an interdependent community of God's people all over the world. [But] this does not mean ... that we cease to be creatures of our cultures.'[29]

The Transformational mandate to hold the creative tension between the global/universal and local/particular comes from an understanding of the biblical reality of the kingdom of God. For Transformationists, the Gospel of the kingdom as delineated in the Bible provides the norm by which Christian mission must proceed. Their commitment to the biblical vision of the consummate kingdom, where peoples from all tribes and nations will worship God (Rev. 7:9-17), compels them to engage in mission that is in scope both global/universal and local/particular.[30] In this light, one sure glocal dimension of Mission as Transformation has to do with maintaining the dialectic between the biblical integrity of the Gospel that provides a unified vision of humanity (orthodoxy) and the cultural currency of the Gospel that affirms human diversity (contextualization).

Indeed this commitment to both biblical orthodoxy and contextualization is a hallmark of Mission as Transformation. Transformationists have insisted from

---

[27] Schreiter, *The New Catholicity,* 4.

[28] 'Constants in Context', is the title of Stephen Bevans and Roger Schroeder's book (Maryknoll, N.Y.: Orbis, 2004), which many consider the best overview of the Christian mission since Bosch's *Transforming Mission.*

[29] Maggay, *Jew to the Jew, Greek to the Greek,* 55.

[30] Maggay, *Jew to the Jew, Greek to the Greek,* 49-56.

the very beginning that Christian mission must stay true to the biblical historical person of Christ while taking seriously the different incarnations of his Body, the Church, within the world's cultures. Samuel defended this conviction in reflecting on discussions at the 1988 Lambeth Conference when he said, 'Some are willing to risk everything for the sake of context. ... They will even risk Christ for the sake of the context ... [But] a Christ who does not make any real difference to the context is no Christ; he is an idol.'[31] Samuel went on to affirm the words of Gutierrez, who also attended the conference, that 'authentic and biblical God-talk is a language that is ready to risk anything *except* Christ.'[32] Mission as Transformation strives at once to remain resolutely faithful to the traditional understanding of the person of Christ (via the biblical text) and thoroughly committed to the cultural lenses through which one must peer to understand the good news of Christ (context). Lapiz summarizes this glocal conviction when he calls for 'every tribe and nation ... to evolve a brand of Christianity whose spirit is biblical but whose body is indigenous'.[33]

The objective of conference after conference sponsored by Transformationists on all levels, national, continental, and inter-continental, attests to the commitment to work out this creative tension between orthodoxy and contextualization. Grounded firmly in the soil of the evangelical tradition, Transformationists have sought to discern the meaning of biblical mission *interculturally*. It is in this idea of going about mission *interculturally* that biblical truth, which is applicable to all, and the polycentric or pan-local nature of global Mission as Transformation meet. Since no one culture has an advantage to interpret the Bible for mission, the global Church together has to do the hard work of intercultural biblical hermeneutics. The first INFEMIT consultation on Christology in 1982 at Bangkok set the precedent. In the introductory paragraphs of the conference findings, the twenty five participants, representing twenty one nations, stated:

> We were deeply conscious of our continuity not only with historic evangelicalism, but also with the different Christian traditions, both of western and of non-western origin, which exist in the Two Thirds World. ... We worked with a common commitment to Scripture as the norm, not only in matters of faith and conduct but also for theology. We were, however, also deeply aware that the agenda for our theological activity must be given to us by our respective contexts. In these contexts, it is always necessary to reflect on the biblical passion for justice, the

---

[31] Cited in Sugden, *Gospel, Culture and Transformation*, 4.

[32] Sugden, *Gospel, Culture and Transformation*, 5. Italics mine.

[33] Lapiz, 'Filipino Indigenous Liturgy', 26.

biblical concern for the 'wholeness' of salvation, and the biblical concept of the universality of Christ.[34]

Transformationists have never detoured from this commitment to both orthodoxy, as it is interculturally interpreted, and contextualization in their desire to bring the kingdom of God to bear upon the kingdoms of the world. The integral links between Transformation, biblical interpretation and cultural analysis describe the very innards of Mission as Transformation.[35]

A glocal theology of mission, one that seeks to remain true to tradition (in the best sense of the word) and cultural context, proclaims a message that offers people substantive hope. It offers solid ground upon which to stand amidst the quicksand of postmodern theologies, which have rightfully deconstructed the fallacy of modernist Christian universalism, but which have also not bothered to offer anything other than disconnected floating islands of local theologies in its place. Responsible theologians of mission cannot settle for extreme theological and cultural relativism as the answer to the fallacy of Enlightenment based Christian universalism. Now more than ever in a world cracked at the foundations, the Church in mission must remember its head - the biblical historical person of Jesus Christ in the power of the biblical Holy Spirit - and offer to the world nothing less than solid rock, who is Jesus himself, upon which people can stand and have hope (Matt. 7:24-25). Any missionary message to the world that does not have this Jesus at the centre compromises the integrity of a world vision that claims to be Christian.

But if the good news of the biblical historical Christ does not flow out of an intercultural understanding - in other words, if only one corner of the world interprets the Gospel for the rest and Christian mission turns into the mechanism by which that interpretation is diffused - then the Church is back to colonial square one. The Church must safeguard against retreating back to modernist models of mission that fall pathetically short of the authentic universal vision of the biblical kingdom just as adamantly as safeguarding against succumbing to postmodern forces that water down the Gospel. Only a theology of mission that is glocal, the kind that maintains fidelity to both intercultural biblical orthodoxy and contextualization, the kind that missiologies like Mission as Transformation exemplify, can adequately minister in today's world.

The next three glocal dimensions draw out how Transformationists have *practiced* the 'whole church' in mission together. Glocalization comes practically in our attempts at missionary equality and mutuality, i.e., partnership in mission between churches across cultures. A cursory review of

---

[34] 'Towards a Missiological Christology in the Two Thirds World', *Sharing Jesus in the Two Thirds World*, 277.

[35] Sugden, *Gospel, Culture and Transformation*, 4.

twentieth century missiological literature would reveal that the missionary enterprise across traditions has reflected much upon partnership, quite extensively in fact since the 1928 Jerusalem Conference of the International Missionary Council (IMC). That conference marked the first time the Church grappled seriously with the theme of partnership.[36] So there is certainly nothing new about the discussion surrounding cross-cultural partnership, but there is also nothing finished about it! Sadly enough, the global Church in mission does not have many examples of genuine intercultural partnership in mission, despite affirming it for over seventy five years.[37]

Missiologists today, at least conceptually, have discarded missionary paternalism where colonial churches abused their power to fashion native churches in their own image. As established earlier, contextual theology has done well to level the playing field, and although the leveling work is far from over, Two Thirds World theologians have come to play. The radical evangelical theologians and missiologists, who make up the Mission as Transformation network first came together as INFEMIT precisely to facilitate this leveling within the evangelical mission community. Sugden reports that,

> They resolved to meet ... as a Two Thirds World consultation. They did not reject partnership with Western Christians, as others had done before them in calling for missionary moratorium. But they wanted to build that partnership on a proper basis of equality and mutuality. ... They wanted a partnership with Western Christians and churches that expressed a relationship of reconciliation and mutual sharing in place of dominance and subservience.[38]

According to Costas, they wanted this type of partnership in an effort 'to help the evangelical movement in general and our respective churches in particular to bear a more biblically faithful, spiritually authentic, and socio-culturally relevant witness to Jesus Christ in the Two Thirds World'.[39]

This Transformational commitment to true partnership has generated at least three interrelated glocal dimensions that define practical partnership in mission: incarnational dialogue, post-colonial reconciliation, and collaborative action. These three glocal dimensions serve as the categorical umbrellas under which many other issues of genuine practical partnership fall. Space will not allow us to discuss in detail very important, on the ground partnership issues such as leadership and power (who controls what and why?), money and accountability (where are the finances coming from and how do we keep an accounting?),

---

[36] Philip L. Wickeri, 'Partnership, Solidarity and Friendship: Transforming Structures in Mission', a study paper for the Presbyterian Church USA, (2002), 1-2. Available at http://www.pcusa.org/marketplace/item.list.jsp.

[37] Wickeri, 'Partnership, Solidarity and Friendship', 2.

[38] Sugden, 'Wholistic Evangelism', 38.

[39] Costas, 'Proclaiming Christ in the Two Thirds World', 4.

theology and education (who sets the agenda?), and so on. However, getting a handle on the missiological dimensions of dialogue, reconciliation and collaborative action provide the guidance for intercultural partnerships to deal with these practical issues in ways that befit the kingdom. As such, these glocal dimensions warrant further discussion.

Incarnational Dialogue

For Transformationists, the possibility of partnership in mission between Western and non-Western churches rests upon the effectiveness of cross-cultural dialogue. Equality and mutuality stand a chance when churches across cultures open themselves up to the process of listening, sharing, reasoning, disagreeing and struggling with one another, and thus sharpening and enriching one another. Transformationists seek this kind of dialogue.

After their first consultation in Bangkok, Transformationists recognized 'the necessity not only for dialogue between mission theologians from various regions, but also for a proper interaction with the philosophical presuppositions, cultural values, social structures, mission histories and religious traditions of our contexts'.[40] Toward that end, Transformationists have created structures to facilitate international dialogue. Chapter 3 featured INFEMIT, the Oxford Centre for Mission Studies (OCMS) and several publishing initiatives, including Regnum Books and the journal Transformation, as making up these structures. The 'Editorial' section of the maiden issue of Transformation includes the following:

> A majority of Christians now live outside the Western industrialized nations. Our problems today are global. It is imperative therefore to improve the exchange of ideas among all parts of the church worldwide.
>
> *Transformation's raison d'etre* is the promotion of that global discussion. ... If evangelicals worldwide are to avoid disastrous fragmentation, if we are to work together to avoid global disaster, we must listen carefully to the developing views on social ethics in all parts of the world. *Transformation* exists to facilitate that international evangelical dialogue.[41]

Transformationists then have identified from the outset international dialogue as the open door through which the Church worldwide must enter in order to achieve practical partnership in mission. This could not be truer today in a globalized world where opportunities for cross-cultural encounters come much more readily.

---

[40] 'Towards a Missiological Christology', *Sharing Jesus in the Two Thirds World*, p. 279.
[41] 'Editorial', *Transformation* 1.1 (1984), 1-2.

Maggay has pointed out recently however, that genuine dialogue across cultures, where cultural parties truly engage one another, is easier said than done. As a presenter at the American Society of Missiology in 2004, she stated that 'cross cultural contact does not necessarily lead to cross cultural understanding.' She continued:

> It is one thing to see other cultures on TV, with their exotic habits and colorful costumes; it is another thing to see them invading our living spaces and smell their cooking. Once contact becomes real rather than virtual; once it engages that part of us which has to do with perceptions, values, beliefs and world views, coming together becomes awkward, tense, messy and often painful. This is the kind of discomfort we all go through once we truly cross cultures.[42]

Genuine cross-cultural dialogue, where all parties truly begin to understand and accept one another, entails a willingness to go through a very real level of discomfort. It entails going beyond surface contact and a mere exchange of words. For churches across cultures, it entails going beyond the 'business of mission' and actually getting to know one another on a deeply personal level out of which intercultural mission then flows. Genuine missionary dialogue is incarnational dialogue.

As established earlier, Transformationists have taken the incarnational principle to a profound level by applying it relationally, especially among the poor. As for both foreign and national missionaries working together, I have reflected upon my own experience of working with Filipinos in community transformation and celebrate the fact that:

> We not only worked together, we also played together; we not only designed community development strategies together, we also shared family problems together; we not only organized projects in impoverished areas together, we also went on retreats in the mountains together. Sharing intimately with each other that went beyond the 'workplace' was a good indication that the incarnational principle was more than a theological concept - it had become an integral part of our daily realities.[43]

Genuine dialogue between God's intercultural people occurs in the context of genuine relationships; not just of the shallow polite variety, but relationships that demonstrate a deep commitment to one another as fellow persons before they are fellow missionaries. Genuine dialogue for mission goes beyond words and manifests itself in the context of relationships that find their roots in the deep practical application of the incarnation.

---

[42] Maggay, 'Engaging Culture', 62.

[43] F. Albert Tizon, 'Team-Building in a Cross-Cultural Context', in Roger Heuser (ed.), *Leadership and Team-Building* (Matthews, N.C.: CMR, 1999), 254-255.

Post-Colonial Reconciliation

In addition to incarnational dialogue, authentic partnership in mission also requires reconciliation, a rich theological and socio-political concept that the limits of this study cannot take up fully here. For this dimension, we limit our remarks to the practical necessity of reconciliation between churches across cultures that seek to work together for Transformation.

Some may well ask, 'What exactly needs reconciling?' The short answer is the colonial past, which includes the part that missions played in it. To face up to the undeniable link between colonialism and missions should disturb any conscientious Christian.[44] Indeed the sins of the colonial missions era have left open sores on the Body of Christ, and the band-aid remedies of Christian niceties will not do. Trite phrases like 'Let bygones be bygones' or 'It's under the blood now' or 'Why can't we all just get along?' mock genuine reconciliation in Christ, especially when it is the missionaries from formerly colonizing nations who say them! The process of reconciliation, contends Schreiter, needs to come from the lineage of the victims, not of the oppressors.[45]

In light of this sobering truth, any talk of intercultural partnership in mission necessitates, more often than not, a reconciliation of a post-colonial kind, that is, a reconciliation based upon confession of, and forgiveness for, the sins of the colonial era. An occurrence at the 1996 Urban Poor Network Consultation in Hong Kong exemplifies this kind of reconciliation between churches across cultures. Many Transformationists, including Viv Grigg, Corrie De Boer, and other members of the SANGKOP alliance in the Philippines, led the consultation.[46] One night during worship (while singing a song entitled 'Break Dividing Walls' based on Eph. 2:14), a participant from Japan walked up to a woman from Korea, stood in front of her, and publicly apologized to her. The man said he needed to do so, on behalf of his country, because of the atrocities his forefathers committed in the 1940s and 50s against Korean women who were forced to 'comfort' Japanese servicemen. After getting over the awkwardness of the moment, the Korean woman teared up and suddenly embraced the Japanese man in a visible act of forgiveness. Their confession-forgiveness exchange set off a domino effect among the rest of the participants. For the next thirty minutes or so (while the band continued to play 'Break

---

[44] Tizon, 'Team-Building', 16. I do make the point in this chapter, however, that the colonialism-missions connection is only half the story. Indeed documentary evidence also points to many missionary endeavours that sided with native peoples against the evils of colonialism (16, 25-26).

[45] Robert J. Schreiter, *Reconciliation: Mission and Ministry in a Changing Social Order* (Maryknoll, N.Y.: Orbis, 1992), 45.

[46] I was privileged to be part of this consultation, and my primary source for the comments made in this section is my personal experience.

Dividing Walls'), Americans approached Filipinos and confessed their sin against them, the English did the same to the Indians, the Dutch to the black South Africans, and so on, all in the name of Jesus Christ through whom God promised the reconciliation of all things (Col. 1:20). The consultation program had Jackie Pullinger, founder-director of the St. Stephen's Society in Hong Kong, scheduled to speak that night, but she decided to forgo her message; for all concurred that the Spirit of God had already spoken a word - the word of reconciliation - to which the people of God could only respond.

This momentous event in Hong Kong happened spontaneously. Perhaps the coming of age of the post-colonial era calls for a more intentional effort at practical reconciliation between One Third and Two Thirds World churches. And I will go as far as to say that Transformationists are poised to lead the way. For example, the local Filipino dimension of critical consciousness discussed in Chapter 8 at least admits to the unease and suspicion that exist among Filipino Transformationists toward foreigners in general and foreign missionaries in particular based upon the colonial past. But these real feelings of unease and suspicion have not resulted in enmity against foreigners; they have rather served as motivation for Filipino Transformationists to create concrete avenues through which foreigners can learn more about Filipino church, culture and communication patterns.

These Filipino Transformational avenues reflect the efforts at work on the global level as well. INFEMIT formed precisely to strengthen the theological voice of Two Thirds World evangelicals long squelched by colonialism, in order at once to say 'no more dominance!' as well as 'let us work together'. These two sentiments equal a call for genuine reconciliation. Sugden writes of the original members of INFEMIT, 'They understood that reconciliation between different races and cultures was an important expression of the Gospel.'[47] They knew that the very nature of the Gospel prevented them from severing ties with the West, but Western Christians had to know that the age of dominance was over. Or to say it more positively, the God of reconciliation compelled these missiologists to continue seeking ways to work hand in hand with their Western counterparts as a witness to the global/universal Gospel.

These examples of facing up to the reality of a wounded past point the way toward more intentional efforts at reconciliation between churches that once patterned their relationships after the colonial model. For only through taking head-on the reality of the wounded colonial past, in contrast to glossing over it or too easily dismissing it or simply ignoring it, can a deep healing process of reconciliation ever take place.

---

[47] Sugden, *Gospel, Culture and Transformation*, 38.

Collaborative Action

To the extent that relationally based incarnational dialogue and post-colonial reconciliation occur, genuine intercultural partnership can mature into collaborative action. Whereas dialogue and reconciliation, as they are presented here, seek to set right intra-Church relationships toward genuine partnership, action fulfils the purpose of the partnership, namely, to go outside the Church and engage the world with the Gospel. The intercultural partnership of churches must at the end of the day take action, for 'faith without works is dead' (James 2:26).

Action, or 'works' in the language of *James*, finally takes the full implications of the Gospel to the ends of the earth; *collaborative* action envisions this to happen by an intercultural Church working together: *the whole Church* taking the whole Gospel to the whole world. In light of the hard challenges of dialogue and reconciliation, to rush into attempts at collaborative action seems ill-advised. On the other hand, if the Church waits for the fruit of dialogue and reconciliation to ripen before it takes action, it might never take the first step! Collaborative action needs to move forward, but with ongoing ministries of dialogue and reconciliation also in motion. In any case, if intercultural partnership between churches worldwide seeks to reflect the Gospel of Christ, then it must ultimately develop into a partnership of action.

Examples of collaborative action abound among Transformationists. Most if not all of the 'case studies in wholistic mission' featured in *Transformation* implicitly, if not explicitly, model intercultural collaboration. Sergio Sanchez, founder-director of the Mexican Association for Rural and Urban Transformation of Mexico City (AMEXTRA), claims that AMEXTRA is the product of ongoing dialogical input from groups like the International Fellowship of Evangelical Students (IFES) and the Latin American Theological Fraternity (LATF).[48] Ronald Klaus, pastor of the Living Word Community in Philadelphia USA, describes the Living Word as a racially and ethnically heterogeneous congregation. He says, 'We see this kind of modeling relationships and love across societal boundaries to be a crucial foundation to our social outreach.'[49] John Perkins' Voice of Calvary Ministries, based in race conscious Mississippi, 'has a congregation almost equally black and white and corresponding leadership' to lift up the possibility of racial reconciliation for the society at large.[50] Andrea Zaki Stephanous reports that the Coptic Evangelical Organization for Social Services (CEOSS) in Egypt, of which he

---

[48] Cited in McAlpine, *By Word, Work and Wonder*, 83.

[49] McAlpine, *By Word, Work and Wonder*, 87.

[50] McAlpine, *By Word, Work and Wonder*, 92.

serves as publications manager, 'cooperates with other development organizations at local, district, and national levels, as well as internationally'.[51]

Focusing on the Filipino Transformational scene, the SANGKOP-ACDA network, essentially an alliance of evangelical activist groups among the poor, includes in its membership non-Filipino organizations like SERVANTS, International Justice Mission, Norwegina Missionary Alliance, Open Doors with Brother Andrew, and others. The National Coalition for Urban Transformation (NCUT) also models cultural border crossing on the practical level as it works with the likes of American Ray Bakke and the International Urban Associates, New Zealander Viv Grigg, American Herb Schneider, S.J., and others. Moreover, individual missionaries from foreign denominational and interdenominational groups have joined Filipino organizations in their respective ministries. For example, Mission Ministries Philippines, Samaritana, LIGHT Ministries, and other Filipino organizations have had at one point or another non-Filipinos serve on their respective staffs. These examples of intercultural collaborative action in the Philippines and beyond demonstrate the possibility of genuine partnership in mission.

Collaborative action on the concrete local level, however, comes with a caveat. The very word 'collaboration' denotes equality, but applying it missiologically and locally should carry with it the idea of 'home field advantage'. Missionaries are guests, Bernard Adeney reasons, and 'as guests, we must always remember that our hosts are superordinate. We are on their turf.'[52] In the practical missionary context, the idea of guest translates into that of an invited co-worker who follows the lead of the host Church. This posture flies in the face of Western missionary condescension that comes from a sense of cultural superiority. This sense, which manifests in an unacceptable leader-teacher-trainer complex, unfortunately continues to contaminate cross-cultural relationships to this day.

Louder than ever before, the coming of age of the post-colonial era calls for an end to this kind of relationship between foreign and national missionaries, and again, Transformationists seem poised to demonstrate a radically different kind of relating. For example in the Philippines, a waste management project, located at the site of the infamous Smokey Mountain, has involved international participation, but the leadership undoubtedly comes from Filipino NCUT visionaries, primarily Fr. Benigno Beltran. The mission agency SERVANTS provides another example, or rather many examples, as its commitment to incarnational presence in the slums has resulted in many Filipino-initiated Transformational projects in which SERVANTS missionaries merely participate. Jennie Craig's volume *SERVANTS Among the Poor*

---

[51] Andrea Z. Stephanous, 'Coptic Evangelical Organization for Social Services, Egypt', *Transformation* 11.3 (July/September 1994), 18.

[52] Adeney, *Strange Virtues*, 51.

documents many of the collaborative efforts surrounding these projects, which range from planting holistic churches to establishing pre-schools to obtaining legal electricity for a squatter community.[53] These examples demonstrate the very real possibility of intercultural collaborative action in which national churches take the lead and international partners support, encourage and participate.

Table 4: Glocal Dimensions

Missiology (Theology and Practice)	Glocal Dimensions of Mission as Transformation
Mission Theology	1. orthodox and contextual
Mission Practice	2. incarnational dialogue 3. post-colonial reconciliation 4. collaborative action

These proposed glocal dimensions of mission theology and practice, derived from the way in which Transformationists worldwide have gone about doing mission, hold promise in guiding the whole Church in the worldwide missionary task (Table 4). Comparing the glocal dimensions with the global and local dimensions of Mission as Transformation shows all three lists as essential and standing on their own. In other words, the glocal does not make obsolete the global and the local. Rather, its glocal dimensions come into play by always keeping the other two lists in view, and the three lists - global, local and glocal - exist interdependently. For the whole Church to take the whole Gospel to the whole world, it must keep all three lists in view. Broadly speaking, its global dimensions keep the big picture of God's universal kingdom for the whole world; its local dimensions ensure contextual relevance with a local appropriation of the whole Gospel; and its glocal dimensions urge the whole Church to work together in the missionary task.

---

[53] Craig, *Servants Among the Poor.*

Conclusion

Against the backdrop of the once raging debate within the Christian missionary movement concerning the place of social concern, a worldwide network of radical evangelical mission theologians and practitioners sought to bring the full implications of the Gospel to bear upon a complex needy world. Their reflections found harbour in the notion of 'Mission as Transformation', a missiology first articulated at the Consultation on the Church in Response to Human Need in Wheaton, IL in 1983.

I have traced the historical and theological developments of this missiology worldwide as well as in the Philippines, and have done so through a global-local grid. The contemporary world scene has compelled us to use such a grid as it pulsates both with forces of economic, cultural, political and technological globalization and local responses to them. Missiology, an applied reflection-action inter-discipline that is intercultural and international by its very nature, must also re-conceptualize reality in terms of the global and the local if it seeks to maintain its relevance.

I have identified eight global dimensions and nine local Filipino dimensions of Mission as Transformation, seeking ultimately to understand the interplay between its global and local understandings. Utilizing the concept of 'glocalization', I have also identified four *glocal* dimensions, ultimately arguing that in order effectively to address the global-local complexities of today's world with the Gospel, the Church will have to go about its mission *glocally*. Championing global/universal notions of the Gospel at the expense of the local/particular (the modernist fallacy) or asserting local/particular expressions at the expense of the global/universal (the postmodern fallacy) will not do. The model of holistic mission developed by the network of Transformational theologians and practitioners around the world provides a missiology that affirms both levels, thus offering a viable way of doing mission in the twentieth first century.

As its history and global and local theologies have shown, Mission as Transformation represents one of the most progressive missionary movements among evangelicals since Lausanne '74. Consequently, some sectors within evangelicalism might be inclined to write it off as some kind of left of centre fringe movement on which the Church needs to keep a watchful eye. However in light of the advances made by this missiology - lifting up Two Thirds World voices, cantering the poor and oppressed on the missionary agenda, integrating evangelization, social justice and charismatic renewal, and other accomplishments - a dismissive response on the part of the evangelical community, or for that matter, of the larger Christian community, would be a travesty. For in light of these advances, we cannot help but conclude that Mission as Transformation has contributed significantly to the cause of the *missio Dei*, and it deserves a place among exemplary models of mission that have sought to serve a complex needy world in Christ's name.[1]

Issues for Further Exploration

Such an affirmation does not intend to announce the arrival of a perfect and flawless missiology. Being a 'missiology on the road', i.e., a process rather than a goal, a journey rather than a destination, Mission as Transformation is in constant flux, informing new issues that arise in particular situations as well as being informed by those same issues. For example, by sympathizing with liberations movements of the 70s and 80s and thus taking on much of their ideas and passions, has evangelical Transformational theology placed itself unwittingly alongside the dying embers of liberation theology, and thus is dying out too? Certainly, ministry to the poor, contextualization, and the integration of evangelism and social concern are enduring biblical calls upon the church, but Transformationists may need to find new language that speaks to, and resonates with, emerging generations of missionaries, development workers and pastors.

Another area that requires further development among Transformationists is the role of spirituality in holistic mission. How do worship, liturgical theology, preaching and mission inform one another? Transformationists are not totally unaware of these issues, but they have yet to make a significant impact on their missiological understanding. Despite continued disillusionment over the institutional church among so called Generations X and Y, a renewed hunger for genuine spirituality that includes the element of justice has only increased.[2] It would behoove Transformational mission theologians, for example, to look closely at the emerging phenomenon of what has become known as 'the New

---

[1] Some have certainly recognized Mission as Transformation as such. See for example, Scherer and Bevans' inclusion of the 'Wheaton '83 Statement on Transformation' in their *New Directions in Mission and Evangelization 1,* 281-291, and Bosch's discussion of it in *Transforming Mission,* 407-408.

[2] Mike Booker and Mark Ireland, *Evangelism—Which Way Now?* (London: Church House Publishing, 2004), 174-188.

Monasticism', a movement among a younger generation of evangelicals who are recovering ancient practices of mysticism, simplicity and radical mission.[3]

Somewhat related to spirituality is the issue of self-care. Perhaps due to an underdeveloped spirituality, not a few holistic practitioners through the years have been stricken with compassion fatigue. Transformationists have not dealt very deeply with the need for self-care among activists and missionaries. Transformationists must reflect further on this if they want to sustain the movement, drawing from the works of missionary mystics such as Christine Sine and Marva Dawn, who both emphasize the desperate need to establish a biblical, Sabbath rhythm in order to be truly productive for the kingdom. Dawn's rhythm of ceasing, resting, embracing and feasting forms the essential art of Sabbath keeping, an art that gives God's people, not an escape from the world, but 'a larger perspective for plunging into its needs and sufferings more deeply'.[4] Sine echoes this when she writes that the Sabbath 'means joining in the worldwide song of liberation, a song whose vibrations cut through our own forms of bondage and awaken us to the need of all people for freedom and justice.'[5] Such insights into Sabbath keeping give biblical ways for Transformational practitioners to sustain in the hard, intense, and often lonely journey of holistic ministry.

A Brief Word on Methodology

I did not intend at the outset to propose a generalized missiological method, but the methodological path that this study took, as it sought to understand Mission as Transformation through a contemporary global-local lens, perhaps points in a viable direction for doing missiology in a globalized world. After painting the necessary historical background of the movement in Part I, the first task consisted of discerning its global developments. A comprehensive review of Transformational literature gave a clear picture of the shape that Mission as Transformation took through the years after Lausanne '74 and especially after Wheaton '83. Samuel's eight components of Mission as Transformation provided the key ingredients, which Part II interpreted, reorganized, developed and identified as its eight global dimensions.

The next essential task entailed understanding how this missiology works 'on the ground', on the concrete local level. Any context would have theoretically worked, but as this study has revealed, the contextual theologizing

---

[3] See for example, Scott A. Bessenecker, *The New Friars: The Emerging Movement Serving the World's Poor* (Downers Grove, Ill.: IVP, 2006) and Shane Claiborne, *The Irresistible Revolution* (Grand Rapids, Mich.: Zondervan, 2006).

[4] Marva J. Dawn, *Keeping the Sabbath Wholly* (Grand Rapids, Mich.: Eerdmans, 1989), 200.

[5] Christine Sine, *Sacred Rhythms* (Grand Rapids, Mich.: Baker, 2003), 159.

that has occurred among Filipino Transformationists has contributed significantly and uniquely to the movement. Part III mined the history of the Filipino Church in mission in the context of the peoples' sustained struggle against the injustices of colonial rule, identifying four historical threads that served as sources of nine local dimensions of Mission as Transformation in the Philippines.

But if theoretical premises of the likes of Schreiter, Robertson and others have any merit, then the global informs the local and reflexively, the local informs the global. These levels did not and do not develop independently from each other; rather, an ongoing interdependent relationship exists between them, and their relationship does not have to be antagonistic. Lest the danger of the 'global *versus* local' predicament be allowed to develop fully, the relationship between the global and the local requires a negotiation. Part IV attempted to do that, as it appropriated Robertson's concept of glocalization to missiology. We showed how the organic nature of the global-local relationship can symbiotically and positively determine the form and destiny of both realms. We then discovered four glocal dimensions - one theological and three practical - derived from examples of intercultural partnerships in mission between Transformationists around the world. These four glocal dimensions encourage the whole Church in its mosaic of diverse races, cultures and traditions to participate together in the holistic mission of God.

From the global to the local to the glocal: Can this sequential process of understanding a given phenomenon serve as a roadmap (albeit unrefined at this stage) to guide other missiological investigations of similar social movements? The compressed, globalized nature of the world certainly warrants it (or something like it); for what local expressions of faith have global forces not yet touched? And what global forces of faith have local expressions not yet reflexively affected? Indeed a full understanding of any missiological phenomenon will require global, local and glocal lenses.

The Globalization of the Gospel: Challenging the Giant Redwood

Beyond methodology, what does Mission as Transformation offer? Quite simply, it offers the Church a biblically sound, culturally relevant and holistic way forward in mission, as it proclaims an authentic version of the Gospel. This Gospel challenges the ultimately false promises of ideological globalization. Talk of globalization still primarily revolves around the American based market culture - the values, the lifestyle, and the goals of neo-liberal capitalism - flooding every nook and cranny of the rest of the world; and appropriately so since 'the American way' continues to dominate the world scene on both the popular and elite levels. Sociologists James Hunter and Joshua Yates posit that in spite of the presence of 'many globalizations' in the world, 'at the end of the day ... we are still faced with the present reality of America's powerful if not dominant role in processes of globalization.'[6] They explain further:

> So much of what we know as globalization is, in both source and character, undeniably American. Whether McDonald's (serving 20 million people worldwide each day), MTV (reaching half a billion people per year), Coca-Cola (serving 1 billion people worldwide everyday), Hollywood (from which 85 percent of the most watched films in the world come), Michael Jordan, himself a global icon (generating over $10 billion just over the course of his playing career for an array of global commercial ventures), and so on, the popular culture, food, and status symbols of America are ubiquitous.[7]

This description only covers the pop culture level of the Americanization of the world; Hunter and Yates go on to describe America's dominance over the world's elite business, philanthropic, educational and religious spheres.[8] So despite the fact that many other nations and movements have taken advantage of advanced technologies to globalize their respective agendas (hence, the reason for the claim that there are many globalizations), American based market culture is still ... the biggest game going and it will likely stay that way for the foreseeable future.'[9] Or to use another analogy, which I prefer, the American based market culture is 'the giant redwood' in the globalization forest.

Does this giant redwood serve the rest, or does it take over the forest as it serves its own interests? As established earlier, globalization, at least in its unrestricted, ideological form, resembles colonialism in at least the following ways: 'The imposition of a foreign structural system [into traditional situations]... the disregard for the richness of diverse cultures, the exploitation of natural resources, and the marginalization of the majority of a population.'[10] Furthermore, 'this dimension of globalization represents a new kind of political-economic religion with its own idols and gods, [and] it is ultimately destructive of all religions and cultures.'[11] Regarding its inherent idolatrous nature, Maggay writes, 'It is not the first time in history that we see the

---

[6] James D. Hunter and Joshua Yates, 'In the Vanguard of Globalization: The World of American Globalizers', in Peter L. Berger and Samuel Huntington (eds.), *Many Globalizations: Cultural Diversity in the Contemporary World* (Oxford: Oxford University Press, 2002), 325.

[7] Hunter and Yates, 'In the Vanguard', 324.

[8] Hunter and Yates, 'In the Vanguard', 324.

[9] Peter L. Berger, 'Introduction', in Peter L. Berger and Samuel Huntington (eds.), *Many Globalizations: Cultural Diversity in the Contemporary World* (Oxford: Oxford University Press, 2002), 2-3.

[10] Tizon, 'Remembering the Missionary Moratorium Debate', 23.

[11] 'The People of God Among All God's People', *The People of God Among All God's People*, 15.

ascendancy of Mammon.... More than any other idol, money rivals God in the comprehensiveness with which it is able to exact allegiance from us'.[12] It may not be the first time Mammon has tried to compete with God, but in light of the technological capabilities to globalize itself, it may be its strongest attempt yet. In this sense, God's people must actively resist (in their own lives as well as in the world) the seduction of ideological globalization.

But rather than hitting up against it violently, like some fundamentalist Muslim groups have done (the 9/11 tragedy is but one of many attacks), the Church in its worldwide missionary mode must engage in a different kind of globalization. The idea of 'many globalizations' helps here; for it challenges the monopoly of the forest that the giant redwood may think it has, and it allows for alternative agendas to become globalized. Referring to world religions in general, Held and colleagues claim that they 'unquestionably constitute one of the most powerful and significant forms of the globalization of culture in the premodern era, indeed of all time.'[13]

I ultimately propose here that the globalization of the Gospel by means of missiologies like Mission as Transformation offer a subversive alternative to the behemoth tree in the middle of the forest. Samuel declares that the globalization of the Gospel through holistic mission constitutes the only Christian response, for 'the Gospel is far more powerful than any free market globalization'.[14] The manner in which Transformationists have proclaimed this Gospel - holistically (refusing to evangelize without also engaging in liberation for the poor and oppressed), faithfully (refusing to compromise the biblical and historical roots of the faith), and glocally (refusing to embrace a world Christian vision without also affirming the richness of local contexts) - bears witness to the very nature of the Gospel. It has liberated the Gospel's power to transform lives and communities, especially those victimized or left behind by the intimidating presence of the giant redwood, the globalization of the American Dream.

As such, the Gospel that Transformationists have preached threatens this presence, but it does so by way of 'the mustard seed' - small, seemingly insignificant activities that reflect the kingdom of God and, by the cultivation of God, grow disproportionately to overtake the forest (Mk. 4:31-32). Itself a mustard seed, considering its disproportionate influence relative to its size, Mission as Transformation has catalyzed local movements around the world that have empowered God's people to initiate social as well as personal change. And no matter how insignificant these small movements may seem, 'to deal

---

[12] Maggay, 'Our Text in Context: Shaping a Life-Giving Word for Today', 18.

[13] Held, McGrew, Goldblatt and Perraton, *Global Transformations*, 333.

[14] Vinay Samuel, 'Evangelical Response to Globalization: An Asian Perspective', *Transformation* 16.1 (January/March 1999), 6.

locally with real people in real communities tackling real problems plays an important role in the battle against globalization'....[15]

The Mustard Seed in the Philippines

In light of the long-term relationship between the Philippines and America dating back to the end of the nineteenth century, we can build a case that Filipinos have put up with the giant redwood for a long time. Processes of globalization, as dominant America began fulfilling its 'manifest destiny' among the subjugated Filipino people, started in the Philippines long before the contemporary age of globalization dawned upon the world. But as Filipino church history has shown, resistance against it also dates back as far. Filipino Transformationists have simply continued in the best of the Filipino Church's contributions to that resistance as they have walked in step with the themes of subversion, nationalism, church unity with a purpose, and mobilization of the poor. The nine local dimensions developed under these four themes have defined how Filipino Transformationists have fleshed out the Gospel in their particular historical, socio-political and cultural context.

Filipino Transformationists have certainly not shied away from speaking boldly against the effects of ideological globalization in their country. ISACC's *Patmos* has served as a regular forum to warn people of its false promises. It published an article by former UCCP Bishop Ben Dominguez who wrote, 'The problem with the global village is ... the real, true-to-life village is not part of the agenda.'[16] He cited the plight of the grape farmers in La Union as an example and said, 'In the past, they profited from their grape farms because they were able to sell their produce. This year, however, the same farmers ... saw their produce go to waste. They were not able to sell them [because] the grapes from other countries that flooded the country were sold at very low prices.'[17] In another *Patmos* article, Ed De la Torre, a progressive former Catholic priest turned grassroots activist, reiterated this loss of local significance when he accused ideological globalization of defining for the local people what it means to be fully human and to be fully happy.[18]

The inclusion of such articles in *Patmos* from the likes of Dominguez and De la Torre, outsiders to the evangelical fold, testifies to the Transformational slant regarding ideological globalization. But they only serve to strengthen 'insider' perspectives. Articles like Miranda-Feliciano's 'Megamall, Here I

---

[15] Tizon, 'Revisiting the Mustard Seed', 22.

[16] Ben Dominguez, 'Eto Na Po Sila: Globalization and the New Trinity', *Patmos* 13.1 (November 1997), 10.

[17] Dominguez, 'Eto Na Po Sila', 10.

[18] Ed de la Torre, 'Globalization and Governance', *Patmos* 13.3 (April 1998), 24.

Come!'[19] and Maggay's 'Beyond Globalization'[20] clearly spell out a Transformational critique of ideological globalization in the Philippines. 'From where I sit,' Maggay bemoans, 'things look more and more like a "slave new world."'[21] These articles vocalize the resistance that Transformationists have mounted in the Philippines, and they play a part in the mustard seed activities germinating subversively throughout the forest amidst the powerful, seemingly invincible presence of the giant redwood.

These mustard seeds growing in the Philippines, however, merely represent what is growing in many other parts of the world. Tom Sine's *Mustard Seed Versus McWorld*[22] not only documents many of these global activities, it also points out the fact that together, they undermine the power of ideological globalization. Mustard seed and McWorld are rival movements, and Sine makes it clear which of these he thinks will prove victorious. He writes, 'The power of this new global economic order is awesome, and it has brilliantly demonstrated its ability to market not only its products but its values all over our small world. But I am still betting my life that God's mustard seed agenda, with a very different approach to globalization, will win the day.'[23] These small, seemingly insignificant, kingdom activities testify to the God who has always changed the world by means of the lowly, the poor and the powerless. They constitute a bottom-up, grassroots, global movement that Sine, Sider, Samuel, Sugden, Maggay, Miranda-Feliciano, Escobar, Padilla, Bediako, Gitari, and other radical evangelicals around the world first identified as Transformation.

The rest is history.

---

[19] Evelyn Miranda-Feliciano, 'Megamall, Here I Come! Or Is This the Way to Globalization?' *Patmos* 13.1 (November 1997), 14-15, 24.

[20] Maggay, 'Finding Our Way into the Future',

[21] Maggay, 'Finding Our Way into the Future', 5.

[22] Sine, *Mustard Seed Versus McWorld* (Grand Rapids, Mich.: Baker, 1999).

[23] Sine, *Mustard Seed Versus McWorld,* 22.

Appendix One

Statement on Radical Discipleship at Lausanne '74

Theology and Implications of Radical Discipleship

A number of issues have thrust themselves upon us from papers delivered in this Congress and, from the subsequent wrestling with them under the authority of God's Word, a number of us have felt the compulsion of his Spirit to share this response.

We affirm that . . .

The *evangel* is God's Good News in Jesus Christ; it is Good News of the reign he proclaimed and embodies; of God's mission of love to restore the world to wholeness through the Cross of Christ and him alone; of his victory over the demonic power of destruction and death; of his Lordship over the entire universe; it is Good News of a new creation of a new humanity, a new birth through him by his life-giving Spirit; of the gifts of the messianic reign comtained in Jesus and mediated through him by his Spirit; of the charismatic community empowered to embody his reign of shalom here and now before the whole creation and make his Good news seen and known. It is Good News of liberation, of restoration, of wholeness, and of salvation that is personal, social, global and cosmic. Jesus is Lord! Alleluia! Let the earth hear his voice!

The *communication of the evangel* in its fullness to every person worldwide is a mandate of the Lord Jesus to his community. There is no biblical dichotomy between the Word spoken and the Word made visible in the lives of God's people. Men will look as they listen and what they see must be at one with what they hear. The Christian community must chatter, discuss and proclaim the Gospel; it must express the Gospel in its life as the new society, it its sacrificial service of others as a genuine expression of God's love, in its prophetic exposing and opposing of all demonic forces that deny the Lordship of Christ and kepp men less than fully human; in its pursuit of real justice for all men; in its responsible and caring trusteeship of God's creation and its resources.

There are times when our communication may be by attitude and action only, and times when the spoken Word will stand alone; but we must repudiate as demonic the attempt to drive a wedge between evangelism and social action.

The response demanded by the evangel is that men and women repent of their sin and every other lordship that that of Jesus Christ, and commit themselves to him to serve him in the world. Men are not already reconciled to God and simply awaiting the realization of it. Nor can biblical authority be found for the false hope of universalism; the reality of the eternal destruction of evil and all who cling to it must be solemnly affirmed, however humbly agnostic the Bible requires us to be about its nature.

Salvation is by God's grace on the sole ground of Christ's death and resurrection and is received by obedient faith. Repentance is demanded; men must experience a change of understanding, attitude and orientation. But the new birth is not merely a subjective experience of forgiveness. It is a placement within the messianic community, God's new order which exists as a sign of God's reign to be consummated at the end of the age.

Methods in evangelization must centre in Jesus Christ who took our humanity, our frailty, our death and gave himself in suffering servanthood for others. He sends his community into the world, as the Father sent him, to identify and agonize with men, to renounce status and demonic power, and to give itself in selfless service of others for God. Those who proclaim the Cross must be continually marked by the Cross. With unashamed commitment to Jesus Christ we must engage in the mutual listening of dialogue, the reward of which is understanding. We need to meet men on their own ground and be particularly attentive to the powerless. We must use the language, thought - forms and imagery appropriate to differing cultures. As Christians, we must live in such unity and love that men may believe. We must allow God to make visible in the new humanity the quality of life that reflects Christ and demonstrates his reign. We must respect cultural integrity while being free from all that denies or distorts the Lordship of Christ. God's Spirit overcomes all barriers of race, color and culture.

Strategy for world evangelization in our generation is with God, from whom we eagerly anticipate the renewal of his community, equipping us with love an dpower so that the whole Christian community may make known the whole Gospel to the whole man throughout the whole world. We believe God to be calling us into greater unity and partnership throughout the earth to fulfil the commission of our Lord Jesus Christ.

We confess that . . .

We have been failing in our obedience to the Lordship of Christ and have been refusing to submit to his Word and be led by his Spirit.

We have failed to incarnate the Gospel and to come to men as servants for Christ's sake.

Our testimony has often been marred by triumphalism and arrogance by lack of faith in God and by diminished love for his people.

We have often been in bondage to a particular culture and sought to spread it in the name of Jesus.

We have not been awere of when we have debased and distorted the Gospel by acceptance of a contrary value system.

We have been partisan in our condemnation of totalitarianism and violence and have failed to condemn societal and institutionalized sin, especially that of racism.

We have sometimes so identified ourselves with particular political systems that the Gospel has been compromised and the prophetic voice muted.

We have frequently denied the rights and neglected the cries of the underprivileged and those struggling for freedom and justice.

We have often separated Jesus Christ the Savior from Jesus Christ the Lord.

We have sometimes distorted the biblical understanding of man as a total being and have courted an unbiblical dualism.

We have insulated new Christians fro life in the world and given simplistic responses to complex problems.

We have sometimes manipulated our message, used pressure techniques and been unduly pre-occupied with statistics.

We have allowed eagerness for qualitative growth to render us silent about the whole counsel of God. We have been usurping God's Holy Spirit of love and power.

We rejoice . . .

In our membership by his Spirit in the Body of Christ and in the joy and love he has given us in each other.

In the openness and honesty with which we have met each other and have experienced mutual acceptance and forgiveness.

In the possibilities for men to read his Word in their own languages through indigenous translations.

In the stimulation of mind and challenge to action that has come to us from his Word as we have placed the needs of our generation under its judgment and light.

In the prophetic voices of our brothers and sisters in this Congress, with whom we go forth in humility and hope.

In the certainty that the kingdom of this world shall become the Kingdom of our God and of his Christ. He shall reign forever. Alleluia!

We resolve . . .

To submit ourselves afresh to the Word of God and to the leading of his Spirit, to pray and work together for the renewal of his community as the expression of his reign, to participate in God's mission to his world in our generation, showing forth Jesus as Lord and Savior, and calling on all men everywhere to repent, to submit to his Lordship, to know his salvation, to identify in him with the oppressed and work for the liberation of all men and women in his name.

LET THE EARTH HEAR HIS VOICE!

Appendix Two

Wheaton '83 Statement on Transformation

Transformation: The Church in Response to Human Need

Introduction

For two weeks during June 1983 we have come together from local churches and Christian mission and aid agencies at Wheaton College in the USA from 30 nations to pray about and reflect upon the church's task in response to human need. Some of us belong to churches which are situated among marginalized peoples who live in situations of poverty, powerlessness, and oppression. Others come from churches situated in affluent areas of the world. We are deeply grateful to our heavenly Father for allowing us the privilege of sharing our lives with one another, studying the Scriptures in small groups, considering papers on aspects of human development and transformation, and looking closely at the implications of case studies and histories which describe different responses to human need. Because God hears the cries of the poor, we have sought each other's help to respond (Exod. 3:7-9; James 5:1-6). We rejoice at what we believe the Holy Spirit has been teaching us concerning God's specific purpose and plans for His distressed world and the part the church has to play in them.

As we have faced the enormous challenge before God's people everywhere to alleviate suffering and, in partnership together, to eliminate its causes, we are more than ever aware of the liberating and healing power of the Good News of Jesus. We gladly reaffirm, therefore, our conviction that Jesus Christ alone is the world's peace, for He alone can reconcile people to God and bring all hostilities to an end (Eph. 2:14-17).

We acknowledge furthermore, that only by spreading the Gospel can the most basic need of human beings be met: to have fellowship with God. In what follows we do not emphasize evangelism as a separate theme, because we see it as an integral part of our total Christian response to human need (Matt. 28:18-21). In addition, it is not necessary simply to repeat what the Lausanne Covenant and the Report of the Consultation on the Relationship between Evangelism and Social Relationship between Evangelism and Social Responsibility (CRESR, Grand Rapids, 1982) has already expressed.

What we have discovered we would like to share with our brothers and sisters throughout the world. We offer this statement, not as attempt to produce a final word, but as a summary of our reflections.

Both Scripture and experience, informed by the Spirit, emphasizes that God's people are dependent upon His wisdom in confronting human need. Local churches and mission agencies, then, should act wisely, if they are to be both pastoral and prophetic. Indeed the whole human family with its illusions and divisions needs Christ to be its wisdom as well as its Savior and King.

Conscious of our struggle to find a biblical view of transformation that relates its working in the heart of believers to its multiplying effects in society, we pray that the Spirit will give us the discernment we need. We believe that the wisdom the Spirit inspires is practical rather than academic, and possession of the faithful rather than the preserve of the elite. Because we write as part of a world full of conflict and a church easily torn by strife we desire that the convictions expressed in this document be further refined by God's pure and peaceful wisdom.

Some may find our words hard. We pray, however, that many will find them a help to their own thinking and an encouragement to "continue steadfast, immovable, always abounding in the work of the Lord, knowing that in the Lord your labor is not in vain" (1 Cor. 15:58).

I. Christian Social Involvement

1. As Christians reflect on God's intention for the world they are often tempted to be either naively optimistic or darkly pessimistic. Some, inspired by a utopian vision seem to suggest that God's Kingdom, in all its fullness, can be built on earth. We do not subscribe to this view, since Scripture informs us of the reality and pervasiveness of both personal and societal sin (Isa. 1:10-26; Amos 2:6-8; Mic. 2:1-10; Rom. 1:28-32). Thus we recognize that utopianism is nothing but a false dream (see the CRESR Report, IV.A).

2. Other Christians become pessimistic because they are faced with the reality of increasing poverty and misery, of rampant oppression and exploitation by powers of the right and the left, of spiraling violence coupled with the threat of nuclear warfare. They are concerned, too, about the increasing possibility that planet earth will not be able to sustain its population for long because of the

wanton squandering of its resource. As a result, they are tempted to turn their eyes away from this world and fix them so exclusively on the return of Christ that there involvement in the here and now is paralyzed. We do not wish to disregard or minimize the extensive contribution made by a succession of Christians who have held this view of eschatology, through more than one hundred years, to medical and educational work in many countries up to the present day. Nevertheless, some of us feel that these men and women have tended to see the task of the church as merely picking up survivors from a shipwreck in a hostile sea. We do not endorse this view either, since it denies the biblical injunctions to defend the cause of the weak, maintain the rights of the poor and oppressed (Ps. 82:3), and practice justice and love (Mic. 6:8).

3. We affirm,, moreover, that, even thought we may believe that our calling is only to proclaim the Gospel and not get involved in political and other actions, our very non-involvement lends tacit support to the existing order. There is no escape: either we challenge the evil structures of society or we support them.

4. There have been many occasions in the history of the church - and some exist today - where Christians, faced with persecution and oppression, have appeared to be disengaged from society and thus to support the status quo. We suggest, however, that even under conditions of the most severe repression, such Christians may in fact be challenging society and even be transforming it, through their lifestyles, their selfless love, their quiet joy, their inner peace, and their patient suffering (1 Pet. 2:21-25).

5. Christ's followers, therefore, are called, in one way or another, not to conform to the values of society but to transform them (Rom. 12:1-2; Eph. 5:8-14). This calling flows from our confession that God loves the world and that the earth belongs to Him. It is true that Satan is active in the world, even claiming it to be his (Luke 4:5-7). He is, however, a usurper, having no property rights here. All authority in heaven and on earth has been given to Christ Jesus (Matt. 28:18; Col. 1:15-20). Although His Lordship is not yet acknowledged by all (Heb. 2:8) He is the ruler of the kings of the earth (Rev. 1:5), King of kings and Lord of lords (Rev. 19:16). In faith we confess that the old order is passing away; the new order has already begun (2 Cor. 5:17; Eph 2:7-10; Matt. 12:18; Luke 7:21-23).

II. Not only Development but Transformation

6. The participants at this conference have entered into the current discussion concerning development. For many Western political and business leaders development describes the process by which nations and people become part of the existing international economic order. For many people of the Two-Third World it is identified with an ideologically motivated process of change, called

"developmentalism." This process is intrinsically related to a mechanistic pursuit of economic growth that tends to ignore the structural context of poverty and injustice and which increases dependency and inequality.

7. Some of us still believe, however, that "development," when reinterpreted in the light of the whole message of the Bible, is a concept that should be retained by Christians. Part of the reason for this choice is that the word is so widely used. A change of term, therefore, would cause unnecessary confusion.

8. Other in our Consultation, because of difficulty in relating it to biblical categories of thought and its negative overtones, would like to replace "development" with another word. An alternative we suggest is "transformation," as it can be applied in different ways to every situation. Western nations, for example, who have generally assumed that development does not apply to them, are, nevertheless, in need of transformation in many areas. In particular, the unspoken assumption that societies operate best when individuals are most free to pursue their own self-interests needs to be challenged on the basic of the biblical teaching on stewardship (Luke 12:13-21; 16:13-15; Phil. 2:1-4). People living in - groups based on community solidarity may help these kinds of societies see the poverty of their existence.

9. Moreover, the term "transformation," unlike "development," does not have a suspect past. It points to a number of changes that have to take place in many societies if poor people are to enjoy their rightful heritage in creation.
10. We are concerned, however, that both the goals and the process of transformation should be seen in the light of the Good News about Jesus, the Messiah. We commit ourselves and urge other Christian believers to reject the cultural and social forces of secularism, which so often shape our idea of a good society. We believe that notions alien to God's plan for human living are often more powerful in forming our opinions about what is right for a nation than the message of Scripture itself.

11. According to the biblical view of human life, then, transformation is the change from a condition of human existence contrary to God's purpose to one in which people are able to enjoy fullness of life in harmony with God (John 10:10; Col. 3:8-15; Eph. 4:13). This transformation can only take place through the obedience of individuals and communities to the Gospel of Jesus Christ, whose power changes the lives of men and women by releasing them from the guilt, power, and consequences of sin, enabling them to respond with love toward God and toward others (Rom. 5:5), and making them "new creatures in Christ" (2 Cor. 5:17).

12. There are a number of themes in Bible, which help us focus on the way we understand transformation. The doctrine of creation speaks of the worth of

every man, woman, and child, of the responsibility of human beings to look after the resources of nature (Gen. 1:26-30) and to share them equitably with their neighbors. The doctrine of the Fall highlights the innate tendency of human beings to serve their own interests, with the consequences of greed, insecurity, violence, and the lust for power. "God's judgement rightly falls upon those who do such things" (Rom. 2:2). The doctrine of redemption proclaims God's forgiveness of sins and the freedom Christ gives for a way of life dedicated to serving others by telling them about the Good News of Salvation, bringing reconciliation between enemies, and losing one's life to see justice established for all exploited people.

13. We have come to see that the goal of transformation is best described by the biblical vision of the Kingdom of God. This new way of being human in submission to the Lord of all has many facets. In particular, it means striving to bring peace among individuals, races, and nations by overcoming prejudices, fears, and preconceived ideas about others. It means sharing basic recourses like food, water, the means of healing, and knowledge. It also means working for a greater participation of people in the decisions which affect their lives, making possible an equal receiving from others and giving of themselves. Finally, it means growing up into Christ in all things as a body of people dependent upon the work of the Holy Spirit and upon each other.

III. The Stewardship of Creation

14. "The earth is the Lord's and all that is in it" (Ps. 24:1); "The land is mine" (Lev. 25:23). All human beings are God's creatures. As made in His image they are His representatives, given the responsibility of caring wisely for His creation. We have to confess, however, that God's people have been slow to recognize the full implication of their responsibility. As His stewards, we do not own the earth but we manage and enhance it in anticipation of Christ's return. Too often, however, we have assumed a right to use His natural resources indiscriminately. We have frequently been indifferent, or even hostile, to those committed to the conservation of non-renewable sources of energy and minerals, of animal life in danger of extinction, and of the precarious ecological balance of many natural habitats. The earth is God's gift to all generations. An African proverb says that parents have borrowed the present from their children. Both our present life and our children's future depend upon our wise and peaceful treatment of the whole earth.

15. We have also assumed that only a small portion of our income and wealth, the "tithe," belongs to the Lord, the rest being ours to dispose of, as we like. This impoverishes other people and denies our identity and role as stewards. We believe that Christians everywhere, but especially those who are enjoying in abundance "the good things of life" (Luke 16:25), must faithfully obey the

command to ensure that others have their basic needs met. In this way those who are poor now will also be able to enjoy the blessing of giving to others.

16. Through salvation, Jesus lifts us out of our isolation from God and other people and establishes us within the worldwide community of the Body of Christ. Belonging to one Body involves sharing all God's gifts to us, so that there might be equality among all members (2 Cor. 8:14-15). To the extent that this standard is obeyed, dire poverty will be eliminated (Acts 2:42-47).

17. When either individuals or states claim an absolute right of ownership, that is rebellion against God. The meaning of stewardship is that the poor have equal rights to God's resources (Deut. 15:8-9). The meaning of transformation is that, as stewards of God's bountiful gifts, we do justice, striving together through prayer, example, representation, and protest to have resources redistributed and the consequences of greed limited (Acts 4:32-5:11).

18. We are perturbed by the perverse misuse of huge amounts of resources in the present arms race. While millions starve to death, resources are wasted on the research and production of increasingly sophisticated nuclear weapon systems. Moreover, the constantly escalating global trade in conventional arms accompanies the proliferation of oppressive governments, which disregard people's elementary needs. As Christians we condemn these new expressions of injustice and aggression, affirming our commitment to seek peace with justice. In the light of the issue of the stewardship of creation we have discussed here, we call the worldwide evangelical community to make the nuclear and arms trade questions a matter of prayerful concern and to place it on their agenda for study and action.

IV. Culture and Transformation

19. Culture includes world - views, beliefs, values, art forms, customs, laws, socioeconomic structures, social relationships, and material things shared by a population over time in a specific area or context.

20. Culture is God's gift to human beings. God has made people everywhere in His image. As Creator, He has made us creative. This creativity produces cultures. Furthermore, God has commissioned us to be stewards of His creation (Ps. 8; Heb. 2:5-11). Since every good gift is from above and since all wisdom and knowledge comes from Jesus Christ, whatever is good and beautiful in cultures may be seen as a gift of God (James 1:16-18). Moreover, where the Gospel has been heard and obeyed, cultures have become further ennobled and enriched.

21. However, people have sinned by rebelling against God. Therefore the cultures we produce are infected with evil. Different aspects of our culture

show plainly our separation from God. Social structures and relationships, art forms and laws often reflect our violence, our sense of lostness, and our loss of coherent moral values. Scripture challenges us not to be "conformed to this world" (Rom. 12:2) insofar as it is alienated from its Creator. We need to be transformed so that cultures may display again what is "good and acceptable and perfect" (Rom. 12:2).

22. Cultures, then, bear the marks of God's common grace, demonic influences, and mechanisms of human exploitation. In our cultural creativity, God and Satan clash. The Lord used Greek culture to give us the New Testament, while at the same time He subjected that culture to the judgement of the Gospel. We too should make thankful use of cultures and yet, at the same time, examine them in the light of the Gospel to expose the evil in them (1 Cor. 9: 19-23).

23. Social structures that exploit and dehumanize constitute a pervasive sin which is not confronted adequately by the church. Many churches, mission societies, and Christian relief and development agencies support the sociopolitical status quo, and by silence give their tacit support.

24. Through application of the Scriptures, in the power of the Spirit, we seek to discern the true reality of all sociocultural situations. We need to learn critically from both functionalist and conflict approaches to human culture. The "functionalist socio-anthropology" approach emphasizes the harmonious aspect of different cultures and champions a tolerant attitude to the existing structures. This position is often adopted in the name of "scientific objectivity." By contrast, the "conflict" approach exposes the contradictory nature of social structures and makes us aware of the underlying conflict of interests. We must remember that both approaches come under the judgement of God.

25. Give the conflicting ethical tendencies in our nature, which find expression in our cultural systems, we must be neither naively optimistic nor wrongly judgmental. We are called to be a new community that seeks to work with God in the transformation of our societies, men and women of God in society, salt of the earth and light of the world (Matt. 5:13-16). We seek to bring people and their cultures under the Lordship of Christ. In spite of our failures, we move toward that freedom and wholeness in a more just community that persons will enjoy when our lord returns to consummate His Kingdom (Rev. 21:1-22:6).

V. Social Justice and Mercy

26. Our time together enabled us to see that poverty is not a necessary evil but often the result of social, economic, political, and religious systems marked by injustice, exploitation, and oppression. Approximately eight hundred million people in the world are destitute, and their plight is often maintained by the rich

and powerful. Evil is not only in the human heart but also in social structures. Because God is just and merciful, hating evil and loving righteousness, there is an urgent need for Christians in the present circumstances to commit ourselves to acting in mercy and seeking justice. The mission of the church includes both the proclamations of the Gospel and its demonstration. We must therefore evangelize, respond to immediate human needs, and press for social transformation. The means we use, however, must be consistent with the end we desire.

27. As we thought of the task before us, we considered Jesus' attitude toward the power structures of His time. He was neither a Zealot nor a passive spectator of the oppression of His people. Rather, moved by compassion, He identified Himself with the poor, whom He saw as " harassed and helpless, like sheep without a shepherd" (Matt 9:36). Though His act mercy, teaching, and lifestyle, He exposed the injustices in society and condemned the self-righteousness of its leaders (Matt. 23:25; Luke 6:37-42). His was prophetic compassion and it resulted in the formation of a community which accepted the values of the Kingdom of God and stood in contrast to the Roman and Jewish establishment. We were challenged to follow Jesus' footsteps, remembering that His compassion led Him to death (John 13:12-17; Phil. 2:6-8; 1 John 3:11-18).

28. We are aware that a Christlike identification with the poor, whether at home or aboard, in the North, South, East, or West, is always costly and may lead us also to persecution and even death. Therefore, we humbly ask God to make us willing to risk our comfort, even our lives, for the sake of the Gospel, knowing that "everyone who wants to live a godly life in Christ Jesus will be persecuted" (2 Tim. 3:12).

29. Sometimes in our ministry among the poor we face a serious dilemma: to limit ourselves to acts of mercy to improve their lot, or to go beyond that and seek to rectify the injustice that makes such acts of mercy necessary. This step in turn may put at risk the freedom we need to continue our ministry. No rule of thumb can be given, but from a biblical perspective it is clear that justice and mercy belong together (Isa 11:1-5; Ps. 113:5-9). We must therefore make every possible effort to combine both in our ministry and be willing to suffer the consequences. We must also remember that acts of mercy highlight the injustices of the social, economic, and political structures and relationships; whether we like it or not, they may therefore lead us into confrontation with those who hold power (Acts 4:5-22). For the same reason, we must stand together with those who suffer for the sake of justice (Heb. 13:3).

30. Our ministry of justice and healing is not limited to fellow Christians. Our love and commitment must extend to the stranger (Matt. 5:43-48). Our

involvement with stangers is not only through charity, but also through economic policies toward the poor. Our economic and political action is inseparable from evangelism.

31. Injustice in the modern world has reached global proportions. Many or us come from countries dominated by international business corporations and some from those whose political systems are not accountable to the people. We witness to the damaging effects that these economic and political institutions are having on people, especially on the poorest of the poor. We call on our brothers and sisters in Jesus Christ to study seriously this situation and to seek ways to bring about change in favour of the oppressed. "The righteous care about justice for the poor, but the wicked have no such concern" (Prov. 29:7).

VI. The Local Church and Transformation

32. The local church is the basic unit of Christian society. The churches in the New Testament were made up of men and women who had experienced transformation through receiving Jesus Christ as Savior, acknowledging Him as Lord, incarnating His servant ministry by demonstrating the values of the Kingdom both personally and in community (Mark 10:35-45; 1 Pet. 2:5; 4:10). Today similar examples of transformed lives abound in churches worldwide.

33. We recognize that across the generations local churches have been the vehicle for the transmission of the Gospel of Jesus Christ, and that their primary, thought not their only, role is a threefold ministry: the worship and praise of God, the proclamation in word and deed of the Gospel of the grace of God, and the nurture, instruction, and discipleship of those who have received Jesus Christ into their lives. In this way transformation takes place in the lives of Christians as individuals, families, and communities; through their words and deeds they demonstrate both the need and reality of ethical, moral, and social transformation.

34. All churches are faced at times with the choice between speaking openly against social evils and not speaking out publicly. The purpose for the particular choice should be obedience to the Lord of the church to fulfil its ministry. Wisdom will be needed so that the church will neither speak rashly and make its witness ineffective nor remain silent when to do so would deny its prophetic calling (1 Pet. 3:13-17). If we are sensitive to the Holy Spirit and are socially aware, we will always be ready to reassess our attitude toward social issues (Lk. 18:24-30).

35. Integrity, leadership, and information are essential for the transformation of attitudes and lifestyles of members of local churches. Churches are made up of people whose lives are pressured by the way their neighbors spend their money.

They are often more aware of this than of the suffering and human need in their own and other countries. Often, too, they are reluctant to expose themselves to the traumas of global need and to information which would challenge their comfort. If church leadership fails to adequately stress the social dimensions of the Gospel, church members may often overlook these issues (1 Tim. 3:1-7; Heb. 13:17).

36. We should sensitive and responsive to need within the local church. Windows, prisoners, the poor, and the stangers are people who are particularly the responsibility of the local church (Gal. 6:10). We should attempt to be well informed about local human need and to seek God's will for us in meeting those needs. We should seek to minister to the poor in our local areas who are not members of the church (James 1:27; Rom. 12:17).

37. Our churches must also address issues of evil and of social injustice in the local community and the wider society. Our methodology should involve study, earnest prayer, and action within the normative, ethical guidelines for Christian's conduct set out in Scripture. Within these guidelines there are times, no matter the political system, when protest can be effective. Christians should carefully consider the issues and manner in which they protest so that the identity and message of the church is neither blurred nor drowned.

38. The local church has however to be understood as being a part of the universal church. There is therefore a genuine need for help and sharing (*diakonia*) built on fellowship (*koinonia*) between churches of different localities and contexts. In this connection we considered a model for relating churches in different areas of the world. In such "church twinnings" the relationship should be genuinely reciprocal with giving and receiving at both ends, free from paternalism of any kind (Rom. 15:1-7).

39. Such reciprocal relationship in a spirit of true mutuality are particularly needed in view of the fact that every local church always lives on the edge of compromise with its context (Rom. 12:3-18). Some churches are immersed in the problems of materialism and racism, others in those of oppression and the option of violence. We may help each other by seeking to see the world through the eyes of our brothers and sisters.

40. Within regard to the wider world community, Christian churches should identify and exchange people who are equipped through their personal characteristics, training, and Christian maturity to work across cultures in the name of Christ and of the sending church. These men and women would go as servants and stewards characterized by humility and meekness; and they would work together with members of the Body of Christ in the countries to which they go.

VII. Christians Aid Agencies and Transformation

41. In reflection upon the Christian to human need, we have recognized the central place of the local church as the vehicle for communicating the Gospel of Jesus Christ both in word and deed. Churches around the world have throughout history displayed active concern for the needs around them and countries to serve the needy. We call upon the aid agencies to see their role as one of facilitating the churches in the fulfilment of their mission.

42. We recognize the progress, which in recent years has been made, in our understanding of the Gospel and its social and political implications. We also recognize, however, the deficiencies in our witness and affirm our desire for a fuller understanding of the biblical basis for our ministry.

43. We acknowledge that the constituency of the aid agencies is generally concerned with human suffering, hunger, and need. However, we recognize that this concern is not consistently expressed with integrity. In efforts to raised funds, the plight of the poor is often exploited in order to meet donor needs and expectations. Fund-raising activities must be in accordance with the Gospel. A stewardship responsibility of agencies is to reduce significantly their overheads in order to maximize the resource for the ministry.

44. We are challenged to implement in our organizations a positive transformation demonstrating the values of Christ and His Kingdom, which we wish to share with others. We must, for example, avoid competition with others involved in the same ministry and a success mentality that forgets God's special concern for the weak and "unsuccessful" (Gal. 2:10; Ps. 147:6). We should continually review our actions to ensure biblical integrity and genuine partnership with churches and other agencies. Decisions on ministry policy, including how resources are to be used, need to be made in consultation with the people to be served.

45. We need to ensure that our promotional efforts describe what we are actually doing. We accept the responsibility of educating our donors in the full implications of the way Christian transformation is experienced in the field. The Holy Spirit has led us to this ministry. In accepting the responsibility of education we recognize the process may cause some to question our approach. We will strive to educate with a sense of humility, patience, and courage.

46. In all of our programs and actions we should remember that God in His sovereignty and love is already active in the communities we seek to serve (Acts 14:17; 17:23; Rom. 2:9-15). Agencies, therefore, should give adequate priority to listening sensitively to the concerns of these communities, facilitating a two-way process in communication and local ownership of

programs. The guiding principle is equitable partnership in which local people and Western agencies cooperate together. Many models for development have originated in the Two Thirds World. Christian aid agencies should in every way encourage these local initiatives to succeed. In this way the redeemed community of the Kingdom will be able to experiment with a number of models of transformation.

47. The agencies' legitimate need for accountability to donors often results in the imposition of Western management systems on local communities. This assumes that Western planning and control systems are the only ones which can ensure accountability. Since the communities these agencies seek to serve are often part of a different culture, this imposition can restrict and inhabit the sensitive process of social transformation. We call on development agencies to establish a dialogue with those they serve in order to permit the creation of systems accountability with respect to both cultures. Our ministry must always reflect our mutual interdependence in the Kingdom (Rom. 14:17-18; 1 Cor. 12).

48. In focusing on the apparently conflicting requirements of our action as Christian agencies, we are conscious of our sin and compromise. In a call to repentance we include a renunciation of inconsistency and extravagance in our personal and institutional lifestyle. We ask the Spirit of truth to lead us and make us agents of transformation (Acts 1:8).

VIII. The Coming of the Kingdom and the Church's Mission

49. We affirm that the Kingdom of God is both present and future, both societal and individual, both physical and spiritual. If other have over emphasized the present, the societal, and the physical, we ought to confess that we have tended to neglect those dimensions of the biblical message. We therefore joyfully proclaim that the Kingdom has broken into human history in the Resurrection of Christ. It grows like a mustard seed, both judging and transforming the present age.

50. Even if God's activity in history is focused on the church, it is not confined to the church. God's particular focus on the church - as on Israel in the Old Testament - has as its purpose the blessing of the nations (Gen. 12:1-3; 15; 17; Isa. 42:6). Thus the church is called to exist for the sake of its Lord and the sake of humankind (Matt. 22:23-40).

51. The church is called to infuse the world with hope, for both this age and the next. Our hope does not flow from despair: it is not because the present is empty that we hope for a new future (Rom. 5:1-11). Rather, we hope for that future because of what God has already done and because of what He has promised yet to do. We have already been given the Holy Spirit as the

guarantee of our full redemption and of the coming of the day when God will be all in all (1 Cor. 15:28). As we witness to the Gospel of present salvation and future hope, we identify with the awesome birthpangs of God's new creation (Rom. 8:22). As the community of the end time anticipating the End, we prepare for the ultimate by getting involved in the penultimate (Matt. 24:36-25:46).

52. For this reason we are challenged to commit ourselves to a truly vigorous and full-orbed mission in the world, combining explosive creativity with painstaking faithfulness in small things. Our mission and vision are to be nurtured by the whole counsel of God (2 Tim. 3:16). A repentant, revived, and vigorous church will call people to true repentance and faith and at the same time equip them to challenge the forces of evil and injustice (2 Tim. 3:17). We thus move forward, without either relegating salvation merely to an eternal future or making it synonymous with a political or social dispensation to be achieved in the here and now. The Holy Spirit empowers us to serve and proclaim Him who has been raised from the dead, seated at the right hand of the Father, and given to the church as Head over all things in heaven and on earth (Eph. 1:10, 20-22).

53. Finally, we confess our utter dependence on God. We affirm that transformation is, in the final analysis, His work, but work in which He engages us. To this end He has given us His Spirit, the Transformer *par excellence*, to enlighten us and be our Counselor (John 16:7), to impart His many gifts to us (Rom. 12; 1 Cor. 12), to equip us to face and conquer the enemy (2 Cor. 10:3-5; Gal. 5:22-23). We are reminded that our unconfessed sins and lack of love for others grieve the Spirit (Eph.4:30; Gal. 5:13-16). We therefore fervently pray for our sins to be pardoned, for our spirit to be renewed, and for the privilege of being enlisted in the joyous task of enabling God's Kingdom to come: the Kingdom "of ... justice, peace, and joy in the Holy Spirit" (Rom. 14:17).

Appendix Three

Institute for Studies in Asian Church and Culture

Who We Are

We are a research and training organization specializing with the following core expertise within an Asian context

- Development
- Cross-cultural studies
- Missiology

OUR MISSION is to creatively witness to the Lordship of Jesus in all of life by penetrating culture with the values of the Kingdom and engaging the powers towards social transformation.

The gospel is for the whole person. Witness to it has both a verbal and visible dimension as expressed in prophetic proclamation of the Word as well as in the Spirit's work of transformation in the life of the individual and of nations. We believe that Christ is King, not just over the church, but over nations and peoples. His kingdom makes no distinction between the secular and the sacred; He rules over all of life.

Jesus in saving us became a human being just like us. He identified with a particular culture at a particular time; He was a Jew. In the same way, we believe that the gospel must be in context, immersed in the culture and story of a people. We seek to speak sensitively, according to a people's ways of thinking and feeling, and in a way that truly brings good news to the places where they fear and hurt.

While all, rich and poor, are sinners and need forgiveness, not all are victims of injustice. Power is usually on the side of the oppressor, weakness is often the lot of the poor. While we are told not to be partial to a poor man in his lawsuit and follow justice and justice alone, the prophets also tell us that God's love is particularly focused on the poor.

Institutional Profile

ISACC was established in 1978 as a reflective arm of the church and a catalyst towards biblically - based responses to political, social and cultural issues in the country. Through its 21 years of existence it has evolved from an initially marginal prophetic voice operating within a largely conservative church community into a major influence in the life and witness of the churches, with a reputation for committed and creative responses to issues of national concern among NGOs and other progressive elements in the country.

ISACC maintains a considerable network of individuals and organizations with similar concerns. Its solidarity network ranges from secular NGOs like Freedom from Debt Coalition and Philippine Alliance of Human Rights Advocates to ecumenical church bodies and, internationally, the World Association of Christian Communication, International Christian Media Commission, Partnership in Mission, World Vision, London Institute for Contemporary Christianity, Breakthrough in Hongkong, and friends in the International Fellowship of Evangelical Students (IFES) network.

Some of its main funding sources have been the Evangelische Missionwerk (EMW) of Germany, Tear Fund Australia and UK, Anglican Church of Canada, ICCO of the Netherlands, the Uniting Churches of the Netherlands, and the Philippine government, like the Department of Education and other local sources. ISACC also maintains links with local organizations in media and the arts such as Far East Broadcasting Company and the Day by Day Christian Ministries. It is also a member of the Alliance of Christian Development Agencies (ACDA) and the Philippine Council of Evangelical Churches (PCEC).

Select Bibliography

All Scripture Quotations are from the New Revised Standard Version

Primary Sources

Statements

'(The) Commitment (to Simple Lifestyle)'. In Ronald J. Sider (ed.), *Lifestyle in the Eighties: An Evangelical Commitment to Simple Lifestyle.* Philadelphia, Pa.: Westminster, 1982, 13-19.

'(The) Grand Rapids Report on Evangelism and Social Responsibility: An Evangelical Commitment'. In John Stott (ed.), *Making Christ Known.* Grand Rapids, Mich.; Cambridge: Eerdmans, 1996, 165-213.

'Kingdom Affirmations and Commitments'. *Transformation* 11:3 (1994), 2-11.

'Lausanne Covenant'. In James D. Douglas (ed.), *Let the Earth Hear His Voice.* Minneapolis, Minn.: World Wide Publications, 1975, 3-15.

'(The) Oxford Declaration on Christian Faith and Economics'. In Herbert Schlossberg, Vinay Samuel and Ronald J. Sider (eds.), *Christianity and Economics in the Post-Cold War Era.* Grand Rapids, Mich.: Eerdmans, 1994, 11-30.

Padilla, C. Rene and Chris Sugden, (eds.) *How Evangelicals Endorsed Social Responsibility.* Nottingham: Grove Books, 1985.

— *Texts on Evangelical Social Ethics: 1974-1983.* Nottingham: Grove Books, 1985.

'Statement of Intent'. In Ronald J. Sider (ed.), *Evangelicals and Development: Towards a Theology of Social Change.* Exeter: Paternoster, 1981, 15-16.

'Theology [and] Implications of Radical Discipleship'. In James D. Douglas (ed.), *Let the Earth Hear His Voice.* Minneapolis, Minn.: World Wide Publications, 1975, 1294-1296.

'Wheaton '83 Conference Notebook'. Material distributed at Wheaton '83: An International Evangelical Conference on the Nature and Mission of the Church, Wheaton, Ill., 20 June - 1 July 1983.

'Wheaton '83 Statement on Transformation'. *Transformation* 1:1 (1984), 23-28.

'Word, Kingdom & Spirit'. *Transformation* 11:3 (1994), 1-11, 33.

Interviews

Apilado, Mariano C. San Francisco Theological Seminary, San Anselmo, Calif., 13 April 2004.

Francisco, J. Mario. Jesuit School of Theology at Berkeley, Berkeley, Calif., 23 January 2004.

Maggay, Melba P. Divine Word International, Techny, Ill., 19 June 2004.

Samuel, Vinay K. Eastern University, St. Davids, Pa., 26 July 2003.

Sider, Ronald J. Eastern University, St. Davids, Pa., 25 July 2003.
Sine, Tom Eastern University, St. Davids, Pa., 25 July 2003.

Secondary Sources

History and Theology of Holistic Mission

Bockmuehl, Klaus. *Evangelicals and Social Ethics*. Trans. David T. Priestly. Downers Grove, Ill.; Exeter : InterVarsity; Paternoster, 1979.

Bosch, David J. *Transforming Mission: Paradigm Shifts in Theology of Mission*. Maryknoll, N.Y.: Orbis, 1991.

— *Believing in the Future: Toward a Missiology of Western Culture*. Harrisburg, Pa.: Trinity Press International, 1995.

Cerillo, Augustus and Murray W. Dempster, (eds.) *Salt and Light: Evangelical Political Thought in Modern America*. Grand Rapids, Mich.; Washington, D.C.: Christian College Coalition, 1989.

Douglas, James D., Ed. *Let the Earth Hear His Voice: International Congress on World Evangelization*. Minneapolis, Minn.: World Wide Publications, 1975.

— *Proclaim Christ Until He Comes*. Minneapolis, Minn.: World Wide Publications, 1990.

Hedlund, Roger. *Roots of the Great Debate in Mission*. Bangalore: Theological Book Trust, 1997.

Henry, Carl F. H. *The Uneasy Conscience of Modern Fundamentalism*. Grand Rapids, Mich.: Eerdmans, 1947.

Kirk, J. Andrew. *Liberation Theology: An Evangelical View from the Third World*. Atlanta, Ga.: John Knox, 1979.

— *The Good News of the Kingdom Coming*. Downers Grove, Ill.: InterVarsity, 1983.

Moberg, David O. *The Great Reversal: Evangelism Versus Social Concern*. Philadelphia, Pa.; New York: J.B. Lippincott, 1972.

Nicholls, Bruce J., Ed. *In Word and Deed: Evangelism and Social Responsibility*. Grand Rapids, Mich.: Eerdmans, 1986.

Quebedeaux, Richard. *The Young Evangelicals*. New York: Harper and Row, 1974.

Ro, Bong Rin and Bruce J. Nicholls, (eds.) *Beyond Canberra*. Oxford: Regnum; Lynx, 1993.

Smith, Linda. 'Recent Historical Perspective of the Evangelical Tradition'. In Edgar J. Elliston (ed.), *Christian Relief and Development: Developing Workers for Effective Ministry*. Dallas, Tex.: Word, 1989, 23-36.

Steuernagel, Valdir R. 'The Theology of Mission in Its Relation to Social Responsibility within the Lausanne Movement'. Doctor of Theology thesis. Lutheran School of Theology at Chicago, 1988.

— 'Social Concern and Evangelization: The Journey of the Lausanne Movement'. *International Bulletin of Missionary Research* 15:2 (1991), 53-56.

Stott, John R.W., Ed. *Making Christ Known: Historic Mission Documents from the Lausanne Movement, 1974-1989*. Grand Rapids, Mich.; Cambridge: Eerdmans, 1996.

Taylor, William D., Ed. In *Global Missiology for the 21st Century: The Iguassu Dialogue*. Grand Rapids, Mich.: Baker, 2000.

Tholin, Richard and Lane T. Dennis. 'Radical Evangelicals: Challenge to Liberals and Conservatives'. *Explore* 2:2 (1976), 45-54.

Utuk, Efiong S. 'From Wheaton to Lausanne'. In James A. Scherer and Stephen B. Bevans (eds.), *New Directions in Mission & Evangelization 2*. Maryknoll, N.Y.: Orbis, 1994, 99-112.

Yoder, John H. *Politics of Jesus*. Grand Rapids, Mich.: Eerdmans, 1972.

Mission as Transformation, General Works

Adeney, Miriam. *God's Foreign Policy*. Grand Rapids, Mich.: Eerdmans, 1984.

Bediako, Kwame. *Christianity in Africa: The Renewal of Non-Western Religion*. Oxford: Regnum, 1996.

Cook, William 'I Will Build My Church: Reflections on the Wheaton '83 Conference on the Nature and Mission of the Church'. *Evangelical Review of Theology* 9:1 (1985), 27-31.

Costas, Orlando. *Christ Outside the Gate: Mission Beyond Christendom*. Maryknoll, N.Y.: Orbis, 1982.

— *The Church and Its Mission: A Shattering Critique from the Third World*. Wheaton, Ill.; London: Tyndale; Coverdale House, 1973.

— *The Integrity of Mission: The Inner Life and Outreach of the Church*. San Francisco, Calif.: Harper & Row, 1979.

— 'Report on Thailand '80'. *TSF Bulletin* 4:1 (1980), 4-7.

Covell, Ralph 'Wheaton '83'. *Missiology* 11:4 (1983), 531-533.

Coy, Terrell F. 'Incarnation and the Kingdom of God: The Political Theologies of Orlando Costas, C. Rene Padilla, and Samuel Escobar'. Doctor of Philosophy thesis. Southwestern Baptist Theological Seminary, 1999.

Dempster, Murray, Byron Klaus and Douglas Petersen, (eds.) *Called and Empowered: Global Mission in Pentecostal Perspective*. Peabody, Mass.: Hendrickson, 1991.

— *The Globalization of Pentecostalism: A Religion Made to Travel*. Oxford: Regnum, 1999.

Escobar, Samuel. *Changing Tides: Latin America and Mission Today*. Maryknoll, N.Y.: Orbis, 2002.

Gasque, Laurel and Ward Gasque. '"Third World" Theologians Meet'. *Christianity Today* (27 May 1991), 59-60.

Gitari, David. *In Season and Out of Season: Sermons for a Nation*. Oxford: Regnum, 1996.

Gnanakan, Ken *Kingdom Concerns: A Biblical Exploration towards a Theology of Mission*. Banaglore: Theological Book Trust, 1993.

Hathaway, Brian 'The Kingdom Manifesto'. *Transformation* 7:3 (1990), 6-10.

Lau Branson, Mark and C. Rene Padilla, (eds.) *Conflict and Context: Hermeneutics in the Americas*. Grand Rapids, Mich.: Eerdmans, 1986.

Maggay, Melba P. *Transforming Society*. Oxford: Regnum, 1994.

McAlpine, Thomas H. *By Word, Work and Wonder: Cases in Holistic Mission*. Monrovia, Calif.: MARC, 1995.

Moffitt, Robert 'Biblical Development'. Paper distributed in the course *Basic Wholistic Christian Discipleship* at Asian Theological Seminary, Quezon City, 1993.

Myers, Bryant L. *Walking with the Poor: Principles and Practices of Transformational Development*. Maryknoll, N.Y.: Orbis, 1999.

Nicholls, Bruce J., Ed. In Word and Deed: Evangelism and Social Responsibility. Grand Rapids, Mich.: Eerdmans, 1986.

Padilla, C. Rene. 'Evangelism and Social Responsibility: From Wheaton '66 to Wheaton '83'. *Transformation* 2:3 (1985), 27-33.

— 'Liberation Theology: An Appraisal'. In Daniel Schipani (ed.), *Freedom and Discipleship: Liberation Theology in an Anabaptist Perspective.* Maryknoll, N.Y.: Orbis, 1989, 34-50.

— *Mission Between the Times.* Grand Rapids, Mich.: Eerdmans, 1985

Padilla, C. Rene, Ed. *The New Face of Evangelicalism: An International Symposium on the Lausanne Covenant.* Downers Grove, Ill.: InterVarsity, 1976.

Petersen, Douglas *Not By Might Nor By Power: A Pentecostal Theology of Social Concern in Latin America.* Oxford: Regnum, 1996.

Ringma, Charles. 'Transformational Theology: Some Curriculum Issues'. *Phronesis* 2:1 (1995), 77-91.

— 'Holistic Ministry and Mission: A Call for Reconceptualization'. *Missiology* 32:3 (2004), 431-448.

Samuel, Vinay K. 'The Development Movement: An Overview and Appraisal'. *Transformation* 13:4 (1996), 12-16.

— 'Evangelical Response to Globalization: An Asian Perspective'. *Transformation* 16:1 (1999), 4-7.

Samuel, Vinay and Albrecht Hauser, (eds.) *Proclaiming Christ in Christ's Way: Studies in Integral Evangelism.* Oxford: Regnum, 1989.

Samuel, Vinay and Chris Sugden, (eds.) *AD 2000 and Beyond: A Mission Agenda.* Oxford: Regnum, 1991.

— *The Church in Response to Human Need.* Oxford; Grand Rapids, Mich.: Regnum; Eerdmans, 1987.

— *Mission as Transformation: A Theology of the Whole Gospel.* Oxford: Regnum, 1999.

— *Sharing Jesus in the Two Thirds World.* Grand Rapids, Mich.: Eerdmans, 1984.

Sider, Ronald J.

— *Rich Christians in an Age of Hunger.* Downers Grove: InterVarsity, 1977.

— 'An Evangelical Theology of Liberation'. In *Perspectives in Evangelical Theology.* Kenneth Kantzer and Stanley Gundry, (eds.) Pp. 117-133. Grand Rapids, Mich.: Baker, 1979.

— *One-Sided Christianity? Uniting the Church to Heal a Lost and Broken World.* Grand Rapids: Zondervan, 1993.

Sider, Ronald J., Ed. *The Chicago Declaration.* Carol Stream, Ill.: Creation House, 1974.

— *Evangelicals and Development: Toward a Theology of Social Change.* Exeter: Paternoster, 1981.

— *For They Shall Be Fed: Scripture Readings and Prayers for a Just World.* Dallas, Tex.: Word, 1997.

— *Lifestyle in the Eighties: An Evangelical Commitment to Simple Lifestyle.* Philadelphia, Pa.: Westminster, 1982.

Sine, Tom. *Mustard Seed Conspiracy.* Waco, Tex.: Word, 1981.

— *Mustard Seed Versus McWorld.* Grand Rapids, Mich.: Baker, 1999.

— *Wild Hope: Crises Facing the Human Community on the Threshold of the 21st Century.* Dallas, Tex.: Word, 1991.

Snyder, Howard A. *Models of the Kingdom*. Nashville, Tenn.: Abingdon, 1991.

Stott, John R.W. and Ronald J. Sider, (eds.) *Lifestyle in the Eighties: An Evangelical Commitment to Simple Lifestyle*. Philadelphia, Pa.: Westminster, 1982.

Sugden, Chris. *Gospel, Culture and Transformation*. Oxford: Regnum, 2000.

— 'Modernity, Postmodernity and the Gospel'. *Transformation* 10:4 (1993), 1-2.

— 'Placing Critical Issues in Relief: A Response to David Bosch'. In Willem Saayman and Klippies Kritzinger (eds.), *Mission in Bold Humility: David Bosch's Work Considered*. Maryknoll, N.Y.: Orbis, 1996, 139-150.

— *Radical Discipleship*. London: Marshall, Morgan and Scott, 1981.

Wallis, Jim. *Agenda for Biblical People*. New York: Harper and Row, 1976.

— 'Liberation and Conformity'. In Gerald H. Anderson and Thomas F. Stransky, (eds.), *Mission Trends No. 4*. New York; Grand Rapids, Mich.: Paulist; Eerdmans, 1979.

Mission as Transformation, Filipino Specific

Bautista, Lorenzo C. 'The Church in the Philippines'. In . Saphir Athyal (ed.), *Church in Asia Today*. Singapore: Asia Lausanne Committee for World Evangelization, 1996, 169-195.

Beltran, Benigno P. *Christology of the Inarticulate: An Inquiry into the Filipino Understanding of Jesus Christ*. Manila: Divine Word, 1987.

Callanta, Ruth *Poverty: The Philippine Scenario*. Manila: Bookmark, 1988.

Craig, Jenni M. *Servants Among the Poor*. Manila; Wellington: OMF: SERVANTS, 1998.

Grigg, Viv. *Companion to the Poor*. Monrovia, Calif.: MARC, 1990.

Institute for Studies in Asian Church and Culture. *Sambahaginan: An Experience in Community Development Work*. Quezon City: ISACC, 1992.

— *Courage to Live These Days: Editorials that Matter*. Quezon City: ISACC, 1999.

Lapiz, Ed. 'Filipino Indigenous Liturgy'. *Patmos* 14:2 (1999), 11-12, 26.

— *Paano Maging Pilipinong Kristiano*. Makati City: KALOOB, 1997.

Lim, David S. 'Consolidating Democracy: Filipino Evangelicals in Between People Power Events (1986-2001)'. Unpublished manuscript sent via email to author, 2003.

— 'A Critique of Modernity in Protestant Mission in the Philippines'. *Journal of Asian Mission* 2:2 (2000), 149-177.

— 'The Living God in the Structures of Philippine Reality'. *Transformation* 5:2 (1988), 1-8.

— *Transforming Communities*. Manila: OMF, 1992.

Magalit, Isabelo. 'Church and State Today'. *Phronesis* 7:2 (2000), 49-61.

— 'The Church and the Barricades'. *Transformation* 3:2 (1986), 1-2.

Maggay, Melba P. 'American Protestant Missionary Efforts and Filipino Culture'. *Patmos* 14:1 (1998), 4-7, 26-30.

— 'Early Protestant Missionary Efforts in the Philippines: Some Intercultural Problems'. *Journal of Asian Mission*. 5:1 (2003), 119-131.

— 'Engaging Culture: Lessons from the Underside of History'. *Missiology* 33:1 (2005), 62-70.

— *A Faith for the Emptiness of Our Time*. Mandaluyong: OMF, 1990.

— *Filipino Religious Consciousness: Some Implications to Missions*. Quezon City: ISACC, 1999.

— *The Gospel in Filipino Context.* Mandaluyong: OMF, 1987.
— *Jew to the Jew, Greek to the Greek: Reflections on Culture and Globalization.* Quezon City: ISACC, 2001.
— 'Notes from the Editor: Tidings for the Fisher-King'. *Patmos* 1:1 (1979), 24-25.
— 'Signs of the Presence of the Kingdom in the February Revolution'. In Douglas J. Elwood (ed.), *Toward a Theology of People Power.* Quezon City: New Day, 1988, 62-71.
Miranda-Feliciano, Evelyn. *All Things to All Men.* Quezon City: New Day, 1988.
— 'Megamall, Here I Come! Or Is This the Way to Globalization?' *Patmos* 13:1 (1997), 14-15, 24.
— *Pinoy Nga, Biblikal Ba? Kaugalian, Tradisyon at Paniniwala.* Trans. of *Filipino Values and Our Christian Faith* published in 1990. Manila: OMF, 1995.
— *Unequal Worlds.* Quezon City: ISACC, 2000.
Schwenk, Richard L. *Onward, Christians! Protestants in the Philippine Revolution.* Quezon City: New Day, 1986.
Suico, Joseph R. 'Pentecostalism: Towards a Movement of Social Transformation in the Philippines'. *Journal of Asian Mission* 1:1 (1999), 7-19.
Tizon, F. Albert. 'Filipino Protestant Faith in Revolutionary Times: Historical Elements in an Evangelical Theology of Social Transformation'. *Journal of Asian Mission* 4:1 (2002), 3-30.
— 'Revisiting the Mustard Seed: The Filipino Evangelical Church in the Age of Globalization'. *Phronesis* 6:1 (1999), 3-26.

Global-Local Works

Bankoff, Greg and Kathleen Weekley. *Post-Colonial National Identity in the Philippines.* Basingstoke; Burlington, Vt.: Ashgate, 2002.
Barber, Benjamin R. *Jihad vs. McWorld.* New York: Times Books, 1995.
Berger, Peter L. and Samuel P. Huntington, (eds.) *Many Globalizations: Cultural Diversity in the Contemporary World.* Oxford: Oxford University Press, 2002.
Brecher, Jeremy, Tim Costello and Brendan Smith. *Globalization from Below: The Power of Solidarity.* Cambridge, Mass.: South End, 2002.
Freston, Paul. *Evangelicals and Politics in Asia, Africa and Latin America.* Cambridge: Cambridge University Press, 2001.
Held, David, Anthony McGrew, David Goldblatt and Jonathan Perraton. *Global Transformations: Politics, Economics and Culture.* Stanford, Calif.: Stanford University, 1999.
Hutchinson, Mark and Ogbu Kalu, (eds.) *A Global Faith: Essays on Evangelicalism and Globalization.* New South Wales, Australia: The Centre for the Study of Australian Christianity, 1998.
Robertson, Roland. 'Glocalization: Time-Space and Homogeneity-Heterogeneity'. In Mike Featherstone, Scott Lash, and Roland Robertson, (eds.) *Global Modernities* London: Sage, 1995, 25-44.
— 'Globalization and the Future of "Traditional Religion"'. In Max L. Stackhouse and Peter J. Paris (eds.), *God and Globalization, Vol. 1: Religion and the Powers of the Common Life.* Harrisburg, Pa.: Trinity Press International, 2000, 53-68.
Schreiter, Robert J. *Constructing Local Theologies.* Maryknoll, N.Y.: Orbis, 1985.

— *The New Catholicity: Theology between the Global and the Local.* Maryknoll, N.Y.: Orbis, 1997.

Van Drimmelen, Rob. *Faith in a Global Economy: A Primer for Christians.* Geneva, Switzerland: WCC, 1998.

Wiberg, Pedersen Else Marie, Holger Lam and Peter Lodberg. *For All People: Global Theologies in Contexts.* Grand Rapids, Mich.; Cambridge: Eerdmans, 2002.

Name Index

Subject Index

GLOBAL THEOLOGICAL VOICES
Series Listing

David Emmanuuel Singh (Ed.)
Jesus and the Cross
Reflections of Christians from Islamic Contexts

The Cross reminds us that the sins of the world are not borne through the exercise of power but through Jesus Christ's submission to the will of the Father. The papers in this volume are organised in three parts: scriptural, contextual and theological. The central question being addressed is: how do Christians living in contexts, where Islam is a majority or minority religion, experience, express or think of the Cross? This is, therefore, an exercise in listening. As the contexts from where these engagements arise are varied, the papers in drawing scriptural, contextual and theological reflections offer a cross-section of Christian thinking about Jesus and the Cross.

2008 / 978-1-870345-65-1 / x + 226pp

Sung-wook Hong
Naming God in Korea
The Case of Protestant Christianity

Since Christianity was introduced to Korea more than a century ago, one of the most controversial issue has been the Korean term for the Christian 'God'. This issue is not merely about naming the Christian God in Korean language, but it relates to the question of theological contextualization—the relationship between the gospel and culture—and the question of Korean Christian identity. This book examines the theological contextualization of the concept of 'God' in the contemporary Korean context and applies the translatability of Christianity to that context. It also demonstrates the nature of the gospel in relation to cultures, i.e., the universality of the gospel expressed in all human cultures.

2008 / 978-1-870345-66-8

Young-hoon Lee
The Holy Spirit Movement in Korea
Its Historical and Doctrinal Development

This book traces the historical and doctrinal development of the Holy Spirit Movement in Korea through five successive periods (from 1900 to the present time). The first period (1900-20) was characterised by repentance and revival, the second period (1920-40) by persecution and suffering under Japanese occupation. The third period (1940-60) was a time of confusion and division while the fourth period (1960-80) was a time of explosive revival in which the Pentecostal movement played a major role in the rapid growth of Korean churches. In the fifth period (1980 to the present time), the Holy Spirit movement reaches out to all denominations. The book also discusses the relationship between this movement and other religions such as shamanism, and looks forward to further engagement with issues of concern in the larger society.

2008 / 978-1-870345-67-5

For the up-to-date listing of the Global Theological Voices Series, see
http://www.ocms.ac.uk/docs/Global_Theological_Voices_Listing.pdf.

Regnum Studies in Mission

Academic Monographs on Missiological Themes

(All titles paperback, 229 x 152mm)

Allan Anderson and Edmond Tang (eds.)
Asian and Pentecostal
The Charismatic Face of Christianity in Asia
(Published jointly with Asia Pacific Theological Seminary)
This book provides a thematic discussion and pioneering case studies on the history and development of Pentecostal and Charismatic churches in the countries of South Asia, South East Asia and East Asia.
2005 / 1-870345-43-6 / approx. 600pp

I. Mark Beaumont
Christology in Dialogue with Muslims
A Critical Analysis of Christian Presentations of Christ for Muslims from the Ninth and Twentieth Centuries
This book analyses Christian presentations of Christ for Muslims in the most creative periods of Christian-Muslim dialogue, the first half of the ninth century and the second half of the twentieth century. In these two periods, Christians made serious attempts to present their faith in Christ in terms that take into account Muslim perceptions of him, with a view to bridging the gap between Muslim and Christian convictions.
2005 / 1-870345-46-0 / xxvi + 228pp

Kwame Bediako
Theology and Identity
The Impact of Culture upon Christian Thought in the Second Century and in Modern Africa
The author examines the question of Christian identity in the context of the Graeco–Roman culture of the early Roman Empire. He then addresses the modern African predicament of quests for identity and integration.
1992 / 1-870345-10-X / xviii + 508pp

Richard Burgess
Nigeria's Christian Revolution
The Civil War Revival and Its Pentecostal Progeny (1967-2006)
Nigeria has become the arena of one of the most remarkable religious movements of recent times, reflecting the shift in the global centre of Christianity from the North to the South. This book tells the story of one sector of this movement from its roots in the Nigerian civil war to the turn of the new millennium. It describes a revival that occurred among the Igbo people of Eastern Nigeria, and the new Pentecostal churches it generated, and documents the changes that have occurred as the movement has responded to global flows and local demands. As such, it explores the nature of revivalist and Pentecostal experience, but does so against the backdrop of local socio-political and economic developments, such as decolonisation and civil war, as well as broader processes, such as modernisation and globalisation.

2008 / 978-1-870345-63-7 / xxii + 347pp

Gene Early
Leadership Expectations
How Executive Expectations are Created and Used in a Non-Profit Setting
The author creates an Expectation Enactment Analysis to study the role of the Chancellor of the University of the Nations-Kona, Hawaii, and is grounded in the field of managerial work, jobs, and behaviour, drawing on symbolic interactionism, role theory, role identity theory, and enactment theory. The result is a conceptual framework for further developing an understanding of managerial roles.

2005 / 1-870345-30-4 / xxiv + 276pp

Keith E. Eitel
Paradigm Wars
The Southern Baptist International Mission Board Faces the Third Millennium
The International Mission Board of the Southern Baptist Convention is the largest denominational mission agency in North America. This volume chronicles the historic and contemporary forces that led to the IMB's recent extensive reorganization, providing the most comprehensive case study to date of a historic mission agency restructuring to continue its mission purpose into the twenty-first century more effectively.

1999 / 1-870345-12-6 / x + 140pp

Tormod Engelsviken, Ernst Harbakk, Rolv Olsen, Thor Strandenæs (eds.)
Communicating the Gospel in the 21st Century
Essays in Honour of Knud Jørgensen
Knud Jørgensen is Director of Areopagos and Associate Professor of Missiology at MF Norwegian School of Theology. This book reflects the various main areas of Jørgensen's commitment to mission. At the same time it focuses on the main frontier of mission, the world, the content of mission, the Gospel, the fact that the Gospel has to be communicated, and the context of contemporary mission - the 21st century.
2008 / 978-1-870345-64-4 / 472pp

Tharcisse Gatwa
The Churches and Ethnic Ideology in the Rwandan Crises 1900-1994
Since the early years of the twentieth century Christianity has become a new factor in Rwandan society. This book investigates the role Christian churches played in the formulation and development of the racial ideology that culminated in the 1994 genocide.
2005 / 1-870345-24-X / approx 300pp

Gideon Githiga
The Church as the Bulwark against Authoritarianism
Development of Church and State Relations in Kenya, with Particular Reference to the Years after Political Independence 1963-1992
'All who care for love, peace and unity in Kenyan society will want to read this careful history by Bishop Githiga of how Kenyan Christians, drawing on the Bible, have sought to share the love of God, bring his peace and build up the unity of the nation, often in the face of great difficulties and opposition.' Canon Dr Chris Sugden, Oxford Centre for Mission Studies.
2002 / 1-870345-38-X / xviii + 218pp

Samuel Jayakumar
Dalit Consciousness and Christian Conversion
Historical Resources for a Contemporary Debate
(Published jointly with ISPCK)
The main focus of this historical study is social change and transformation among the Dalit Christian communities in India. Historiography tests the evidence in the light of the conclusions of the modern Dalit liberation theologians.
1999 / 81-7214-497-0 / xxiv + 434pp

Samuel Jayakumar
Mission Reader
Historical Models for Wholistic Mission in the Indian Context
(Published jointly with ISPCK)
This book is written from an evangelical point of view revalidating and reaffirming the Christian commitment to wholistic mission. According to Jayakumar, the roots of the 'wholistic mission' combining 'evangelism and social concerns' are to be located in the history and tradition of Christian evangelism in the past; and the civilizing purpose of evangelism is compatible with modernity as an instrument in nation building.
2003 / 1-870345-42-8 / x + 250pp

Julie Ma
Mission Possible
Biblical Strategies for Reaching the Lost
Written as Julie Ma hiked the mountains to share God's news, this is a missiology book for the church which liberates missiology from the specialists for every believer. Nevertheless, it serves as a textbook that is simple and friendly, and yet solid in biblical interpretation. This book links the biblical teaching to the actual and contemporary missiological setting, thus serving two important purposes. Examples are clearly given which aid understanding, and the biblical development is brought in to our contemporary setting, thus making the Bible come alive.
2005 / 1-870345-37-1 / xvi + 142pp

Myung Sung-Hoon and Hong Young-Gi (eds.)
Charis and Charisma
David Yonggi Cho and the Growth of Yoido Full Gospel Church
This book discusses the factors responsible for the growth of the world's largest church. It expounds the role of the Holy Spirit, the leadership, prayer, preaching, cell groups and creativity in promoting church growth. It focuses on God's grace (charis) and inspiring leadership (charisma) as the two essential factors and the book's purpose is to present a model for church growth worldwide.
2003 / 1-870345-45-2 / xxii + 218pp

Jemima Atieno Oluoch
The Christian Political Theology of Dr. John Henry Okullu
This book reconstructs the Christian political theology of Bishop John Henry Okullu, DD, through establishing what motivated him and the biblical basis for his socio-political activities. It also attempts to reconstruct the socio-political environment that nurtured Dr Okullu's prophetic ministry.
2006 / 1-870345-51-7 / xx + 137pp

Bernhard Ott
Beyond Fragmentation: Integrating Mission and Theological Education
A Critical Assessment of some Recent Developments in Evangelical Theological Education
Beyond Fragmentation is an enquiry into the development of Mission Studies in evangelical theological education in Germany and German-speaking Switzerland between 1960 and 1995. This is carried out by a detailed examination of the paradigm shifts which have taken place in recent years in both the theology of mission and the understanding of theological education.
2001 / 1-870345-14-2 / xxviii + 382pp

Bob Robinson
Christians Meeting Hindus
Analysis and Theological Critique of the Hindu-Christian Encounter in India
This book focuses on the Hindu-Christian encounter, especially the intentional meeting called dialogue, mainly during the last four decades of the twentieth century, and mainly in India itself.
2004 / 1-870345-39-8 / xviii + 392pp

David Emmanuel Singh, Bernard C Farr (Eds.)
Christianity and Cultures
Shaping Christian Thinking in Context
This volume is a way of marking an important milestone in the relatively short story of the Oxford Centre for Mission Studies (OCMS). The papers here have been exclusively sourced from Transformation, a quarterly journal of OCMS and seek to provide a tripartite view of Christianity's engagement with cultures by focusing on the question: how is Christian thinking forming or reforming through its interaction with the varied contexts it encounters? As Christianity has taken and still takes shape in multiple contexts, it naturally results in a variety of expressions and emphases. One can gain an appreciation of these by studying different strands of theological-missiological thinking, socio-political engagements and forms of family relationships in interaction with the host cultures.
2008 / 978-1-870345-69-9 / x + 260pp

Christopher Sugden
Seeking the Asian Face of Jesus
The Practice and Theology of Christian Social Witness in Indonesia and India 1974–1996
This study focuses on contemporary wholistic mission with the poor in India and Indonesia combined with the call to transformation of all life in Christ with micro-credit enterprise schemes. 'The literature on contextual theology now has a new standard to rise to' – Lamin Sanneh (Yale University, USA).
1997 / 1-870345-26-6 / xx + 496pp

Christopher Sugden
Gospel, Culture and Transformation
A Reprint, with a New Introduction, of Part Two of Seeking the Asian Face of Jesus
Gospel, Culture and Transformation explores the practice of mission especially in relation to transforming cultures and communities. Vinay Samuel has played a leading role in developing the understanding of mission as transformation, which he defines as follows: 'Transformation is to enable God's vision of society to be actualised in all relationships: social, economic and spiritual, so that God's will may be reflected in human society and his love experienced by all communities, especially the poor.'
2000 / 1-870345-32-0 / viii + 152pp

Al Tizon
Transformation after Lausanne
Radical Evangelical Mission in Global-Local Perspective
Lausanne '74 inspired evangelicals around the world to take seriously the full implications of the Gospel for mission. This was especially true of a worldwide network of radical evangelical mission theologians and practitioners, whose post-Lausanne reflections found harbour in the notion of "Mission as Transformation". This missiology integrated evangelism and social concern like no other, and it lifted up theological voices coming from the Two Thirds World to places of prominence. This book documents the definitive gatherings, theological tensions, and social forces within and without evangelicalism that led up to Mission as Transformation. And it does so through a global-local grid that points the way toward greater holistic mission in the 21st century.

2008 / 978-1-870345-68-2 / xx + 281pp

Hwa Yung
Mangoes or Bananas?
The Quest for an Authentic Asian Christian Theology
Asian Christian thought remains largely captive to Greek dualism and Enlightenment rationalism because of the overwhelming dominance of Western culture. Authentic contextual Christian theologies will emerge within Asian Christianity with a dual recovery of confidence in culture and the gospel.

1997 / 1-870345-25-8 / xii + 274pp

For the up-to-date listing of the Regnum Studies in Mission, see
http://www.ocms.ac.uk/docs/Regnum_Studies_In_Mission_Listing.pdf.

regnum
Regnum Books International
Regnum is an Imprint of The Oxford Centre for Mission Studies
P.O. Box 70, Oxford, OX2 6HB
Web: www.ocms.ac.uk/regnum

In partnership with
Paternoster
Web: www.authenticmedia.co.uk/paternoster

June 2008